Odessa: A History,
1794 – 1914

Patricia Herlihy
Odessa: A History,
1794–1914

Distributed by Harvard University Press
for the
Harvard Ukrainian Research Institute

Publication of this volume was made possible
by a generous donation from
Mykola L. Hromnycky.

The Harvard Ukrainian Research Institute was established in 1973 as
an integral part of Harvard University. It supports research associates and visiting scholars who are engaged in projects concerned with
all aspects of Ukrainian studies. The Institute also works in close
cooperation with the Committee on Ukrainian Studies, which super-
vises and coordinates the teaching of Ukrainian history, language,
and literature at Harvard University.

To the Cherished Memory of My Mother
Irene Rigby McGahey
(1898 – 1985)

Preface

Among the great cities of the world, Odessa can claim certain distinctions. A new town, founded only in 1794, it grew rapidly, to become by the late nineteenth century the largest city in the Ukraine and the fourth city of the Russian Empire, after St. Petersburg, Moscow, and Warsaw. (It is now third in the Ukraine and twelfth in the Soviet Union.) Its location on the Black Sea made it a kind of commercial and cultural interface between the Russian Empire and the outside world. Its population came to include an extraordinary mix of ethnic, cultural, and religious communities—Ukrainian, Russian, Greek, Jewish, Western-European, and Asian. For this reason too, its history intersects with the history of many peoples, within and outside the Russian Empire. For example, a large part of the American-Jewish community traces its immediate, Old World origins to Odessa and its environs.

This book surveys the history of Odessa from its foundation until the outbreak of the First World War in 1914. I might have carried the story forward until the present, but Odessa's recent history is difficult to trace, and it raises an entirely different set of problems from those I examine here. The resulting book, at all events, would have been either too big or too superficial. I might have stopped at the great turning point of 1917. But Odessa did not in fact figure very largely in the revolutions of that year, and to treat them I would have had to recount events transpiring in large part outside of the city. The outbreak of the First World War seemed the best point of termination. It represented a breakdown of a seemingly stable system of international relations. It followed upon a breakdown within Odessa of a seemingly stable social system. An old world was disintegrating; it is best to end with sunset.

There is no single method of urban history, and I apply no single method here. I have used administrative and statistical records when they were available, and was fortunate in the opportunity, provided by the U.S.A./USSR cultural exchange program, to work in the Odessa State Archives. I also made considerable use of the reports of foreign consuls serving at Odessa (American, British, French, Tuscan, and Austrian), some published, most not. Travelers' accounts proved particularly illuminating, especially for the early period. The precise, concrete, and colorful contemporary descriptions give a sense of what the city was like in the nineteenth century. They present Odessa not as an abstract urban entity but as it really appeared to those who lived or visited there, from its muddy, dusty streets to its Italianate opera. The use of consular and travelers' reports might result in excessively anecdotal history, but I hope I have controlled this tendency by frequent recourse to statistical data.

The theme of the book is the experience of a city that grew in the course of the nineteenth century *ex nihilo* to become a European metropolis. In the course of that growth, Odessa faced formidable material, economic, social, political, and cultural problems. I examine the factors which in the first half of the century helped Odessa achieve a considerable measure of success: an excellent harbor, attractiveness to immigrants, the developing hinterland, the booming grain trade, effective leadership, liberal government, and social tolerance. I also examine the factors that limited or undermined that success in the latter half of the century: the changing international conditions of the grain trade, slow development of economic infrastructures, slow industrialization, unemployment, ethnic tensions, and inadequate support from the imperial government.

Like the empire itself, Odessa was composed of many ethnic and cultural communities. But perhaps even more urgently than the empire itself, it had to seek a social and cultural accommodation among those communities. Its history offers an exceptional opportunity to observe how this problem imbedded in the tsarist empire was addressed at the local level, to record the substantial successes and the disappointing failures, and to suggest reasons for them.

My research has taken me to many archives and libraries in the Soviet Union, Western Europe and the United States, and I am grateful to the staffs for their assistance. A grant from the International Research and Exchange Board made possible my research in Odessa itself. My children, Maurice, Christopher, David, Felix, Gregory, and Irene helped along the way, and the last three spent part of their vacation in Madrid correcting proofs. My husband

David has been of inestimable help from the beginnings of the project to this the finished book. He has my deepest thanks.

Odessa's history between 1794 and 1914 is unique, fascinating, and significant; I hope that the following effort to reconstruct its course does justice to it.

Patricia Herlihy
Mather House
March, 1986

Table of Contents

Table of Tables

Table of Maps

Maps 1.1 and 3.1 are based on maps prepared by Geoffrey
J. Matthews in Paul R. Magocsi, *Ukraine: A Historical
Atlas* (Toronto: University of Toronto Press, 1985).

Table of Figures

A Note on Transcription

In transcribing Ukrainian and Russian terms a modified Library of Congress System was used. Soft signs were dropped when they occured at the end of words but retained when they appeared within words.

A Note on Geographic Terms

The term, Novorossiia (New Russia), is here utilized in its official administrative sense. In 1804, it designated the three *gubernias* of Kherson, Taurida, and Katerynoslav; in 1812, it came to include Bessarabia as well. In 1874, it ceased to represent an administrative unit, but the name was still used informally to identify this region. The name, South Ukraine, is exclusively a geographic term, including approximately the same area but not Bessarabia. Many foreigners in the nineteenth century used the term South Russia, but the meaning is essentially that of the South Ukraine. Ukrainian placenames are used for all geographical references in the Ukraine (see sample list below), except when standard English forms exist, such as Kiev, Odessa, Dnieper and Dniester.

Ukrainian	*Russian*
Boh River	Bug River
Chernihiv	Chernigov
Ielysavethrad	Elizavetgrad
Ievpatoriia	Evpatoriia
Inhulets River	Ingulets River
Katerynoslav	Ekaterinoslav
Mariiupil	Mariupol
Molochna River	Molochnaia River
Mykolaiv	Nikolaev
Ochakiv	Ochakov
Podillia	Podoliia
Tyraspil	Tiraspol

Street and district names in Odessa will be transliterated from Russian, the official language of city administration in the tsarist period.

A Note on Weights and Measures

The metric and United States equivalents of the Russian weights and measures used in the sources quoted here are as follows:

Russian	Metric	United States
1 *chetvert*	2.099 kilograms	5.7719 bushels
1 *pud*	16.38 kilograms	36 pounds
1 *verst*	1.065 kilometers	0.663 miles
1 *desiatina*	1.09 hectares	2.7 acres
1 *sazhen*	2.13 meters	7 feet

CHAPTER ONE

Beginnings, 1794–1803

> The resumption of this ancient navigation [on the Black Sea] is a notable event in modern history; in commerce it has effected a great revolution.
> —Anthoine de Saint-Joseph, French merchant in the Black Sea, 1805

Of the major cities of contemporary Europe, Odessa, officially founded in 1794, is among the youngest, and no other European city can match its rate of growth in the nineteenth century. But it also developed in an area of the continent that possessed an ancient tradition of trade and a long if discontinuous history of urban settlement. Geography favored this region. The depression to the north of the Black Sea offers an easy, indeed the widest, path through the mountain chains that divide Europe north from south. Moreover, the Black Sea itself, linked through the Straits with the Mediterranean, offers a convenient maritime route to western lands. The northern littoral of the Black Sea is thus superbly placed to serve as a line of contact and exchange, between south and north, west and east.

Patterns, Ancient and Medieval

The conditions for commercial prosperity in the region were preeminently two: the presence of a stable political regime in the hinterland, protecting the overland routes from producers to ports; and access to a network of overseas trade, maintained by merchants who knew both distant markets and where the characteristic products of the steppe and forest economy could be sold. In the ancient world, the establishment of steppe empires—those, for example, of the Cimmerians and the Scythians—and the penetration into the Black Sea of Mediterranean, preeminently Greek, merchants fulfilled these conditions. Greeks founded colonies along the northern littoral of what they called the Euxine ("Hospitable") Sea.[1] Among them were Olbia (Ol'biia) on the right bank of the South Boh River, near present-day Mykolaiv and Tiras on the shore of the Dnistrovyi Lyman (estuary). The bay of present day Odessa is almost a halfway stop between the sites of these two Greek settlements.

The Greek colonists sought the characteristic products of the northern forests and steppes—honey, wax, amber, furs, skins, slaves, and, perhaps most important of all, wheat. They offered in exchange the oil, wine, and luxury products of the Mediterranean world. But the same easy avenues over land and sea that served merchants and travelers could also, in the absence of stable political regimes, invite pillagers and pirates. The agony of the ancient world and the disappearance of stable government disrupted peaceful, productive exchanges through the Black Sea ports. From the third century after Christ, a stream of invaders—Goths, Huns, Avars, Magyars, and others—fought for possession of the steppes, and the violence undermined the security of the overland routes.

The conditions of trade grew favorable again in the period from the ninth to the twelfth centuries. The unification of Kiev and Novgorod into the principality of Kievan Rus' lent vitality to the trade route that "connected the Varangians [i.e. Vikings] with the Greeks."[2] But in this commercial exchange the steppes were more a zone of transit than of production. Kiev and other towns on the fringes of the steppe were the chief staging points, where the commercial expeditions were organized and directed to the south. And the route itself, down the Dnieper River to the Black Sea, remained vulnerable to the incursions of the steppe nomads. In the early twelfth century, the Cumans (Polovtsi) successfully wrested the steppes from the control of Kievan Rus' and permanently divided Greeks from Varangians.

The full revival of Black Sea commerce awaited the thirteenth century, when again a stable empire ruling the steppe came into contact with Mediterranean traders. These traders were in the main Italian merchants, from the booming ports of Amalfi, Venice, Pisa, and Genoa, who established permanent commercial colonies in the Black Sea. The Venetians placed their first such settlement on the Crimean peninsula near the ancient Greek colony of Tanais; it was called Tana, and later Azov. The Pisans chose their first commercial base near present day Taganrog. Most active of all Italians were the Genoese, who, in 1282, built the capital of their Black Sea commercial empire, Caffa in the Crimea, on the site of the ancient city of Teodosiia.[3]

In these same years, the Mongol prince Ghenghiz Khan brought under his sole authority a huge stretch of the Eurasian continent, from China to Eastern Europe. Under Mongol auspices, western missionaries and merchants (among them, Marco Polo) could travel in safety all across Asia, even to fabled Cathay.

Along the northern shores of the Black Sea, the political empire of the Mongols met the commercial empire of the Italians. Once again, the steppe yielded to Mediterranean countries its characteristic products—wheat, salt, hides. Still more distinctive was the active export of slaves—Circassians, Slavs, even Tatars. Some—chiefly young girls—were shipped to western Europe for employment as household servants. But most were carried to Mameluke Egypt, where they filled the ranks of the slave army and administration, the twin supports of the Mameluke regime. Cereals too regained their ancient prominence as an article of export; grain from the steppes helped feed Constantinople and even the cities of distant Italy. In the early fourteenth century, a Florentine named Francesco Pegolotti advised his fellow merchants on the qualities of wheat to be found in the regions of the Black Sea.[4] In the fifteenth century, even grain from the far-off Kingdom of Poland, carried over the rivers of the Ukraine, was reaching the Black Sea and the Mediterranean beyond.[5]

The Italians called the future site of Odessa "Ginestra," for the colorful broom that grew along the coast. We first hear of the Tatar name of the location, Khadzhibei, in 1415. But by then the structures sustaining trade were disintegrating. The break-up of the Mongol Empire in the fourteenth century into several rival and warring hordes undermined the security of the overland routes into the continent. Plagues, wars, and economic depression in western Europe reduced the attention and resources that the Italian merchants could invest in this distant trade. The fall of Constantinople jeopardized commerce through the Straits, and the tiny Italian colonies were in no position to resist the overwhelming power of the expanding Ottoman state. Caffa clung to independence until 1475, but its inevitable surrender marks the end of the medieval period of Euxine commercial history—a period remarkable both for the brilliance achieved and the promise left unfulfilled.

The Modern Revival

During the early modern period the currents of long distance trade largely bypassed the Black Sea. The Ottoman Porte, controlling the Straits, was capricious in its policies and wary of foreigners, and it favored its indigenous merchants—predominantly Greeks, Armenians, Jews, and Arabs. Perhaps an even greater brake on commercial development was the disturbed political status of the Ukrainian steppes. Numerous peoples contended for supremacy over them— Tatars, Poles, Lithuanians, Ukrainians, Cossacks, and Russians, as well as the Turks themselves. The Ottomans recognized the need to fortify their exposed northern borders. In 1764, they built a line of fortresses along the northwest coast of the Black Sea. One they erected on a promontory overlooking its waters, at Khadzhibei, about halfway between the mouths of the Dniester and Boh Rivers; they named the fort Yeni-Dunai, "New World."[6]

The Turkish forts primarily defended against Russian expansion, which had been gaining momentum since the seventeenth century. As early as 1687, Empress Sophia, the clear-eyed, ill-fated elder half-sister of Peter the Great, tried to gain control of the entire course of the Don River to its opening on the Sea of Azov. Peter eventually replaced his sister but kept her policy, and in 1696 wrested from the Ottomans a small area on the Sea of Azov, including the like-named town. He celebrated his triumph by founding a city, Taganrog, which he intended to make into a naval base, the promise of Russian supremacy on these southern waters. But the Ottomans were not yet beaten, and by the peace settlement of 1711, Peter grudgingly surrendered the port. A subsequent ruler, the Empress Anne, took the town but agreed not to fortify it and not to launch armed Russian ships on Azov's waters. The town was soon lost again, and not until 1769 were Azov and Taganrog finally reconquered.

Empress Catherine II (1762–1796) made the wide and lasting breakthrough onto the waters of the Black Sea. She waged several successful wars against the Ottomans. In 1774, the Treaty of Kuchuk-Kainarji granted to the Russian Empire a stretch of coast properly on the Black Sea, between the South Boh and Dnieper Rivers.[7] Russia also gained two other sections of coast along the Sea of Azov. The littoral included the future sites of Mykolaiv, Kherson, and (on the Sea of Azov) Mariiupil (now Zhdanov). The treaty also delivered the Crimea to the feeble rule of a Tatar principality. Catherine claimed full sovereignty over the peninsula in 1783. The Russian Empire absorbed the entire Azov coastline, including the strategic Straits of Kerch, which open onto the Black Sea. And Catherine, unlike Peter, kept what she had conquered.[8]

Catherine actively sought to promote commerce within the newly acquired lands. In 1778, only four years after the Treaty of Kuchuk-Kainarji, she founded the city of Kherson at the mouth of the Dnieper River, ninety miles east of the future Odessa.[9] In her design, the new town would become the chief port of the region and the "St. Petersburg of the South." Set upon a marshy delta, ringed and divided by canals and ditches, it looked to some visitors more like a southern Amsterdam. The principal architect of the city was I. A. Hannibal, the black great-uncle of Alexander Pushkin.[10] The toponym, Kherson, evoked the name of the ancient Greek town of Chersonesus, which the scholarship of the time erroneously placed in the vicinity of the new city.[11] The name also bore strong Christian overtones. In pious belief, Prince Volodimer, who first led ancient Rus' into the Christian faith, was baptized at Korsun, medieval Chersonesus.

Intent on establishing her control over the new regions with fortresses and ports, Catherine built Mariiupil on the Sea of Azov in 1779.[12] In 1788, she founded Mykolaiv, at the mouth of the South Boh River, 15 *versts* north of the site of the ancient Greek colony of Ol'bia.[13]

The success of these new foundations was critically dependent on the resources and resolution of their Russian rulers. But it depended no less critically on another factor: commercial links to the world beyond the seas, which would bring life to the harbors and send demand for produce rippling back into the hinterland. The tsarist generals, garrisons, administrators, and clerks who came into the new towns met almost at once arrivals from another direction, from Mediterranean communities. They were chiefly merchants, and in the earliest years they were for the most part Ottoman subjects (who were thus able to ship through the Straits with relative ease). Most of them were Greeks. In the seventeenth and eighteenth centuries, Greeks from the Aegean Islands, and especially Chios, had woven a tight commercial network stretching across the Mediterranean, much as the Italians had done in the twelfth century. Along the northern littoral of the Black Sea, a strong political regime once again came into contact with a vital commercial empire.

Two years after the foundation of Kherson, Greek merchants were already actively trading there. They did not, however, long remain alone. Five non-Greek, foreign companies and twelve "branches" (*kontoras*) were active at Kherson between 1781 and 1788. Austrians and French were especially prominent. Two of their number, Johann Weber and Anthoine de Saint-Joseph, have left us glowing reports of the town and its prospects.[14] The French in particular saw in the opening of the Black Sea an opportunity to outflank the trade routes through the Baltic and White Seas, which England dominated.[15] In the first six months of 1787, nineteen ships left Kherson for Marseilles.[16] As a mark of his special interest, Emperor Joseph II of Austria accepted the invitation of Catherine to visit Kherson in 1787.[17]

The chief produce these merchants sought from the hinterland was wheat. The long-term population growth in western Europe and the short-term impact of wars (those of the French Revolution and those of Napoleon) drove up the price of wheat in western markets, and also kindled the ambitions of merchants, who sought it in ever more distant regions. Table 1.1 gives the volume of wheat exports through the principal Black Sea ports of the Russian Empire from 1792 to 1794. Exports tripled between 1792 and 1793, but fell in 1794, cut by crop failures, by a plague of locusts, and at one point by a government prohibition against the export of grain.

Table 1.1

The Export of Wheat
Through Black Sea Ports, 1792–1794 (In *Chetverts*)

	1792	1793	1794
Ochakiv	8,875	46,615	33,390
Kherson	14,812	29,399	2,758
Mykolaiv	15,682	26,010	6,511
Taganrog	5,326	32,328	20,483
Totals	44,695	134,352	63,142

Source: Vol'skii, 1854, p. 61.

But these early foundations were also handicapped in serving as entrepôts between the hinterland and the hungry western markets. The Sea of Azov was shallow and difficult to navigate. Its ports (Taganrog, Mariiupil, Azov) attracted only the most skilled and confident—and venturesome—captains. Kherson and Mykolaiv, both Black Sea ports of great potential, were founded upon lowlands; the proximity and extent of marshes worsened conditions of hygiene and obstructed land traffic with the hinterland. By 1794, the newly resuscitated trade with the West had not found a satisfactory port to link sea and steppes.

Novorossiia and Its Capital

In 1764 Catherine formed the territories newly acquired in the southwest of her empire into a province, which she called Novorossiia.[18] In the course of the war waged between 1787 and 1791, Don

Joseph de Ribas, a soldier of fortune born in Naples of Spanish and Irish stock and one of many adventurers in Catherine's service, stormed the fortress of Yeni-Dunai at Khadzhibei.[19] The date was September 17, 1789, and the newly conquered territory was added to the province of Novorossiia.

The Treaty of Jassy (1792, new style), which ended the war, also profoundly reshaped the political geography of the Black Sea littoral. Russia was conceded full sovereignty over the Crimea, which she had claimed since 1783. Moreover, the Porte recognized her rule over the section of coast between the South Boh and the Dniester, including the site of Khadzhibei.

Catherine apparently considered making the port of Ochakiv, near the mouth of the Boh River, the effective capital of Novorossiia.[20] But Ochakiv lacked a good natural harbor. On the other hand, de Ribas and a close collaborator, a Dutch engineer named Franz de Voland, recommended Khadzhibei as the site of the region's principal port. Its harbor was deep and nearly ice-free. Breakwaters, on the model of those found at Naples, Livorno, and Ancona, could be cheaply constructed and would render the harbor safe even for large fleets. The governor general of Novorossiia, Prince Platon Zubov—one of Catherine's favorites—lent crucial support to this latter proposal. On May 27, 1794, Catherine gave it her approval.[21]

She immediately sent twenty-six thousand rubles to de Ribas and de Voland to build a harbor. This new settlement was given the name Odessa. The reasons for this choice are obscure. According to one report, the august Academy at St. Petersburg first proposed it.[22] Catherine doubtless consulted with many advisers, but there seems no reason to doubt the old tradition that the final choice was her own, as was confirmed by an Italian merchant resident in Odessa only a few years after its founding.[23] Significantly, the name of Odessa, like that of Kherson, has strong Greek connotations. It was named after the ancient Greek settlement Odessos built almost forty-five *versts* to the east of Khadzhibei on the left bank of the Tylihul's'kyi Lyman. According to A. Orlov, an early historian of Odessa, Catherine ordered that the name be written not Odessos, but Odessa, "in the feminine gender."[24] She reportedly made the statement at a court ball on January 6, 1795.[25] Perhaps too, as other historians have surmised, she hoped that a Greek name would attract Greek merchants and settlers to the new foundation, for their presence would be critical to its prosperity.[26]

And the new town did prosper. It provided the required entrepôt, where merchants from abroad could bid for products brought in from

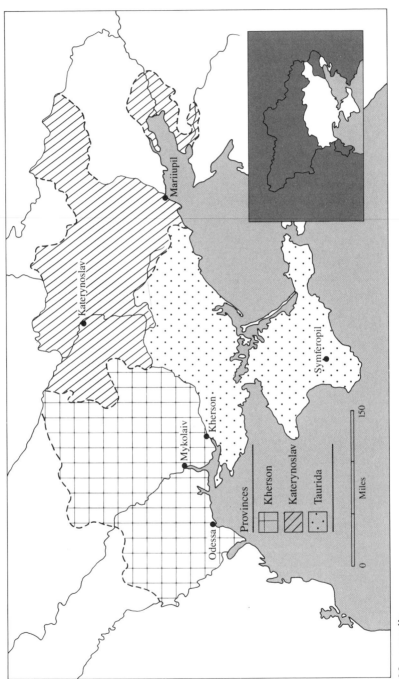

Novorossiia

a politically stable and economically productive hinterland. In fact, Odessa proved to be the most successful of Catherine's many foundations; in its rapid growth it much resembles what Gunther Barth has called an "instant city."[27] In the metaphor of one Russian historian, Odessa "rose like a mushroom after a heavy rain"; in the view of another, this was a city that "had no infancy."[28] In 1889, a German engineer claimed that such rapid growth was "unheard of in Europe."[29] The advantages that gave it this remarkable growth were several—an excellent location, intelligent planning, the favor of the imperial government, the appeal of the city to settlers of many nationalities, and, above all, the continuing expansion of foreign trade.

Site

Not the least of the new town's advantages were aesthetic. The city was founded upon an outcropped promontory, rising to a height of almost two hundred feet above the Pontine plain. Nearly every traveler who approached the city by water commented upon its striking location. An English visitor wrote in the 1840s:

> A view of Odessa from the sea is very commanding. A majestic line of stone houses of Grecian architecture, forming a handsome "boulevard" built on the edge of a cliff about 200 feet high, the abrupt termination of the steppe,. . .[30]

In 1862, Timothy Smith of Vermont, appointed to serve as United States consul in the city, wrote enthusiastically of his first view of Odessa:

> It stands upon a bluff or ridge of soft stone, of a yellow color, which rises almost abruptly about one hundred fifty feet from the shore, leaving a margin below available for storehouses, dock yards and heavy trade.[31]

The approach from the hinterland also possessed dramatic qualities. Travelers had to traverse the wide, monotonously flat and nearly deserted Ukrainian steppes:

> Our approach to Odessa [wrote a visitor in the 1820's] had a wild and dreary aspect. Oceans of steppe appeared everywhere, without a vestige of cultivation or wood.[32]

Inevitably, the similarity of steppe and sea suggested itself to these early travelers. The steppe was itself an "ocean" and the canvas-covered wagon that navigated across it "looked like a ship with sails."[33] Odessa was a port twice-over, looking out to the empty sea, looking inward to the seemingly empty land. It was also a center of movement, of bustle and of life, which contrasted with the solitude and the stillness of both steppe and sea.

> Arriving at Odessa from the steppe [a German visitor observed], as in our case, it is scarcely possible to trust the senses, when the rows of splendid houses, whose outline becomes constantly more distinct, gradually rise to view, and after having seen nothing for a length of time but sky and steppe, we suddenly behold the busy scene in all its magnificence.[34]

The bustling city presented itself in a riot of color. The plains, in contrast, were monochromatic—brown in spring, green in summer, gold in autumn, and white in winter. Odessa's site, set between solitudes, no doubt influenced even its cultural life. Both to immigrants and to distant observers, it seemed a point of concentrated action, of vital movement, surrounded by inert steppe and empty sea. Things were done at Odessa, and life was lived intensively. As the poet Vladimir Mayakovsky once exclaimed: "It happened/ In Odessa, it happened. . . ."[35]

Among the further advantages of the city was a comparatively mild climate and a good natural harbor. Its mean annual temperature is 50.4° F. (10.2° C.). January, the coldest month, averages 27.3° F. (−2.6° C.). July, the hottest month, has a mean temperature of 73.4° F. (23° C.). The site is, however, exposed to shifting winds and to spells of unusual heat and cold.[36] Average annual rainfall is slight (431.3 mm. or 17 inches) and also erratic. Some years it is only 200 milimeters, or less than 9 inches. A climatological factor of prime importance at Odessa was wind. The uninterrupted flatlands to the north made the region a wind channel between two weather systems, the Mediterranean and the continental.[37] The promontory upon which the city was set held it high into the course of these shifting currents.

The lively air usually quickly dissipated spells of dead heat or dead cold, which were the bane of lowland towns. But they also, quite literally, stirred up an acute problem for the populace. That problem was dust. The limestone soil—formed by layers of cockleshells and the porous debris of other shellfish—was easily friable, and the winds of the summer distributed a suffocating dust through the town.[38]

Windows or doors, even when tightly fitted, offered scant protection. The rains of winter cleared the air but transformed the dust into ubiquitous mud, nearly as obnoxious. Still, these annoyances did not constitute major hazards to health, and Odessa's turbulent air was, on balance, a benefit.[39]

In an area nearly devoid of trees, the Pontine limestone, which largely formed the seaside bluffs, offered a satisfactory building material. The stone was soft enough for a hachet to cut, and, as one traveler noted, it was "very favourable for the more showy purposes of the architect."[40] The limestone hardened under weathering and its light color set the hues of the new and growing city. Imbedded in the limestone were so many cockleshells that many of the houses had "the rough appearance of an artificial grotto."[41] The promontory was itself mined in building the city, resulting in "catacombs" underlying its surface.

The limestone was also easily penetrated by wells reaching down to the water table, set upon impervious clays. The ravines, cutting into the limestone, uncovered natural springs, and in 1792 the well water available on Odessa's future site was described as "fresh and good."[42] But already in 1805 an Italian merchant found that the water was bad and very scarce in summer.[43]

The limestone cliffs gave Odessa its beauty, but the narrow stretch of coastal plain between the cliffs and the sea made its fortune. The same Italian merchant who complained about the drinking water in the city praised the waters of its harbor. "Its port has one of the easiest approaches and furnishes excellent anchorage of a depth of 11 meters."[44]

The harbors of the Sea of Azov were all shallow, as were those of the Black Sea located on or close to river deltas. In Odessa's deep harbor, large ships could load and unload their cargoes without the use of lighters. Tides were insignificant; changes in depth responded to variations in river flow (and sometimes to winds) but were never substantial. Comparatively mild temperatures kept the harbor free from ice for most of the year. Typically, ice formed in the harbor about January 4, and its closing could be expected between January 27 and February 19. But the spring thaw came early, and usually the port was open once more in early March. In about one out of three years, the harbor did not close at all. To be sure, the weather was erratic, and a sharp cold wave could unexpectedly close the port. In 1803, the waters froze within twenty-four hours—a remarkably brief period. Ice held sixty ships laden with grain destined for western Europe in its unyielding grasp.[45]

The Black Sea remained, of course, a challenge to sailors. According to an observer writing before 1819, November was the most dangerous month for ships, with violent storms and dense fogs to harass navigators.[46] But Odessa shared these difficulties with every other Black Sea port. Given the risks of the open water, mariners no doubt found her excellent harbor all the more welcome.

Planning

As a new foundation, Odessa was from its origin a planned city; its early history reflects not only military and commercial needs, but the esthetic sense of the epoch. The two chief architects of the town were de Ribas, the Spanish-Irish soldier of fortune; and de Voland, the Dutch engineer. The honor for drawing the city's design has traditionally been awarded to de Ribas, whose name still today decorates one of Odessa's principal thoroughfares. Catherine gave him chief responsibility for the town administration, and he successfully presided over the city's early growth. But by de Ribas's own testimony, de Voland built the port "according to his own projects and plans," which received the approval of Prince Platon Zubov, commander of the Black Sea fleet.[47]

The terrain imposed many constraints upon the builders. The coastal plain became perforce the port district of the city—destined to contain wharves, the quarantine, customs house, and warehouses—but it was too small to include a large residential area. The city was chiefly laid out atop the high promontory, which gently sloped to the southeast. Two ravines cut into the surface, and the uneven terrain prevented the implementation of a rigorously symmetrical layout.

De Voland's plan for Odessa was "in keeping with other western ideas of the time."[48] Because of the ravines, de Voland laid out two gridirons intersecting at a forty-seven degree angle. To preserve uniform rectangularity in the city blocks, the principal gridiron had to be set at an angle to the shore. This grid pattern was a popular contemporary form, chiefly because it rendered the tasks of surveying and subdividing relatively straightforward. It often appears, for example, in the new towns of the American West. De Voland's design envisioned spacious streets one hundred feet wide; an esplanade was to separate the old Turkish fort from the residential area.

Soldiers from the local garrison began constructing the city and port on August 22, 1794, a date traditionally celebrated as Odessa's official birthday.[49] At the request of Platon Zubov, the imperial government provided the substantial sum of a little less than 2 million rubles, to be spent over a five-year period. These funds were to be used for the construction of the port, the admiralty, barracks, and warehouses. The Platon Mole commemorated the name of the city's benefactor. In 1796, the city received an additional 312,135 rubles to pay for the construction of a hospital, cathedral, and administrative offices.[50]

The young city was divided into two sections, the Military and the Greek. The Military section occupied fifty-two blocks with 560 lots. The Greek section included sixty-five blocks with 720 lots. De Ribas was given authority to assign the lots. He took two for himself and built a house, and other lots were given to various Russian nobles, military personnel and merchants.[51] In providing port facilities, state buildings, private homes, churches, gardens, and markets, de Voland and de Ribas faced constant frustrations. Shortages of building materials, difficulties in transporting needed supplies, faulty plans, hasty construction, and misappropriation of funds obstructed their work. Still, at the age of one year, Odessa boasted a customhouse, a quarantine station, police offices, and other administrative bureaus. The foundations were laid for St. Catherine's Orthodox Church in 1794; in the following year, construction began on the Greek church of the Trinity. De Voland's reputation grew with the city. In 1795, an English woman who visited the new town expressed the sanguine opinion that, as it was de Voland's work, the city was destined for greatness.[52] By 1796, Odessa had a stock exchange and an office of censorship—both indicators of a lively commercial and cultural life.

Empress Catherine had favored both Odessa and its architects, and her death in 1796 introduced a dark interlude in its young history. Her son and successor Emperor Paul hated his mother and all her works. He purged her chief administrators in Novorossiia, including de Ribas, and forced the resignation of de Voland. The two went on to active, even turbulent, careers; de Ribas was implicated in a plot to assassinate the emperor in 1799. But neither one is subsequently involved in the history of Odessa.[53]

The city's growth did not rigorously conform to de Voland's original plan, but Odessa continued to reflect in its wide streets and regular grid his basic conceptions.[54] Perhaps not surprisingly, a visitor from the New World, Mark Twain, detected in the 1860s resemblances to midwestern America:

I have not felt so much at home for a long time as I did when I "raised the hill" and stood in Odessa for the first time. It looked just like an American city; fine, broad streets, and straight as well; a stirring, business-look about the streets and the stores; fast walkers; a familiar *new* look about the houses and everything; yes, and a driving and smothering cloud of dust that was so like a message from our own dear native land that we could hardly refrain from shedding a few grateful tears and execrations in the old time-honored American way. Look up the street or down the street, this way or that way, we saw only America.[55]

An earlier visitor, a German doctor, also noted Odessa's broad streets and its position between two solitudes:

The streets are, like all new Russian streets, immensely broad, and so completely open that one can often see the sea at one end and the steppe at the other, and look from the middle of the city at once into the waste of waters and the waste of grass.[56]

Odessa, with its long and wide streets and distant vistas, was designed for expansion. The city, in a way, looked outward. This characteristic may have handicapped the coalescence of an integrated urban community. Later observers noted, as we shall see, that Odessa's society was highly segmented. On the other hand, the same characteristic easily tolerated the existence of differing ethnic and cultural groups within the city; the forces of assimilation worked feebly. Its physical layout thus may have reinforced one of the chief features of the new town—a cosmopolitan society and culture.

It is a commonplace of urban history that the government dominated urban development in the Russian Empire, whereas western European and American towns grew spontaneously.[57] Catherine did indeed decree that a town should rise on the site of Khadzhibei, but the central government in St. Petersburg had difficulty retaining tight control over its distant creation. Catherine's charter of towns, issued in 1785, provided for the election of city councils through complex procedures, but they exercised little power. At Odessa too, the participation of the citizenry in government remained very limited.[58] In Novorossiia, chief authority rested with an appointed official, the governor general, whose office was created in 1775. In 1802, Tsar Alexander I established the administrative mechanism under which the city would be governed for the next eighty years. The head of the urban government was called "city chief" (*gradonachal'nik*), and the area under his jurisdiction was the *gradonachal'stvo*.[59] He was appointed by the tsar—an indication of his importance—but answered to the governor general of Novorossiia and through him to the minister of internal affairs. The chief, or mayor, supervised the work of urban officials, although these too were largely selected by the central government.

Characteristically, however, these officials enjoyed greater autonomy than their commissions might suggest. The officials located on this distant frontier did not follow the strict bureaucratic routines required of their counterparts in the central provinces.[60] They could consult with St. Petersburg only on the most pressing matters, and sometimes had to act before an answer was received. The system remained authoritarian in theory, but under a capable and energetic administrator, it could be liberal in practice.

Moreover, with only trivial exceptions, the imperial government did not force serfs from the older provinces to settle upon the land and in the cities of Novorossiia—as it had in the early development of St. Petersburg.[61] Rather, it tried to encourage spontaneous settlement by offering land under favorable terms and by promoting commerce.

The early settlers of Novorossiia were predominantly free, or at least lived as free men. Among them were soldiers, including Cossacks, who garrisoned the fortress towns. Many, after their terms of service, remained as civilian residents in the towns they had guarded. Developers and speculators also figured prominently among the first arrivals, as they sought to take advantage of the wide, fertile, empty lands of the southern steppe. The frontier further attracted runaway serfs from the central provinces. At least three thousand Russian and Ukrainian serfs found freedom near Odessa in the last years of the eighteenth century.[62] One historian calculated that in 1797, one-third of Odessa's population was either without passports (which meant they had immigrated illegally) or were foreigners.[63] These people presented a special problem. Should the government chase them down and send them back to old Russia or quietly welcome their valued labor? Initially, the active policy seems to have been inaction; unless strongly prodded, the government did not pursue these fugitives. In an *ukaz* dated December 12, 1796, and promulgated after her death, Catherine allowed runaway serfs settled in the southern Ukraine to remain there in freedom.[64] The lure of liberty would attract—Catherine seems to have hoped—abundant labor to these sparsely settled lands. This policy marks an early limit set on the reign of serfdom in Russia, and perhaps an incipient awareness of its deficiencies. [64]

We do not, of course, know how many serfs availed themselves of this route to freedom, but contemporaries imply that they were many. To travelers, Novorossiia looked to be a European Australia, a dump of fugitives and criminals, "an asylum for the refuse of neighboring countries."[65] By 1819, three-quarters of Odessa's petty tradesmen and even some of its great merchants were said to be runaway serfs.[66] According to Baron von Haxthausen, these fugitives were known as *neznaiushchie* or "know-nothings." In reply to any query concerning their origins, they always replied, "Ne znaiu" (I don't know).[67] Serfdom, to be exact, was not entirely banned from the soil of Novorossiia. Landowners (*pomeshchiks*) could transfer their serfs to Novorossiia if they owned land there; but few did so in the eighteenth century.[68]

Catherine also actively recruited free colonists from beyond the borders of the empire. In general terms, Catherine offered to the foreign immigrants attractive terms that included land, tax exemptions, loans, religious toleration, and other privileges. She invited, for example, two to three hundred Greek, Albanian, and Moldavian veterans of her Turkish wars to settle in Odessa. Some twenty thousand *desiatina*s were allocated for these colonists.[69] The imperial government promised each family a house and a loan to help it build its new life. If the family constructed its own house, it received a bonus of 150 rubles. The government further donated two thousand rubles toward the erection of a small church. The colonists could bring through customs without tariff their household possessions and even goods for sale, up to a value of three thousand rubles. Beyond that sum, they were charged only one-fourth of the normal tariff on the goods they imported. They were freed from all duties and services for ten years, and were forever exempt from military conscription and from billeting soldiers.[70]

The religious toleration, promised to all immigrants, had a further purpose. Many—Greeks, Bulgarians, Albanians, Moldavians, Armenians, and others—were former Turkish subjects, and they retained national and cultural animosities against the Ottomans. The preservation of their cultural identities would make them, it was hoped, stalwart defenders of the frontier against any Ottoman resurgence.

According to A. A. Skal'kovskii, Catherine persuaded half a million Jews to settle in Novorossiia along with lesser numbers of German, Swiss, and Portuguese colonists.[71] Some failures accompanied these successes. Thus, Catherine hoped to found two colonies on the Sea of Azov, large enough to offer asylum to six thousand French émigrés, fugitives from the revolution in their native country.[72] But the émigrés seemingly had more attractive invitations, and they never came.

Also, because of the vast distances, the central Russian government could not always deliver the help and rewards it had promised. In 1783, for example, a ship crowded with 195 prospective settlers set sail from Genoa, destined for Kherson. The archives of Turin contains a list of their names and professions.[73] Some 164 were of Italian origin, and they included peasants, artisans, soldiers, and sailors. They seem never to have received in their new home the aid promised them, and their enterprise ended in failure. "I saw the bad outcome," an Italian consular agent tersely reported, "of the Italian colonists transported to Kherson, where those unfortunates, abandoned by the government, died of starvation."

Other colonies succeeded, and their success brought not only people, but capital, into Novorossiia. A document, dated August 1799, allows us to examine the composition of the merchant class of Odessa.[74] The list gives us the name, age, capital, guild membership, and provenance of nearly all the male heads of family and mentions also the names and ages of their wives and offspring. Of the 208 Odessan merchants so described, 126—about 40 percent—came from abroad, and the remaining 82 were Russian, or at least born within the empire. Most of those of foreign extraction came from Ottoman territories, and among them Greeks predominated.[75]

Eager to promote trade through the new port, the government adopted commercial policies remarkably liberal for the epoch. In 1782, Catherine reduced all duties on imports and exports through the Black Sea ports (then Kherson, Sevastopol, and Teodosiia) by one-quarter. In 1784, she declared those ports open to the flags of all nations with which the empire had concluded trade agreements.[76] Two years later, she freed all the Crimean ports from tariffs for a period of five years. A milestone in the liberalization of trade was the conclusion of a commercial treaty with France in 1787, from which the Black Sea ports drew the principal profit.[77]

To be sure, in a tumultuous epoch, trade remained a hostage to political events—to revolutions, wars, alliances, and even changes in regimes. The revolution in France (1789), the declaration of a republic (1792), and the execution of Louis XVI (1793) impelled Catherine to sever both diplomatic and commercial relations with the Gallic regicides.[78] Her son Paul (1796–1801) was by nature xenophobic, and events in Europe did little to reassure him that light came from the West. In 1797, he published a new tariff schedule, which revised rates sharply upward. But even Paul did not break entirely with the favorable policy that his mother had adopted in regard to the southern harbors. He conferred on the Crimean towns of Teodosiia and Ievpatoriia the status of free ports for thirty years.[79] His son, Alexander I, (1801–1825) returned fully to the enlightened principles of his grandmother. He professed admiration for that apostle of economic liberalism, Adam Smith. The new tsar found a spirit kindred in thoughts, if not in origins, in the new ruler of France, Napoleon. Skilled in the councils of peace as well as war, Napoleon promoted the commerce of France, and his keen eye discerned the extraordinary promise of the Black Sea trade. On February 16, 1802, seeking to revive the commercial treaty of 1787 abrogated by Catherine, he wrote to Alexander:

> The states of Your Majesty and of France should have a direct commerce by way of the Black Sea. . . . It would be one of the most profitable flows of commerce, inasmuch as it is the most direct and sure of seas and is always navigable. . . . We would carry directly from Marseilles the products of our colonies and of our manufactures, and in return [bring] wheat, wood and other products, which could arrive with ease along the great rivers which empty into the Black Sea.[80]

The treaty with France was signed, and in 1803 Alexander further decreased by 25 percent the duties of imports and exports through the Black Sea ports. He was in effect restoring the conditions of trade which his grandmother had established. To be sure, wars with Turkey and with France itself affected commerce. But, clearly, the central thrust of governmental policy was to favor commerce through the new ports on the Black Sea, including Odessa.

The government thus played an important, but still restricted, role in the early growth of Odessa. The fiat of rulers did not fill the fields with settlers nor pack the port with ships. Rather, the government sought to encourage spontaneous resettlement, to promote the natural swell of commerce into the new and fertile regions. Perhaps the state's chief contribution to the growth of Novorossiia and of Odessa was its willingness to let things pass. The colonists remained for the most part unharassed; goods were traded under fewer encumbrances and charges than elsewhere in the empire.

Two political events gave further stimulus to commerce. In 1801 the Ottomans granted unhampered passage through the Straits to flags deemed to be friendly—those of England, Russia, Naples, Ragusa, Holland, and the Seven Ionian Islands. And the general European peace of 1802 brought still larger numbers of vessels.[81] In 1803, the construction of two breakwaters was completed; they extended into the sea a distance of 250 *sazhen*s (about 532.5 meters) and divided the harbor into three parts. It was now also possible to run grain-laden carts along embankments, and to load the grain (and other forms of freight) directly onto the ships.

In 1794, only seven ships ventured into the harbor; in 1795, thirty-nine ships. In 1796, eighty-six ships weighed anchor in the port and sixty-four departed.[82] Table 1.2 gives the value of Odessa's imports and exports in silver rubles, over the years from 1795 to 1802.

Table 1.2

Odessa's Imports and Exports, 1795–1802
(In Silver Rubles)

Year	Imports	Exports	Totals
1795	43,065	24,824	67,889
1796	92,559	79,422	171,981
1797	129,492	79,091	208,583
1798	117,888	90,977	208,865
1799	303,822	111,258	415,080
1800	264,651	287,540	552,191
1801	501,820	519,906	1,021,726
1802	719,982	1,534,114	2,254,096

Source: Compiled from Druzhinina, 1959; Zolotov, 1963; and Sirotkin, 1970, p. 79.

Initially, imports exceeded exports. Odessa had to bring in by sea the building supplies and furnishings it needed for its many new constructions. But the register of exports shows from the start a greater buoyancy, and after 1801 they substantially surpassed in value the quantity of imports. This favorable balance remained characteristic of Odessa's maritime commerce for decades thereafter.

This buoyancy also carried Odessa to first position among the Black Sea ports. In 1798, Taganrog, with imports valued at 447,657 silver rubles and exports at 858,705 rubles, still far surpassed Odessa. But by 1805, the two ports handled approximately equal volumes.[83]

To maintain perspective, it should, however, be noted that the Black Sea commerce still represented only a fraction of Russia's total foreign trade. From 1793 to 1797, that trade was valued at 76.9 million rubles. Of this sum, ports on the Baltic Sea accounted for 71.3 million rubles, and those on the White Sea, 3.7 million. The Black Sea carried Russian commerce to the value of 1.9 million rubles—a mere 2.5 percent of the total.[84] But if the volume appears small, there is no mistaking its movement. By 1802, the Black Sea trade had come to account for some 4 to 5 percent of the total. By then 16.3 percent of all the wheat exported from the Russian Empire was moving through these southern outlets.[85]

With growing trade came a growing population. In 1795, according to a survey taken by de Ribas, 2,349 persons were settled on the 30,700 *desiatinas* of land which made up the original circumscription of the town.[86] This census did not include nobles, civil servants, the garrison, or a special contingent of Greek and Albanian soldiers. There were registered some 1,679 petty tradesmen (*meshchane*), 146 merchants, 240 Jews, 224 Greeks, and 60 Bulgars. Of the 1,845 Russians, fully one-third were runaway serfs.

Two years later, the population was officially recorded as 3,153. The figure, however, included 337 Greek and Albanian soldiers and 404 Cossacks. The true increase in population over two years was thus 269. We know further that in 1797 there were approximately 800 Italians residing in Odessa, then forming about 25 percent of the population.[87] The city was also growing in a physical sense. According to a survey dated 1799, it contained 60 state buildings (22 of stone), 353 private houses, 234 earthen huts, 416 shops (174 of stone) and 101 magazines.[88] These and other surveys give some sense of the society of the new town and also of its economy. The great merchant families inhabited the stone houses. Twelve of these families accounted for a trade in goods worth 300,000 rubles annually. At the other end of the social scale, port and construction workers, "those who supported themselves in labor," inhabited the earthen houses.[89]

Apart from work in the port itself, construction was the chief support of the laboring population. The survey of 1799 records the presence of three brick yards, employing eighty workers and four limestone works, employing twenty-four. Among other visible industries there was one macaroni factory and one powder (cosmetic) manufactory.[90]

Odessa had enjoyed remarkable growth in the first decade of its life. But not all the visitors to the town in 1803 or 1804 expressed optimism for its future. Some pointed to looming problems of housing, water, public services, and civic culture. Odessa had lacked consistent, central direction—a leader who could channel its surging energies and give its physical structures harmonious shape as a city. These were the accomplishments of the remarkable man who in 1803 came to preside over Odessa's destinies—the duc de Richelieu.

CHAPTER TWO

The Regime of Richelieu: Enlightenment and Growth in Novorossiia, 1803–1814

[The] Duke de Richelieu . . . the founder and benefactor of Odessa, his name can never cease to be regarded with reverence.
—George Gordon Lord Byron, 1822

In 1803, Tsar Alexander I named as *gradonachal'nik* or "city chief" of Odessa a young French émigré, then thirty-six years old, the duc de Richelieu. Eighteen months later, in 1805, the tsar enlarged his authority by appointing him to serve simultaneously as governor general of the then three provinces of Novorossiia. In the eleven years of his administration, the duc de Richelieu acquired an extraordinary reputation for statesmanship and sense, both abroad and in Russia. To the English writer, Lord Byron, he was a figure of high romance, in part a model for his fictional hero, Don Juan.[1]

In Russia his reputation has remained bright and untarnished through changing times and regimes. Tsar Alexander I allegedly remarked that the French Revolution could not have been all bad, as it bestowed on Russia the services of Richelieu.[2] Soon after the duc's return to France, the grateful citizens of Odessa commissioned the sculptor Ivan Petrovich Martos (1754–1835) to execute a bronze statue of the governor. Finished in 1826, it was placed (and still stands) at the top of the majestic sweep of stairs—now called the Potemkin steps—that lead to the coastal plain below.[3] Clothed inexplicably in a toga, the statue points to the sea, presumably to indicate the source of Odessa's riches.

The Making of an Administrator

The duc de Richelieu was born in 1766 near Bordeaux, France, a scion of a distinguished noble lineage.[4] The famed Cardinal Richelieu, chief minister of Louis XIII in the seventeenth century, was his great-uncle. He was educated at the College du Plessis, which his great-uncle had founded, and did brilliantly. His family betrothed the fifteen-year-old lad to the daughter of Count Louis de Rochechouart, Rosalie, age twelve. He set forth soon after for a tour of Italy, Switzerland, Germany and Austria (1783–1784). Upon his return to France, he discovered that his fiancée was deformed (a hunchback). But still he married her and departed once again for Austria and Russia. His wife never joined him in his long and lengthy peregrinations abroad.[5] Like many young and ambitious officers from the West, he was drawn to the service of Empress Catherine in 1789 and fought against the Turks under the command of Suvorov. He joined in the successful assault on the Turkish fortress at Ismail in 1790 and suffered a slight wound. For this display of courage, Catherine decorated him with the Cross of St. George, and he earned a reputation at the imperial court. He returned briefly to France in 1801 and 1802. When Napoleon insisted that he serve France exclusively, he once more went abroad. In part his dislike of the upstart Corsican, in part his friendship for the new tsar, Alexander, brought him back to Russia.

Although Byron viewed him as a romantic figure, the duc de Richelieu was very much a child of the Enlightenment. He was cool and calculating and brave in battle, but he avoided all acts of personal flamboyance. As chief of Odessa and governor of Novorossiia, he resided in a modest five-room house with simple furnishings, always living within his means.[6] To contemporaries and later historians, he has had the appearance more of a commoner (*raznochinets*) than the highborn noble he was. Druzhinina attributes his austere regimen to a "Puritan" upbringing.[7] He rose early in the morning to get a quick start on the day's business. His cousin and aide has left us this description of the *gradonachal'nik*'s daily schedule:

> . . . he rose at six, summer and winter, and took a cup of *café au lait* at 8 o'clock. Then, except on Sundays and festivals, he gave audience for an hour to anyone who wished to see him; after this, he would work with his three civil secretaries until 12:30. At one he dined, then worked or went out until evening; he had supper at nine and went to bed at 11:00.[8]

Thanks partially to his early travels, he was fluent in numerous foreign languages—Russian, German, English and Italian as well as his native French. He listened attentively to the petitions and complaints of citizens and liked to wander through the city on foot, making observations, inviting conversation, sensing moods.

In his personal relations, the duc was friendly and approachable, but avoided passionate attachments or aversions to favorites or foes. No shadow of scandal touches his life. A contemporary described him as tall and lean, with fine curly hair; he had "dark, kind eyes, and a very pleasant white face without a beard, like a woman."[9] He seems to have been near-sighted. According to his friend Sicard, the duc would always ask a companion if he should greet an oncoming woman on the street, as he could not tell whether he knew her or not.[10]

This sociable, gentle, and modest man was apparently as much appreciated by foreign citizens of his city as by Russians themselves. The Nogai Tatars were said to have "loved and respected him as a father."[11] He was solicitous in settling them into permanent communities. To this end he "had a mosque and a house for the mullah and his family built in each of their camps." He was aided in his work by the comte de Maisons, formerly president of the Parlement of Rouen, who devoted thirty years without pay to caring for the Tatars.[12] The Jews also revered his person and his memory. The elders of the community recounted with wonder his goodness and tolerance, blessing his name.[13]

One French historian characterizes his rule as one of "enlightened despotism," or the "dictatorship of honesty."[14] Like many men of the Enlightenment, he had abounding faith that reason, founded upon close observation, could resolve even the most truculent human problems. No detail of administration—or corner of social life—was so menial as to escape his direct attention. He gave seemingly equivalent energies to every aspect of government, the grand and the trivial. He envisioned a countryside filled with free and prosperous farmers, exporting their surpluses through a city filled with free and prosperous merchants and artisans.

The Peopling of Novorossiia

From his integrated perspective, Richelieu recognized that the growth of Odessa depended upon a growing hinterland—upon a supportive regional structure of farms, local markets, roads, and thoroughfares pumping the blood of commerce to and through the port.[15] Critical in the development of Novorossiia was the establishment of a stable administration over its region. Acquisitions of extensive territories along the Turkish frontier, changes in rulers and changes in the whims of rulers were breeding administrative confusion. Through an *ukaz* promulgated on October 8, 1802, Tsar Alexander I brought comparative stability into this regional government. He permanently divided Novorossiia into three *guberniias*. Two of them took their names from cities: Katerynoslav, "the glory of Catherine," founded in 1786 by her favorite Potemkin; and the port Mykolaiv, later replaced by Kherson. This latter *guberniia* included Odessa. The third division of Novorossiia was called Taurida, from the ancient Greek name for the Crimea.[16] The administration of these three provinces was originally confided to a single governor general. The duc de Richelieu, who accepted the commission in 1805, was the second governor general, and the first to combine that post with appointment as chief of Odessa.[17]

Richelieu's chief task as governor was spelled out in the emperor's mandate. He was "to seek to increase the population by extending all encouragements and privileges to foreigners. ..." With the indispensable support of Emperor Alexander, Richelieu offered immigrants the inducements of fertile and nearly free land, grants and loans, tax exemptions, and religious toleration. The resultant flow of immigrants moving into Novorossiia can be divided into two principal currents: "internal" migrants, that is, those coming from areas already forming part of the empire; and foreigners, those attracted from beyond its borders. Both groups helped to give the region that extraordinary mixture of nationalities, languages, and religions that thereafter marked its history.[18]

Internal Migration

Among Russians and Ukrainians, the great spur to migration south was continuing population growth and land crowding in the central provinces of the empire. The Russian government possessed the authority to move peasants—technically, serfs—settled upon state lands into the new regions. Thus, between 1807 and 1812 the government transferred 3,002 peasants from the overcrowded province of Smolensk into the Crimea.[19] But Richelieu opposed forcible transfers of laborers as he recognized that only willing workers could subdue the challenging steppe.[20] The voluntary flow of state peasants grew slowly. They came, for example, in family groups of five, ten, or fifteen from the province of Chernihiv—another crowded area—to settle in the Crimea.[21] Between the years 1806 and 1809, over one thousand state peasants sought permission to migrate to Novorossiia. In June 1812, at the recommendation of Richelieu, Alexander exempted all state peasants who settled in Novorossiia from taxes for a period of five years. They were also eligible for cash subsidies and loans. After 1812, the movement of peasants from the crowded center—especially Smolensk—swelled; many contemporary steppe villages—Bel'manka, Haichul, Temriuk—owe their origin to this influx. By 1860, at least 4,115 state peasant farmsteads had been transferred to the South Ukraine.[22]

The frontier, with its aura of freedom, was especially attractive to religious dissenters. Among them were the Dukhobors, a sect characterized by pacifism, by a communal way of life, and by their energetic and productive husbandry. On governmental invitation, Dukhobors, who were technically state peasants, settled along the Molochna River in 1802.[23] The privileges accorded to them were exceptionally generous. Each "soul" (in the definition of the census taker) was given fifteen *desiatina*s of land and a loan of one hundred rubles, to be repaid over twenty years, beginning in 1812. They were also excused from taxes for the usual five-year period. Like the Mennonites and the Old Believers, who had settled the region in Catherine's time, they were also exempt from military service.

These state peasants—both Orthodox and dissenters—did well in Novorossiia. Exemption from military service (though only for a time) and from onerous state taxes conferred upon them a status nearly equivalent to that of free colonists. Many became substantial farmers. Contemporaries compared their prosperity with that of the German settlers—high praise indeed, as the Germans were supposed to serve as models of good husbandry on the steppe.[24]

Cossacks also moved south; they had long been settled along the Russo-Ukrainian frontier facing the Tatars and Turks. From 1806 to 1809, 7,165 Cossacks from the provinces of Chernihiv, Poltava, and elsewhere migrated to Novorossiia.[25] The benefits given them under the *ukaz* of 1812, however, were fewer than those received by the state peasants; their exemption from taxes, for example, lasted for only one and one-half years. And the allotments of land accorded them were also smaller. Richelieu himself invited a group of Ukrainian Cossacks to settle in the military area east of the Sea of Azov, although their new home lay beyond the borders of Novorossiia.[26] An even more exotic group of settlers were the former slaves, called *iasyr*s, who once belonged to Tatars.[27] Alexander I emancipated them in 1808 and provided them with loans and land in the Crimea.

Jewish Colonies

Jews formed a special group within the category of "internal" migrants. Jews had lived in the region of Odessa even before the founding of the city. Their settlements were scattered among the small villages near the fort of Khadzhibei. Jews were also numerous in the large cities of the Ottoman Empire, where they earned their living primarily as artisans and retail merchants. Odessa possessed a Jewish cemetery soon after 1794. The first synagogue was built in 1798. Skal'kovskii gives the Jewish population as 240 out of a total population of 2,349 in 1795, although Smol'ianinov gives a lower figure of 135 Jews for 1797.[28] When Richelieu assumed the governorship, he made special efforts to attract Jewish immigrants, not only to the cities, but also to the countryside of Novorossiia.

By far the largest single source of early Jewish immigration was the region of Belorussia (White Russia).[29] The Russian Empire obtained sovereignty over the area through the successive partitions of Poland in 1772, 1793, and 1795. The Jewish inhabitants numbered more than sixty thousand, and they worked chiefly as artisans, petty merchants, or tavern keepers (Polish law had forbidden them to engage in agriculture). Russian policy imposed further restrictions upon them. According to a *Polozhenie* or Ordinance of December 9, 1804, Jews could not live in villages outside a prescribed area or "pale." They also were no longer allowed to own or operate taverns. These were severe blows to their economic fortunes and came at a time when their own numbers were increasing.

Recognizing their plight, a Latvian administrator, I. G. Frizel, devised a plan to move a certain number of Jews out of their overcrowded villages to the empty steppes of Novorossiia. Like other colonists, these Jews would receive land, enjoy various exemptions, and in turn would establish farms and villages. Richelieu endorsed the idea, and from 1806 warmly received Jewish emigrants into Novorossiia. The state contributed the sum of 310,000 assignat rubles to meet the costs of relocation. Each family was to receive 125 rubles for the construction of a farmhouse and a daily food allowance of 5 kopecks, until the land became productive.

By 1809, eight Jewish colonies were established, most of them distributed along the Inhulets River in the Kherson *guberniia*. By 1810, according to a survey made that year, 1,691 Jewish colonial families, containing 9,757 individuals, were working the soil.

In spite of these auspicious beginnings, this experiment in Jewish agrarian settlement ended in failure. Ten years later, the number of colonial families had declined to only 417. The Jews abandoned the land, not because they were unaccustomed to agricultural pursuits, but because so little of the promised subsidies ever reached their hands. As S. Ia. Borovoi has shown, chicanery and peculation marked this project more than most.[30] Many Jews faced starvation, and many more decided to seek employment in villages and cities where their special skills were readily marketable. In particular, Odessa and other port cities easily absorbed Jewish artisans and traders.

Foreign Colonists

Even more than his grandmother Catherine, Tsar Alexander (and his chief lieutenant in the south, the duc de Richelieu), wished to attract settlers from abroad onto the steppes.[31] Alexander eagerly recruited new colonists from a remarkable variety of peoples. The neighboring Ottoman Empire contained numerous Christian peoples—Bulgarians, Gaguazy, Moldavians, Serbs, Greeks, Armenians and others—who had reason for disgruntlement with Turkish rule.[32] From all these communities, some migrants enlisted in the Russian army and fought in special national battalions. Others settled in the cities as merchants and tradesmen, and still others joined agricultural communities. Many sought a home in Bessarabia (incorporated into the Russian Empire in 1812), traditionally a haven for fugitives. One Bessarabian village in Alexander's time counted among its residents, Ukrainians, Moldavians, Russians, Bulgarians, Jews, French, Greeks, Armenians, Poles, Gypsies, Serbs, Albanians, Germans, Hungarians, Turks, and others.[33]

Bulgarians first appeared in the South Ukraine as early as the 1760s, but the largest influx came between 1801 and 1812. The French consul at Odessa has left an apt description of the movement:

> ... in this same period [1802–1819] the Bulgarian colonists likewise came. These were inhabitants of Rumelia [European Turkey along the shores of the Black Sea] of Greek religion and origin. Their compatriots and some Greek merchants of Constantinople, through emissaries who were also their compatriots and who had been for many years settled in Odessa, came to persuade them to come as colonists to Russia. The bonds of religion, the hope for a better future, the assurance to a jealous folk that their wives and daughters would be protected, the exemption from conscription and the promises of subsidies made to them, did not fail to persuade these Christians, who were as slaves in Turkey, to flee their oppressors and to escape their

yoke. Thousands of these Bulgars moved away; they were taken on board ships along the coasts and brought to Odessa. Here, they have colonized the environs and the interior of the steppes to a distance of 15, 20 and 50 leagues. Among all the colonists of different races and nations, they farm the most diligently and gather in better wheat than the Russians, the Poles and the Germans.[34]

The immigration of these Ottoman subjects to the Russian Empire strained its relationship with the Porte. In 1801, clearly in response to Ottoman pressure, Alexander issued the curious command that Russia would no longer receive immigrants who crossed the Danube River, which marked the inland frontier with Turkey. If the émigrés arrived in Odessa by ship, however, they would be granted Russian citizenship, assistance, temporary residence in Odessa, and land to farm.[35]

Serbs were also settling in the region from the middle eighteenth century, but their numbers also swelled in the first decade of the nineteenth century.[36] In 1804, twenty-two families arrived at the port of Odessa. They eventually settled along the river Balaichuk; each family received the generous allotment of 150 to 500 *desiatinas* of land. In 1815, another group of sixteen Serbian families arrived; they received only 65 *desiatinas* of land per family—a reduction which no doubt reflected the diminishing extent of uncultivated soil.

Among those fleeing the domination of the Turks were Greeks and Armenians.[37] In the eighteenth century, many "Greeks" from the Crimea settled in the Azov region, especially around Mariiupil. In the early nineteenth century, new waves of Greek immigrants arrived from the Balkans and the Archipelago. They had difficulty communicating with the Mariiupil Greeks, who had long since adopted the Tatar language and dress. The Greek farmers learned from their neighbors on the steppes how to raise livestock and plant orchards and vegetable gardens. A flourishing Armenian colony also grew up at Hryhoriopil on the Dniester.

Eager to develop as many specialized industries as possible, the duc de Richelieu invited Moldavians to settle in a region near Tyraspil on the left bank of the Dniester. He had discovered that the mulberry tree flourished there and somehow learned that Moldavians were skilled in the art of raising silkworms. Agents were dispatched to buy up the land from its private owners for redistribution to the Moldavian colonists. At first only twenty-four families responded to his invitation, but by 1808, fifty-nine families were industriously engaged in the production of silk.

Even some Muslim subjects of the Ottoman Porte sought out homes in Novorossiia. Here the most important group was the Nogai Tatars, who are often mistakenly confused with the Crimean Tatars.[38] As early as the 1770s they were settling on the land between the Don and the Kuban Rivers. By the end of the century colonies of Nogais were established along the left bank of the Molochna up to the Tokmak River on a stretch of land some 353,000 *desiatina*s in extent. They then numbered about 5,000 souls. The traveler and naturalist P. S. Pallas encountered these people on his trip through southern Ukraine in 1793 and has left a detailed description of their culture. Catherine II granted them virtually the same benefits she extended to other foreign colonists, but Paul enrolled them as state peasants. He also attempted to enlist them into the Cossacks, but the effort proved unsuccessful. At one time nomads, the Nogais developed an economy of settled agriculture, fishing, viticulture, and sheep-raising. Their relative freedom and considerable prosperity attracted additional immigrants from Turkish territory. By 1805, about seventeen thousand Nogais from the frontier region of Budiak—many of whom had fought on the Russian side in recent wars—moved northward. By 1806, they numbered over twenty-one thousand. Although they were technically state peasants, they enjoyed many of the privileges extended to foreign colonists.

Former Turkish subjects—both Christian and Muslim—made up the larger part of the foreign immigrants in Novorossiia. But Alexander, like Catherine before him, actively recruited western Europeans as well. They would, he hoped, not only colonize the steppe, but provide examples of good husbandry to the native settlers.

Germans and Swiss

By far the most numerous of these immigrants from the west were Germans.[39] Not only the lure of fertile soil, but also the hope of religious freedom, brought them to Russia. The social and political disruptions of the Napoleonic period, the frequent wars, taxes, and conscriptions worked to loosen their bonds to their native soil. The Russian government, for its part, was particularly eager to attract Germans. The duc de Richelieu, for example, hoped to recruit substantial numbers to the vicinity of Odessa. With the tsar's permission, he purchased more than eighteen thousand *desiatina*s of land from such great landlords as Count Potocki and General Kislinskii.[40] German colonists settled on this land would, he expected, assure the city an abundant supply of fruits, vegetables, butter, and other comestibles.

The government was therefore willing to offer the Germans exceptionally generous terms.[41] The colonists who responded came as communities rather than as individual settlers—a reflection of the strength of the religious factor in promoting immigration. In 1803 alone, nearly three thousand Mennonites left Ulm for the promised land of the steppe, and their experiences were similar to those of many other immigrants. The Russian officials did not provide them suitable quarters for the winter. As a French resident of Katerynoslav reported to Paris, the colonists who arrived before October had a comparatively easy time, as they could prepare for winter. On the other hand, those who did not arrive until November or December often fell ill and died.[42] After the bitter winter some Germans returned to their homeland; others, like a group at Ovidiopil, lodged complaints against the Russian officials, who had allegedly packed them into crumbling buildings "like herring."[43] Even worse, when some of the leaders tried to make their protests heard, they were physically beaten. As with the Jewish colonists, officials were slow to deliver the promised subsidies. The colonists were supposed to receive a daily allotment of forty kopecks per person, but were lucky to receive ten. Mysterious diseases ravaged the settlements. In one small colony, 150 persons died in a single day in February 1805. The duc de Richelieu personally visited the devastated town and successfully restored the morale of the settlers. The colonists, we are told, came to revere him "as a father."[44]

The loneliness of the steppe was itself a danger. Mennonites, for example, settled on the virgin soil along the Molochna River; they were on an exposed plain, and during the harsh winter were without neighbors to aid them. Many perished. Still, persistency and industry eventually paid rewards. By 1818, there were 958 Mennonite families in Novorossiia with more coming annually. In 1820, another 179 families sought a new home on the plains. The Mennonites not only produced wheat, but grew fruits and vegetables, raised cattle, and engaged in small manufacture such as cloth-making. Their neat cottages, trim fences, and bursting granaries so impressed the government that it attempted to settle other German émigrés, less experienced in agriculture, near them. Political exiles in particular were settled on adjacent lands, in hopes that they would emulate their industrious neighbors.

Catholic Germans also responded to the invitation to take up farming on the steppe, albeit in smaller numbers. Thus, Roman

Catholics made up the entire population of Kleinliebenthal and Josephsthal—two colonies established in 1804.[45] Located about twelve *versts* from Odessa, Kleinliebensthal was founded by Johann Snoger and Anton Schliech, but named by the duc himself. The settlement grew slowly—forty-eight families arrived in the first year, and only thirty-one over the following three. A hundred years later, the population of the colony, still Catholic, was 2,397 persons.

Josephsthal was likewise founded on empty lands inhabited only by wild animals. The immigrants—116 strong—passed their first Russian winter (1803–1804) in Odessa; the duc gave them employment and sent for a German-speaking pastor, since all the Catholic priests in the city were Italian and knew no German. The pastor who came to serve them, Joseph Korizky, has left a description of the settlement's difficult early days. The air, he believed, was harmful, especially to newcomers unaccustomed to stiff winds from the sea. The lack of forests meant a shortage of firewood, and this compounded the rigor of the winter. The Germans burned seaweed to warm themselves and cook their food. Snakes and rats infested their huts and fields. In early October 1815, more than one thousand German colonists were reported ill, most from unknown diseases.

Some colonists used up their allotted funds but failed to make their farms productive. In 1811, fifty German families fled from a colony near Odessa, but were caught and returned. One of the leaders among the Germans, Pastor Schabel, reported in 1815, "I found the poor colonists in total desperation. Hundreds of them were dying of hunger and cold."[46] And yet the colonies survived.

Swiss immigrants came from both the German-speaking and (in smaller numbers) the French-speaking cantons. Many were artisans skilled in the manufacture of silk, paper, and muslin. The economic disruptions of the Napoleonic wars prompted them to seek a new home in which to ply their trades. One group from Zürich founded a village in the Crimea about sixteen kilometers from Teodosiia and named it Zürichsthal, for their homeland. In 1805, no fewer than forty-nine Swiss families found their way to the Crimea. With its stately mountains and forests, it must have reminded them of their homeland. They also faced formidable difficulties in building a new life. They lived in flimsy Tatar huts until they could build sturdy houses. There was no market for their manufactures, and they depended chiefly upon farming, fishing, and forestry. But the site was a good one, and Zürichsthal soon attracted colonists from Germany as well as Switzerland. By 1820, it included 145 households.

French-speaking Swiss settled on the right bank of the Dniester River in Budiak.[47] A noted botanist, Louis-Vincent Tardan, had previously reconnoitered the region and recommended settlement on a strip of land along the river near Akkerman. The land, he affirmed, was excellently suited for vineyards. The French Swiss called their settlement Chabeau, from the Turkish *ashaba*, meaning "lower gardens." Each family received sixty *desiatina*s, and the community was given common lands to the extent of seven hundred *desiatina*s. The settlement was one of the smallest in the southern Ukraine, but its economy seems to have flourished. Even in the 1960s, descendants of the Swiss settlers were still to be found in the region; they retained French names and spoke the French language. They also spoke Russian, Ukrainian, Moldavian, and German—an indication that they maintained close relations with their neighbors on the steppe.

Did this policy of recruiting foreign settlers to farm the steppe make a substantial contribution to the development of Novorossiia? Both contemporaries and modern historians have voiced differing opinions. According to Mary Holderness, an Englishwoman who visited the region about 1820, many Bulgarian and German colonies had clearly failed, despite the privileges they had received.[48] Although land was abundant, their houses were packed together; plague and other diseases easily spread among them. Excessive drink and poor preparation for the winter took heavy tolls. Skilled artisans—carpenters, shoemakers, cabinet makers, blacksmiths, and tailors—were allowed to settle in cities to the deprivation of the rural villages. On the other hand, some colonies flourished.

The Mennonites seem by all accounts to have been the most successful. Still according to Mrs. Holderness, the Mennonites residing near Perekop in the Crimea were wealthy, knowledgeable in business affairs, sober, and industrious. They built large farmhouses, planted extensive orchards, laid out great gardens, and bred the finest cows in the country; they also produced a great abundance of wheat. In her words, "They are a most industrious and religious class of people, deservedly held in high estimation."[49] According to an article in the *Journal d'Odessa*, dated January 1828, there were then 11,714 Mennonites settled in sixty-five colonies; they were celebrated for their well-built houses, cleanliness, beautiful gardens, prosperity, and hospitality.[50] About a decade later, Anatole Demidov painted a bright picture of Mennonite life: well-cultivated fields, well-maintained houses, immense stocks of corn, blooming acacias.[51] The Mennonites deserved commendation for transforming the desert into a land overflowing with milk, vegetables, fruits, and fine wheat flour.

Did the colonists serve as models of good husbandry for the indigenous peasants? This too was a principal goal of the settlement policy, but here the results were meager. Both administratively and culturally, the colonies remained isolated from the general population. They were initially placed directly under the minister of internal affairs, who governed them through a central authority (located first in Katerynoslav and then in Odessa) and through a system of resident inspectors. Later the colonial administration was placed under the minister of crown domains. But consistently, they escaped the jurisdiction of the normal administrative apparatus; even the governor general of Novorossiia had no direct authority over them. He could not therefore develop a fully integrated policy of settlement within the region, which might have encouraged cultural exchanges. As E. I. Druzhinina points out: "Although the settlers assumed Russian citizenship, the largest number of them bore the name 'foreign colonists'; they were separated from the surrounding population by language, religion, habits, and especially by their distinctive juridical status."[52] Another twentieth-century historian, K. Waliszewski, gives an even more negative assessment:

> The colonies thus founded formed so many little islands cleanly separated from the surrounding environment, with which the presumed *Kulturtraeger* has only the most indispensable contacts. . . . they strove to keep themselves as close as possible to their country of origin. . . .[53]

J. Kohl, a German doctor, was more optimistic:

> It is a common thing to hear the Russians in the vicinity of a German colony say . . . 'that's the way the Germans do,' and this alone would be enough to convince me that the example of my countrymen has not been altogether thrown away.[54]

Novorossiia was nearly unique in allowing pockets of foreign settlements to be excluded from the general administration of the area. In the United States and Canada, ethnic and religious groups clustered in certain regions, but as quickly as they settled, their lives were subsumed under the general laws for administering the populations at large. Juridical distinctiveness in Novorossiia helped preserve cultural diversity; the colonies long preserved their own languages, religion, and customs and successfully resisted assimilation.

While its cultural repercussions may have been slight, the policy of recruiting and assisting colonists—both native and foreign—did succeed in filling up the land. Richelieu left one million more souls in Novorossiia than he found there in 1803.[55] Land values in the province increased ten times, from about one ruble per *desiatina* to ten or more. By 1817, no more uncultivated land was available for free distribution to colonists. The duc had carried out his mandate to settle the steppes. The words he addressed to Alexander I expressed satisfaction with the results:

> Never, Sire, in any part of the world, have there been nations so different in manners, language, customs, and dress living within so restricted a space. The Nogais occupy the left bank of the Molochna; families from Great Russia, the right bank; then, higher up, are the Mennonites, facing the Germans, who are half Lutheran, half Catholic; higher up again at Tolmak, the Little Russians [Ukrainians], members of the Greek religion; then a Russian sect, the Dukhobors.[56]

The City

When the new administrator arrived at Odessa in 1803, needs were pressing. The duc himself had difficulty finding lodgings among the earthen huts, in which many citizens still resided. He finally located in a single-story house, but had to wait patiently for six weeks until furnishings—including chairs—could be found for him at Kherson.[57]

His friend Sicard, who arrived in Odessa soon after (in 1804), paints a dismal picture. No land was cultivated for forty leagues around it. There were almost no wells, and water was insufficient; wood, whether for fire or construction, was in short supply.[58] Mrs. Guthrie, who visited the city about the same time, comments that its houses were "poorly built."[59] According to Pingaud, in 1803 only about "4500 souls vegetated in Odessa," and the city revenues did not meet expenses.[60] A Russian historian has called Odessa in the days before Richelieu "more like a pirate colony than a well-built city."[61] The government buildings, erected only a few years before, were falling apart, the cathedral unfinished, port facilities inadequate, and the houses sunk in mud.

Planning and Building

Richelieu built and encouraged building, and his policies inspired a veritable boom in construction. Keeping alive the traditions of de Voland and de Ribas, he laid out a symmetrical city and favored the clean and elegant neo-classical style; his work gave Odessa the harmonious aspect it has in part since retained. Much of his success was due to his abilities at raising money. In 1812, Baron Stieglitz donated 100,000 rubles to the city to meet the costs of construction.[62]

To supervise public constructions, the duc hired the noted Russian architect A. I. Mel'nikov.[63] His best-known works are the two charming, semicircular buildings that still stand above the monumental stairway leading down to the shore. Later, the statue of Richelieu was appropriately set between them. The entire complex today forms the city's aesthetic heart.

The source of almost equal pride was the municipal theater, built by a local architect, Frappoli, according to the design of the noted architect of St. Petersburg, Toma de Tomon.[64] Begun in 1803, it was finished in 1809. Consisting of three rows of loges, a stage similar to that of the Opera House in Paris, and a ground floor, the theater could seat eight hundred persons with more room for standees. The building was, to be sure, without heat, and the lighting system—oil lamps and candles—proved to be a fire hazard and ultimately the ruin of the structure. In 1873, the edifice burned down; on its site stands the present Opera House.

The grand opening of the original theater was celebrated with the performance of the twenty-first symphony of the Ukrainian composer M. D. Ovsianiko-Kulikovs'kyi, who conducted his own serf orchestra. The early plays were put on by Polish actors. Subsequently, Italian companies and ballet groups came to the theater. Soon amateur companies were formed; one performed in French and one in Italian. The leading French amateur actress was the proprietress of a French *boutique* in Odessa; she had the further distinction of being the daughter of Leonard, the hairdresser of Queen Marie-Antoinette.[65] In order to make the downtown area more attractive, in 1811 the duc arranged for its illumination by two hundred street lights. Richelieu was not unmindful that the theater attracted rich Polish landlords into the city.[66] Those who came to play might stay to trade.

Richelieu also laid out the wide boulevard at the very edge of the promontory overlooking the sea. The great merchants allegedly raised loud protests, as their houses now had to be built far back from the promontory's edge; they could no longer view with satisfaction their ships coming into port.[67] But the citizenry as a whole was given ready access to a splendid prospect over sea and harbor.

To private builders, the governor offered free home sites, laid out along straight and wide streets, on condition that they build upon them within two years. If they did not do so, then the sites reverted to the government. A "Committee of Administration," funded by tax revenues, was authorized to give loans to builders at the rate of 6 percent per annum.[68]

Richelieu placed great store upon the planting of trees, both in the city and in its immediate environs. Trees would offer protection against sun and wind, reduce dust, and give the city something of the qualities of an oasis, arising out of the treeless steppe. A Frenchman, the Chevalier de Rosset, is supposed to have planted Odessa's first tree, a poplar near the quarantine.[69] The duc himself imported acacias from Vienna at his own expense, and gave them free to all who promised to plant and care for them.[70] Should a citizen fail to water the trees in front of his house, the watchful duc would call upon him to remind him of this civic duty. Colonists who received twenty-five *desiatina*s of land near Odessa had to plant three hundred trees within two years. To this day, Odessa is known as the city of the white acacias.

The duc also encouraged the planting of private gardens, for a distance of thirty to forty leagues around the city.[71] The first public garden was donated to Odessa by Felix de Ribas, brother of the city's founder. However, the best-known urban park was the "Duc's Garden," where Richelieu collected samples of various flowers and plants, both native and foreign.[72] Even after his own departure from Odessa, he continued to ship slips of various plants to enhance the garden's beauty and interest.

Visitors to Odessa waxed lyrical about the city's rapid progress. After only five years of the duc's rule, reported Mrs. Guthrie, the city was unrecognizable. The air, she claimed—perhaps too sanguinely—was good, the streets were wide and straight, and lined by two-storied houses built of stone.[73] Storage facilities, also built of stone and as elegant as houses, could hold three thousand *chetvert*s of wheat. The population had grown to between eighteen and twenty thousand.

Another visitor to the city, the Frenchman de Lagarde, praised giant melons, grown in the Crimea, that he had eaten at the duc's table. He too waxed lyrical over the city's progress:

This city is a marvel when one thinks of the rapidity with which it has grown; all the houses are built in stone, most of them with two stories; the streets are wide and straight.[74]

Difficulty in obtaining stone, he admitted, had delayed the paving of the streets, but sidewalks, lined by rows of trees, had been constructed. Among the city's principal edifices were Russian churches and a Catholic church. (The Orthodox cathedral, designed by Frappoli in the classical style, was completed in 1809.) There was a *gymnasium* (high school) harboring one hundred boarders, an institute for young ladies, and a hospital. De Lagarde admired the botanic gardens and the well-equipped port, and described the barracks. He set the population at twenty-five thousand, and, like most other visitors, wondered at its polyglot character. One routinely encountered on the streets of Odessa, Russians, Ukrainians, Jews, Greeks, Armenians, Turks, Tatars, Poles, French, Germans, Italians, and Englishmen. Some wore their native costumes, and this added to the color of the passing parade.

Richelieu himself, in his memoirs, drew up a balance of his own achievements.[75] When he arrived at Odessa in 1803, the population numbered between seven thousand and eight thousand (Pingaud, it should be remembered, thought it was more nearly forty-five hundred), settled in some four hundred houses. When he left eleven years later, the city contained thirty-five thousand persons; the number of houses had grown remarkably, to twenty-six hundred. He further located the basis of this substantial progress: overseas trade, the city's chief source of wealth, had continued to grow, and his own government had used its incremented resources wisely and well.

Commerce

Richelieu gave much attention to the construction of good port facilities. The imperial government granted a loan of 200,000 rubles for harbor improvements; a large mole was built extending into the harbor, dividing the port into two parts—one for ships coming down the Dnieper River and plying the coastal waters; and the other for larger ships coming through the Straits and subject to quarantine. The quarantine facilities were modelled after those of Marseilles. To ease conditions for foreign sailors and travelers, he converted the old Turkish fortress into quarantine quarters, where the new arrivals could wait out their period of confinement in reasonable comfort. Storage facilities were also greatly enlarged.

Still in the interest of promoting commerce, Richelieu sought to establish a supporting infrastructure of credit and insurance institutions. In 1804, a commercial bank with a capital of 750,000 rubles was founded under his auspices, although financed through private subscription. A merchant could bring to the bank bills of exchange or promissory notes endorsed by two other merchants. The bank would discount the bills for a term of nine months at a charge of 6 percent per annum. Merchants could borrow cash against stocks of goods, which had to be sealed in warehouses. The money granted represented no less than one-third nor more than three-quarters of the fair market value of the merchandise.[76] Insurance too was a needed service for a commercial city, and in 1806, again under Richelieu's prompting, a joint-stock company called the Imperial Chamber of Insurance was formed. Capital was sought from private persons—chiefly local landlords. Navigating in unknown waters, the company soon was paying out more in settlements than it collected in premiums and was forced to close down.[77] It retained the distinction of having been the first maritime insurance company founded in Russia.[78]

Of more lasting service was Richelieu's establishment of a commercial court, which offered quick and reasoned settlement of commercial disputes. Its first director, Armand Emmanuel Saint-Priest, was the second son of François Saint-Priest, a prominent statesman of monarchical France. Richelieu actively cultivated the nobles of Poland, and through his persuasion, "they soon commenced the erection of a number of houses and granaries. . . ." [79]

His name alone attracted merchants from the west, especially from France. He advertised the advantages of Odessa among potential men of commerce—both in the Russian Empire and abroad. One of them, Charles Sicard, wrote that in 1804:

> . . . I was in Marseilles. They scarcely spoke of Odessa, having no idea of the city nor of the country, and consequently, knew nothing of its commerce. I saw three or four expeditions directed to Odessa on the basis that the then young duc de Richelieu was governor there. It was for this same reason that I myself decided to go there for several months, but then I settled there. That is, in a word, the history of nearly all the foreigners established in Odessa.[80]

The Napoleonic conquests also helped to direct the eyes of merchants eastward. The Genoese merchants Gattorno, Andriccia, Franchi, and Bellari relocated their firms in Odessa, allegedly to escape the French hegemony over their native city. By 1809 there were at least ten Italian firms exporting grain.[81]

Richelieu knew most of the foreign merchants personally. He visited them, kept abreast of their business, and listened to their complaints and suggestions. He also encouraged the establishment of permanent foreign consulates in the city. At least seven of them were founded during his tenure in office, representing, respectively, France, Austria, Spain, Naples, England, the Republic of Ragusa, and the Seven Ionian Islands.

Important too for a growing commerce were favorable tariffs. By an ordinance of March 5, 1808, Odessa's merchants obtained the right to store goods in warehouses for up to twelve months without paying duties. Richelieu's greatest—and parting—gift to the city was status as a free port. He had always been sympathetic to Adam Smith's arguments in favor of free trade, and a plague at Odessa in 1812 showed another advantage. As long as duties were high, contraband would be substantial. Smuggled goods escaped the quarantine regulations and rendered the city more vulnerable to contagion. In 1814, the governor petitioned Alexander to make Odessa a free port. In 1817, the tsar granted his request, but by then Richelieu had returned to France.[82]

Trade through Odessa boomed. In 1803, about 550 ships came to its port. They carried off some 600,000 *chetvert*s of grain, valued at five silver rubles per *chetvert*.[83] European capital also drifted eastward to the Black Sea regions, since war in the West was limiting opportunities for investment.[84]

Table 2.1 shows the value of exports from Odessa over the years 1804 to 1813.

Table 2.1

Odessa's Exports by Sea, 1804–1813

Year	Rubles	Year	Rubles
1804	2,339,509	1809	1,776,290
1805	3,399,291	1810	3,146,994
1806	822,927	1811	7,747,544
1807	336,022	1812	5,855,045
1808	1,975,013	1813	8,861,956

Source: Morton, 1830, p. 257. Morton learned this information from Prince Trubetskoi, then Director of Customs at Odessa.

Figure 2.1: Odessa's Exports, 1804–1813

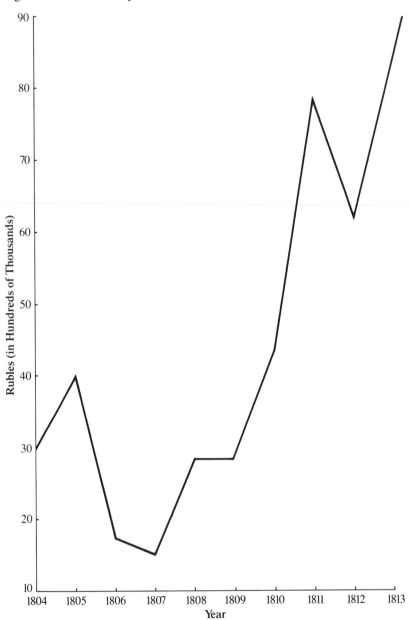

The wide swings in exports evident in Table 2.1 reflect the constant disturbances in international politics. War, to be sure, sometimes stimulated, sometimes repressed, and nearly always redirected trade. Napoleon's "Continental System," for example, proved an unexpected benefit to Odessa. It severely restricted commerce through the Mediterranean ports of the French Empire and diverted some of it to overland routes. Odessa was well placed to capture much of this redirected flow. It was connected by land routes through Brody on the frontier of the Austrian Empire to Austria, Prussia, and France itself; its port gave maritime contact with Turkey, Persia, Egypt, and the Middle East. Cotton fabrics shipped through Odessa alone reached the value of about 11 million rubles per year.[85] The ever-alert Richelieu worked mightily to take advantage of this unexpected boon. In 1808, he reduced the quarantine period, enlarged the storage facilities, and otherwise promoted Odessa's role as entrepôt between East and West. Eventual peace in Europe reduced this transit trade, but compensated for it through reopening Mediterranean ports.

On the other hand, Russia and Turkey were at war between 1806 and 1807, and again between 1809 and 1812. Trade, to be sure, did not altogether cease, even with the Ottomans. According to Sicard, who writes about the first of these conflicts:

> ... while Russian and Turkish soldiers were battling along the Danube, Russian and Turkish businessmen were peacefully trading in all the ports of the Black Sea.[86]

But trade clearly suffered. Only 279 ships arrived at Odessa in 1806, down from 643 in the previous year, and the price of wheat fell to a quarter of its former level.[87]

In the subsequent Turkish war, the imperial government ill-advisedly prohibited the export of cereals to and through Constantinople, in hopes of starving the Turks into submission. But Constantinople found new suppliers in Egypt, Cyprus, Sicily, and elsewhere, and Odessa itself faced depression. Journeying to St. Petersburg in 1811, Richelieu pleaded with the tsar to rescind the prohibition. He gained what he sought; characteristically, he carried the good news back to Odessa in secret, lest its premature diffusion create disordered conditions in the city's commodity markets.

In spite of revolutions and wars, Richelieu carefully built up at Odessa the material and social supports needed for a vigorous commerce. In 1804, commerce brought in about 2 1/4 million rubles. When he left in 1814, the total was 25 million.[88] Aided by this expanding economic base, he was also able to give the city liberal and enlightened government.

Schools and Culture

The duc also played a significant role in promoting schools and cultural activities within the new city.[89] Before 1804, there were no public schools at Odessa; each national or religious community trained its own children. Thus, Jewish schools existed virtually from the foundation of the town. Richelieu himself founded a school in 1805, called the Institute for Nobles, intended for the education of upper-class children, who could afford the high tuition; and then a second school, called a *gymnasium*, supported exclusively by private donations and open to everyone. Sons of merchants, soldiers, officials, *meshchane*, and the like were instructed in philosophy, law, commerce, and military science. Alexander was favorably impressed by the training it imparted; by an *ukaz* issued in March 1808, he allowed its graduates to enter the Cadet Corps at St. Petersburg.

By 1811, in accordance with the duc's wishes, the *gymnasium* became a government school. In reforming its curriculum, he enlisted the aid of a French émigré named Jeudy-Dugour, who had settled in Russia and adopted the name Dugurov. He was also a former professor at Kharkiv University and rector of St. Petersburg University. In spite of his foreign origins, Dugurov was convinced that Odessa's children should receive a common education, in which the Russian language would predominate.

Richelieu took a personal interest in the school; he quizzed those students who aspired to a military career and often conducted examinations himself. The duc also drafted notices in French to be sent out to the hinterland of Novorossiia. The school, these advertisements stated, offered excellent preparations for military or civil service, for trade, or for any other occupation that appealed to the student. By 1814, however, instruction was no longer gratuitous; the student was charged 750 rubles per year for tuition and 200 rubles for books—fairly substantial costs.

Although the institute was successful, Richelieu sensed the need for a school which would directly serve the commercial community of Odessa. Commercial *gymnasia* of this sort already existed in Taganrog and Katerynoslav. He chose as head of the *gymnasium* a French Dominican, Abbé Nicolle. Richelieu prescribed not only the study of the ancient languages, but of modern Greek and Italian. He deemed the mastery of these languages invaluable in Novorossiia, "where all trade is found in the hands of Italian and Greek merchants having a close connection with the southern cities of Europe."[90] The new school also offered training in statistics and bookkeeping—valuable mercantile skills. No tuition was charged, and poor as well as rich students who wished to prepare for a business career could apply for admission.

For young ladies, the Italian de Pozzis and his Russian wife directed an institute. The feminine counterpart of the male *gymnasium*, the school was expensive and clearly designed to serve the upper classes. The girls were instructed in the Ten Commandments, languages, geography, history, art, music, dance, painting, sewing, and household economy. Later, after the duc's departure, a rich merchant, Iakov Protasov, grew dissatisfied with the education available to girls and founded a new school for young ladies. While supervised by the government, the school was largely supported by the substantial merchants of the city.

In June 1816, the future tsar, Nicholas, paid a visit to Odessa and inspected the schools. Students at the *gymnasium* addressed him in Russian, French, Latin, and Italian. He was much impressed. In the following year, the *gymnasium* and the Institute for Nobles, founded by Richelieu, were superseded by a lycée, to which, appropriately, the name of Richelieu was given. In 1818, the famous poet K. N. Batiushkov wrote to his friend, A. I. Turgenev, the director of spiritual affairs in the ministry of spiritual affairs and public education, about the school:

> I tell you honestly speaking, the lycée is the best ornament of Odessa, just as Odessa is the best city after the capital.[91]

Richelieu's work for education was thus acknowledged. According to a contemporary, Odessa's schoolchildren loved him as their patron.[92] The Richelieu Lycée attracted children of the aristocracy even from the capitals.

Books abounded in early Odessa, perhaps because the national communities were intent on preserving knowledge of their particular languages and cultures. In 1810, a visitor to Odessa remarked on the number of Russian and French bookstores and on the volume of Jewish literature, shipped there from Poland.[93] Richelieu's lycée also contained the first library in Odessa. Richelieu himself, by then in France, donated his personal library as well as thirteen thousand francs to maintain it.[94] The collection eventually formed part of the library of Novorossiia University, which was founded in 1865.

The first printer's shop in the city opened in 1814. As a prosperous commercial port set on the borders of Europe, Odessa, in Richelieu's view, offered great promise as a center of the book trade. Even after his departure, he recommended to Alexander I in 1818 that he establish a large press in Odessa. This would satisfy not only the local demand for books, but could sell volumes in Greek and Armenian through the Balkans and Asia Minor. His suggestion seems to have borne no fruit, but he was right in his assessment that Odessa was well located to serve cultural as well as commercial exchange.[95]

The common commercial language, and very nearly the *lingua franca* of the city, was Italian, as it was in many port cities of the eastern Mediterranean basin. At Odessa, the earliest street signs—and also those of many shops—were in both Italian and Russian. Notarial documents were redacted in Italian, as were passports, bills, receipts, commercial correspondence and books, price lists, and even theater notices. The first publication by a local press was a sonnet in Italian.[96] Because nearly everyone attended the Italian opera and because of the many Italians on the docks, even common people sprinkled their speech with Italian words. Cab drivers offered rides to "Signori." Stevedores asked for "quaranti" kopecks, and clerks in shops spoke to their customers in Italian.[97] Under Richelieu and his successor, Langeron, French understandably grew in importance; the Jews preferred German; and Greek was second only to Italian as a language of commerce. But in this polyglot community, Italian long retained a certain preeminence. In 1811, an Italian opera company, directed by the famous musician Montovani, visited Odessa to play in the new theater.[98] In 1818, the poet K. N. Batiushkov, a guest of Saint-Priest, wrote to his aunt how much he loved the Italian opera, and indeed, he exclaimed, "Odessa is a wonderful city, made up of all the nations of the world, and flooded by Italians."[99]

Plague and war ended the performances and closed the theater between 1812 and 1814. When it reopened, Ukrainian and Russian plays were performed regularly, but Italian opera retained a special appeal. An Italian, F. Fiorini, was the maestro. So pleased was Alexander I at one of the productions that he personally congratulated the impressario. Thereafter, Montovani and another Italian conductor, Zamboni, brought over the best Italian companies annually.

Civic Affairs

Not the least of Richelieu's achievements was fiscal reform. Before his arrival, municipal finances had been in chronic deficit, and profiteers had looted public monies with apparent immunity. Richelieu took direct charge of finances, which he supervised with the aid of a financial board. The revenues that accrued to the city came from three principal sources: its control over the distillation of vodka, its claim to one-tenth of the customs, and a charge of 2.5 kopecks (raised to 5 in 1813) on every *chetvert* of exported wheat. These incomes grew with population and with trade. In 1808 alone, the city gathered in 130,000 rubles from the consumption of spirits.[100]

A constant, critical problem faced by the governor was the health of the citizens; as a port, Odessa was more exposed than most towns to infections of every sort. With characteristic diligence, Richelieu established a hospital and formed a Committee for the Prevention of Smallpox. But the greatest test his government faced was plague. In August 1812, a plague epidemic struck the city, and the battle against it constitutes a dramatic episode in Richelieu's crowded career.[101]

As soon as the dimensions of the epidemic became known, the duc divided the city into five districts, each with an inspector and a doctor, to monitor the course of the malady and to impose quarantine. Four of the five doctors died of the disease. Cossacks were used to seal off infected areas. For about one hundred *versts* around the city, from the Boh to the Dniester Rivers, the government established a *cordon sanitaire*. Provisions could enter the city only along one, well-supervised route. Stores, shops, the theater, the stock exchange, inns, schools, and churches were all closed. Normal life in the city ceased. I. A. Stemkovskii, an aide to the duc, likened the city to "an enormous tomb—a sorrowful silence reigns over the empty squares and streets of the city which only a short while ago were lively and noisy."[102] Once the duc himself, collapsing upon a rock in his own courtyard, reportedly proclaimed: "I can no longer stand. My heart is melting to have to use all my authority to make these streets deserted when I have spent ten years populating and bringing them to life."[103]

William Wilkinson, the British consul general at Bucharest, who happened to to be in Odessa at the time, spent his period of confinement writing his valuable book on Moldavia and Wallachia.[104] He also studied Greek. Two colleagues, similarly detained, learned

Arabic and Russian, respectively. The Austrian consul allegedly resisted the enforced confinement, saying he would rather "die of infection than of boredom."[105]

The panicked populace did what little it could to ward off the contagion. Some tarred their clothes—especially those who carried provisions into and through the city. Many took baths in the sea and washed not only their clothing, but also goods that came into their possession. Money in changing hands was soaked in bowls of vinegar. Bonfires were built to cleanse the city's air! And still the deaths increased over the winter and spring. The inhabitants viewed with dread and grief the many carriages rolling by their houses with a black flag signifying death, or a red one, warning of a diseased passenger. After six months the toll reached 2,632; at its height in the spring of 1813, the plague carried off several dozens of persons per day. A huge sepulchral mound containing the victims gave solemn reminder of the tragedy.[106]

Under conditions of panic, Richelieu struggled to maintain both discipline and morale and to reduce contagion among the citizens. One section of the city, nearest to the dock (the suspected source of the infection), was burned down in a futile effort to limit its spread. The houses of plague victims were marked with red crosses. Convicts dressed in black leather suits soaked in oil, and still wearing chains, were sent into the contaminated houses to clean them out twenty days after the dead were removed. By November, all citizens were confined to their homes, unless they had special authorization to depart. Over the winter of 1813, the plague lost its virulence; in February 1814, the city was declared "plague-free," although sporadic cases continued to appear until August. This was the last crisis the duc had to face in Odessa.

Richelieu's Departure

Inspired by enlightened principles, confident in the value of clear thought, eager to experiment and reform, Richelieu thus helped impart both physical and cultural form to the new city of Odessa. Under his guidance, the city passed through a period of nearly continuous international tumult and of strong local growth. But the character of the times was changing, even as Richelieu himself gave up the governance of the city.

The duc left Odessa on September 26, 1814, to return to France. A sorrowing group of two hundred people or more saw him off at the first post station. Every vehicle in the city had been pressed into service to convey the ruler's friends and well-wishers to the departure point.[107] They expressed grief over the loss of a man most of them knew personally and all respected. As the authors of a guidebook to the city later commented:

> With every opportunity of enriching himself, the duke is said to have left Odessa with a small portmanteau containing his uniform and two shirts, the greater part of his income having been disbursed in relieving the distresses of immigrants who generally arrived in a great state of destitution. His amiable and charitable qualities endeared him to all classes, and his departure was greatly regretted.[108]

Even after Richelieu returned to France to serve as prime minister under the restored monarchy, he retained cordial ties with the imperial Russian court and with its ambassador in France, Pozzo di Borgo. Indeed, he has been regarded as a puppet of the tsar, a "western minister for Russia," as hostile contemporaries called him.[109] His archrival, Talleyrand, who referred to him sarcastically as "the man in France who knew the most about the Crimea," fully shared this opinion.[110] In the assessment of a modern historian, through Richelieu, ". . . the influence of Alexander on the internal affairs of France remained constant, ever present, and powerful."[111] Still, a defeated France had to act deferentially toward her conquerors, and Richelieu won concessions too. In 1818 at Aix-la-Chapelle, Alexander agreed to reduce both the number of occupation troops in France and the indemnities imposed by the Treaty of Paris. A grateful Chamber of Deputies awarded the duc fifty thousand francs for this diplomatic achievement. Uninterested as always in riches, the duc donated the sum to found a hospital in his native city of Bordeaux.

In 1816, confronting a poor harvest, France was forced to import substantial quantities of grain from the southern Ukraine. Here again, the duc's enemies questioned his motives in apparently promoting trade with a region he once governed. Yet in a memorandum written in 1820, the duc rather showed concern for the French peasants in the face of growing competition from foreign foodstuffs. He recommended that France's own exports of cereals be restricted, to assure an abundance of local grain and to reduce the need of imports.[112] The interests of France and not of Russia were clearly directing his thoughts.

Richelieu died in 1822, at the age of fifty-six, after several years in the service of the restored Bourbon monarchy. He retained his superb administrative abilities, but the true measure of his talents, and the true monument to his life, was the city on the Black Sea, whose early growth he stimulated, directed, and decorated. He called Odessa "the best pearl in the Russian crown." If such it was, the credit for it in large part goes to him, not only for his achievements but also for the policies he initiated. These included the vigorous promotion of agriculture and of trade, the embellishment of the city, and the effort to maintain in Odessa a political and cultural milieu tolerant of diversity. He pointed out the path to Odessa's continuing development.

CHAPTER THREE

The Development of the Hinterland

The land which has merely been tickled with the plough will laugh with a copious harvest.
—George Hume, 1857

The nineteenth century was an age of frontiers, a period during which peoples of largely European extraction pushed into vast new areas of the world—western America and Canada, South Africa, Australia and New Zealand, and South America. Novorossia and the eastern steppes were another such frontier. This expansion of settlement is a central development in the social history of the nineteenth century, and it led to profound changes in the Russian Empire as in many other regions of the world.

Animal Husbandry

In nearly all these frontier lands, the raising of animals dominated the early stages of their economic development.[1] Animal husbandry demanded little capital investment (apart from the costs of the animals themselves) and required little labor, characteristically expensive in the new regions. Few houses, barns, fences, folds, pens, or even roads, had to be constructed, and the herds could graze freely over vast and open lands. So too, in the southern regions of the Russian Empire, the first large grants of land usually went to those who planned to raise livestock upon them.

Sheep

The great steppes stretching to the north and east of the provinces of Novorossiia had long been renowned as pastures. The black soils produced a luxuriant covering of grass, and even the hard continental winter stimulated the growth of thick fleece on the animals, which lived for the most part under the open sky. The introduction of merino sheep in the first decade of the nineteenth century marked a milestone. In the shrewd assessment of a foreign colonist, a German named G. Müller, this famous breed was well suited for the steppe.[2] In 1805 the government granted him twelve thousand *desiatina*s of land near Odessa, a loan of twenty thousand rubles payable in ten years, and the old customs house, which he turned into a wool-washing station. He agreed to bring to Novorossiia thirty thousand head of sheep within three years, one-third of them to be pure merinos.[3] Müller and others systematically interbred the merinos with local breeds, in hopes of acclimating offspring of these animals to their new home. Many settlers recognized the promise of seemingly limitless pasture on the steppes. In 1828, Count Vorontsov brought to his Crimean estates Leicestershire sheep and crossed them with Wallachian and Moldavian breeds.[4]

Hommaire de Hell, a French engineer who visited Novorossiia in 1841, gave credit for introducing the merino sheep to a French émigré named Rouvier. In his account, it was Tsar Alexander I who provided the Frenchman with 100,000 assignat rubles and five thousand *desiatina*s of land in the hilly parts of the Crimea as well as twenty five thousand *desiatina*s of land on the steppes. He even placed at his disposal a man-of-war to fetch the sheep from Spain. Rouvier quickly made a fortune. Hommaire de Hell visited his son-in-law, Poitier, who claimed to count more than twenty thousand merino sheep on his lands. Another son-in-law, called Vassal, similarly prospered. The family's wool-washing establishments gave employment to six hundred men.[5]

In 1834, John Ralli, Greek by birth, but acting as the United States consul at Odessa, reported:

> The steppes nearby feed a huge number of sheep, and wool of all qualities, common and Spanish, are in great abundance, so that wool is of the first importance and is much cheaper here than anywhere else in Russia.[6]

Prince A. A. Prozorovskii, who owned five hundred *shlenskii*s and one hundred Spanish sheep in 1808 in the Katerynoslav *guberniia*, with the help of servile labor produced not only wool on his estates, but also finished cloth.[7] Most of the sheep raisers, however, with flocks ranging from two dozen to nearly two thousand head, utilized hired labor: colonists, rented serfs, vagabonds without passports, and so forth.[8] But they did not hire many. Responding to an inquiry in 1808, a sheep raiser observed that three men could watch from four hundred to five hundred sheep; two, two hundred to three hundred sheep; and one man, up to two hundred head.[9]

As Table 3.1 shows, fine-haired flocks increased substantially if not consistently between 1807 and 1825.

Table 3.1

Fine-haired Sheep on Landlord Estates in Katerynoslav
Guberniia, 1807 – 1825

Year	Number	Year	Number
1807	4,000	1818	35,097
1808	7,490	1819	46,215
1811	14,848	1821	63,172
1812	18,138	1822	79,547
1813	25,752	1823	63,590
1814	27,648	1824	84,567
1815	27,154	1825	77,527
1817	21,855		

Source: Druzhinina, 1970, p. 208.

Great ranchers were not alone in raising sheep, however. Although yearly counts of the number of sheep in Novorossiia do not survive, we do know that in 1823, in the Katerynoslav *guberniia* fine-haired sheep numbered 114,980. Table 3.1 shows that landlords owned 63,590; colonists, state peasants, and others must have been raising about 51,390 sheep.[10] In the provinces of Katerynoslav and Kherson there were over one million head by 1827.[11] In the Crimean *guberniia* sheep-raising registered spectacular gains. Over a thirty-three year period (1823 – 1856), the number of sheep grew from fewer than 500,000 to 11 million.[12]

Flagging demand for other agricultural products lent impetus to wool production and exports. The foreign market for wheat was weakening after the years 1815 – 17, and the French consul at Tiflis foresaw the results:

The agriculturalist alarmed by the fall in grain [prices] will feel the necessity of varying his produce. The income from his land will no longer rest on cereals alone. He will busy himself with plantations; he will multiply his animals; his breeding studs will be more numerous; the breed of his sheep will improve; leather, tallow, salted beef, wool, hemp, wax, tobacco, will then become important articles of export. . . .[13]

The same observer noted the formation in the Black Sea region of gigantic ranches, owned by French, Germans, and Dutch, harboring flocks of from thirty-five thousand to forty-five thousand merinos.[14] Interesting to add, wool was the product most sought after by American merchants in the South Ukraine.[15] Wool was not only shipped overseas, but much of it found its way to Moscow; delivery by cart required thirty to forty days.[16]

In 1825, forty thousand *pud*s of wool were exported through the Black Sea ports.[17] In 1838, wool ranked second behind wheat as the area's most important export, and its total value added up to a third of that represented by cereals.[18] In 1841, exports from the southern ports had grown to 236,630 *pud*s—more than 50 percent of Russia's total wool exports. Odessa led all other ports in the volume of wool shipped abroad (135,000 *pud*s). The city was unique, too, in that merino wool accounted for the larger part of the wool shipped abroad (86,000 out of the 135,000 *pud*s). In all other ports of the Russian Empire, the export of ordinary wool far surpassed that of the fine Spanish variety.[19]

Still, wool was never really able to challenge wheat as the most important export. Wool was widely produced in the world and easily transported, and Russian wool had little competitive advantage over that provided in ever greater quantities from the Americas and Australia. In 1841, Hommaire de Hell attributed the fall in the price of sheep (500 to 600 francs a ram in 1834–1835 to 250 to 300 in 1841) to Russia's prohibitive tariff system.[20] If merchants could not sell, they would not come to buy a product available elsewhere on the world market.

The chief reason, however, for the shrinking size of the sheep industry was simply that raising wheat became more profitable. And the flocks diminished even in the Crimea, the province that once contained the largest count of sheep. In 1880, there were only 138,000 head of sheep compared to the 11 million found there a quarter of a century earlier.[21]

Later in the century, crude, rather than fine, wool found an outlet, especially for the making of rugs in the United States. But wool export was limited and eventually was cut by a phenomenon which, in the twentieth century, would ultimately limit Russia's importance as a wheat exporter too—Russia's need and ability to use its wool (as well as its wheat in increasing amounts) at home, as its own industries and industrial population grew.

Cattle and Tallow

Along with sheep, cattle were a principal support of the economy of the southern steppes. As early as 1807, Katerynoslav province alone contained 643 cattle farms.[22] The Mennonites raised Dutch cows, especially for dairy purposes. The Mariiupil Greeks owned 45,463 head of cattle in 1810, which had increased to 116,077 head by 1824 or about 2.1 to 4.3 cattle per person.[23] The foreign colonists as a whole in 1825 possessed many fewer cattle—only 7,320 head or just under one per person.[24]

Cattle were at times raised and then driven to internal markets— even Moscow—for slaughter and sale. The imperial army and navy were big customers. There were difficulties as well as advantages in raising cattle: they were periodically attacked by epidemics, which wiped out entire herds. Spells of bad weather reduced fodder, and winters may have been getting colder on the steppe as human settlement spread and the land lost its natural cover of vegetation. Water was frequently lacking or contaminated. Nonetheless, during the first quarter of the century, the number of cattle grew. By 1844, there were 2,500,000 head in Novorossiia. However, disease in 1848–1849 reduced the number to 1,950,000 head.[25] A chief reason for investment in cattle was the high prices that foreign markets offered for cattle products, especially tallow. Tallow was, in fact, the fourth principal export of Novorossiia. It was used for machine grease, candles, fuel for lamps, and soap; the introduction of the stearine lamp in the 1820s further expanded demand. Because of its large herds, Novorossiia could aspire to become a principal supplier to the world of this versatile fat. Moreover, the yellow tallow produced from its oxen—distinct from the white tallow obtained from sheep—was especially favored in world markets. In 1838, J. G. Kohl, the German traveler quoted above, inspected the slaughter houses of the South Ukraine, which provided the carcasses destined to be boiled down into tallow. He was appalled by the gory procedure, but impressed with the export statistics:

> . . . about 250,000,000 pounds of tallow are furnished to the rest of the world, providing the chief supply of soap and candles to England, France, Germany, Scandinavia, Italy and the other countries of Europe. This is without including the extra quantity which the Russian themselves consume. Now, nearly the whole of this enormous quantity is furnished by the Pontine steppes, which may, therefore, be looked on as the main enlighteners and purifiers of the civilized world.[26]

One is reminded, in reading these reports, of the early Californian economy, as described, for example, by Henry Charles Dana in *Two Years before the Mast*. The first intensive use of the dry California grasslands was for cattle, and the first exports that brought ships, including Dana's *Pilgrim*, to its shores were hides and tallow.[27]

The Ottoman Empire took large quantities of Russian tallow, for the uses mentioned above, and also, in the case of better qualities, for human consumption. But Russia's best customer was industrial England. In the 1830s some 90 percent of England's imported tallow was Russian in origin.[28]

Conditions of both production and marketing affected the making of tallow in the South Ukraine. If bad weather reduced the supply of fodder, the herds had to be thinned; tallow, naturally enough, became plentiful and cheap, while wool grew scarcer and dearer.[29]

Meat prices followed those of tallow and hides. With increased slaughter of animals, meat supplies grew more plentiful. Visitors to Novorossiia were frequently surprised at the low cost of meat.[30] Eventually, however, the foreign market for tallow lost its buoyancy. The product could be transported easily, and competition from other countries, including the United States, soon became brisk. Moreover, the uses of tallow were diminished by the development of mineral oils and paraffin. By 1837, its importance as an item of export was already declining.[31] In 1852, the French consul reported to Paris that the Russian Empire was exporting diminished quantities of tallow. England was purchasing it more frequently from the colonies and America. Then too, with the expansion of agriculture in the southern Ukraine, fewer animals grazed on the open steppe.[32]

Vegetables, Fruit, Oil, and Wine

As settlement expanded on the steppes, the producers understandably turned to more intensive uses of the land. Observers noted a considerable development in the South Ukraine of garden farming. According to Skal'kovskii, in the environs of Odessa alone there were in 1843 some 611 country houses and villas, nearly all with fruit and vegetable gardens. Fruit trees were in special abundance and some dachas earned their owners from 150 to 700 silver rubles each year.[33] Kohl reports that numerous locales in the Ukraine, the Crimea, the Caucasus, and even the Asian steppe contained *bastan*s, a Tatar term for "gardens." The gardens produced sunflowers, onions, beets, gourds, and cucumbers in all imaginable shapes, sizes, and colors. But their chief glory was the watermelon.[34] So abundant were these melons that they appeared at almost every meal, even in winter (they were preserved, through packing them with clay and storing them in cellars). In lieu of sipping liquid, the diners nibbled from watermelon slices. Kohl marveled that the dry steppe could produce these large, natural containers of succulent juices.

In garden farms, peas, beans, and corn were also raised, and our observers noted some slowly developing commercial possibilities. In 1858, the *Journal d'Odessa* reported that peas and beans, once sold locally, were exported to Marseilles, Genoa, and Livorno.[35] Maize (*kukuruza*) had for years been raised in quantity in Bessarabia, but the kernels were ground into a type of corn meal or *polenta*, called *mamaliga*, and consumed locally. In 1844, only 19,161 *chetverts* were exported. By 1857, favorable prices abroad induced a quick increase in production and export to a substantial 632,252 *chetverts*.[36]

One such product for which foreign demand was consistently strong was linseed. The chief customer for Russia's vegetable oil was England. Its growing industries had many uses for this multipurpose product. It served as a base for paint and varnishes, for inks and soaps, and as a lubricant for engines. Moreover, Russian linseed was regarded with particular esteem by foreign importers. Late in developing, the cultivation of linseed and similar oil-producing plants advanced with seven-league strides in the late 1820s and 1830s.[37]

In 1834, the United States consul at Odessa reported that the prospects for linseed production seemed so bright that "landlords and peasants [were] cultivating it as more profitable than corn [wheat]."[38] Over the years from 1831 to 1845, Russia supplied about 80 percent of the oil imported into England.[39] Americans also purchased from Russia small, but stable, quantities.[40]

In spite of auspicious beginnings, the production and overseas sale of Russian linseed encountered early limits. Costs of transporting the seeds from hinterland to port remained high. In 1844, the French consul in Odessa noted that the price of linseed depended less on the abundance of the harvest than the going costs of transport. Cart costs, he noted, varied widely and unpredictably.[41] By the 1840s, oil from India was claiming a large share of the world market. And Russia itself was absorbing more and more of its own production, leaving correspondingly less seed and oil to be offered for sale on foreign markets. Sunflower seeds and oil were produced on a large scale after 1845, but most of the output was consumed locally.[42]

Another agricultural product that attracted considerable interest but achieved only limited development was wine. The Russian government actively promoted viticulture in the south, in the hopes of restricting an expensive import, and perhaps even of earning currency abroad. In the 1840s the minister of the domains of the empire, P. D. Kiselev, invited Odessa's Agricultural Society to propose means of encouraging the planting of vineyards. The minister suggested that the German colonists be required to put aside a certain portion of their land for the cultivation of the grape. Capital would also have to be supplied to the entrepreneurs, as the slips would not produce useful grapes until six years after planting. Cellars would also have to be built to age the wine. And tariffs on Greek and Romanian wines would have to be raised.[43] A decade later, to stimulate local production, tariffs on all foreign wines consumed in Odessa were raised from one-fifth to three-fifths of the rate imposed on wines shipped into the interior.[44]

With characteristic detail Skal'kovskii wrote of the situation in 1846:

> Viniculture and the cultivation of grapevines constitute one of the favorite occupations of the inhabitants of Odessa. There are almost no gardens or country houses (*khutors*) where vines have not been planted. Wine-making constitutes an important branch of suburban industry. Within the environs of the city in 1843 there were six million vines, for the most part French or Spanish, producing each year (since 1837) from 30 to 32 thousand *vedros* (from 78,750 to 84,000 gallons) of white and red wine, with a quality similar to Moldavian wine, but sometimes stronger and better. A thousand silver rubles of the product is sold each year. Wine made from berries sells for 200 to 300 silver rubles per year. From the founding of the city up until 1815, factories produced spirits made from wine and liqueurs similar to the Italian *rossoglio* and *maraschino*, but with the establishment of licensing, they ceased to exist.[45]

Grapes did particularly well on the sunny hills of the southern Crimea. With characteristic enterprise, Count Mikhail Vorontsov planted vines on a large scale on his Crimean estates. In 1838, his income from wine sales was already eighty thousand rubles.[46] But the undertaking remained hostage to the climate. The frosts of one bad winter destroyed forty thousand out of sixty thousand vines.[47] An English visitor has left a vivid description of Vorontsov's vineyards in 1839. French and German vintners worked them. The count acquired some prized French slips in Vienna, originally ordered by an American who failed to claim them. To the Englishman's taste, the Vorontsov champagne surpassed the vintages of all lands saving France itself. Could it but travel, the wine, in his estimation, would find an enthusiastic reception in England. Vorontsov himself, still according to our reporter, showed little confidence in his product; he allegedly labelled his bottles so that they would pass as French. And he allegedly sold them in Moscow at inflated prices as authentic imports.[48] On the other hand, the French consul conceded in 1843 that, while some Russian vintners pasted false French labels on their bottles, Vorontsov had the good grace to put "Crimean" on his.[49]

This interest in viticulture, warmed by the government's mild protectionist policies, induced some notable results. As early as the 1830s, an English visitor observed:

> Some traffic also now takes place in the wines of the Crimea, which are fast rising into repute, though we cannot agree with the Russians in thinking that they will supplant the wines of Oporto. The annual sales of the Crimea, including those of the *Kokour* wine, now generally average 12 million bottles.[50]

In the sixteen years before 1848, the extent of grapevines in the Crimea had allegedly multiplied six times.[51] The French understandably grew concerned both for their own exports to Russia, and at the prospect of confronting a new rival in the world market. In about 1850, they noted that the Crimea produced 83,798 hectoliters of wine—only 1/250 of the French production, but likely to grow.[52] In 1854, another study of the Crimean wine production appeared in the French press. The author expressed confidence that the quality of the Russian product would never duplicate that of the French.[53]

All these products so far considered—wool, tallow, linseed, wine—had considerable commercial importance. In 1838, they together constituted slightly over half of the region's total export. A report written in 1835 speculated that the shipments abroad of "wool, wax, hempen cordage, flax, linseed, hempseed and other oil seeds" had so increased in quantity that one day they might surpass grain as the king of the export market.[54] The prediction proved wrong. Even though the late 1830s were not favorable to international cereal sales, wheat retained its preeminence.

Cereals

The fertility of the black soil of the Ukraine and southern Russia is proverbial. As early as 1573, a French traveler, Blaise de

Vigenère, remarked on their extraordinary qualities:

> They say that the land of the country [Podillia] is so good and fertile
> that if one leaves his plow in the field, the grass grows so fast around
> it that after two or three days the plow can hardly be found.[55]

Moreover, the black soil was deep. A. Shmidt, in his survey of the
province of Kherson, calculated that the soil averaged fourteen
inches in depth.[56]

An official report made to Tsar Nicholas I in 1835 stated that
cereal crops "often yield to the grower a produce of twenty-fold
upon the quantity of seed sown."[57] Skal'kovskii's records for the
years 1845 through 1851, however, reveal that such abundant yields
were not as frequent as the report implied. During that period, the
worst year, 1845, gave only 1 3/4 as much as sown, and the yield for
the best year, 1851, was only a bit more than thrice. Earlier, again
according to Skal'kovskii, for the period 1832 through 1836, the
worst year, 1833, failed to render the quantity sown, while the best
year, 1836, gave 4 1/2 times the seed.[58]

Just as important as the natural fertility of the soil of Novorossiia
was its vast extent. The more northerly black-soil provinces were, to
be sure, among the most thickly populated areas of the empire. In
1856, Podillia, with a density of 47.68 persons per square *verst*,
ranked only behind the *guberniia* of Moscow.[59] Poltava with 41.32
persons and Kiev with 40.25 persons to the square *verst* ranked fifth
and sixth in population density among the provinces within the
empire.

As late as 1856, the territory of Novorossiia had less than half the
population density of the more northern, black-soil region. Taurida
(the Crimea) ranked fiftieth among the provinces with only 12.31
persons to the square *verst*; Kherson, thirty-sixth with 17.83 persons;
Katerynoslav, thirty-fifth with 18.02. Bessarabia, the most densely
settled of the lands of Novorossiia, counted only 29.23 persons per
square *verst*. The easterly regions of the steppes in 1856 were comparatively deserted. The Territory of the Don Cossacks had only
6.25 person to the square *verst*, and the land of the Black Sea Cossacks only 5.51.

Haxthausen reported that in 1841 only one-third of the Katerynoslav and Kherson *guberniia*s was cultivated. He attributed the slow
development to three obstacles: "the unfavorable nature of the climate, the want of springs and fresh water, and the scarcity of
wood."[60] As the demand abroad for wheat grew, however, more
and more land was put under the plow. From 1881 to 1886, the area

of sown land in the Crimea grew 16.2 percent, reaching two million *desiatina*s. In the Kherson *guberniia* the area of sown land reached 3 million *desiatina*s.[61] As late as 1862, the United States consul, Timothy Smith, was surprised to find so much uncultivated land in the vicinity of Odessa:

> The surrounding country, unfortunately to the distance of two to five hundred miles, is for the most part uncultivated steppe or prairie. . . . Within a circuit of fifty miles from Odessa are several German colonies which have succeeded in cultivating the steppe and have prospered very well. Beyond that distance, however, it is for the most part an uncultivated waste.[62]

The kinds of wheat that flourished on these black soils were of excellent quality.[63] The wheat was either hard (*tverdaia pshenitsa*) or soft (*miagkaia pshenitsa*). The soft wheat found its best market in England, France, Spain, and the north of Europe, as consumers there favored it for their bread and biscuits. In the Mediterranean markets (including Constantinople, Greece, and the Ionian Islands), and notably in Italy, hard wheat was preferred, as it is particularly suitable for pasta. Moreover, of the hard wheats available to the Mediterranean consumer, Russia's was recognized as among the best. Its glutinous content was particularly high; an expert who compared the hard wheat of the Azov region with that produced in France found that it contained 40 percent gluten, while the French wheat contained only 30 percent.[64]

To be sure, the dark color of hard wheat put off some customers—the Spanish, for example—but others bought it expressly for its resistence to moisture. Not only did it produce a long-lasting pasta, but also bread and biscuits that kept over long sea voyages. It grew with particular abundance near Taganrog. So too did the popular winter red wheat; Dearborn described it in 1817: "It is esteemed the best wheat in the world, being very large, heavy and clean."[65] Dearborn claimed that the yield at that time was forty times the seed. Of the hard wheat cultivated, the most important was arnaut (*arnautka*), a spring wheat distinguished by its exceptionally long grains. Arnaut in Russian sources is also called by a number of other names: *turka, beloturka, kubanka, krasno-turkaia pshenitsa*, or simply *russkaia pshenitsa*.

Most of the soft wheat cultivated was of the winter variety (*ozimaia pshenitsa*) and was both red and white. The white seems to have been the more widespread, as it was considered less sensitive to the cold. With the extension of cultivation to the east and north into the steppes, spring wheat assumed greater importance, as it did not have to pass the harsh winter in the ground and was ready for export in late summer or in the autumn. A milestone in grain cultivation in Novorossiia was the introduction in the 1840s of soft red *girka* wheat. Both winter and spring varieties existed, but the spring was by far the more important. The dark red *girka* produced a fine flour.[66] Another soft, spring wheat was *sandormirka*. Of Polish origin, this strain was widely cultivated in the northwestern parts of Podillia, Volhynia, and Kiev. Of these types, the red wheat was of better quality than the white and sold at the same price as winter wheat. These were hardy strains, able to survive in years of low rainfall. In 1856, the French consul at Odessa reported that two-thirds of the soft wheat exported came from Voronezh, Saratov, the Caucasus, and even from the banks of the Volga; this last source had only been recently developed.[67]

Travelers in the steppe regions noted the occasional practice of the three-field system (*trekhpol'noe khoziaistvo*) of crop rotation, which was commonly followed in other Russian regions.[68] According to this regimen, a given field supported in turn a winter crop, then a spring crop, and then lay fallow. The Mennonite colony on the Molochna used a four-year crop rotation system. First year: barley, hemp, millet, or potatoes; second year: wheat; third year: barley or oats; fourth year: fallow.[69] To produce crops in two out of three or three out of four years, however, the land required manuring, and this called for a system of mixed farming with fairly large animal herds and considerable capital investment in houses, barns, and the like. A shortage of capital limited the application of such systems in Novorossiia. By far the most common method in the open steppes was the varied field system (*pestropol'noe* or *raznoklinnoe khoziaistvo*). Skal'kovskii called it "the many-field system," which was hardly a system at all. Many of the fields received no artificial fertilization. As the United States consul, Smith, noted:

> The soil is rich, black and deep, requiring no manure and yields in very wet seasons a most luxuriant vegetation and generally in the spring of the year presents a beautifully green and flowery aspect.[70]

If manure was used at all, it was placed on the field only in the first year of cultivation, after which crops would be sown for an extended period. Manure was scarce, as dry dung mixed with straw was also used as fuel, even by the nobles.[71] According to Shmidt, when the steppes of the Kherson province had first been cultivated, the practice was to sow the land for four or five years on end, then to leave it fallow for ten years.[72] The demand for wheat, he noted, had resulted in scaling down the period of fallow and increasing the time that the land bore cereals. P. Köppen observed that the steppes in the Don River basin were cultivated nine to twelve years on end, then rested for a decade.[73] Haxthausen once visited Count Lambert's estate near Mykolaiv, which spread over thirty thousand acres of good soil. There, the peasants planted virgin land in the spring with millet; in the second and third years, they planted spring wheat. After the harvest and autumn plowing, they sowed winter wheat. The following autumn, however, they planted rye or barley. No manure was ever applied, but after repeated croppings, the land was allowed to lie fallow for an extended period.[74]

This loose system of crop rotation required little start-up capital; indeed, the cultivator, with abundant land at his disposal, invested in hardly more than the cost of seed and a few simple tools. The ease of wheat cultivation on the steppes and the small capital needed to produce it made the supply of grain highly elastic. Ultimately, of course, these primitive modes of cultivation stagnated Russian agricultural techniques on deplorably low levels. But for a country chronically short of capital, the cheaply produced grain earned abundant returns on foreign markets. In feeding western Europe, exported wheat fed Russia with hard currency.

Fertile and accessible, the southern regions of the Russian Empire seemed destined to become the granary of Western Europe. But there were also obstacles to expanded cereal production. Foremost among them was the climate. The southern regions of the empire are dry. Precipitation averages about one-half meter a year, and falls off rapidly in the direction of the east. This is close to the minimum needed for wheat (ca. 42.5 centimeters), but fortunately, the rain chiefly falls when the growing plant most needs it—in the spring.[75] Observers, including the Tuscan, French, English, and United States consuls in Odessa, reported often on the weather; they scanned it carefully from month to month, in order to estimate the abundance of the coming harvest.[76] Their words could launch or redirect a thousand ships.

In the areas of winter wheat, the most favorable conditions included snow in the late autumn, and, in winter, cold temperatures that conserved it. The snow blanket protected the seedlings from the ravages of deep frost and kept moisture in the ground. In January 1835, the United States consul, John Ralli, reported the presence of such an auspicious blanket:

The experience of years has proved that when snow falls in abundance in this country during the winter and remains a sufficient time on the surface of the earth, as is the case here at present, a good crop seldom or never fails to follow.[77]

The lack of snow, or a mild winter including a "false spring," often proved disastrous to the plant, which flourishes best when temperatures in the critical spring months increase evenly and smoothly. If the snow remained on the ground long into the spring, it could prevent the sowing of spring wheat. Then too, rains had to be plentiful in the autumn and again in the spring (March and April) to water the rapidly growing plants. According to the French consul, harvests were always aleatory; in his estimation the cultivator could count on only one good year in six.[78] Too many things could go wrong. For example, heavy rain storms late in the season might rot the ripened grain before it could be harvested. Hail storms in July menaced the standing plants. The hailstones were allegedly large enough to smite men and beasts.[79] At Tulchyn in 1824 there supposedly rained hail "the size of bantams' eggs."[80]

Excessive heat threatened the flocks and herds with drought. Haxthausen was impressed by the extremes of heat and cold, drought and precipitation, on the steppes. For twenty months in the Crimea in 1832–1833, so much rain fell that the grain rotted and grass could not be made into hay. Usually, however, winds quickly dried the bare steppes. Few lakes, ponds, or woods trapped the precious moisture.[81] The winter of 1862, lacking snow and rain, was again disastrous. According to George Hume, an expert in the agriculture of Novorossiia, one good crop came every three years and one bumper crop in seven.[82]

Locusts joined the weather in threatening the crops. Many witnesses have left us descriptions of the terrifying black clouds of insects that swooped down on the grain and hungrily devoured it. One traveler wrote:

The neighborhood of Odessa is very bleak and much infested by locusts which come in immense bodies, covering entire acres and in an hour after they have alighted, every vestige of verdure is effaced.[83]

A long-time resident of the Ukraine claimed that once the locusts were so thick that they stopped a train. A certain kind of fly was reputed to be the natural enemy of the locust, but apparently the numbers of these allies were insufficient. The chief method for combating locusts was to make as much noise as possible. Several

travelers described the din and the weapons: shouts, cries, the ringing of bells, the banging of drums, shovels, pots, pans, the firing of
guns—anything to chase them away.[84] "It was a real battle," said the
Countess Rzewuska.[85]

The German colonists established a "locust policeman" to give
the alarm at an approaching swarm. They too used noise as a
weapon and also invented a machine drawn by horses that dragged a
bar with fingers designed to grind up the insects.[86] Another method
of extermination was to drive the locusts into ditches and then set
them afire. Crude instruments were devised to roll along the
ground, crushing the eggs.[87] Still another strategy was to drive the
locusts into the sea, where their bodies formed floating islands.[88] In
1828, a Mr. Blonskii wrote to the *Journal d'Odessa* and advised farmers to have little boys, too small to work in the fields, dig up the
eggs and expose them to the air to kill them.[89]

Whatever the method adopted, the locusts remained a periodic
plague. Certain years were noted for the advent of the locust: 1824,
1825, 1828, 1829, and 1862.

The famed poet Alexander Pushkin was once sent on an official
assignment to investigate locusts. Governor General Vorontsov
suspected that the bored exile had been courting his wife; he chose
the advent of the locusts as an excuse to send him the following
order on May 22, 1824:

> I make you responsible for visiting the districts of Kherson, Ielysa-
> vethrad, and Oleksandriia. Upon your arrival in those towns, you
> must obtain the following information: in what places have the locusts
> been killed, how many were there, what were the orders for their
> extermination, and the means used to obtain their elimination. Once
> you have learned that, then you are to inspect the places where the
> locusts were the most numerous in order to evaluate the efficacy of
> the present methods for clearing them out. You are to study if the
> measures taken by the provincial committees are sufficient. All that
> you observe is to be reported to me personally.[90]

Pushkin strenuously solicited an excuse (he claimed a terminal
aneurism) from higher authorities, but was constrained to go and
inspect the locust situation. His official report, if indeed he made
one, is not extant, but tradition has it that he composed the following verses in summary of his observations:

        The locusts flew, flew
        Then they alighted
        Crept along, devouring all
        And once again, flew away. [91]

His observations on the locusts were thus accurate, if not especially profound. The problem persisted. At the end of the 1850s Count Tolstoi, vice chairman of the South Russian Agricultural Society, headed a "committee for the battle against locusts."[92] Although the locusts were by far the most pesty menace on the steppe, man had to fight the Hessian fly, the Hungarian or Austrian beetle, the marmot, the jerboa, snakes, spiders and tarantulas as well.

Mice and other rodents also scoured the land. In 1830, the French consul at Odessa was astonished that a group of men surrounding the wheat stack were able to flush out and kill four thousand mice![93] Mice infested the grain carts, in which they nibbled their way to port. As the Countess Rzewuska reported in 1836, the fondest hope of the inhabitants of Odessa was that the grain be sold before the rats consumed it.[94]

Inland Transport

Besides offering soil of exceptional fertility and wide expanse, geography also favored Novorossiia by affording fairly good access to distant markets. Geographers routinely praise the great rivers of Russia for their commercial functions. Large and slow-flowing, they radiate from Moscow and the central Russian provinces and form the oldest strands—still important strands—in the commercial web binding together the Russian Empire. Curiously, however, the new lands to the south were not well served by the river system. As early as the middle seventeenth century, a French traveler commented upon the inadequacy of river transport in the Ukraine and its unfortunate economic repercussions:

> The land is so fruitful, it often produces such a plenty of corn that they do not know what to do with it, because they have no navigable rivers that fall into the sea, except the Borystenes [Dnieper], which is not navigable fifty leagues below Kiow or Kovia [Kiev], by reason of thirteen falls on it, the last of which is seven leagues distant from the first, which makes a good day's journey. ... This is what hinders them carrying their corn to Constantinople.[95]

In 1780, an engineer by the name of Faleev tried unsuccessfully to dig a canal around the rapids.[96] In 1801, Tsar Paul I attempted to blow up some of the cataracts, and in 1828 another futile attempt was made to clear them.[97] All to no avail; the course of the Dnieper ran vexed to the sea.

To the west, the Dniester was a convenient waterway for carrying grain from Podillia to the Black Sea, but it was not until 1812 that both banks were included within the Russian Empire. The largest and most important of all Russian rivers, the Volga, had little significance for the grain trade. The steppe regions it traversed remained for long undeveloped, and it flowed into the land-locked Caspian.

Then, too, river transport in the south was affected by the seasons. When swollen with waters from the spring thaw, the rivers easily carried the largest barges. By early fall, when most grain had to be moved, many of the rivers, in many points in their courses, were dangerously shallow. Silting near the mouth was another common problem for the southern river ports. Dredging the channels might have greatly facilitated navigation, but this required capital, and of capital Russia had little to spare. In 1845, a statistician calculated that in bringing grain to Odessa, river transport accounted for only about 25 percent of the volume—no more than half a million out of two million *chetverts*.[98]

The bulk of the grain had to be carried overland—in the great, ox-drawn carts driven by Ukrainian *chumaks*, that had long served as the basic means of transport on the steppe. They were pulled by two oxen in a wooden yoke.[99] The chassis of the cart was made of bark upon which a rough cloth was spread. Five to seven sacks filled with wheat were placed on the cloth and covered with a dried cow skin. The covering did not entirely prevent moisture from seeping into the sacks, but the grain could be dried later.

A cart could carry five to six *chetverts* of hard wheat, six to eight *chetverts* of soft wheat, eight of rye, or ten or eleven of oats—reflecting primarily the respective weights of the cereals. An English traveler calculated that each cart carried eight sacks of wheat, or about three quarters and two bushels.[100] The carts travelled, according to one French source, five to six leagues (about 12.5 to 15 miles) per day, "including nights."[101] Other reporters set their speed at 10, 12, or 15 miles per day.[102] The abundance of fodder growing along the routes provided feed for the beasts. Water was less easily obtained and frequently had to be purchased. This was expensive. As early as 1805, well water was inadequate for the people of

Odessa, and water for the beasts had to be obtained from afar.[103] The French consul estimated that in 1832 it cost 4.5 paper rubles per *chetvert* to deliver wheat to Odessa. About a decade later, Hommaire de Hell stated that it cost 4.6 rubles a *chetvert.*[104]

The terrain was fairly passable only at certain times of the year— only seven months, in fact, according to Hommaire de Hell.[105] The carts started out in late spring or early summer, after the roads had dried and hardened.[106] Much of the traveling was done at night.[107] During high summer, carters were often occupied in the fields and unavailable to serve in carting. Then again in early autumn (after September 1) more caravans of carts would set forth when the roads were reputedly in the best shape of the year. This apparently primitive method could deliver astonishing quantities of grain. In the first decade of the nineteenth century, according to an Italian merchant, from five hundred to a thousand carts arrived in Odessa within a single day.[108] Some years later, in the 1830s, a French traveler counted six hundred carts arriving daily.[109] In 1843, 200,000 carts rolled across the Ukraine, moving in all one million *chetvert*s of wheat and 200,000 *chetvert*s of linseed.[110] Some of the carters at the terminus broke up their wagons and sold them for firewood. Some sold their oxen for slaughter as well.[111]

In 1862, the United States consul described the great caravans approaching Odessa with wheat from the hinterland:

> This produce for the most part has been brought into Odessa from three to five hundred miles, over the steppe, in carts or waggons [sic] drawn by horses and oxen, by roads either very dusty or very muddy. One pair of horses or oxen can take from twenty to ninety bushels of wheat to a load; and one man can generally manage three or four teams which move in caravans or lines from twenty to a hundred in number.[112]

Although the carts, carters, and oxen of the South Ukraine were able to move impressive quantities of wheat, this method of transport had clearly become inadequate even before the 1840s. The deterioration of roads in bad weather meant difficult journeys and high grain prices. The oxen were vulnerable to a number of ailments as well. Around 1845, a serious epidemic broke out among the oxen in Novorossiia.[113] Skal'kovskii asserted that 75 percent of all cattle of Novorossiia died in that year.[114] On one of Voronstov's estates alone some four thousand head of cattle perished.[115] In January 1845, the French consul stated that nearly one-half of the area's cattle had died and the disease was still then raging.[116] Called the

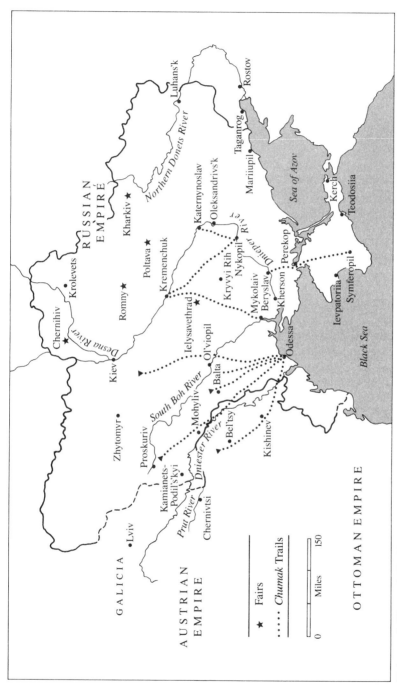

Fairs and *Chumak* Trails

plague of Siberia, it appeared to strike chiefly oxen, although horses were also affected. Sheep remained immune. Three years later, because of an extraordinarily cold winter, the supply of fodder fell to a dangerous low, and this reduced the numbers and sapped the strength of oxen.[117] Under such catastrophes, the cost of carting soared to levels that rendered uneconomical the transport of grain from areas of any distance. In October 1851, the United States consul at Odessa, noting the limited arrivals of grain, attributed it to "the deficiency of draught cattle to convey it to market."[118]

Like drought and disease, the government could reduce the numbers of available oxen. In Polish lands, after the failed uprising in 1830, the government freely requisitioned beasts, carts, and peasant carters into state service. In 1843, the French consul wrote:

... today one pays about twice the amount as formerly in order to transport wheat from the Polish provinces to Odessa.[119]

In 1849 too, when Nicholas I determined to repress the Hungarian revolution, the United States consul at Odessa noted a scarcity of carts: "... the government being in immediate want of carts and draught cattle to transport the ammunition and stores of the troops now in motion."[120]

Finally, even under the best of conditions, the carts could serve only a limited region. Dearborn, to be sure, claimed in 1819 that hard wheat arrived in Taganrog from as far as fifteen hundred or 1,800 *versts* (about 1,000 miles), but part of this long journey was made by river barge.[121] Sauron, the French consul, affirmed that the carts rumbled 560 *versts* (about 400 miles) on their way to port, while the English traveler Jesse claimed that some had covered 700 miles.[122] Still, the average distance travelled by the carts seems to have been from 150 to 300 *versts*, or about 90 to 180 miles.[123] When cereal prices at the ports were buoyant, the high costs of transport were partially absorbed. But when prices were low, profit margins in wheat sales collapsed; producers and purchasers wrangled, but often could not come to terms. Even in boom years, the high costs discouraged distant producers from sending grain to the ports; the crude system of transport showed its inadequacies.

Moreover, this expensive transport required a shift in the use of resources from grain production to grain carting. The cultivators of wheat were, in the main, also the carters, and the job might easily claim some forty days of a peasant's time.[124] Initially, this employment meshed rather smoothly into the normal seasonal cycle of peasant labor. But as the trips grew longer in distance and time, they interfered with properly agricultural duties. Then too, the extension of grain cultivation reduced the open meadows rich in fodder upon which the draft animals fed. By 1859, the French commercial consul at St. Petersburg, Vallat, affirmed that the increase of settled population on the steppes made carting less and less feasible. Moreover, as the distances traversed grew larger, the bad state of Russian roads and bridges imposed even bigger handicaps. For example, the river Boh, which flowed through one of the most productive regions of the southern Ukraine, had only one bridge in 200 *versts* (120 miles) of its course.[125]

By the 1840s the manifest deficiencies of carting evoked pointed complaints, both from Russians and from foreigners engaged in the grain commerce. The French civil engineer Hommaire de Hell reported in 1841:

Unfortunately, the means of communication have been totally neglected, and the government has taken no steps to facilitate transport; in consequence of this, the price of grain instead of falling, is constantly increasing, and merchants are no longer willing to purchase except in seasons of scarcity.[126]

The *Journal d'Odessa* was both indignant and sanguine in 1847:

The difficulty which is sometimes encountered with the means of transporting agricultural products from contiguous provinces is the sole reason for which various other areas can easily compete with us in their prices, and for some time, we have tried to draw the attention of the government to this point of major importance. It is incontestable that improvements of communication by water and land, the construction of good roads, and the perfection of river navigation are essentially indispensable for our trade. And these innovations, which under the paternal care of our government are going forward with great strides in our vast country and are growing on all sides, will establish the wealth of Odessa and the prosperity of the South of Russia on a solid basis for a long time.[127]

The great strides noted by the *Journal* were in large measure imaginary. A traveler to Odessa in 1852 marvelled at the absence of a single macadamized road leading forth from the city in any single direction.[128] In 1858, another visitor claimed that despite the huge production of grain in the Russian Empire, through defective transport "enough wheat to feed the rest of Europe was lost to the market."[129] For this reason, he labelled as illusory the fear that

Russia might some day flood Western Europe with cheap grain, to the ruin of its agriculture. He thus explained:

> There will always remain the difficulty of internal transportation, reduced perhaps, but always calculable in its effects, which will reduce considerably the quantity of exportable cereals. And this difficulty in internal transportation will become more evident to those who consider that the Russian railways pass through long stretches of uninhabited land, and the stations cannot be so close to each other as the Piedmontese and French lines, so that the cultivator must still cover large areas of bad roads just in order to transport his wheat from the field to those places where he might load them on the railroad.[130]

In 1862, the United States consul agreed that more efficient transport to the hinterland was Odessa's great need:

> At present the great want of Odessa, then, is the means of communication with the far interior, the country which really sustains and supports it, by means of railroads and canals.[131]

The effort to solve this problem of inland transport inspired countless pamphlets and many imaginative projects. Early efforts were made to construct macadam roads, but progress was glacial. By the middle of the century, one macadam highway united Kharkiv and Podol'sk and another led from Kiev to Ostrov and beyond.[132] The continuing bad state of roads in the South Ukraine inevitably caught the eye of local humorists. The following passage, from Il'f and Petrov, was written in the early twentieth century, but its point—that modernization left roads unchanged—expresses a reality of life in the South Ukraine.

> Between the village of Udoyevo, founded in *A.D.* 794, and Chernomorsk [that is, Odessa], founded in *A.D.* 1794, lay a thousand years of time and 2000 miles of dirt roads and highways. . . . The life of the country changed with every century. Apparel changed, weapons were improved, and the potato riots were suppressed. People began shaving their heads. The first balloon was launched. . . . The iron twins— the locomotive and the steamship—were invented. Motor cars began sounding their horns. But the road remained exactly as it was during the time of Solovei the Highwayman.
>
> Humped, covered with volcanic mud or coated with dust as poisonous as flea powder, the road wound its way past villages, towns, factories and farms; wound its way like a thousand-mile death trip. By

its sides, in the yellow, defiled grass, lay the skeletons of carts and tortured, expiring motor cars.[133]

A project conceived in 1846 called for railroads with wagons pulled by horses. And a multitude of river and canal projects were excogitated.[134] Ultimately, of course, the railroad provided the most important, if not exactly a complete, solution to the Ukraine's problem of transport—an issue to which we must return.[135] Meanwhile, the carts rumbled and creaked their way to port, while suppliers and purchasers expressed ever-greater impatience with these picturesque, but outmoded, vehicles. The primitive system of inland transport did not serve well, but neither did it totally block, the economic and social development of the southern Ukraine in the first half of the nineteenth century.

CHAPTER FOUR

Producers, Middlemen, and Merchants

Who was the true creator of these enormously beautiful cities, harbors, railroads, highways, the grain elevators and ships, the theaters and the hospitals and the universities? The merchant.
—Vladimir Zhabotinskii

From the beginnings of settlement, foreign trade worked decisively to shape the economy and society of Odessa and of Novorossiia. Under its influence, the growing population came to form three large categories. There were the herders and the cultivators—those who directly exploited the rich resources of the region in order to support themselves and to produce commodities for market; the middlemen, who arranged for the delivery of this produce from the hinterland to port; and the merchants, who maintained contact with the distant purchasers. These groups differed one from the other, not only by reason of their basic employment, but also in their origins and in their culture.

The Producers

Novorossiia in the early nineteenth century experienced an explosive growth of population and expansion of settlement. Although we do not have complete censuses, the imperial government in a series of *reviziia*s counted up the number of taxable male "souls"; it scrutinized virtually the entire peasant population (though not the gentry). The count of peasants, by far the largest class in this society, can serve as a good indicator of the expansion of the total population. (See Table 4.1)

The male population settled in the territory of the Don Cossacks similarly grew from 100,503 in 1782, to 212,574 in 1815, to 393,493 in 1850.[1] This phenomenon of rapid growth, this "frontier" character of Novorossiia, fundamentally influenced regional life and institutions. The new arrivals did not enter an established system of agricultural organization, which in other, older parts of contemporary

Russia, was based upon the manor and upon serfdom. Rather, the settlers were free to fashion their own modes of production in response to the growing market for wheat.

Table 4.1

The Count of Male "Souls" in the
Three *Guberniia*s of Novorossiia, 1782–1857

Year	Male Souls	Year	Male Souls
1782	290,026	1833	1,127,404
1795	519,950	1850	1,283,069
1811	732,500	1857	1,347,265
1815	875,640		

Source: Kabuzan, 1971, pp. 103, 115, 127, 139, 151, 163, 175. The figures derive from the fourth through tenth *reviziia*s, the only ones to include the three *guberniia*s.

People and Land

Only a few settlers in Novorossiia acquired land in full title; there was no recognition of "squatters' sovereignty," no general policy of offering free land to small cultivators who would improve it, as implemented, for example, after 1866 in the American West. The largest number of cultivators worked land technically owned by the State (Treasury). A second group nearly as big was found on the estates of the favored nobility. Only a small number of the cultivators worked the Crown land, or estates that belonged to the imperial family. Since this last category included only one-tenth of one percent of the total population, we will not give it special consideration. In 1801, the settlers on the two largest categories of land numbered as follows:

Table 4.2

Settlers on State and Private Lands in Novorossiia, 1801

State Lands		Private Lands	
Military Personnel	151,373	Non-servile Peasants or	165,759
State Peasants	81,246	"Seigneurial Subjects"	
Colonists	16,448	Traditional Serfs or	28,166
Others	8,094	"Seigneural Peasants"	
Totals	257,361		193,925

Source: Druzhinina, 1970, p. 70.

Figure 4.1: The Count of Male "Souls" in Novorossiia, 1782–1857

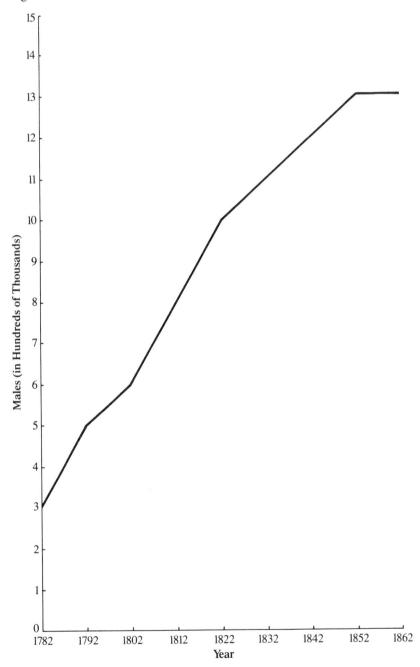

Nearly all the persons enumerated above actually worked the land. Some of the military personnel were not engaged in agriculture, but others were military colonists who were expected to raise enough food to be self-supporting. Although their economic status seems often to have been miserable, these persons remained juridically free.[2]

The State peasants, though technically unfree, enjoyed a comparatively favorable status. They were independent cultivators who paid taxes to the State for the lands they worked, but they were not subject to *barshchina* (labor services) or to other forms of manorial discipline. Even the prospect of passing under private ownership sometimes provoked riots in the villages.[3] Many of these State peasants were settled in the Crimea, a fact that no doubt prompted the traveler, Mary Holderness, to remark around 1820 that "slaves" were not found in that region.[4] And the population settled on State lands was growing in relative numbers—from 57 percent in 1801 to 65 percent in 1817.

The government did not systematically resettle State peasants from old to new lands, but it did provide incentives (for example, five years remission of taxes) to those who voluntarily chose to immigrate. Most State peasants came in small groups, spontaneously, without even applying for special permission and benefits.[5]

Of the peasants settled on private estates, most were fairly evenly divided between the Katerynoslav and Kherson *guberniias*, with relatively few in the Crimean peninsula. Foreign colonists were also found in fairly equal numbers in these two *guberniias*.

The largest category of "private" peasants—indeed, the largest single group of cultivators of any sort in 1801—consisted of *pomeshchik* or seigneurial "subjects" settled upon private estates. Most of them seem to have been recruited from runaway serfs, prisoners, vagabonds, and so forth. Others were emigrants who did not qualify as "foreign." Although many had left their places of origin without authorization, the government officials ignored their provenance or looked at them, in the colorful Russian phrase, "through their fingers." The officials, in fact, could hardly have pursued them vigorously. If harassed, the migrants might have continued their flight beyond the Russian borders, and the empire would have lost their valued services to even newer regions. Typically, these people brought with them little or no capital. Typically too, they leased farms from the landowners.

The government did not favor the transference of private serfs from the old northern manors into Novorossiia. In an *ukaz* of 1796,

Catherine decreed that peasants must remain in their residences of 1795. While the law is usually interpreted as confirming serfdom, its results for Novorossiia were paradoxical. It gave immunity to those escaped serfs who had already settled in the new provinces. And it obstructed the export of Russia's "peculiar institution" into the new lands. The government itself seems to have sensed that the frontier required or recommended free labor.[6] Thus, in 1861, only about one-tenth of the land owned by *pomeshchik*s was worked by servile labor; for the remaining nine-tenths, hired labor was employed.[7] There is an intriguing analogy here with the contemporary opposition in America to the extension of slavery to the western territories.

In 1827, another survey was taken of the then much larger population of Novorossiia; it invites comparison with the divisions of 1801.[8] Four new categories appear: cereal farmers (*svobodnye khlebopashtsy*) living on their own land (1,519 males); landless peasants on State lands (*bobyletskie krest'iane*), for whom no exact count is given; obligated settlers (*obiazannye poseliane*) on private estates (1,312 males); and military colonists (*voinskie poseliane*) on State land, who are also not precisely counted. Unfortunately, however, it is no longer possible to identify the true serfs within the enumerated population. On the private estates of the *pomeshchik*s, no distinction was made between servile and nonservile settlers; this in itself points to the waning (or at least confused) significance of "classical" serfdom. In this and contemporary records, these settlers are variously called "*pomeshchik* peasants and household serfs" (*pomeshchich'i krest'iane i dvorovye*), "*pomeshchik* peasants and subject Ukrainians" (*pomeshchich'i i poddannye malorossiiane*), or simply "settlers on private estates" (*poseliane chastnykh imenii*). To be sure, in the survey of 1827, echoes of bondage remain, particularly in the allusion to "obligated settlers." But of 711,034 males counted, 709,713 were within or on the margins of free status.

The enterprise of Count M. S. Vorontsov (governor general of Novorossiia from 1823 to 1844) gives a concrete example of the transformation of traditional Russian agrarian institutions under frontier conditions.[9] Beginning in the 1820s, he acquired massive areas of land in the southern Ukraine, as well as in the Crimea. He transferred serfs from his estates in central Russia to settle his new possessions (in spite of Catherine's prohibition). Significantly, however, most of the new arrivals became leaseholders in their new homes. In 1827, his father Semen expressed satisfaction that nearly all of Mikhail's peasants had their own homes and lived on the land like "farmers."[10] They were not charged with labor services, but simply paid rents or *obrok*. Under this regimen, père Vorontsov opined, the land would be better cultivated; peasant, landlord, and nation would all profit. Besides these transferred serfs, other immigrants were invited to take the land under comparably liberal conditions. In his viticulture, vegetable farming, and grain cultivation, Vorontsov initially relied predominantly upon hired labor. His model remained the capitalistic agriculture of the West.

According to Zagoruiko, in the early years in the Odessa district (*uezd*), resettled serfs from the central provinces were to be found on no more than twenty to thirty estates.[11] Apparently too, the transplanting of serfs carried considerable risks. In 1832, the French consul observed that one out of four immigrants forcibly resettled soon succumbed to disease and death, because they did not readily adjust to the different climate.[12]

The liberal regime enjoyed by the peasants of Novorossiia in the early phases of settlement evoked approval in a report prepared in 1827:

> Although there are some *pomeshchik*s who oppress peasants with excessive work or subject them to cruel and intolerable punishments, it can be said in general that in the region of Novorossiia, peasants have more complete enjoyment of their legitimate rights than in other Russian provinces, and that they are subjected to repression less than happens elsewhere.[13]

The report goes on to affirm that in Novorossiia, landlords do not even interfere in the marriages of the peasants.

Small Properties

Besides the weak presence of serfdom, a second characteristic of early settlement in Novorossiia was the importance of small and medium-sized estates. Many of these small owners were *meshchane*, "middle people" or "petty bourgeois," although the category also included urban artisans and small traders. In 1801, the *meshchane* in Novorossiia numbered 21,812 males; by 1827, they were 69,669. The cultivators among them characteristically lived on small farms on the outskirts of, or at least close to, cities. They usually held their farms by lease from *pomeshchik*s, and engaged in vegetable farming. A special group among them were the *desiatinshchik*s, named from a measure of land (*desiatina* or 2.7 acres), who were especially numerous in the environs of Odessa. As Skal'kovskii observed as late as 1858, they were recruited from State peasants, colonists, runaway serfs, or religious separatists (*raskolniks*), and enjoyed considerable prosperity on their small, but productive, farms.[14]

With rare exceptions—M. S. Vorontsov most notable among them—even the nobles or *pomeshchiks* of Novorossiia usually owned modest estates and few or even no serfs; in contrast, huge estates worked by great numbers of serfs pitted the landscape of the central provinces. The small *pomeshchiks* of the southern Ukraine typically relied on hired and seasonal labor, and the shortage of workers necessarily limited the size of these enterprises.

Within this category of small cultivators fall also the foreign colonists. Welcomed, as we have seen, in the first years of settlement, they were less courted as the land filled up with people.[15] According to P. Köppen, the number of colonies and foreign settlers in the empire in the year 1839 was as follows:

Table 4.3

Foreign Colonies and Foreign Settlers in Russia, 1839

Province Novorossiia:	Number of Colonies	Foreign Settlers
Bessarabia	105	74,473
Kherson	55	40,591
Katerynoslav	47	13,297
Taurida	80	23,560
Totals	287	151,921
Elsewhere:		
Cis-Caucasian	3	481
Georgia	7	2,388
St. Petersburg	13	3,035
Saratov	102	127,028
Chernihiv	8	1,752
Voronezh	1	1,231
Totals	134	134,315

Source: Adapted from Köppen, "Kornbedarf Russlands," p. 579, Table P.

The colonists characteristically settled in small villages close to their fields.[16] They thus could work their lands intensively without walking great distances from house to field. In size, their farms ranged from medium to large. Foreign settlers in Novorossiia usually received from thirty to eighty *desiatinas* (from about 80 to 210 acres) per family, and the farm could not later be divided.[17] An English clergyman traveling in Novorossiia in the 1830s noted that there were fifteen German villages between Tyraspil and Odessa. Each village contained from one hundred to two hundred houses, each with an allotment of sixty *desiatinas*.[18] In the 1840s, according to the rough but indicative calculations of A. A. Skal'kovskii, the colonists produced about 12 percent of Novorossiia's exported grain.[19]

Still another category of small cultivators in Novorossiia consisted of independent peasants. Effectively, the "State peasants" who were not subject to *barshchina* services functioned as independent cultivators. Then too there were substantial numbers of Cossacks, Tatars, Turks, and others, who had long lived in the South Ukraine, and were not regarded as "foreign colonists." All these independent cultivators together numbered more than 760,000 by 1848.[20] Typically, these independent peasants lived in very large villages; many walked from two to three miles to reach the fields they worked.[21] To increase productivity, by 1850 the government was trying to limit the size of villages in the South Ukraine to twenty-five homesteads.[22] Their methods of cultivating the land were largely limited to the varied-field system already discussed. The return from seed barely surpassed 3:1, and was much poorer than that gained by the colonists and even the Russian *pomeshchiks*.[23] Unlike the colonists and the owners of large estates, these independent cultivators had little capital and scant experience with producing for market. The one "factor of production" in which they were abundantly supplied was land. Their holdings typically spread to the east and north within the black-soil belt.

Frontiers and Freedom

The frontier of Novorossiia thus hosted settlers of varied national and social origins, under an atmosphere of comparative freedom. Table 4.4 shows the percentage of *pomeshchik* serfs found in the total population, in 1833 and 1857, respectively. (In these areas, all non-*pomeshchik* serfs were State peasants.)

We include for comparative purposes data from the north-Ukrainian province of Kiev. As the table shows, *pomeshchik* serfs remained very few in the Crimea—at the limits of the empire—and comparatively few in Kherson and Katerynoslav. Moreover, between

1833 and 1857 the percentage of *pomeshchik* serfs in the total population was declining in both the northern Ukraine (Kiev) and in the southern provinces. On the whole, the percentage of such serfs in Kherson *guberniia* seems to have fallen off more considerably than it did in Kiev.

Table 4.4

Percentage of *Pomeshchik* Serfs in the Total
Population of Novorossiia and Kiev, 1833 and 1857

	1833	1857
Crimea	6.78	6.04
Katerynoslav	36.15	32.71
Kherson	37.65	31.59
Kiev	64.19	60.51

Source: Kabuzan, 1971, pp. 152-53, 176-77, based
on the eighth and tenth *reviziias*.

The serfs of Novorossiia also worked comparatively small estates. Table 4.5 shows the average number of serfs per proprietor (which indirectly indicates the numbers of serfs per estate) on the eve of emancipation, in 1857.

Table 4.5

Number of Serfs per Proprietor
in Novorossiia and Kiev, 1857

	Owners with Serfs	Number of Serfs	Average
Crimea	543	21,144	38.93
Katerynoslav	2,621	158,859	60.60
Kherson	2,813	151,142	53.72
Kiev	1,584	521,245	319.06

Source: Report of the Central Committee of Statistics, reproduced in AMAE, Mémoires et Documents, Russie, Vol. 45, ff. 1–31, 1858.

As late as 1857, the provinces of Novorossiia thus contained relatively fewer serfs, settled on relatively smaller estates, than in the old-settled *guberniia* of Kiev.

To be sure, the decline of serfdom in the Ukraine may not have been as linear and as smooth as these figures imply. The initial big boom in grain exports seems to have prompted some landlords in the old and densely settled areas of the Ukraine to demand new or increased labor services from their peasants. In Podillia, Volhynia, and the district of Kiev, the landlords' exactions of labor services had grown so exorbitant that in 1848 the government insisted on compiling an "inventory," which would stipulate exactly who were serfs and what they owed. The English consul at Odessa commented that in these regions there were places

> . . . where the lords of the soil, stimulated by the great profits arising from the market of Odessa have increased production, by concentrating labor upon large systems of cultivation, affected only by enormous abuses, and an arbitrary disposal of the service of their peasants; so that the latter have been sinking into deeper misery and degradation, while wealth has been flowing in for their masters.[24]

Even the southern frontier was touched by this movement. In the 1830s, M. S. Vorontsov, for all his professed liberalism, was again demanding labor services from resettled serfs and other peasants working his estates.[25] In other words, the booming demand of the foreign market initially at least had this paradoxical effect: the reemphasis, in one of the most commercially oriented agricultural regions of the Russian Empire, on that obligation most characteristic of traditional serfdom and the manorial system—labor services.[26] The pattern is reminiscent of the resuscitation of American slavery, which the invention of the cotton gin (1793) and the soaring market for cotton, generated in the New World.

But it also seems clear that this renewed stress on *barshchina* services was a temporary expedient, a response to a sharply increased foreign demand for grain, which the local producers could not otherwise exploit. The *pomeshchiks* of Novorossiia, of whom Vorontsov is typical, reverted to forced labor out of no admiration for its efficiency. There was this further, big disadvantage. Traditionally, the serf who performed *barshchina* had to be given his own farm; in other words, in return for labor, the lord lost considerable amounts of fertile land, the produce of which went substantially to the serf himself. The trade-off of productive land for indifferent labor was not entirely in the lords' interest. Indeed, in a series of essays published in 1856–1857, a Russian agricultural economist, A. I.

Koshelev, affirmed that a large number of serfs on black-soil estates reduced their value:

> At the purchase of an estate in wheat-raising areas [that is, black-soil], we pay special attention to the quantity and quality of the land, and for the most part, the fewer the serfs the higher the value we give to the land. . . . On the other hand, at the purchase of an estate in industrial areas, we look preeminently at the *obrok* paid by the peasants.[27]

The estate owners of Novorossiia continued to rely primarily on seasonally hired labor where they could recruit it—from among independent cultivators and from State peasants. Even serfs from the central provinces, owing *obrok* payments to their owners, not only labored in city industries, but also worked for wages on the southern, grain-producing estates. They remained technically serfs, but they did not work their masters' land. How much did the serf's own production, on his own farm, contribute to wheat production in the South Ukraine? It is difficult to reach a firm estimate. In the 1840s, according to Skal'kovskii, the wheat delivered directly from the lords to the export market reached 968,000 *chetverts*; sales from serfs yielded only a paltry 48,000.[28] The figures suggest that the lords' lands contributed the lion's share of exports of Novorossiia. But the figures may be misleading. Estate owners, such as Vorontsov, brought grain from their own peasants (and from smaller, neighboring *pomeshchiks*) and marketed it indiscriminately with their own produce. Skal'kovskii's statistics show only that few serfs had direct contact with cereal merchants.

How did the commercialized agriculture and the largely free settlement of the southern Ukraine contribute to the abolition of serfdom in the empire in 1861? Marxist historians and theoreticians have traditionally seen in this growing production for market a principal factor in revolutionizing the "relations of production," in overthrowing "feudalism" and in introducing capitalism in the countryside. "The production of wheat for sale by the landlords," wrote V. I. Lenin, "which had especially developed in the last years of the existence of serfdom, was already a harbinger [*predvestnik*] of the downfall of the old regime."[29] Marxist historians such as P. I. Liashchenko and, more recently, P. A. Zionchkovskii, have consistently associated the development of capitalism in Russian agriculture with the breakdown of the serf system.[30] Non-Marxist scholars such as Jerome Blum, on the other hand, have expressed skepticism concerning the supposed linkages between growing commercialization and the emancipation of the serfs in 1861.[31] To these scholars, the purported causal link from increased market demand to commercialized agriculture, to the disintegration of "feudalism," to legal emancipation, form a defective explanatory model, too simple, too mechanical. Then too, there is the paradox we have already discussed: one social effect of the increased production for market was a return, even if temporary, to *barshchina* obligations.

Still, the great growth in cereal export necessarily affected the organization of agriculture in the empire and the social and juridical status of the peasants. To reach a balanced analysis, historians must consider not only the economic, but also the legal and institutional, factors that pushed the State toward eventual emancipation.

Here, we offer only a few comments. From the late eighteenth century, the population of Novorossiia was already, in its larger part, juridically free, and the degree of freedom grew more pronounced as one approached the imperial frontiers, in Bessarabia and the Crimea. But tensions inevitably developed between traditional bondage in the old-settled areas and freedom on the periphery. The government itself, as we have seen, was willing to tolerate illegal immigration into Novorossiia—violations of its own laws, in sum—in order to populate the new lands. The dichotomy between interior serfdom and peripheral freedom raised many anomalies. What exactly was the status of an illegally resettled serf? What was the status of a serf from the central provinces, who worked as a hired hand in Novorossiia, and still paid *obrok* to his distant master? By the middle nineteenth century, the government was under strong pressures to emancipate the serfs—in effect to bring the vast numbers of its subjects under a uniform and consistent juridical regimen. The alternative was rapidly becoming anomaly, confusion, chaos.

This then, on the most fundamental level, was the contribution that the settlement of Novorossiia made to the eventual emancipation of serfs in the empire: the new regions offered a model of a productive economic system based largely on freedom. The settlers in the south first enjoyed that kind of status that the imperial government would extend to all serfs in the Russian Empire in 1861.

Marketing

Between the producers and the consumers, the wheat of the South Ukraine passed through many hands: harvesters, *chumaks* with their carts and oxen, stevedores and sailors, bakers and shopkeepers; on a different level, the ownership of the wheat also passed by purchase and repurchase among many dealers. Here we examine the movement of cereals at this latter level: who purchased them, and who organized their delivery to market.

The simplest, and always the most attractive strategy of marketing, was for the producer to bring his wheat to port, to sell it directly to the foreign purchasers. The strategy was pursued, but it had its drawbacks. The foreign colonists, because of their proximity to Odessa, their knowledge of business procedures, and their generally high level of cultural and material resources, usually brought their produce directly to port.[32] Many large-scale producers, whether Russian, Ukrainian, or Polish, also dealt directly with foreign purchasers or their agents in Odessa. A German traveler reports in 1838:

> Many of the Polish nobility have counting houses and warehouses in Odessa, and the produce of their lands passes immediately out of their hands into those of the captains of vessels, without any intervention of the merchants.[33]

These large-scale producers, for the most part Polish, took advantage of their selling expeditions to enjoy the amenities of the city. They visited the spas, the seaside, the fancy shops and restaurants, and at times the gaming tables as well. One English traveler commented in 1839 that some two hundred "invalids" were in Odessa taking the baths. They were mostly landlords from Podillia who, "having disposed of the produce of their estates, carry off as many foreign luxuries as they can either smuggle or afford." On this gold coast, many gambled away their newly won profits. Even lady proprietors came to sell grain, and to buy millinery and the latest Parisian fashions.[34]

But not all these great proprietors were wastrels. Some of them built warehouses at Odessa, many of which were designed to look as decorative as the palaces they adjoined. A contemporary describes their elegance:

> . . . but what struck me as especially pleasing were the corn magazines, through whose handsome airy windows the golden blessings of the fields might be seen heaped up in rich masses. These magazines are built with the same elegance as the dwelling-houses, and indeed are frequently metamorphosed into them. Some are really magnificent; in particular, those of Count Potocki, and those which, before the Polish insurrection, belonged to the count Sabanski.[35]

Count Sabanski—eventually exiled from Odessa, we might mention, because of his sympathies for Polish liberty—could place in his warehouses thirty-six thousand *chetverts* of wheat. Other storehouses could hold from fifteen to twenty thousand *chetverts*.[36] The number of these graceful magazines grew even as Odessa's trade; 345 in 1827, they were 448 in 1846 and 720 in 1857.[37]

For their part, the captains of the foreign vessels were authorized to offer cash for cereals. In 1832, the French consul at Odessa described how cargoes were obtained; already the figure of the middleman was looming large:

> There arrive Greek and Genoese and sometimes Austrian ships which carry funds of cash or letters of credit. If it is in cash, then it consists of strong Spanish piasters. They don't have cargo agents; the captains themselves simply own, or have equipped, or have a share in the ship. They remain in quarantine, give the purchase orders to the merchant to procure for them a sample of wheat before they make a purchase.[38]

The foreign purchasers soon learned the advantage of offering advances on the purchase of wheat yet to be harvested; they thus paid but a low price for assured supplies. In 1855, an English prisoner of war in Russia noted that the flow of cash made June a busy and festive season in Odessa:

> All the rich land proprietors come from the interior to make the best bargain they can for the produce of their land. At these seasons they receive immense sums in anticipation of their next harvest. . . .[39]

Still, only a few privileged producers—those close to the ports, those familiar with complex commercial practices, those with vast estates and means—could bargain directly with the foreign purchasers. In spite of the importance of foreign colonists and great landlords, the southern Ukraine in particular remained an area of small estates and farms, of producers who could not deliver their produce directly to purchasers at the ports. In consequence, the growing demand for wheat was a bounty for middlemen, for persons who could talk with both the local producers and the foreign purchasers, who could link, as it were, two worlds.

In those parts of the Ukraine where they were numerous, Jews were exceptionally well suited to take advantage of this growing commercial opportunity. Many were literate, with some experience in petty trade. Jewish peddlers had long sold Levantine goods on the Polish-Ukrainian markets. They were helped by a supporting network of co-religionists (and sometimes relatives), which overlay a large part of the grain-producing region and extended into the ports. Indeed, the absence of a Jewish population in some areas seems to have been a handicap to marketing.

In 1832, Sauron, the French consul at Odessa, prepared a particularly thorough description of the methods by which exporters at the ports ordered, paid for, and secured the delivery of wheat from the hinterland. Specifically, he distinguished five common means by which the grain was ordered and delivered:[40]

1. Importing firms abroad place orders for wheat with exporting companies at the ports. They in turn contract with middlemen (usually Jews) in the countryside for deliveries of wheat to Odessa in the months of May, June, or July. The middlemen are paid one-half the value of the order in advance, at the time of the contract.

2. Export firms retain their own agents in the countryside to buy wheat in advance. These agents usually hire local Jews to inspect the wheat "on the stalk" (at harvest) and seldom "in the blade" (before harvest). These Jews also are responsible for sewing up the sacks of grain and for engaging carts for transporting the produce. The agents also receive an advance of one-half the total purchase price.

3. Exporters go directly to the countryside to buy grain from the peasants or from petty buyers who already possess grain in storage. Brokers then draw up contracts calling for future delivery. Buyers advance from one to five rubles per *chetvert* (the amount is based on estimated future price). Full payment is made upon delivery. In these cases the purchaser arranges and pays for transporting the grain to port.

4. Exporters buy and pick up the grain in the countryside as in retail sales.

5. Exporting firms establish permanent branches in the grain-producing regions, such as Kherson and Mykolaiv, and their own employees make the purchases. In 1832, according to the consul, Jews were still not numerous in the eastern steppes. For this reason, the great mercantile houses in the ports had to establish their own branches in the new regions—to erect, so to speak, their own infrastructure supporting wheat exports.

It should be noted that only the fourth method made use of fairs; these were largely concentrated in the North Ukraine and were not of major importance in cereal exports. Much grain was of course sold at the fairs, but most of it was purchased for local consumption; speculators also claimed a share of it, in expectation of profitable resale. But the conclusion of M. K. Rozhkovoi, that the bulk of the Ukrainian grain trade for export moved outside the fair network, seems right, as against the opinion of E. I. Druzhinina.[41] A principal reason for this is that as exports grew, most grain was sold and partially paid for in advance of the harvest. The harvest was already committed before the fairs were held.

To pay for the wheat, the merchants of Odessa sent large sums of money by insured mail to their correspondents and agents. They paid the postal authority one percent of the value of such remittances. Bank notes sufficed for payment made in Odessa, but silver rubles were required in the hinterland. The costs of transporting the wheat to port and of incidental expenses were generally the same as in the Polish provinces.[42]

One means of marking the evolution in marketing arrangements within Novorossiia is to note the movements of the place of delivery, the point where the primary producer gave up ownership of the wheat. In 1832, the French consul observed that in former years the proprietors had delivered the grain to Odessa. Recently, this had changed. Now the merchants assumed the "expense, perils and risk" of transport. In other words, with the development of Novorossiia, the loci of primary deliveries tended to move out from the ports, toward the centers of production.

There were several reasons for this. As settlements extended, distances to the ports also grew, and transport became more expensive. Small producers in particular, who loomed ever more important as the market expanded, did not have the capital and the means to transport their own produce to the ports. Institutional reasons also counted. The merchants of Odessa generally insisted that all disputes regarding the transaction be litigated before the Commercial Court at Odessa, and that its judgments be binding. But the producers feared that the ruling would seldom be in their favor. Consequently, whenever possible, the proprietors contracted to deliver the grain no farther than their own domains. If a dispute should arise, the case would then be heard before their own local (and presumably more sympathetic) commercial courts. Another recourse was to have local Jews act as the primary purchasers (standing in for the Odessa merchant); then too, in case of dispute, the local court, not the Commercial Court of Odessa, would have jurisdiction.

The producers who sought to market the grain at Odessa itself encountered many difficulties, which the French consul again describes in detail. They had to bring their grain to Odessa in May, June or July. The more needy owners sold their harvest immediately for cash; those who could afford to wait stored the cereals for a period ranging from one to three months. This sometimes meant that they did not sell the wheat before the last convoy of ships had departed, as it usually did in November. Some owners mortgaged their wheat until April and May, with the hope of selling it more advantageously early in the new season. They mortgaged only as much as was absolutely necessary, to pay their taxes and their more pressing debts. Still others were forced to sell their wheat by December, in order to pay off debts contracted at the summer fair of Kiev.

These were involved procedures, and cultivators of an even moderate importance could hardly supervise both their fields and the complex operations of the Odessa market. Producers were consequently reluctant to take their own produce directly to exporters, to negotiate for themselves its terms of sale. The result was a gradual retreat of the primary sellers back from the ports. The dispersion of these loci of primary delivery into the countryside heightened the need for competent middlemen; Jewish traders in particular responded with alacrity to this golden opportunity. This process of diffusion also implied that commercial relations were penetrating deep into the hinterland. Many cultivators of the southern Ukraine remained steeped in poverty, but nearly all of them were gaining some familiarity with commercial markets.

Merchants

The opening of the Black Sea brought the lands of the southern Ukraine into direct contact with a trading network, knitting together the shores of the Mediterranean Sea. While the Russian government welcomed exports from the South (and the hard currency those exports earned), still it viewed with misgivings the intrusion of foreign merchants into its national territory. To counter their presence, it sought to assure that Russian nationals would also participate in and perhaps take the leadership of the booming Black Sea trade.

Imperial commercial policy amply documents this official ambiguity toward the foreign businessman. In 1807, the government forbade foreign firms from purchasing directly from the inland producers.[43] The foreigners responded by making their purchases through local brokers and effectively circumvented the purposes of the law. In 1842, in desultory pursuit of this exclusionist policy, the government again required that only Russian citizens could accept commissions to make purchases, but again it retreated before a sea of protests, rising particularly from the English and the Dutch. Finally, on December 17, 1845, even as cereal exports were booming, foreign merchants were allowed to buy grain under the same conditions as Russian nationals.[44] The volume of trade, the government evidently concluded, was more important than the nationality of the traders.

Who were the merchants who forged the links between the Black Sea ports and the world beyond? The question has been much examined, both by contemporaries and by modern historians. Among the latter, E. I. Druzhinina has studied the issue with characteristic thoroughness for the years of Novorossiia's settlement to 1860. She cites several surviving official lists of Odessa's merchants, and comments:

> The almost complete absence of Ukrainian and Jewish names from these lists strikes one's eye; Russian names are also very rare. Does that mean that representatives of those peoples did not play an essential role in the Black Sea Trade? [45]

No, she responds. Native-born middlemen in the hinterland, *chumaks* or carters, were essential to the trade. And Jewish dealers too, most of them Russian subjects, played a vital if still restricted role. Still, for these early years, Druzhinina is at a loss to show a significant Russian (or even Jewish) presence among the greatest merchants. They were, for the most part, foreigners. Their external origins, their capital, their familiarity with distant markets and foreign languages gave them critical advantages in leading Odessa's early commercial development:

> The diverse national composition of the merchants guaranteed the success of trade relations of Russia with various countries. All of this contributed to the primitive accumulation of capital in Russia.[46]

When the emperor Nicholas I visited Odessa in 1829, he asked the mayor, I. V. Avchinnikov, why Russians were not occupied with Odessa's foreign trade. The response from the mayor was to the point: "Sire, if we use our capital for [foreign] affairs, what would remain here for internal trade?" [47]

Most contemporary visitors to Odessa affirmed that Russian merchants were *rarae aves* in the early nineteenth century. François Sauron, French consul in the city, surveyed the export firms in 1832:

> There are forty foreign firms, established by Greeks, Italians, Slavonians, Triestians, Genoese, French, German, English, Swiss and Spanish. These enterprises are all regular and permanent. . . . The Greeks are the most numerous and the richest.[48]

The report presented by Julius de Hagemeister to the tsar in 1835 makes these observations:

The foreign trade is almost exclusively in the hands of persons of foreign origin, the greater part of whom are Greeks and Italians. The merchants of Russian origin are comparatively few in number, and are chiefly employed in the sale of the different manufactures of the country, such as cordage, glass and iron and copper articles. . . .[49]

Russian observers also noted the scant participation of their own nationals in the booming overseas trade. A statistician named Protopopov, who amassed a huge amount of statistics on Russian trade in the period, concluded that not a single "authentic" (*korennyi*) Russian commercial house was engaged in the export trade from Odessa.[50] He strongly deplored the failure of Russians to take a more active role in the lucrative business. In his view, a program of mercantile education ought to be instituted, to create an indigenous class of overseas merchants.

Not all contemporaries accepted these observations, however. In particular, citizens of Odessa seem to have feared that animosity toward "foreigners" might provoke restrictive government policies and injure the commercial prosperity of their city. One of the most learned and energetic advocates of the Russian character of Odessa's trade was A. A. Skal'kovskii, historian of Odessa, editor-in-chief of the Central Statistical Committee of Novorossiia, and secretary of the city's Chamber of Commerce.[51] In 1844, this "Herodotus of Novorossiia" published a pamphlet in Russian, entitled "The Commercial Population of Odessa." In the following year, the *Journal d'Odessa* published a French translation in its pages. His statistics on the composition of the commercial classes of Odessa are the best available even today, and the conclusions he draws from them are worth regarding.

Skal'kovskii investigates the commercial classes primarily on the basis of guild records. By law, all merchants trading at Odessa had to inscribe in one of three guilds.[52] Those in the first guild were permitted to trade with unlimited capital in both the interior and foreign lands. In 1856, the members paid a steep yearly fee of 979 rubles 15 kopecks (then worth about $736.20).[53] Members of the second guild could also transact business both in the interior and abroad, but the value of their foreign transactions could not exceed 90,000 rubles ($67,669.17). The yearly fee collected from members was 401 rubles 97 kopecks ($302.23). The third guild included the small merchants, who were restricted to trade within the empire; they paid 108 rubles 50 kopecks ($81.58) yearly. Up to 1859, foreigners resident in Russia had to join the first guild.

On the basis of guild membership, Skal'kovskii counted the total commercial population of the city, and arrived at the figures given in Table 4.6.

Table 4.6

The Commercial Population of Odessa, 1840–51

Year	Total Population	Commercial Population
1840	68,765	3,199
1841	73,888	3,163
1842	77,778	3,041
1851	96,443	5,676

Source: A. A. Skal'kovskii, 1845, for the first three years, and *Odessa*, 1895, for 1851.

Making up only 4 to 6 percent of the total population, the commercial classes at Odessa at first appear surprisingly small.[54] According to Skal'kovskii, however, the figures do not include approximately two thousand small shopkeepers and porters. On the assumption that each merchant supported a family of five, he calculated that some twenty-five thousand persons, or roughly a third of the population of Odessa, lived directly from commercial enterprises.

How many of these businessmen were "authentic" Russians? Judging on the basis of citizenship, Skal'kovskii affirmed that the great majority of Odessa's merchants were Russian, loyal and productive subjects of the tsar. Table 4.7 recapitulates his figures.

Table 4.7

Russian Citizens and Foreigners (*Gosti*) in Odessa's Guilds

Year	1837	1838	1839	1840	1841	1842	1843	1844
Merchants in the guilds	765	765	738	693	719	702	704	700
Classification according to citizenship:								
Russian	598	602	589	578	582	584	589	588
Foreign	167	163	139	115	127	118	115	112
Classification according to religion:								
Christians	586	584	550	499	518	480	482	468
Jews	160	168	177	183	190	215	214	221
Karaite Jews	19	13	11	9	11	7	8	11

Source: Skal'kovskii, 1845, p. 3.

Skal'kovskii concluded on the basis of his data that foreign houses were yearly diminishing in number in comparison to those owned by Russian subjects. He drives this point home, against unnamed skeptics:

> And now we may demand . . . on what are founded the phrases of certain so-called patriots, who complain and state that Odessa is entirely a foreign town, outside of the great Russian Empire? Perhaps they take the boundary of the free port for a line of separation between the city and the Empire.[55]

By 1844, only a sixth of the commercial houses in Odessa technically belonged to foreigners; Skal'kovskii's arguments from citizenship are irrefutable. But a survey on the basis of national origins or culture, as we have seen, gives a much different picture. According to a series of articles in the *Odesskii vestnik* in 1845, there were sixty-six to seventy-seven merchants dealing in overseas trade; apart from Novikov, all were of foreign origins. The author urged Russians to awake from their lethargic dreams, to acquire education, to study foreign languages and commerce, and to put a commercial career over that of becoming government officials.[56]

These foreign merchants were recruited from an extraordinary range of peoples, most of them with an already established familiarity with Mediterranean trade. They included Armenians, Moldavians, Slavs from Ragusa and Trieste, Italians, French, and some few Germans, Danes, and English. The largest group was the Greeks. As a modern historian, E. Druzhinina, observes: "The role of the Greek merchants in the Black Sea trade was exceptionally great."[57] Konstantin Skal'kovskii, a native of Odessa, wrote in his memoirs that from the 1820s, the Greeks in commerce ousted the Italians, and took the place of the French, who had been invited by the duc de Richelieu.[58]

In 1817, a contemporary identified the ten richest Greek merchants at Odessa and estimated their combined fortunes to be about 10 million rubles.[59] Some ten years later, four Greek houses of Odessa—the Serafino, Iannopulo, Marazli, and Paleologos—were reckoned among the richest mercantile establishments in the entire Russian empire.[60] Dimitrios Inglesi—scion of another, smaller but still prominent commercial house—served as mayor of Odessa from 1818 to 1821.[61] In 1820, the famous Greek patriot Alexander Ipsilanti visited the city; among the rich merchants who gave him welcome and support were members of the Inglesi, Marazli, Mavros, and Khristodulo families.[62] These names persisted in Odessa's records across the decades of the nineteenth century, indicating a high degree of stability among the resident Greek merchants.

In the middle years of the century, among the most prominent Greek commercial firms at Odessa were the Ralli brothers. In 1845, the Ralli firm was cited as the largest trader in Odessa combining imports and exports.[63] In a ranking of Odessa's merchants, prepared in 1847, fifth on the list according to wealth was the Greek merchant John Ralli.[64] His colorful career is typical of the entrepreneurial Greek merchants, who were instrumental in building up Odessa's international commerce.

In his own words, written in 1854, Ralli was "a Russian subject, born on the Island of Scio [Chios] in the Archipelago, and was by birth of Greek origin."[65] He was born on November 3, 1785. His father, named Stephen, was also born at Chios thirty years earlier. He too was a merchant, and he died at Marseilles in 1827. John married an Italian girl, Lucia, who was born in Pisa in 1794. They were married in Odessa, but we do not know the year. Their only child, Stephen, was born in London in 1821. John as a young man was clearly accustomed to moving frequently!

In 1838, an American visitor to Odessa wrote that Ralli had left his native island as a boy and had visited every European port as a merchant, before settling permanently in Odessa about 1830.[66] In fact, John left London in 1827.[67] It is likely that the death of his father at Marseilles in the same year called him, as the eldest son, back to the Mediterranean, the center of the family's already far-flung interests. John decided to settle in the booming city of Odessa. In 1826, before his own arrival there, the Ralli company at Odessa was already importing and exporting goods to the value of 290,524 rubles. In 1827, the amount fell to 149,342 rubles. Under John's immediate supervision, however, by 1846, the company traded yearly in commodities, chiefly cereals, worth more than 1.5 million rubles.

From 1832 until his death in 1859, John served as consul for the United States at Odessa, although he was never an American citizen.[68] An American diplomat, Charles Rhind, who recommended him for the appointment without ever having met him, described him as "rich and respectable."[69] Some American travelers who met Ralli in 1835 praised him for his courtesy.[70] They seem to have been the first "authentic" Americans whom the American consul met in Odessa. In spite of the time he spent in England, Ralli still spoke English with difficulty.

Ralli fulfilled the duties of consul with high competence, as his long tenure suggests. His dispatches to Washington were always informed and written in faultless English (by a secretary). He alerted the government to commercial opportunities for American ships in the Black Sea and stressed the profits to be made by shipping colonial products directly to Russia. In his assessments, he had the advantage of information flowing to him from his offices in Rostov, Taganrog, and other Azov towns, as well as from his numerous connections in the West. As an example of his good commercial sense, he advised the United States to increase grain shipments to Europe during the Crimean War, to take advantage of the prohibition against cereal exports which the Russian government had recently imposed.[71]

In 1857, the American government tried to prohibit its consuls abroad from engaging in private commercial ventures. Ralli appealed the decision to President Buchanan, and described his own career:

> I have been a merchant for a great number of years. . . . I have not only a commercial house at Odessa, and branch houses in other parts of Russia, but likewise houses in England, France, Turkey, Persia and also the East Indies.[72]

To retain his consular post, Ralli was willing to renounce his stipend, but he would not end his commercial career. He reminded the president of his father's friendship with him, when both had been together at the Court of St. James's. His petition was favorably received, but John died soon after, in 1859, while abroad in Paris. His widow went to Paris to live but died in 1873 in Livorno, in the country of her birth.

The commercial firm of Ralli Brothers continued to play a prominent role in international trade (the London office, founded by John and four younger brothers in 1818, survived until 1961).[73] At various times, the company maintained branches in the Danubian Provinces, Persia, the East Indies, and America, besides the Russian Empire. The vast trading network the partners erected has elicited the following comment from a recent historian, S. H. Chapman:

> In their migration westward the more successful Greek houses spawned new branches, and tracing these reveals the pattern of extension of their interests. Ralli Brothers, the Chian family in the vanguard of the migration, opened branches at Odessa, Marseilles, London and Manchester (1828), and were soon exporting cotton twist to Germany as well as the Levant. In 1865, at the summit of their mercantile achievement, the Rallis were operating through interlocked partnerships in fifteen centres, spread across Europe and the Middle East.[74]

John Ralli and numerous other Greek merchants, such as Marazli, Rodocannachi, Papudov, Mavrokordato, and Zarifi, played a central role in the early growth of Odessa's international commerce. After mid-century, the participation of Greeks in Odessa's trade precipitously declined. We shall subsequently investigate the reasons.[75]

The Greeks and most other foreign merchants were already actively involved in international commerce before settling in Odessa. Jewish merchants, on the other hand, had a much different origin. Important as middlemen in the hinterland, Jews were slow to penetrate the ranks of the great export merchants.

Jewish commercial houses at Odessa were gaining importance by the decade of the 1830s. Between 1837 and 1844, as Table 4.7 shows, the number of Jewish commercial houses grew from 160 to 221, while Christian firms diminished in number. Skal'kovskii saw the opening of the Odessa Bourse in 1837 as a principal reason for this.[76] Like St. Petersburg, Trieste, and other great commercial cities, Odessa now had its own money market. The opportunity to act as brokers attracted Jews. Because their operations ranged from small to middle scale, they clustered in the second and third guilds. Overwhelmingly, they were Russian subjects. "And when have the Jews," asked Skal'kovskii, "not been humble, faithful and often useful subjects of the Russian state?"[77] Still, by 1848 Jews do not figure prominently among the largest firms. An article in the August 1848 issue of the *Journal de la Haye* listed them last after Greeks, Italians, French, English, and Germans active in Odessa's commerce. Not until the 1850s did the favorable political climate attract wealthy Jews from Austria. By the 1850s, Jewish firms, such as Efrusi and Raffalavich, had more than one million rubles in total trade.[78]

Unlike the other merchant groups that tended to depart from Odessa after the initial boom in cereal exports had spent its course, the Jews remained. They were destined to play an ever larger commercial role in the export trade over the second half of the century. To this theme we shall return.

CHAPTER FIVE

Foreign Trade and Domestic Industry, 1814–1861

... the [Napoleonic] war removed thousands of hands from agriculture, and famine years capped the misery of the land, at one time so rich and so flourishing. With these pressing needs, people thus had recourse to the southern provinces of Russia.

—Thom, Austrian consul at Odessa, 1826

From the late eighteenth century, western Europe faced a growing scarcity of cereals and was forced to search for them in widening circles. The vagaries of weather, the altered use of land, the long-term growth of population, the mobilization of millions in search of new jobs and new homes—all heightened the demand for cereals in western Europe without stimulating a proportionate increase in their local production. The western search for cereals was, in fact, creating an integrated, worldwide market in grain. In that market, Odessa was foreordained to become a principal participant.

The Swell of Cereal Exports

The Euxine steppes were ideally placed to serve this mounting demand emanating from the West for cereals. They were close to the growing market; indeed, in the entire world, no other large and new agricultural area, capable of massive wheat production, was so near to western consumers. The steppes were, moreover, easily reached. Even slow sailing vessels could deliver the wheat with relative ease and expedition. In fact, the slowness of sailing ships long shielded the steppes from the competition of equally fertile, but much more distant areas—the United States and Canada, for example, or Argentina.

With Richelieu's departure from Odessa in 1814, the business community understandably feared for the future of its commerce. As it happened, the simultaneous movements of another Frenchman—Napoleon—had a larger effect upon the city's economic fortunes. He was forced into exile to Elba in 1814, but slipped away from the tiny kingdom and returned to Paris, and for one hundred days Europe was in an uproar. The sudden, unexpected remobilization of huge armies in the West shot the demand for Black Sea wheat skyward. Happily too, the political obstacles to the free flow of trade had also diminished; in particular, the Ottomans who controlled the vital Straits, were becoming more accommodating to the passage of foreign vessels. The last years of the Napoleonic adventure defined a pattern of commerce that persisted over nearly the entire course of the nineteenth century.

To be sure, the course of international trade does not always run smooth. Napoleon's violent and dramatic exit from politics was very soon followed by what one historian calls "the last great subsistence crisis" of European history.[1] Beginning in 1816, torrential rains swamped the grain fields of western Europe. Protracted belligerence had disrupted European production and had already exhausted local reserves. Europeans hungered. Speculators in the West hoarded supplies in expectation of still higher prices, and venturesome merchants sought the treasured cereals in the Euxine regions. In 1817, Odessa shipped nearly one and one-half million *chetvert*s of wheat to the West.

In 1815, some 1,500 ships entered the Black Sea, principally in search of grain; only thirty-nine ships had called at Odessa's port in 1795, and only 552 in the previous high year of 1803.[2] The Austrian representative at St. Petersburg was amazed at this outpouring of Russian wheat and expressed alarm at the highly favorable balance of payments it assured the Russian Empire.[3] The price of a *chetvert* of wheat at Odessa soared to forty-five rubles in 1816 and 1817 and may have briefly reached fifty-two.[4] It would not regain this value for decades. The Neapolitan consul at Odessa, de Ribas, cynically compared the city to a doctor, who prospered when others were ill.[5] But Doctor Odessa could not assure his own good health. Exports slumped badly in 1818 and 1819. The price of a *chetvert* of wheat at Odessa dwindled to ten rubles and below.[6] Crops in the Ukraine failed in 1820 and 1821; plagues of locusts and outbreaks of smallpox harassed the harvesters and disrupted harvests throughout the decade. Nature, which had severely taxed western farmers in the previous years, was righting its balances. In the West, political instability in Greece and Italy disturbed the trade routes. Even restored peace in the West did not help. England, France, and other western powers reerected tariff barriers to protect native farmers against the cheap and abundant Russian production. In retaliation, in 1821 Russia raised its tariffs on wines, liquors, silks, and cottons—characteristic imports from the West. The customs officials at the port could show growing revenues. In 1824, customs amounted to 2,980,314 rubles, and in 1825 they rose to 3,220,575 rubles.[7] The effect of restrictive policies of protectionism in both West and East squeezed the arteries of international commerce, however.

In 1826, the august Academy of Sciences offered a prize for the best essay in explanation of the collapsing prices for Russia's agricultural produce, especially wheat. The winner, A. Fomin, advanced the straightforward thesis that Russian production was too great, and western demand too little.[8] Also in 1826, the Austrian consul in Odessa offered his analysis of grain trade after the boom year of 1817.[9] Too many speculators had entered the business. Their failures discouraged more prudent merchants from establishing trading companies. Further, the guild charges were too high, and long-term credit was too scarce. Wealthy landowners, he claimed, did not put their capital into commerce; instead, they squandered it in luxurious living and frequent trips abroad. No doubt all of these observations were accurate, but Fomin's explanation of diminished demand is the most persuasive.

To be sure, there were small gains. In the euphoria of 1817, the government declared that Odessa would become a free port, and the decision was implemented two years later, in 1819. The delay was necessary, as the government needed to construct walls and gates around the city, to stop smugglers from carrying the duty-free goods off into the hinterland. The hope was that Odessa would become the great entrepôt for western goods in the regions of the Black Sea. The status conveyed advantages, but not the full prosperity that the government expected. Most western merchants doubted the possibilities of making large and profitable sales at Odessa; ships arrived in ballast. An institutional change of far greater significance was the opening of the Turkish Straits to merchant ships making peaceful passage.

Rights of Passage

The importance of the Straits for Odessa's commercial prosperity impressed every merchant and traveler. In 1819, a passing English preacher commented: "So long as the Dardanelles and the Bosphorus remain in the possession of the Turks, the commerce of Odessa must be subject to great fluctuations."[10]

Even in times of peace, ships from western nations could not sail through the Straits without express permission from the Porte. Since 1774, Russian ships could enter the Straits, but they were few in number. And the Ottomans used their strategic control over this major trade route for political purposes. During the uprising against their rule in the Greek Islands in 1821, the Ottomans repeatedly challenged even Russian ships. They suspected that the fomenters of the Greek revolution were going and coming under the protection of the Russian flag.[11] They also frequently requisitioned wheat cargoes, as they could no longer rely on Greek carriers. Freight rates and insurance rates soared with the risks of search and seizure. If trade was difficult in peace, it was impossible in war. Hostilities between Russia and the Porte from 1828 to 1829 closed the Straits entirely. Some three hundred Triestine and four hundred Genoese ships reportedly languished in their home ports, awaiting the return of peace. The war represented the capstone to the trade depression of the 1820s.

Still, the Russian government labored mightily to facilitate passage through the Straits. Until 1824, it readily conferred the Russian flag on foreign ships so that they could enjoy the special privileges that the Porte was by treaty obligated to confer on Russian carriers. Even when this dubious practice was discontinued (in 1824), Russia consistently used its good offices with the Porte to gain concessions for foreign shipping. The Austrian consul at Constantinople observed in 1829:

> This cabinet [of St. Petersburg] is the government which has the greatest interest in having the Black Sea open to all flags indiscriminately and in the manner most advantageous for them. This for the reason that the production of the south of the Empire should find the widest possible outlet, the more so because Russia does not have a national merchant marine.[12]

Thus, the Russians aided the Danes, Spaniards, and Neapolitans to gain a treaty with the Porte.[13] The negotiations, by which the Grand Duchy of Tuscany won similar concessions, illuminate these procedures. The Treaty of Adrianople, concluded between Russia and the Porte in 1829, extended to ships of all nations at peace with the Porte the right to pass the Straits.[14] In practice, the Turks continued to harass the ships of those states with which they had no formal treaty. The Tuscan captains sometimes escaped this difficulty by raising the flag of a privileged power, usually the Austrian. Either the Turks were confused by the similarity of the Tuscan and Austrian flags, or, more likely, they overlooked this irregularity in order to collect the required fees. Other Tuscan captains managed to navigate the Straits under their own colors.[15] But the Grand Duchy still wanted the security for its ships which only a treaty could provide. In 1823, the Austrian consul at Constantinople gave helpful advice to the Tuscan government.[16] To gain a treaty, it would have to cultivate the chief ministers of the Porte. Cash might be offered to the grand vizier and other personages in key positions. If cash payments seemed too crass, the officials were known to be partial to gold tobacco cases set with diamonds. But beyond cultivating the sympathies of these high-placed Ottomans, the Grand Duchy needed to enlist the help of the Russians:

> The Court of Russia will willingly take an active part in the negotiations. It must increase the number of ships able to anchor at its ports in the Black Sea, and especially at its emporium at Odessa, a market with which the port of Livorno is in active correspondence. And it would be useful to Russia if our [i.e. the Tuscan] flag might be among those admitted to trade in that sea.[17]

Treaty or no treaty, ships were required to stop at Constantinople to obtain written permission (a *firman*) to sail the Straits. In 1830, the procedure still took several days and cost 108 piasters.[18] But the Ottomans were becoming progressively more liberal in granting the permit. The Tuscan consul at Constantinople reported in 1832:

> It is true that for two years the Turkish authorities located at the Dardanelles have abandoned their traditional vigor, so that no visits are made upon ship arrivals, no delay or trouble is caused them.[19]

The consul, however, laid stress on the uncertainties inherent in the situation and on the critical need that representatives, such as himself, be employed to protect the interests of the passing merchants. He predicted darkly:

The old practices could be renewed, and could cause critical injuries to those navigators who might lack in such a place consular agents ready to give them efficacious aid.[20]

For twenty-five years after the Treaty of Adrianople (1829), the Ottomans did not return to the old policies. Seemingly, the Ottomans learned that the expeditious release of ships increased fees and not foes. At least by the 1850s, consuls or representatives of shipping companies at Constantinople were applying for *firmans* in advance of ships' arrivals, thus minimizing delays.[21] The ships were still subject to numerous charges—to maintain lighthouses and horns, for example. And health regulations, punctiliously enforced, cramped free-moving traffic.[22] Still, from the 1830s shipping moved through the Straits with unprecedented facility.

Law and Technology

Expeditious passage through the Straits was a necessary but not sufficient condition for the revival of massive cereal exports from the South Ukraine. Local harvests obviously mattered, and harvests were poor from 1830 to 1834. Indeed, 1834 was long remembered as a "black year," when people hungered and a few speculators grew rich. For example, in testimony given before a committee of the British House of Commons, an English merchant told how he had purchased wheat at St. Petersburg in August and shipped it to Newcastle. From there he exported it to Odessa, and he earned three times the money he had paid for the wheat in northern Russia.[23] Exports of grain to Odessa resembled shipments of coal to Newcastle: international trade took unlikely turns!

Harvests increased from 1835; trade improved in 1836, when western Europe in its turn endured scarcity. Ralli, the Greek merchant serving as American consul at Odessa, reported in 1837 that there had been considerable demand for cereals from Italy, France, Austria, England, and even America.[24] Later, taking the peak year (1847) as his point of departure, a writer for the *Journal d'Odessa* declared that 1835 marked the turning point in the commercial fortunes of the city.[25] To be sure, the road to the new pinnacle had no uniform slope. Plague struck the city in 1837, and the winter of 1837–1838 was unusually cold, closing the port from mid-December until the end of February.[26] In 1839, exports surged to over a million *chetverts*, but slumped again in 1840, 1841, and 1842. From 1843, the ascent in exports was renewed and now continued. In 1846, Odessa shipped abroad nearly two million *chetverts* of wheat, earning nearly 15 million silver rubles. Observers at Odessa could scarcely believe that such production was possible.[27] But exports in the following year, 1847, rose again, reaching 2,798,183 *chetverts* from Odessa alone.[28] The Tuscan vice-consul regarded the European famine of 1847 as so exceptional that exports would never again equal, much less surpass, the volume of that extraordinary year.[29]

In 1849, when the vice-consul penned this prediction, statistics seemed to lend it credibility. Exports in 1848 slumped to nearly the levels of 1845; they would also fall in the immediately succeeding years, sliding into a kind of trough in 1851. Here, slack demand rather than available supplies was at fault. Improved harvests in the West, competition from other grain-producing areas, and political turmoil in many European countries dampened demand. But a corner was turned in 1852, to the surprise of many observers. A writer for the *Journal d'Odessa* rejoiced:

> Odessa's commerce has again in 1852 resumed the progress which after 1847 (a truly exceptional year and almost unique in its annals) it seemed to have abandoned decisively. . . . Odessa's commerce might have its time of stoppages and even its setbacks, but it cannot be denied that its progress is upward.[30]

In 1853, the last year before the Crimean War (1853–1856) cut off grain exports altogether, the volumes shipped from Odessa surpassed even those of the *annus mirabilis* of 1847, which nearly every commentator had called "exceptional," not likely to be equalled again within a lifetime. Harvests in the South Ukraine were good, and speculative purchases played an important role. Rumors of impending war between Russia and Turkey reverberated through western markets, and speculators scrambled to place orders for wheat, wool, and other regional produce. They hastened to move their purchases through the Straits before a war should close them. Allegedly, there were not enough ships to deliver the wheat, to satisfy orders emanating "from Leghorn, Marseilles, Trieste and Genoa and also from Holland, Belgium, and England."[31]

Several developments were of particular importance in exciting this demand. The great consuming countries were abrogating "corn laws" restricting the importation of foreign wheat. Moreover, the newly invented telegraph made possible the wide and rapid dissemination of market information, and the newly developed steamship permitted a rapid response, on the part of producers, to favorable, though distant, markets. The market for cereals was becoming integrated on a worldwide basis. Consumers no longer relied primarily on local producers for their needs. The peasant of the South Ukraine was entering into direct competition for the same markets as the farmer of Iowa. Initially at least, proximity and cheap production gave the South Ukraine a prominent place in the newly fused international cereal market.

England best illustrates the tergiversations in official policy regarding grain imports. In 1773, 1791, and 1793, Parliament passed the first comprehensive Corn Laws. To assure stable home supplies and prices, the law allowed exports of wheat only when the price dropped below a certain threshold (forty-four shillings per quarter), and imports when the price moved above forty-eight shillings. Still, home producers complained about foreign competition, and the Corn Law of 1804 set the tariff on imported wheat at so high a level (twenty-four shillings two pence per quarter) as virtually to exclude foreign importation altogether, save during years of famine.[32] In a new Corn Law of 1816, the government forbade importation completely when the home price was under eighty shillings per quarter, and lifted all restrictions on imports when the home price surpassed that figure.

The ultimate refinement in the Corn Laws was the "sliding scale," implemented in England in 1828 and soon widely imitated on the continent. The scale of import fees was designed to attract enough foreign grain, but only just enough, to keep local prices from varying beyond certain limits. As local prices rose in response to shortages, the tariff fell. Foreign grain was then admitted in sufficient quantities to stabilize the price. As the local price dropped, the tariff was gradually raised, importation slowed, and home prices returned to the chosen equilibrium. The sliding scale was thus ingeniously contrived to assure consumers reasonable and stable prices for wheat and to protect the cultivators from ruinous competition. Continental states quickly followed the English example; Sweden in 1830, France in 1832, Belgium in 1834, Holland in 1835, and Portugal in 1837 all adopted the strategy of variable tariffs.[33] Prussia and the other states of the German Zollverein retained the older system of fixed tariffs, perhaps in deference to their own, politically powerful grain producers. The sliding scale represented, after all, a step toward liberalized grain trade.

But the ingeniously contrived system of the sliding scale did not work as expected, and it produced some unwanted results. In England in the 1830s, to everyone's surprise, grain prices continued to fluctuate erratically, from thirty-six to ninety shillings per quarter. Lured by the promise of protected markets for wheat, capital flowed into marginal land, cereals were produced in excess, home prices sank, and the surplus grain had to be exported. Moreover, the system promoted widespread speculation.[34] Importers often held grain back from the market, storing it within or outside England, in expectation of a rise in prices. When prices reached an attractive level, they dumped massive quantities on the market. They even resorted to market manipulations, arranging to buy small quantities of grain at exaggerated prices at the local markets, thus affecting the official price indices. The tariff would be lowered, and again massive quantities of wheat would flood the market.

The international trade in cereals under the system of the sliding scale thus retained a highly speculative cast. This had two results. The possibilities it offered of huge (if occasional) sales and great profits invited investments in ships, port and storage facilities, and the whole organizational infrastructure required in long-distance trade. At the same time, the lion's share of profits fell to the speculating importers, not to the primary producers. The cultivators of the southern Ukraine were in no position to claim a principal share of the profits from the delivered grain. The producers were thus not rewarded with the share of the profit that might have been expected from their labors.

The organization of this commerce in cereals I call "the deposit trade."[35] Grain exported from Odessa in the early nineteenth century moved slowly. From Odessa, sailing ships required as many as five or six days to reach Constantinople; twenty to twenty-five days to Messina; twenty-five to thirty days to Naples; thirty-five to forty days to Trieste, and thirty-five to fifty days to Marseilles, Genoa, or Livorno. A direct shipment to England from Odessa required fifty to seventy days. Grain was therefore usually not delivered directly to its ultimate purchasers and consumers. In the 1840s, it appears that of the grain from Odessa ultimately destined for England, only 2 percent was shipped directly there.[36] Most of the grain was taken to intermediately placed ports, where it might be stored for lengthy periods, until its owners learned through slow communications where it could most profitably be sold.[37]

Odessa maintained close contact with the chief deposit ports of the Mediterranean region. Hagemeister names them in 1835:

> Trieste, Leghorn, Genova and Marseilles are the great marts of Southern Europe, and corn is brought there from all quarters, the shipowners being content with almost any rate of freight that will afford them common interest for their capital.[38]

The destination of wheat exported from Odessa in 1838 is shown in Table 5.1.

Table 5.1

Destinations of Wheat Exported from Odessa, 1838
(in *Chetvert*s)

Livorno	446,842	Holland	28,914
Genoa	177,099	Belgium	16,909
Marseilles	93,758	Gibralter	4,348
England	82,453	Ionian Islands	3,829
Trieste	58,326	Greece	2,215
Malta	44,486	Austria	1,230
Constantinople	30,455		

Source: ASF, Affari Esteri, Filza 2528, 29 February 1839

According to another source, the five chief recipients of grain from the Black Sea region in the early nineteenth century were, in order of importance: Marseilles, Trieste, Constantinople, Genoa, and Livorno.[39] Certain of these cities (Marseilles and Livorno) enjoyed the status of free ports, and this was highly advantageous in their function as intermediate places of storage.

Lists of ships, by number and by flag, calling at Odessa have survived sporadically, up to 1839 and nearly continuously thereafter.[40] The lists are, to be sure, usually misleading. Captains were willing to raise almost any flag or declare any nationality, if it meant quicker passage or lower fees. Yet the distributions by flag do tell us something of these ships and of the nature of Odessa's commerce.

Consistently the largest number of ships calling at Odessa were of Austrian registry. To say "Austrian" is to mean ships owned and manned by two groups of Austrian subjects: South Slavs and, above all, Italians from Trieste. Sardinian ships, sailing out of Genoa, were usually second or third in the list of flags; they give further indication of the large Italian participation in the Black Sea trade. The *Corriere mercantile* of Genoa boasted on November 3, 1829:

All the Russian ports of the Black Sea are in debt to the Italians for their prosperity; since of the thousand ships which go to export their products, about 800 are captained by Italians. This Black Sea, marvel of Europe, was rendered hospitable by Italians and above all, by sailors from the Adriatic gulf, who, twenty years ago, navigated the Black Sea in all kinds of weather under the French flag. And from what nation are indeed the captains and crews of the larger part of the ships which with the Russian flag navigate the Black Sea, if not Italian? The pilots who take them to Constantinople, from what nation, if not from the Italian?

The Ottoman Empire was notable for its slight representation within the Black Sea commercial fleets; in fact, the modest merchant marine Turkey possessed was staffed largely by Greeks, and Greek firms—the Ralli and Rodocannachi, for example—dominated the Porte's large export trade, even with England.[41]

Ships of Russian registry present a particular problem. They visited the Black Sea ports by the hundreds every year, but it remains difficult to judge how many were authentically Russian. The imperial government itself pursued ambivalent policies toward its merchant marine. Peter the Great loved ships and tried to inculcate in his people maritime skills and traditions. On the other hand, in the view of a visitor writing in 1829, the authorities "were apprehensive that they [the sailors] may, if in the habit of visiting foreign ports, imbibe strange ideas about the rights of man and so forth, and perhaps may not be inclined to return home."[42] In 1834, the governor general of Novorossiia, Count Vorontsov, created a "Society of Voluntary Sailors" (*Obshchestvo vol'nykh matrosov*) at Nykopil and Aleskhi. State serfs who enlisted were freed of taxes and military service.[43] But in the 1850s, the "voluntary sailors" numbered only 1,842; spending most of their time farming, they had yet to acquire much maritime experience. The government further sought to assure that at least 50 percent of the crews of all ships sailing under the Russian flag be native Russians. But the regulation proved unworkable. Serfs reluctantly took to the sea, even with the promise of freedom. They believed, it seems, that they would sail for life, and serfdom at home seemed preferable to serfdom on distant waters.

As late as 1856, an observer noted that the "great number of ships which sail into the Black Sea under the Russian flag belong to Greeks or to Slavs from the Adriatic."[44] In 1853, at the outbreak of the Crimean War, eight owners of "Russian" ships sold their crafts to Tuscans, lest they be confiscated as prizes of war. Their names were Wukland, Sandborg, Castrem, Gralmi, Giovanni, Instrom, Lindblom, and Candellino. Some of these owners might have been Russian subjects, but not one seems to have been a Russian native. The captains (three are named) were Tuscans and the crews either Finnish, Swedish, or "Austrian."[45] In sum, the ships of Russian registry involved in the Black Sea trade belonged in large part to the traditional mariners of the eastern Mediterranean—Greeks, South

Slavs, Italians primarily—who were either stateless or loosely attached to states. They had no qualms in raising the Russian flag, which assured them passage through the Straits and a welcome in the Black Sea ports.

By the decade of the 1850s, the deposit trade was at last giving way to direct exports. In 1846, the English government, amid much political turmoil, moved to abolish the corn laws. They were completely surpressed in 1849 in favor of a small, fixed tax on imported grain, and even this tax was abolished in 1869.[46] Holland similarly abolished the sliding scale in 1847, and both Belgium and Holland gave full freedom to grain importation in 1850. Portugal in 1854; Sweden, Sardinia, and the Papal States in the 1850s; and the German Zollverein in 1864 followed. France, with a powerful agricultural bloc to consider, acted more cautiously. It suspended tariffs on cereals in 1846, restored them, suspended them again in 1853, restored them in 1859, and finally abolished them in 1861. The age of free grain trade had arrived.

Trade between England and the Black Sea ports drew immediate benefit from this liberalized policy. In 1846–1847, the southern Ukraine had directly supplied only about 2.8 percent of England's imported grain; on the eve of the Crimean War, the portion surged to over 50 percent.[47] Assured of free and open markets, shippers now sought to reduce costs by bringing the grain directly to consumers, without storing it at intermediate ports. They could take further advantage of the development of steam navigation, to move large stores of grain quickly and cheaply.

If the Russians were laggard participants in wind-powered navigation on the Black Sea, they quickly took to the new steam technology and developed a small, but technically advanced, fleet. As early as 1833, the "Black Sea Steamship Company," organized as a joint stock enterprise, was offering regular voyages between Odessa and Constantinople.[48] According to the Tuscan consul at Constantinople, in 1843 the Russian government had commissioned four steamships to be built in England; two had just arrived at Constantinople and were proceeding to Odessa. The ships were to service a line between "Odessa, Constantinople and several ports of the Mediterranean."[49] By May of 1857, a company called the "Russian Steam Navigation and Trading Company" was maintaining regular service to Kherson, Mykolaiv, and several ports of the Crimean coast and the Sea of Azov; it expected to include ports of the Mediterranean Sea by the spring of 1858.[50] The company published its own newsletter in Italian.[51] In 1857, thirty-three Russian steamers called at Odessa, nearly as many as Austrian (forty-two) and English (forty-six). In 1858, the number of Russian steamships soared to sixty-six, now surpassing the forty-one Austrian and twenty-five English steamers.[52] Although sails still predominated on Black Sea waters in the decade of the 1850s, steam was making rapid progress.

Also in the fifties, the telegraph linked Odessa to its foreign customers. To be sure, as late as 1858, the telegraph link to the outer world ran to St. Petersburg, and from there to western markets and capitals.[53] A Tuscan official noted in 1853:

> Some ships which leave [Livorno] for the Black Sea go directly from there for England, and some of these sail again directly from England for the Black Sea. . . . All of this is a consequence of Great Britain's commercial reform which promoted direct commerce, and thus has diminished the resources in this marketplace, which used to come from the deposit of cereals especially.[54]

In 1858, the captain of the port of Livorno gave this clear analysis of these commercial changes:

> Our port has felt the general consequences of the commercial transformations caused by steamships and the telegraph. Since large deposits were made impossible after the almost universal adoption of free trade, traffic had to be limited to consumption, especially after speculation disappeared because of the rapidity with which the telegraph carries the news of the price of goods.[55]

Though fading in the 1850s, the deposit trade had boosted Odessa to the status of a major supplier of wheat to the world market and prepared the port for equally spectacular advances in the decades to come.

The Development of Local Industries

Odessa's access to rich sources of raw materials (particularly agricultural products) invited the formation of local industries. Many factories were established in the city during the first half of the nineteenth century. Still, the crucial problem is not to explain why some industrial development occurred, but why it remained so limited. The comparative lack of industry in this large port city caught the eye of many contemporary observers, and it still perplexes historians.

In examining the industrial growth of ports, economists sometimes distinguish between "induced" and "substitution" industries. An "induced" industry is one that converts traditionally exported raw materials into products for sale abroad. The production of flour out of grain, candles out of tallow, rope out of hemp, cigars out of tobacco, would be examples of induced industrialization. "Substitution" industrialization rather produces for sale in the hinterland commodities traditionally imported from abroad—in Odessa's case, fine wines and foods, clothing, fuel, and the like.[56] Normally, induced industries are the first to develop, and this was true at Odessa. But factors peculiar to Odessa placed severe restrictions on the development of substitution industries, and this was to leave the city with a relatively narrow industrial base.

The first factory in Odessa seems to have been a plant manufacturing powders for cosmetic purposes, founded in 1799 by a French émigré, Captain Pichon; it was an early and rare effort at industrial substitution.[57] Soon after, a macaroni factory, a brewery, and a distillery were founded. By 1802, eighteen small enterprises employed some one hundred workers.[58] These latter were free, hired workers. "Possessional" serfs in factories seem never to have been employed, at least in any number, at Odessa.[59]

By 1827, the macaroni factory was producing four hundred *pud*s of pasta per year. The tobacco industry, produced 52 *pud*s for 2,720 rubles in the same year. Not all enterprises succeeded. A French subject by the name of Jean-Baptiste Davalion attempted in 1825 to establish a wool-washing works on the *khutor*s (farm) of Colonel Poniatowski near the Moldavanka, but it failed to earn sufficient profit and closed in 1826.[60]

Industrial enterprises became more varied as the century progressed, but induced industries retained a prominence. Two entrepreneurs named Meshkov and Novikov founded a rope factory. A man named Santsenbakher undertook the manufacture of soap and candles. Two Greek merchants, Georgii Sarnaki and Georgii Sakelari, similarly entered the soap and tallow business, as did some Bulgarians and Old Believers. Clearly, the low cost and high quality of locally produced tallow made these ventures attractive. Enough soap was produced to ship abroad, notably to the Ottoman empire.[61]

Table 5.2 provides an industrial profile of Odessa in the middle decades of the nineteenth century. The census of industries it offers is no doubt incomplete, but the distributions are still indicative of industrial activities in the city.

Table 5.2

Number and Type of Factories in Odessa, 1833–1856

Type	1833	1835	1837	1845	1856
Rope	7	4	5	—	—
Tile	9	6	5	10	8
Brick	14	7	9	8	16
Soap	—	1	3	3	—
Tallow	6	4	9	3	3
Candles	10	5	5	—	4
Tobacco and cigars	—	2	2	—	3
Hats	1	1	1	1	1
Macaroni	3	4	4	4	8
Founderies	—	1	1	2	2
Wool washing	—	—	3	1	—
Leather	1	—	—	3	1
Sheepskin	15	—	—	7	—
Jute	—	—	—	4	—
Distillery, brewery	1	—	—	2	1
French cotton-wool	—	—	—	1	—
Limestone ovens	—	—	—	12	—
Gingerbread	—	—	—	—	1
Totals	67	35	47	61	48

Sources: Compiled from industrial censuses reported in *Zhurnal MVD* no. 3, p. 575, for 1833 and 1835; ibid. no. 8, p. 304, 1839; ibid. no. 14, p. 247, 1846; and NACRO, 12 July 1856.

Skal'kovskii noted that there were 540 factory workers in 1835 who produced 4.5 million rubles of goods; two years later some 672 workers manufactured 5 million rubles of products.[62] For 1858, we have a total of sixty-five enterprises, which drops to fifty-three the following year. Some 1,015 workers produced 3,374,750 silver rubles of goods in 1858, the same year that the Russian steamship company, ROPiT, opened ship repair yards, which soon became one of the largest employers in the city.[63] Another big enterprise was the mechanical works of Bellino-Fenderikh, founded in 1860 and destined for considerable growth.[64]

As these censuses and descriptions show, the most prestigious were substitution industries (such as the manufacture of pianos), but the most remunerative remained in the category of induced manufactures. Most of Odessa's industries engaged in processing locally supplied raw materials. From animal products came leather, tallow, soap, candles, wool, and sheepskins. In 1858, the French consul observed that the candle business was thriving:

> The export of candles, especially stearine, is making great progress; this is due to the activity of M. Pitancier's establishment which grows with each day.[65]

So also, plant products were the basis of the rope, jute, cigar, cigarette, macaroni, gingerbread, and brewing industries. At mid-century, among the most successful businesses were the rope works of Novikov, the mechanized bakery of Bukovetskii, and the tobacco works. The latter consumed more than 100,000 *pud*s of Bessarabian, Crimean, and Mingrelian tobacco, and were coming to import large quantities of Turkish and American leaves (35,000 *pud*s in the 1850s).[66] An English visitor informs us of the disposition of some of this tobacco:

> The gentlemen of Odessa rival the Turks themselves in their passion for smoking. Nor are they here the only lovers of the narcotic weed for ladies of rank also use it. Several of the most distinguished Russian countesses frequently smoke small cigars, and among the Polish ladies in Odessa the practice is still more common.[67]

An inhabitant of the city, more than a decade later, reproved the women of Odessa for smoking not pipes, but cigars and cigarettes just to show that they were "progressive."[68]

Mineral resources supplied the limestone kilns and the still small metallurgical works. By 1856, manufactories supported some 5,850 workers, who with their families made up probably more than a fourth of the population of 104,162.[69]

Still, most visitors to Odessa were impressed rather by the lack of industries in the bustling port. In 1836, Kohl, the observant German traveler, reported:

> The only manufactories which I was able to discover in Odessa, were a few rope walks and some places where macaroni was made. In the former, many ropes are made for the Turkish fleet, and I knew one ropemaker who sent every year 20,000 puds of ropes to Constantinople. These ropes are sometimes made of the enormous thickness of a Berlin ell in diameter. The macaroni factories send their goods all over the Black Sea and the grassy sea of the steppes, where dried bread and ships' biscuits are often as necessary as on the wide ocean.[70]

Hommaire de Hell, writing a few years later, was even less impressed at the industrial achievements of the South Ukraine:

> Witness South Russia where all manufacturing attempts have hitherto failed, notwithstanding the advantages it derives from its sea-ports. The three governments [*guberniias*] composing it reckon at this day but two thousand workmen, even including those who work in the rope works and the tallow houses.[71]

In the early 1860s Skal'kovskii, the observant statistician, reported to the authorities that the city's total production, valued at about 5 million rubles, came from a steam flour mill, bakeries (the city consumed some twenty-five *pud*s of bread a year), tobacco factories, stearine candles, tallow melting works, rope and vodka factories, manufactories of macaroni and sea biscuits, and wool-washing establishments. If this list is compared with Table 5.2, it can be seen that virtually no progress had been made in a decade.[72]

How can we explain the failure of Odessa to develop a large industrial base, particularly substitution industries, to match its commercial vitality? Problems dogged its industrial development in three principal sectors: labor, energy sources, and capital. All were problems dating from Odessa's origins; all grew with the city's expansion; and all became especially pressing in the latter half of the nineteenth century, when Odessa and its region undertook a major push towards industrialization. We shall look at them in detail in Chapter 8. Here, we shall mention only two structural obstacles which hampered the early implantation of industries in the city: Odessa's status as a free port and the structure of the internal commercial economy of the Russian Empire.

The free admission of foreign goods into Odessa no doubt contributed to its commercial prosperity, but there was a penalty. Its own manufactures were treated as foreign goods and were subject to heavy tariffs once they passed beyond the limits of the free port. To be sure, the smuggling of goods into the hinterland was a major business at Odessa. The chief of customs of the city once explained:

> A large part of the *pomeshchiks* of the neighboring *guberniias* come expressly to the city of Odessa in order to stock up on clothing, shoes, linens for themselves and linens for the table, and above all, for various small articles of luxury which they carry into the empire.[73]

K. A. Skal'kovskii also recollected in his memoirs how gentry carriages, piled high with contraband, departed for the hinterland.[74] In the view of the Soviet historian Zolotov, the business of smuggling huge quantities of goods into the region, was the chief reason for the slow development of local industries.

But smuggling, almost by definition, is difficult to measure, and its ultimate results are hard to evaluate. Smuggling certainly encouraged the importation of foreign luxuries, but it could not have significantly enlarged the market for local manufactures. No entrepreneur would have started a factory in hopes of selling its production illegally.

The status as a free port thus created a trade-off: it stimulated Odessa's foreign trade, but it severely restricted its access to the huge market that the empire represented.

Even after Odessa lost its status as a free port, structural difficulties remained. The old-settled regions of the empire, particularly the central Russian and the Polish *guberniias*, had big populations and were the oldest centers of manufacture. They could take advantage of economies of scale, and the network of fairs distributed their products with considerable efficiency across the Ukraine. Their competition hampered Odessa's own industrial development, as it did that of other Ukrainian regions. Odessa could not take advantage of the big internal market to which it had apparent access.

The failure of Odessa to develop a large industrial base in the early nineteenth century invites comparisons with the histories of other great port cities of a distinctive type, such as Naples, New Orleans, Buenos Aires, and Baltimore.[75] All were large and active ports, and all were the sites of large mercantile houses, banks, and pools of capital. All had access to abundant raw materials. But all lagged in the course of industrialization. The reasons for this were several. The natural resources they commanded were often poorly balanced; Odessa, as we shall further discuss, was critically lacking in wood, fossil fuels, and even fresh water. The activities of the port competed for labor with the young manufactures and drove up its costs. And the wealthy merchants were more inclined to place their monies in commercial enterprises or in land—which they knew well—than in the seemingly more risky factories. And government policy, if it did not assure balanced economic development, had at least promoted the efficient use of the city's chief resource, the port itself. This in turn produced and maintained acceptable levels of prosperity.

CHAPTER SIX

The City Grows, 1815–1861

Odessa [is] a most extraordinary place and seemed as if created by a magical wand.

—Ribeaupierre, 1838

The nineteenth century witnessed a revolution in urban life. People were gathering in cities in unprecedented numbers, and these numbers raised unprecedented demands for housing, services, and space. The experience of Odessa differed from that of other great cities only because its growth was so fast. From a tiny village in 1794, it was, by 1861, a commercial metropolis.

Organizing Growth

The duc de Richelieu's departure for France in 1814 left the city he had governed for eleven years in panic. Without his leadership, without his weighty influence with the tsar, what would befall the still young city? As if to confirm the worst apprehensions, the tsar, preoccupied with the last phases of the war against Napoleon, appointed Major General Koble, the military commandant of the city, as the temporary city chief. There was a sense of drift during this interregnum. But optimism was soon restored; a friend of the duc, a fellow Frenchman, Count Alexander F. Langeron, took office as governor general of Novorossiia and as city chief of Odessa on January 1, 1816.

In 1790, this young French officer had volunteered his services to the Russian army. Like his companion Richelieu, he fought heroically on the battlefield; Paul I rewarded him in 1799 with the title of count. After the death of his first wife, he courted several Russian noble ladies, and he married a Trubetskaia. According to K. A. Skal'kovskii, however, he never learned to speak Russian.[1] As a young man, he wrote verse and dramas in French. One of his tragedies, five acts in verse, was published. Supposedly he gave some of his manuscripts to Pushkin to read when he was in Odessa, but the famous poet never deigned to look at them.[2]

Unlike his friend and predecessor, Langeron was little suited to be sole administrator of the huge domain of Novorossiia. Within three years, he petitioned the tsar to reduce his duties. In 1819, the count wrote an interesting document, preserved at the Ministry of Foreign Affairs in Paris and entitled "Reflections on the Necessity of Concentrating and of Reducing the Immense Administrations Given to the Governors General in Russia:"

> I am the governor general of three enormous *guberniias*, those of Kherson, of the Crimea, and of Katerynoslav. In addition, I have under my orders the very extensive lands of the Cossacks of the Black Sea, and those of the Circassians—difficult to subdue and always restless. [I have command of] a fleet to transport food to the fortresses of Mingreliia and of commissions for food supplies for the provisioning of troops placed in New Russia, Bessarabia, and in Poland, etc., of the infantry regiments, of the artillery, of the Cossacks for the customs service and of the quarantines, of veterans, of battalions, of garrisons. [I administer] more than one hundred colonies of various nationalities. Finally, I am the head of the city of Odessa which is a separate administration and which gives me as much work as all the other duties. All the territory entrusted to me is as large as all of France and is populated by ten different nationalities and by many foreigners. There are to be found also ten different religions and all ten are practiced freely. One can judge the work which burdens me and the absolute impossibility of my doing it all.[3]

In 1820, he was relieved of his position as city chief. It was given to a member of the Commercial Court, N. Ia. Tregubov, who retained the post for two years.[4] The two positions of governor general and city chief were never again entrusted to the same person.

Langeron did not develop a close, personal relationship with Alexander I, although he won some favors. The tsar visited Odessa for the first time (in 1818) when Langeron was governor general.[5] (Richelieu had always discouraged an imperial visit for fear that the young city might disappoint the tsar.) But Alexander was charmed by the city his grandmother had called to life on the Black Sea shore. As a token of his satisfaction he gave the city forty thousand rubles for the improvement of the quarantine and for the construction of an aqueduct (over fifty years were required to finish it!). He ordered the Black Sea fleet to carry paving stone from the Crimea to Odessa.[6]

Langeron, much as Richelieu before him, saw as his principal task the colonization of Novorossiia, and he sought a change in its character. In 1818, he complained that Odessa was filled with vagrants, fugitives, and pirates rather than with men with capital, which the city badly needed.[7]

But Odessa remained a haven for fugitives. Langeron himself proposed that a two-year limit be placed on the right to reclaim serfs. If, at the end of that time, masters found their serfs, they could not remove them but could ask for compensation from the owners of the land upon which they had settled. If the runaways eluded their owners, however, then they would simply be declared residents of wherever they had settled. Langeron (like his successor, M. S. Vorontsov) feared that unrestricted rights to reclaim serfs would drive needed settlers into Turkish territory, to the detriment of Novorossiia.[8]

Langeron was not happy in his office. His expenses were double his salary. Apart from the financial drain of the office, many other burdens weighed upon him. He had to travel through Novorossiia twice a year to inspect his territory; the plague visited the port twice during his regime; and he quarreled continuously with the bureaucracy in St. Petersburg. Locally, he had constant difficulties with the dissident religious sect, the Dukhobors. They blamed him for the capricious State laws that oppressed them.[9]

During the six and a half years of his administration, Langeron presided over the city's continued growth, but seems to have bobbed with the currents and did not dominate or divert them. The great boom years of exports (1816 and 1817) and the great ensuing sag (1820–1822) occurred during his tenure. To do him justice, it should be noted that Langeron proposed that the ports on the Sea of Azov be closed in order to draw more trade to Odessa.[10] In the judgment of Grand Duke Nicholas, he was "just as zealous as his predecessor, [but] he was not as talented."[11] The Russian literary critic Alekseev pronounced that he was "a valorous general, a good and just man, but absent-minded, a droll fellow, and not at all an administrator."[12] His papers convey the impression that he was inherently a military man.

Often weighing resignation, he at last gave up the office in 1822. After retirement, he returned briefly to France and then was called back by Nicholas I to sit on the high court that tried the Decembrists. He died of cholera in 1831 at age sixty-eight in St. Petersburg. His remains were returned to Odessa and laid to rest in the Catholic church.

Langeron's immediate successor was Lieutenant General Ivan N. Inzov. He held command over Novorossiia for nearly a year—from July 1822 to May 23, 1823.[13] He had been an exceptionally humane supervisor of foreign colonists (Germans, Bulgarians, Serbs, and Gypsies), and showed much interest in agricultural development. Viticulture especially interested him.[14] His close ties with Pushkin illuminate his career. The then banished poet lived with the governor's family in Kishinev, and although Pushkin was a troublesome charge, Inzov loyally supported him.[15] Finally, after numerous petitions from the young poet in exile, Inzov granted him permission to leave Kishinev. Pushkin was delighted to quit the dreary Moldavian outpost for Odessa, which he considered "already Europe."[16] It was also Inzov who initiated a fund-raising campaign to erect a bronze statue of Richelieu.

In the estimation of several historians, Inzov was the last of the governors of Novorossiia to exercise great autonomy vis-à-vis the central government. After his regime, in the words of one of them (Pingaud), "les Russes ont bel et bien reconquis la Nouvelle Russie."[17] The writer Vigel quipped that with Vorontsov's appointment, the authorities "wanted New Russia at last to be Russianized."[18]

Vorontsov

The succeeding governor general was Mikhail S. Vorontsov (1823–1845). He is the prime example of the successful entrepreneur, a man who through land speculations on the frontier, through shrewd exploitation of its resources, parlayed a moderate fortune into one of the empire's largest.

To be sure, his family had achieved prominence since 1674. In the eighteenth century, the house had acquired extensive lands in the provinces of central and northern Russia. R. I. Vorontsov, Mikhail's grandfather, owned, at his death in 1774, 4,500 serfs.[19] Mikhail's father, Semen, was the Russian ambassador to England from 1785 to 1806. The young Russian consequently grew up and studied in England. Vorontsov *père* seems to have absorbed some of the entrepreneurial drive and daring then flourishing in England in the early stages of the Industrial Revolution. In a letter addressed to Mikhail on his nineteenth birthday, his father directed him to study languages and to speak English whenever possible; he was already conversant with French and Russian. He pointedly reminded his son that Charles V, the Holy Roman Emperor, spoke English, Flemish, French, German, Spanish, and Italian.[20]

After taking his degree at Cambridge, Mikhail returned to Russia and accepted a commission in the army in the Caucasus. By the time he was thirty he was a major general and an active participant in the war against Napoleon. After the war he returned to England, but Alexander I summoned him home to help reorganize the administration of Bessarabia, acquired by Russia in 1812. He thus developed an intimate awareness of Novorossiia and praised its potential to his father. On December 17, 1819, the elder Vorontsov replied in French:

> I see from the little you told me about it, the importance of that new outlet of our southern provinces. ... If they are complaining at Odessa about the stagnation of commerce this year despite the fact that they sold 700,000 *chetvert*s of wheat, what will be the exportation in the years which will be called favorable to exportations? [21]

Semen was obviously impressed by Odessa's potential; with his support Vorontsov *fils* embarked on a program of massive land purchases in the southern provinces, near Odessa and Taganrog and in the Crimea. In August 1822, Semen urged him to go to Odessa, and then to proceed to the Crimea where he could perhaps purchase the duc de Richelieu's former estates and gardens.[22] He did purchase the duc's house, set on a bluff overlooking the sea. This was the kernel of his magnificent villa at Alupka.

Not surprisingly, given the family interest in the development of the region, Alexander I appointed Mikhail as governor general of Novorossiia and vicegerent of Bessarabia on May 7, 1823. Writing from England to congratulate his son on the appointment, Semen advised him to be wary of Bessarabia, a potential trouble spot because of its proximity to Turkey.[23] The elder Vorontsov asked his son to consider how the Dnieper could be made navigable and how canals might join the Don and the Volga rivers so that the Black Sea and the Caspian might be linked as well. He was eager to learn whether the coal deposits near Katerynoslav might not be better exploited. This concern for the development of the region was not unrelated to the family's increased holdings in Novorossiia. Indeed, Vorontsov actively used his official position to favor his economic position. As Indova noted:

> The activities of Vorontsov as a landlord are shot through with entrepreneurship. Acquiring lands and organizing their economy, from the very first steps he accomplished all that was necessary to assure the future realization of marketable products. Routes of

communication had a vital significance for his Crimean possessions. Using his position as governor general, in the first year after his nomination in that post, he began the construction of a road linking the southern shore with Symferopil: Symferopil-Alushta (1824–1826), Alushta-Simeiz-Baidary (1827–1829).[24]

His interest in communication also prompted him to plead as early as 1844 for a railroad to link Odessa with the interior.[25]

Unlike the kindly Richelieu, Vorontsov appeared haughty to many of his contemporaries. We have already noted the scornful verse dedicated to him by Pushkin, who further called him "a scoundrel, a court boor, and a petty egoist."[26] One merchant affirmed, "He spoke English as well as if he had studied it at Oxford."[27] He seems not to have realized that Vorontsov had indeed studied, not at Oxford, but at Cambridge. One of the French consuls was annoyed that Vorontsov issued all his commercial instructions in English.[28]

An American presents this assessment in 1838:

> The count is a military looking man of about 50, six feet high, with a sallow complexion and gray hair. His father married an English lady of the Sidney family, and his sister married the Earl of Pembroke. He is a soldier in bearing and appearance, held a high rank during the French invasion of Russia, and distinguished himself particularly at Borodino; in rank and power he is the fourth military officer in the empire. He possesses immense wealth in all parts of Russia, particularly in the Crimea; and his wife's mother, after Demidoff and Scheremetieff, is the richest subject in the whole empire. He speaks English remarkably well.[29]

Much in contrast to Richelieu (an advocate of the simple life), Vorontsov chose to live in splendor. A French civil engineer reported: "Count Vorontzof is a veritable *grand seigneur*, and spends more than 6,000 pound a year in pomps and entertainments."[30]

One of the great surviving monuments to Vorontsov's seigneurial style of life is his showcase villa of Alupka in the Crimea. Its splendor testifies to his cosmopolitan culture, grandiose tastes, and huge personal fortune. When Tsar Nicholas I visited the villa in 1837, he is said to have remarked: "He is competing with the tsars."[31]

The plans for the palace were drawn up by an Englishman, Edward Blair, and the building was carried out by Henry Hunt, another English architect. The marble, the masons, and the sculptors came from Italy. The diorite walls have withstood many earthquakes. The palace itself follows in silhouette the pattern of the Crimean peak, Ai-Petri, which stands behind it. The southern entrance resembles the gate to the Great Mosque in Delhi; the northern facade, on the other hand, is in English Gothic. The decoration of the palace took nearly ten years to complete. Enchanted with the palace, gardens and surroundings, a Russian visitor exclaimed, "This is paradise, this is Eden!"[32] Winston Churchill recalled the English background of Vorontsov and the British architects when the United Kingdom delegation stayed at Alupka during the Yalta Conference in 1945.[33]

Vorontsov's father worried about his son's expenditures. In 1824, he wrote to him that he feared that the family would soon be in debt and that they would be forced to sell some of their land. Should his position as governor general continue to run him into debt, he should resign.[34] But Semen Vorontsov also raised his son's allowance from 50,000 rubles to 160,000 rubles per year. His son's health was also a matter of concern and he advised him to resign immediately as vice-gerent of Bessarabia. Vorontsov did not resign from his official duties in the South for another twenty years.[35]

Vorontsov occupied himself not only in opulent living, but also in constructing better roads and in exploiting the natural resources of the country. Following his father's suggestion, he interested himself in the findings of the engineer Hommaire de Hell, who had been part of an expedition to search for coal and iron. Hommaire de Hell had found some iron deposits at the foot of the Dnieper cataracts. When he had finished his earlier commission, he was hired by Vorontsov to continue his explorations. He began in Bessarabia, but encountered only disappointment there. After finding mediocre deposits of coal in various places, he reported excitedly that some forty thousand square kilometers in the region of the Don and the Sea of Azov held good anthracite. He advised Vorontsov to invest heavily in developing the mines with modern methods of drainage and steam engines for extraction. With proper care, these deposits could liberate Novorossiia from dependence on English coal.[36]

Prompted no doubt by Hommaire de Hell's reports, the government built a road from Oleksandrivs'k to Berdians'k near the deposits. And some sixty thouand serfs were liberated in exchange for their settling in the area and working the mines. They were also to raise cattle for transporting the coal from the mines to the Sea of Azov.[37]

How ought we then to assess Vorontsov's administration? He was obviously not beloved by his subjects in the manner of Richelieu, but was not despised either. In a moving passage, Konstantin Skal'kovskii describes Vorontsov's final departure from Odessa in

1845, to assume his new post as commander of Russian forces in the Caucasus. The boulevard overlooking the sea was lined with well-wishers; Jews turned out in great numbers, and hailed him as "our father, our benefactor."[38] Most contemporaries remembered his administration as a productive one. The French consul, who might not be expected to admire a quasi-Englishman, wrote in 1834:

> All the consuls and the foreigners who live in this city find much to praise in this man. He stands out by his extreme courtesy and the nicest manners and he smoothes away as much as he can the difficulties frequently raised by the Russian administration which is in general bothersome.[39]

No doubt Vorontsov applied to Odessa some of the examples of benevolent societies he had come to know in England. Under his administration such societies proliferated: the Women's Society for the Needy; the Home for the Poor; the Orphanage; the School for Deaf-Mutes; the Charitable Religious Home for Women; the German, Swiss, and French Charitable Societies; the Aleksandrovskii Orphanage Asylum; the Almshouse of the Compassionate Sisters, the Hospital for Outpatients; the Home for Aged and Infirm Women; and so forth.[40] He encouraged the founding of the principal newspaper of the city, the *Odesskii vestnik.* His vast collection of books even today forms an important part of the Odessa State University Library.[41] One society, the Imperial Agricultural Society of South Russia, erected a statue of him in 1857 at the cost of three thousand rubles. It still stands on Soviet Army Square (once Cathedral Square).[42]

As private entrepreneur and as governor general, Vorontsov thus manifested conflicting, even contradictory, qualities. He possessed an eye for profit and high entrepreneurial energies, which perhaps he copied from English models. K. A. Skal'kovskii's one criticism of him was that he was too partial to foreigners. Moreover, he retained the taste for extravagant, wasteful living that the old Russian gentry had long cultivated.

For about a half century then, Odessa had been blessed with exceptional leadership and had enjoyed more autonomy than the two capitals of the empire. Perhaps the most significant tribute to Vorontsov's stewardship is that, at his accession to office in 1823, Odessa had 30,000 inhabitants. When he resigned in 1844 (he lived until 1854), the population had more than doubled to 77,778 persons.

Vorontsov's career raises the problem of the distinctive contribution of liberal regimes to Odessa's development. In spite of his strong rule, contemporaries found the atmosphere in Odessa freer than elsewhere in the empire:

> Several families used to living in France and Italy preferred coming to live in Odessa rather than Moscow and St. Petersburg because there is more freedom here than in those two cities, and they find themselves here with a larger number of foreigners.[43]

An Englishman attributed this freedom directly to Vorontsov:

> There is perhaps more political freedom enjoyed in this town than in any other in the empire. This, probably, arises from the high and liberal character of Count Woronzov, the present Governor-General of New Russia.[44]

The leading Soviet historian on Odessa's past, Saul Borovoi, made this judgment:

> Here one felt freer than in the rest of Russia—national oppression and the arbitrary rule of the police were felt less. Vorontsov was unquestionably one of the most liberal administrators of Nikolaevan Russia.[45]

K. A. Skal'kovskii comments: "Under the influence of foreigners and such enlightened leaders as Richelieu, Langeron, Vorontsov, and Levshin [city chief, 1831–1837], life in Odessa was distinguished by such freedom, the like of which could not even be understood in the capitals."[46] A Russian historian of Odessa, D. Atlas, affirms that "in the early nineteenth century, the unbearable yoke of reaction in the capitals compelled Russian liberals to search for escape in Odessa."[47] The administration of these early governors was indeed liberal. But their style was also a response to Odessa's special needs. The city's prosperity required the contributions of many communities, not all of them subjects of the empire. To attract foreign colonists and merchants required a free and open social atmosphere. These early governors recognized the need and worked effectively to meet it.

Population and Society

Between 1811 and 1861, the population of the Kherson *guberniia*, of which Odessa was the principal city, grew by 259 percent. The comparable population growth for all forty-nine *guberniia*s of European Russia was 46.3 percent.[48]

Between 1815 and 1861, the size of the city more than tripled—from about 35,000 to nearly 116,000 inhabitants. The average annual growth rate of the city (compounded) between 1795, when its population was 2,345, and 1815, when it claimed about 35,000 inhabitants, had been 14.47 percent. But, of course, this high rate reflects Odessa's status as a new town, its growth from nearly zero population. The compound annual rate of growth dropped considerably in the period of this chapter, while remaining high by any absolute measure. To carry the population from 35,000 in 1815 to 116,000 in 1861 required an annual rate of 2.6 percent. (Between 1861 and 1914, the continual expansion of the city from 116,000 to 630,000 represented an average annual growth rate of 3.2 percent.) Immigration accounted for the greatest part of this increase.

Who came to live in Odessa? There were a few prominent Russians. The mistress of Alexander I, Naryshkina, brought their daughter Sofia to Odessa for a cure; she took up residence in a lovely palace on the Primorskii Boulevard. The Rozumovs'kyi family and Countess Edling similarly made Odessa their home.[49] But to most observers, Russians and Ukrainians seemed less visible than foreigners.[50]

The variegated garb and picturesque speech of these foreigners attracted the eye and ear. In 1839, an English visitor marveled at the colorful costumes of the Armenians; the blue breeches of the Greeks and Albanians; the fezzes and turbans of the Turks; the Circassians, Karaites, and other Jews; and the pink pelisses and white turbans of the Tatars; even the Russian *muzhik*s could be seen in pink shirts and blue pants.[51]

A Swiss, accustomed to multiple languages, remarked that in Odessa at least twenty languages were spoken as well as ten religions practiced. The passing parade captivated him:

There [Odessa] the Russian jostles against a Turk, a German against a Greek, an Englishman against an Armenian, a Frenchman against an Arab, an Italian against a Persian or a Bucharestian. . . . Everything surges and mixes together: the dress coat, the swallow tail coat of the West European mixes together with the kaftan and robes of the oriental. Here there is glimpsed within the colorful mass, the modern hat of a Frenchman, the high towering cap of a Persian and the turban of an Anatolian and the fez of a Morean and a Dutch sailor in a wide-brimmed low hat.[52]

According to K. A. Skal'kovskii, the various nationalities concentrated in particular trades. Thus, Armenian Catholics were barbers; Bulgarians, gardeners; Moldavians, colliers; Greeks, bakers and fruit merchants; Karaite Jews, dealers in manufactured goods; and Jews, brokers, glaziers, and peddlers. Great Russians were carpenters, coopers, stove makers, plasterers, water carriers, and coach drivers; Italians, fishermen and stevedores. Ukrainian and Polish women worked as nursemaids.[53]

Jews

This stream of immigration carried Jews in large numbers into the city. Eventually this would give Odessa one of the largest concentrations of urban Jews to be found anywhere in the world. During the period from 1815 to 1861, the Jewish population rose from under four thousand to well over seventeen thousand individuals. In 1854, seven thousand Jews were citizens of Odessa, while six thousand other Jewish residents were officially considered to belong to other Russian towns.[54] An English traveler observed: "The Jews form the largest portion of the foreign population. . . . A few are very rich and engage in the banking business; many make large purchases of imported goods from the foreign merchants and sell them retail in their own shops."[55]

Many Jews came from other areas of Novorossiia (where they had been permitted to settle since 1791) and from Volhynia, Lithuania, and Belorussia. At the end of the eighteenth century, some three hundred Jewish families, mostly from Galicia, settled in Odessa.[56] This was the start of a steady flow of emigrants from Galicia—Brody in particular. A leading Jewish scholar in Odessa in 1855, Joachim Tarnopol, wrote that the Jews from Brody combined the virtues of industriousness with commercial skill. Many of them became bankers, merchants, and brokers.[57]

In 1843, during one of its sporadic anti-Semitic campaigns, the Russian government sought to restrict the activities of foreign Jews in the empire. Vorontsov petitioned the authorities in St. Petersburg to exempt Novorossiia from the regulation. He argued that many of the bankers in Odessa were Austrian Jews, whose departure would disrupt the business of the city.[58]

As the Jewish community grew, so did its institutions. In 1826, a secular Jewish school, one of the first in the empire, was founded in Odessa.[59] The curriculum included Hebrew, Talmudic studies, Russian, German, French, mathematics, physics, rhetoric, history, geography, calligraphy, and civil law. In 1835, a similar school for Jewish girls was established. In addition to the subjects taught to the boys, they learned needlework. Soon there was a fashionable boarding school for the daughters of wealthy Jews. The founders were men like S. Pinsker, M. Finkel, and I. Hurowitz, members of the Haskalah, or "Enlightenment," who had to overcome the objections of more conservative Jews of the Hassidic community. In 1837, Tsar Nicholas I visited the Jewish schools and expressed his satisfaction with them. At times Count Vorontsov himself went to examine the youngsters.

In 1841, a large synagogue was founded, mostly by Jews from Brody. Like the progressive school, the synagogue became renowned for its liturgical and organizational innovations. About a decade later, Morandi the city architect, constructed a new building in the Florentine style for another synagogue (the *Glavnaia*); it soon came to be regarded as one of the most magnificent edifices in the city.[60]

In addition to founding synagogues and prayer houses, Jews organized medical services. A Jewish hospital of 75 beds cared for 450 patients each year. Indigent Jews could come into town from the villages to obtain free advice and medicine from one of the city's dozen Jewish doctors. Various philanthropies served the community as well: a friendly society and institutions for educating orphans and indigent children, feeding transients, and clothing the poor. Each year the community collected thirty-seven thousand silver rubles to support these charities.

Not only did Odessa offer Jews unprecedented economic opportunities and freedom to pursue their own cultural interests, but its liberal atmosphere allowed them some participation in political affairs—a rare prerogative in tsarist Russia. In the 1850s, eleven Jews served in city offices.[61] Both Vorontsov and his successor Stroganov insisted that Jews participate fully in all aspects of the city's life. This steady influx linked the urban population through familial and other networks with the Jewish settlements in the hinterland. This laid the basis for still more massive immigration after 1861.

Greeks and West Europeans

Only three years after the founding of Odessa, twenty-five Greek families settled in the town, and by 1798 there were at least twenty-one more.[62] One Greek resident explains Odessa's attraction for his fellow nationals:

How is it possible to leave Odessa, a land where milk and honey flow, where trade flourishes, where the rule is mild, where there are the fullest tranquility and freedom and where the plague does not bother us?[63]

As we have already noted, Greeks played the most important role in the grain export business of Odessa during the period prior to 1861. Greeks were also prominent in the hotel and restaurant business. In 1822, an Italian merchant wrote that Greek was the tongue one heard most often in the streets of Odessa, "because of the great number of Greeks who live there."[64] Two years later, an English traveler also affirmed that among the city's many foreigners, the Greeks were the most numerous.[65] Greek merchants bought much property in the city. With obvious distaste, Shmidt, drawing up an official report for the Russian army, claimed that if one looked at the inscriptions over the gates of the best houses in Odessa, one chiefly saw names ending in "afi," "aki," "pudo," and "pulo."[66]

Greek institutions came early. In 1814, a Greek theater was founded, and, from all accounts, it flourished.[67] A Greek school was opened with great fanfare in 1817, with Governor General Langeron, the metropolitan, and all the Greek notables in attendance. The curriculum included commercial subjects, the Russian language, ancient and modern Greek, religion, natural sciences, the humanities, and Italian. It soon enjoyed the reputation of being the second-best school in Odessa, after the Richelieu Lycée. Supported entirely by the local Greek community, it attracted students from other Greek colonies and from the homeland itself. Three Greek insurance companies were established in Odessa; like the Jewish charitable institutions, they also served as benevolent aid societies.

Like the Jews, Greeks participated in the civic life of the city. Some obtained offices in municipal government (one of the early mayors was a Greek), others served as consuls for foreign states, and nearly all of them participated in some measure or other in the economic development of their adopted city.

Italians continued to come to the city as merchants and traders. They were also numerous in professions such as hairdressing, music, banking, medicine, and as we shall see, architecture. Like the Greeks, they were prominent in the management of hotels and restaurants.

In 1836, the French consul noted in his report to Paris that there was a small French colony at Odessa of about 350 to 400 men, women, and children. Primarily doctors, merchants, watchmakers, and booksellers, they lived in easy circumstances. Some returned to

France as rich men.[68] An English traveler noted, "the least numerous, but not the least important, part of the foreign population is composed of English merchants . . ."[69] Foreigners clearly appreciated the commercial opportunities and liberal atmosphere of this easy-going southern town.

Rich and Poor

Recently, the Soviet historian Zagoruiko asserted that there were two Odessas—one a golden city and the other a vast slum:

> In Odessa, as in no other city in the country, in its architectural aspect, in its organization of public services, in its living conditions and all its mode of life, did luxury and misery combine in so great a contrast.[70]

Economic contrasts are found in all large cities, but Odessa in the first half of the nineteenth century, riding a heady wave of expansion, was bound to attract the poor and hopeful, if for no other reason than that rich merchants resided there and the idle rich came to vacation there. The lucrative grain trade was a magnet drawing stevedores, cabdrivers, builders, bartenders, prostitutes, vagabonds, runaway serfs, marginal traders, thieves. All hoped to find a place in the city's bustling economy. The hasty construction of the boom town, the proliferation of taverns to accommodate well-paid laborers, sailors in port, vacationing rich—the influx of rich and poor in large numbers, in sum, gave rise to starkly different neighborhoods. A German visitor remarked that the city was one of palaces and huts. He noted that many houses were half ruined already, or half finished or collapsing. Some shingle-roofed huts had fallen-in windows and broken doors and shutters. He surmised that some had been thrown up in haste, others never finished.[71]

The construction material itself, the local limestone, contributed to early deterioration. An English traveler brings this to our attention:

> The principal houses are built of a stone so soft as to be easily shaped with a hachet and are therefore soon run up; the roofs are of iron and zinc, and being painted green, have a cheerful appearance. They are much in the Italian style, and though showy when new, soon become shabby, and have a very cheerless appearance from the stucco falling off after hard rains and frost.[72]

The large number of bars—by 1850 there were 554 wineshops, 174 pubs, 102 taverns—gave the city a vulgar appearance, especially near the docks:

> Odessa might be thought uninhabited at night, but for the drunken roars from low wine shops, called caves and under ground. Wine is cheap and corn brandy even cheaper.[73]

One of the shabbier quarters was the Moldavanka, first a suburb, and then, as the city expanded, a district on the outskirts of the city. This area and some of its shady characters have been made famous by Jewish writers, especially Isaac Babel, who wrote about the city a century later. It was dirty, poor, noisy, overcrowded, and dangerous. It came to be thickly settled with poor Jews. Hommaire de Hell described the miserable houses there. He noted that the palaces were lined up fronting along the shore, thus putting the city's best face forward to the sea; poverty was carefully hidden in the rear of the town. Of the fringes of the Moldavanka, Hommaire de Hell wrote:

> Could we even grace with the name of town the place where we then were and the streets we behold? It was a great open space without houses filled with carts, and oxen rolling in the dust in company with a mob of Russian and Polish peasants, all sleeping together in the sun in a temperature of more than 98.[74]

Community

The motley character of the population put a strain on social relationships. Contemporaries noted that people did not mingle easily at Odessa. Its citizens formed their sets of social relationships within their own ethnic groups. In an article entitled "Two More Words About Odessa," which appeared in an almanac for 1839, M. Markevich offered a perceptive picture of the city's social life. Society in Odessa was formed of overlapping circles, and no single circle contained the entire citizenry. Even though the city was new, its citizens, in the author's estimation, did not manifest the open hospitality for which, he claimed, old-fashioned Moscovites were famous. The aristocratic circle included the Vorontsovs and other Russian, Polish, and foreign nobility. Few others were admitted into their company. Whoever comes to Odessa, he warned, had better find a hobby, or he will become rather quickly bored. Merchants, he explained, especially foreign ones, were often clever, enlightened,

kind, and, if not formally educated, at least possessed of outward
marks of education. Yet even they were not at all welcomed into the
higher echelons of society. Consequently, many merchants gravi-
tated toward their ethnic communities. Within them, they founded
their own clubs, churches, and benevolent societies. Even the
winter charity balls held at the Stock Exchange were attended by one
ethnic or social group at a time. However, the author continued,
most people were absorbed in a life of domesticity; they limited their
entertainment to the theater, or they sought pleasure in driving
around the city and in picnicking or fishing in the environs. Merchants who could afford the dues went to the English Club; there
they chatted, played cards, and read magazines. Or they joined the
Karuta casino, where they could rent a room, play cards or billiards,
drink coffee, and read periodicals. The "plain people," he averred,
kept altogether to themselves, while the affluent *beau monde*—noble
families owning from three to four houses—who vacationed on the
shores of the Crimea or in Constantinople, moved in a very narrow
circle indeed.[75] This exclusiveness had several consequences, as
Countess Rzewuska observed:

> Idleness and boredom have given the society of Odessa the habit of
> gossiping, of spiteful teasing, a malicious curiosity devoted to finding
> out family secrets. . . . Odessan society is composed of people who
> detest each other and betray each other. Interest in their pleasures
> was the sole tie which made them respect convention, and if they
> avoided quarrels, it was only so that they would not be excluded from
> a ball, or be given a less favorable reception by Vorontsov. . . . Such
> motives scarcely guaranteed a solid peace; thus hidden tiffs fed gossip
> and unfaithful relations inflamed them.[76]

A Russian émigré summed it up:

> I cannot say that the society of Odessa was the most agreeable.
> Through this mixture of nationalities, there were a great many closed
> circles and coteries, and no extensive society.[77]

All the ethnic communities resisted assimilation, but all were
touched by the city's cultural ferment. Odessa, for example, was an
early home of reform movements within Judaism and of Zionism.
The Greek society for national liberation, the Hetairia, also found a
supportive atmosphere in the city. Nationalists—Bulgarians, Poles,
Ukrainians—as well as Decembrists formed conspiratorial groups in
the city. Italian stores exhibited signs such as "Evviva Garibaldi,"
or "Evviva l'unità d'Italia."[78] When, for example, a Masonic lodge

was founded in Odessa in 1817, its membership included several government officials—even Langeron! A German doctor declared that Odessa was the freest city of all Russia. In St. Petersburg, he noticed, it was forbidden to smoke on the street, to go about with unbuttoned uniform jackets (no matter how lowly the office), or even to wear a flower in one's buttonhole. To appear in public with glasses or a beard raised suspicions of radical sympathies. In Odessa, by contrast, even the cab drivers smoked; debonair youths strolled in the latest European fashions, flower in the buttonhole. The streets were noisy with gay chatter and impromptu musicals—such camaraderie was unthinkable in the capital.[79] In the view of Nicholas I, Odessa was a "nest of conspirators."

But there were disadvantages in this cultural mix as well. The ethnic communities, looking inward, never formed a united and effective political front. As the German Dr. Kohl observed:

> The heterogeneous character of the population may perhaps account for its more than common deficiency in public spirit.[80]

The cosmopolitan composition of the city, which charmed so many visitors, hampered but did not halt the city's physical and cultural development.

Public Improvements

Commercial cities depend for their vitality on the quick movement of goods, their safe and secure storage, and a healthy environment for their inhabitants. Young Odessa had to overcome serious difficulties in all of these areas.

Nearly all travelers stressed the great deficiency of Odessa's streets.[81] In 1839, the Countess Rzewuska dwelt on an all too common theme:

> Upon our arrival in Odessa, we were enveloped by clouds of dust which scattered a hail, the granules of which were the size of pigeons' eggs. Odessa is not yet paved nor sheltered either by mountains nor by any forest. The circulating air carries into the houses a fine and tiny sand which covers all the furniture and against which one takes care to hermetically seal doors and windows.[82]

In 1831, the city chief Levshin attempted to stem the dust by planting twenty thousand trees at the Peresyp, but this measure evidently did not help the center of the city. Even Skal'kovskii, who devoted much of his life to praising Odessa, recalled that he had difficulty in breathing when he first came to live there in June 1827.[83]

As early as April 1827, the *Journal d'Odessa* carried advertisements to the effect that if captains would bring in ballast stones suitable for paving streets, they would be paid fifteen rubles per square *sazhen*.[84] Vorontsov set up a committee to discuss how the streets might best be paved. According to a visiting Englishman, however:

> . . . as soon as the committee met, instead of directing their attention to the foregoing minutiae, upon which alone information was required, they began entering into discussions as to which would be the best species of road—one proposing Macadamization, another paving, and a third suggesting that the work should be performed with stone from Italy, while a fourth preferred materials to be found at some other place.[85]

This visitor made no effort to pave over the committee's confusion. Another visitor alluded darkly to the self-interest behind some strange decisions:

> Trieste stones! with so much granite on the banks of the Bug [Boh] and Dnieper! On inquiry, I found that this was to accommodate a gentleman, one of the paving committee, who had furnished some of the other members with private loans, given good dinners, etc., and who carried on an extensive business with that town.[86]

The same observer felt that anything would be preferable to the local limestone material, which, because of its friable composition, changed into dust when ground by passing vehicles. Some claimed that the dust caused diseases of the eye and lung. People took to wearing white and yellow clothes to disguise, or cloaks to deflect, the dust. Hommaire de Hell reported in 1835 that a French engineer was going to pave the streets with wood.[87] According to a later report (1843), a Frenchman by the name of Barberot had persuaded Vorontsov to allow him to apply his invention of paving in wood. He claimed to have already had success with his process on the road from Paris to Versailles and in parts of St. Petersburg. By the end of the summer of 1842, about 150 meters of Richelieu Street were paved in wood.[88] But wood was expensive, and the central government at St. Petersburg ordered Odessa to cease and desist from laying its wooden streets. Instead, some of the main streets were paved with flagstones from Trieste and Italy or stones from Malta.

Dust and mud continued to plague the people of Odessa, however.[89] In 1861, the French consul sent to Paris a report on the most recent project and observed that the city remained only partially paved. He attributed the lack of progress to the excitement raised over the emancipation of the serfs, which had diverted the government's attention.[90]

By the 1830s, an even more serious deficiency than street paving loomed before the city government. Supplies of potable water were proving insufficient, and even nonpotable water, needed to flush the city's primitive sewer system, flowed in inadequate quantities.[91] Writing at the end of June 1831, the French consul reported that cholera had broken out in the city, and he blamed "poor well water."[92] Short supplies of water seem to have aggravated morbidity and mortality in the city. July, the hottest and driest month in Odessa, also witnessed the highest death rate.[93]

Carters and importers of grain had to cope with scant supplies to water the cattle that brought grain to port. The abundant irrigation necessary for vegetable gardens in the city and environs further depleted supplies. Lack of water also raised the risks of conflagration. Although few of Odessa's houses were constructed of wood (given its scarcity), the porous limestone was inflammable as well. In 1839, an English traveler described the watch towers in each of the quarters of the city. They were equipped with fire engines and manned by firemen, but water was lacking.[94]

The shortage had been worsening for some time. In the 1820s, a traveler stated, "There is a great scarcity of fresh water."[95] In 1819, a missionary complained that the water in the deep wells was "hard and brackish."[96] Most of the city's waters came from two springs: one was seven *versts* distant and the other twelve. By the end of the 1820s, an English engineer was commissioned to build a canal, in order to bring water to the city. But this project, like many others, led to nothing. A few years later, another English traveler attributed the lack of water to "the grossest mismanagement in the local government."[97] He commented further that the cost of water was rising and that the need to dampen down dust in the streets consumed the precious liquid.

Vorontsov licensed a joint-stock company, organized by a Swede named Hartbal, to bottle mineral water. Formed in 1828, the company had a capital of ninety-five thousand rubles.[98] Although it helped to provide good drinking water, it did not solve the problem. The Countess Rzewuska noted the lack of good water and attributed the stunted trees of the city to salty water.[99] A British traveler was no less critical:

> The artesian wells have failed here, and only a few of the best houses have reservoirs in their court yards, which are supplied by the rain, led in by pipes from the roof; but many of these fail entirely in the dry season. The general supply for the inhabitants is brought into the town in large barrels, placed on a cart, and drawn by a wretched horse. The *vodovozy*, or water carriers, fetch it from springs at a distance of from three to six *versts*; these sometimes fail, and the large stagnant ponds near the suburbs are then put in request. The *vodovoz* goes from house to house and the price of a *vedro*, a small stable pail, is two copecks, but they generally supply persons by the month, the expense of a family of four being about five rubles; in the winter, six or seven, but for washing, or baths, the charges are extra.[100]

These water carriers, mostly Russians, were at times undependable in their deliveries. Sometimes it would take an hour or more to seek out a water carrier. Moreover, the water carriers sometimes cheated their customers. Instead of fetching pure water from the Fountains (Large, Middle, or Small), they substituted more available water of dubious quality. The expression, "Not Fountain," referring to the impure water, arose among housewives. In the city to this day the phrase, *Ne Fontan*, is used to denote any article not thought to be genuine.

Water shortages persisted into the 1860s. A German explained in 1860 that the cistern system was inadequate. Wells had to be dug at least 180 feet deep. Yet the water drawn from them was so hard and calcified that it was barely potable.

Finally, construction began on an aqueduct. Steam pumps were to move water from several subterranean sources through iron pipes extending for more than a mile; the pipes would discharge the water into reservoirs, from which it would be distributed throughout the city. In September 1861, the emperor had just approved the formation of a company to bring water from the Dniester to Odessa. It would still be some time, however, before a satisfactory water system was completed.

City Buildings, City Life

Within Odessa, Vorontsov built another palace, almost as magnificent as his villa at Alupka, previously discussed. The Sardinian architect Boffo completed it in 1830. Placed to great advantage at the northern end of the boulevard overlooking the sea, it was visible to those approaching the city by water. In the opinion of several travelers, its Ionic columns and classical style gave it the appearance of an ancient Roman temple.

Italian artists had adorned the walls with frescoes and the floors with intricate parquet. An American arriving in 1848 was impressed:

> The palace is a magnificent building, and the interior exhibits a combination of wealth and taste. The walls are hung with Italian paintings and for interior ornaments and finish, the palace is far superior to those of Italy; the knobs of the doors are amber, and the doors of the dining room are from the old imperial palace of St. Petersburg.[101]

The Countess Rzewuska also described the elegant palace and its furnishings. The magnificent ballroom possessed trellises climbing to an upper story. At one great fête, the countess felt drops of liquid falling upon her. Given the sumptuous surroundings, she wondered whether the mysterious liquid might not be *eau de cologne.* But Madame Vorontsov soon diabused her of that happy surmise. The palace, it seems, had a leaky roof! [102]

Wickoff, an American traveler, regarded it as the equal of the imperial palaces of St. Petersburg.[103] According to an English visitor in 1838, the count entertained frequently in this palace during the winter season. Twice a week, balls were held for noblemen and for civil and military officers. These occasions brought forth an extravagant display of dress, cosmetics, and jewelry. The guests heard music, danced, and played at card games, especially whist; the stakes were high, and fortunes were made and lost. Our source expressed amazement at the sums expended: "The fancy ball given at the Count's after Easter, was very splendid; the milliners' bills were said to have amounted to 50,000 rubles, and the tailors' to half as much."[104]

In addition to the sumptuous palaces, Odessa was graced by many humble, but attractive, homes. Lord de Ros wrote in 1835:

> Odessa is a rather handsome town, with some large churches and buildings; most of the houses have light green roofs which look gay and pretty.[105]

A German observer agreed:

> [Odessa] has a pretty aspect, both in the interior as well as from the outside. In the direction of the sea, it is particularly ornamented by a row of splendid houses and palaces, which would do honor to the

finest city. Prince Woronzoff, and the principal government officers and wealthy merchants, reside in this part of the town. A handsome walk, planted with trees in the form of an avenue, occupies a considerable space between this row of houses and the ridge of the hill, where it descends somewhat precipitously; so that, especially on beautiful autumnal evenings, hundreds of pedestrians enjoy the pleasant and refreshing sea air, and the prospect of the wide sea, that faithful image of eternity.[106]

Vorontsov's palace was at one end of the Primorskii Boulevard, which a French engineer, Poitier, had begun constructing in the 1820s. A handsome avenue running along Odessa's cliff top, it won admiring approval from travelers then as now.[107] At the other end of the boulevard was the stock exchange, a large classical building with an exterior frieze depicting ships' prows and bales of goods—the symbols of Odessa's prosperity. Inside, painted ceilings graced the large mercantile chambers. Stephens admitted that, "Even in Italy or Greece I have seldom seen a finer moonlight scene than the columns of the Exchange through the vista of trees lining the buildings."[108]

This entire street evoked high praise from an American in 1838:

The city is situated on an elevation of about 100 feet [actually, closer to 200] above the sea; a promenade three quarters of a mile long, terminated at one end by the exchange, and at the other by the palace of the governors, is laid out in front along the margin of the sea, bounded on one side by an abrupt precipice, and adorned with trees, shrubs, flowers, statues, and busts, like the garden of the Tuilleries, the Borghese Villa or the Villa Recali at Naples. On the other side is a long range of hotels built of stone, running the whole length of the boulevard, some of them with facades after the best models of Italy. A broad street runs through the center of the city, terminating with a semicircular enlargement at the boulevards and in the center of this stands a large equestrian statue [the duc was not on horseback!] erected to the Duke de Richelieu; and parallel and at right angles are wide streets lined with large buildings, according to the most approved plans of modern architecture. The custom which the people have of taking apartments in hotels causes the erections of large buildings, which add much to the general appearance of the city.[109]

The semicircular buildings marked the beginning of Catherine Street (now Marx). In one of the fine buildings was housed the Hotel St. Petersburg; in the other, the chancellery of the military government, the museum, and the public library. The museum contained antiquities dug up at the ancient Greek colony of Ol'biia. The library founded in 1830, was the first local public library in the Russian Empire. Its librarian, according to an Englishman, was "a little octogenarian, more celebrated from philandering than his learning."[110]

The city boasted large churches as well. The French engineer Hommaire de Hell found attractive "the churches with the green roofs and the gilded domes, the theatre, Count de Witt's pretty Gothic house, and some large barracks, which from the Grecian architecture, one would be disposed to take for ancient monuments."[111]

In 1824, Boffo built the Lutheran church. The Italian architect Toricelli built the Church of the Purification in Russian-Byzantine style (1842–1847). He also designed the Sabaneev Bridge, a handsome Roman-style arch over the Military Slope in the city. Still more ambitious was his "Palais Royal," a huge U-shaped complex with some forty-four stores facing on three streets. In the middle stood a garden with a fountain.

The Orthodox Cathedral of the Assumption with its five domes was begun in 1855, but not completed until 1869. By 1850, there were twenty-three Orthodox churches in Odessa. Some observers felt that this was too few for a city of its size—a reflection of the mercantile and materialistic tenor of its life.

The Italianate palaces and churches (including the synagogue) prompted one visitor to remark in 1835, "I was almost tempted to believe that, by some hocus-pocus, we had tumbled on an Italian town. . . . There was little or nothing Russian about it."[112]

Odessa was one of those rare cities in the Russian Empire that could boast of its lodgings for visitors.[113] Many travelers, upon arriving by sea at Odessa, were required to spend time at the quarantine, a kind of hotel or hospital where new arrivals by sea waited out the period before they could enter the city. Odessa's quarantine was constructed at the foot of the town's principal bluff. Some foreigners found the place obnoxious. An English visitor wrote:

> From Constantinople, I proceeded to Odessa and passed through the ordeal of a disgusting quarantine, and finding nothing sufficiently attractive to detain me in the city or neighbourhood, embarked on a British schooner to return to the southward.[114]

Not all travelers found so much fault. A Madame Craven wrote to her father in France that they were well treated in confinement. "Quelle agréable quarantaine!", she exclaimed, happy to see her mother-in-law, various friends, and even Count Vorontsov himself.

Although parts of her letters had been obliterated in the fumigation process, we are told by Mme Craven that the lazaretto was "un lieu complètement magnifique."[115] Even Governor Vorontsov himself kindly sent French newspapers to the detainees daily. A friend sent a cook who had to remain in quarantine with Mme Craven and her party, but he was deemed "excellent."

An American traveler agreed that the quarantine station, surrounded by acacias, offered lovely views. However, he considered it a bit unnerving to be greeted by soliders, armed with bayonets, who then took innocent travelers for their prescribed stay in quarantine. He noted that in the station with him were Turks, Jews, Christians, Russians, Poles, Germans, English, French, Italians, Austrians, Greeks, Ilyrians, Moldavians, Wallachians, Bulgarians, Sclavonians, Armenians, Georgians, and Africans. They were all stripped, and examined under the arms and at the groin for nodules symptomatic of the plague. They were given flannel gowns, drawers, stockings, and a woolen cap, which they wore until their own clothes were fumigated with sulfuric acid for twenty-four hours. Their outgoing letters were also "purified."[116]

Although Hommaire de Hell also enjoyed the view and the acacias, he said that he felt so grotesque in his borrowed garb that he laughed aloud. The quarantine at Odessa, he felt, was a model of its kind, however. Travelers were detained for a fortnight, merchandise was cleansed for forty-eight hours with chlorine. Compared with the old-fashioned *lazaret* of Marseilles, Odessa's was most effective, he averred.[117]

One English inmate grumbled about the high rates charged for the quarters.[118] Another found out that the Italian who managed the quarantine was also the manager of the Italian Opera House. The more rampant the diseases in the eastern Mediterranean, the more money was accumulated for the support of the opera and for the salaries of famous singers. "It was rumored," our source relates, "that in the event of another unusually severe plague at Constantinople, the manager had expressed his intention of engaging Rachel [a popular diva of the day]."[119]

Complaints in the 1830s centered on the high per diem rates for lodgings, the quaint garb, and the stripping procedure. K. A. Skal'kovskii observed that, aside from the red tape required to obtain permission to travel abroad, Russians thought twice about sailing from Odessa, knowing that they would have to spend from two to six weeks in quarantine upon their return.[120] But conditions had vastly improved since 1819. In that year, the Reverend Pinkerton described the quarantine as a damp and cold place with small stone cells only sixteen by thirteen feet; the ceiling was only ten feet high. There were two small windows measuring four by two feet. At that time, the detainees had to cook their own food. If they retained their own clothes and kept their luggage with them, they remained forty-two days. They could gain release in fourteen days if they surrendered their goods to criminals who handled the fumigation, and if they put on the borrowed clothes. Furthermore, they were locked up from sunset until nine in the morning and were allowed visits from no one.[121] In the 1850s, an English visitor declared, "The Quarantine at Odessa is one of the best."[122] Clearly, with increasing traffic to Odessa, measures were taken to make quarantine a tolerable experience.

Once released from quarantine, the traveler had a choice of luxury hotels. In the 1820s, the Hotel du Nord, established by the Genoese shipping magnate, Venzano, was the smartest inn. The famous Donati restaurant was part of this hotel. John Moore, an English traveler, recommended it in 1824; in 1828, the entourage of Tsar Nicholas I was lodged there.[123] Another large hotel run by an Italian was the Hotel du Club; it featured a terrace overlooking a courtyard and offered hot baths.[124]

By the 1830s and at least through the 1860s, the most fashionable establishment was the St. Petersburg, which occupied the elegant semicircular building near the statue of Richelieu. One Englishman who lodged there for three months reported that the owner was a Greek who spoke French and Italian. He found some fault, however, with the small size of one apartment. Nonetheless, the hotel was a vast improvement over the Hotel de la Nouvelle Russie from which he had transferred, declaring the latter to be a "terrible place." Hommaire de Hell also found the Nouvelle Russie expensive at eight rubles a day with no linens or even a bed without extra payment. There were also no bells to summon servants, and no servants to respond! In fact, many visitors to Odessa's hotels were amazed to find that a ruble extra was charged for sheets. An American traveler was baffled to find in his room a bedstead, but no bed. When he complained about the lack of a mattress, he was told that all "seigneurs" brought their own. Apart from the sparse furnishings, he found his hotel in size and appearance "equal to the best in Paris."[125] In summertime, the after-theater crowd savored ices at the Hotel St. Petersburg. Odessa's western flavor astonished an American visitor:

... looking from the window of the café, furnished and filled up in a style superior to most in Paris, upon the crowd still thronging the boulevards, I could hardly believe that I was really on the borders of the Black Sea.[126]

Many in the crowds thronging the boulevards were shoppers. Hommaire de Hell explains why Odessa had great appeal to visitors in search of bargains:

Odessa possesses one grand attraction for the Russian and Polish ladies in the freedom of its port, which enables them to indulge their taste for dress and other luxuries without the ruinous expense these entail on them in St. Petersburg. Odessa is their Paris.[127]

Among the attractive shops was the German firm of Stiffel Brothers, which offered to its clients china, glass, paper, porter, tea, and drugs of English, French, and Swiss manufacture, but "at fabulous prices."[128] French shops such as those of Ventre Frères, Rueaud, Guérin, Neuman, Béranger, and Martin, similarly sold their sumptuous goods to the wealthy. Hommaire de Hell felt that Odessa was a real Eldorado:

Odessa is a town of pleasure and luxury, where the ladies, it is said, ruin their husbands by their profuse and extravagant love of dress.[129]

A Russian woman visited Odessa in 1832. She described in minute detail exactly what kind of good could be obtained where and who sold it. Thus we learn that Greek Street (where the merchants were mainly Jews) specialized in tea, sugar, coffee, cocoa, dried fruit, sail cloth, tents, lemons, limes, pomegranates, chestnuts, apples, grapes, and pears. Turkish and Persian wares were to be found on Catherine Street, including amber, silks, cotton goods, pipes, cigarettes, and so forth. Gold and silver objects, even custom made, could be purchased cheaply from the many Jewish artisans. From food to finery, all was of good quality and a bargain. She was enthusiastic: "I do not know another place in all of Russia where it is possible to live cheaper, more comfortably, or more agreeably."[130] An English prisoner of war describes Odessa in June:

This was the gay season for Odessa. ... The rich here, more than elsewhere, vie with each other in their extravagances; and I was often struck with the number of carriages, filled with ladies dressed in the first fashions of the day. Gentlemen in all kinds of costumes, not unlike those which are represented in the tailors' books of fashion.

. . . All the ladies must have their carriages and attendants. Their lace and bonnets must come direct from Paris, and with the last fashions; and their dresses must be of the richest texture; and as to the trimmings, they must be of the most unquestionable gentility.[131]

In addition to its palaces, churches, hotels, shops, museums, library, and schools, the city built a monument that has since become its best-known symbol: the giant stairway now known as the Potemkin steps. This city on a hill needed direct access to the harbor below it. Winding paths and rude wooden stairs served until the decision was made in 1837 to construct a "monstrous staircase." Using sandstone from Trieste, the Russian architects A. I. Mel'nikov and Pot'e laid 220 stairs.[132] A man by the name of Upton executed the project. Gradually, the Trieste sandstone was replaced by granite from the Boh region.[133] The number of stairs was reduced to 192, with ten landings. The staircase extended for 142 meters, and cost 800,000 rubles to build. The width of the stairs was so gauged that the staircase gives the illusion of even greater length. A person looking down the stairs sees only landings, while an observer looking up sees only steps. The top step is 12.5 meters wide, while the lowest is 21 meters wide. Through Eisenstein's famous film of the 1920s, the "Battleship *Potemkin*," the stairs were made familiar to movie-goers all over the world. Koch commented: "A flight of steps unequalled in magnificence, leads down the declivity to the shore and harbour."[134]

Inevitably, this bold and costly enterprise elicited criticisms. One detractor was an English visitor:

From the centre of the Boulevard, a staircase called the "escalier monstre" descends to the beach. The contractor for this work was ruined. It is an ill-conceived design if intended for ornament; its utility is more than doubtful and its execution so defective, that its fall is already anticipated. An Odessa wag has prophesied that the Duc de Richelieu, whose statue is at the top, will be the first person to go down it.[135]

The French engineer Hommaire de Hell was similarly outspoken. He complained that workers had wasted two or three years in erecting this gigantic staircase to the beach. "This expensive and useless toy," he concluded, "is likely to cost nearly forty thousand pounds."[136] Yet the staircase did not collapse, and it has remained a fixture of the city.

Odessa attracted visitors and charmed most of them not only through its lovely or impressive buildings; it also beguiled citizens and strangers with rich cultural fare.

Cultural Life

The theater in Odessa was one of the early foci of its cultural life. Theater came to be housed in a building designed and erected by the architect Boffo in 1822. It was a small construction, but its style and interior appointments distinguished it from all other provincial buildings of comparable function. From Richelieu's period, productions attracted large and enthusiastic audiences. Pushkin delighted in hearing Rossini's latest operas. The poet Batiushkov considered the theater at Odessa to be better than that of Moscow, and almost better than the Petersburg theater.[137] Adam Mickiewicz, the famous Polish poet, also frequented Odessa's theater. The actor M. S. Shchepkin played on its stage. The noted literary critic V. G. Belinsky came to see him. The cosmopolitan public favored plays in Polish, vaudeville in French, and operas in Italian.[138]

Franz Liszt came in 1847 to play six piano concerts. In the early fifties N. V. Gogol lived in the city. While he was there, he supervised the performance of his comedy *The Inspector General.*[139] In 1842, when the population of the city was 76,862, it included forty-five male and thirty-two female actors. These people earned substantial livings. One historian noted: "The inhabitants divide their time between the office and the opera." A contemporary confirms this impression. The public in Odessa loved opera so much, he said, "that it would be entirely correct to call Odessa the musical city of Russia." He claimed that common people sang Italian arias on the street. K. A. Skal'kovskii confirmed this impression. According to his memoirs, even the *chumaks* sang "La donna è mobile."[140] Another Russian remarked:

> The new city on the Black Sea contains many French and Italian residents, who are willing to give all that is not necessary for food and clothing for the opera; the Russians themselves are passionately fond of musical and theatrical entertainments, and the government makes up for deficits. All the decorations are in good taste, and the Corinthian columns, running from the foot to the top, are particularly beautiful.[141]

Each spring, new Italian singers would arrive in Odessa and the music lovers would form factions supporting one diva rather than another. These factions would assume the last name of the singer. Thus there were bitter rifts among the "Montechellisti," the "Tassistristi," the "Carraristi," and so on. Usually, Greeks and Italians supported one side and the Jews another. Sometimes these music lovers got out of hand; shouts turned to shoves and pinches and even to blows. The Italian theater was nearly the only arena where all national groups met, and there ethnic tensions were expressed.[142]

For a while it seemed that the famous composer Donizetti would come as conductor of the Italian Opera, but he sent a substitute instead. Italian divas received as much as 500 silver rubles per year; tenors commanded about 340 rubles; basses about 300; baritones about 250 rubles. The city itself contributed as much as 38,000 rubles to help support the Italian opera.[143]

For entertainment and instruction, the citizens of Odessa could look to an ever-growing stream of newspapers and books printed in the city. Despite the stagnation of commerce after 1817, the first commercial newspaper was issued as early as 1820. This was the *Messager de Russie ou feuille commerciale*, published biweekly in French by Devallon.[144] Even earlier (1818) a group called the "Bureau of Russian and Foreign Subjects" weighed the possibility of issuing commercial newspapers for the southern Ukraine.[145] The plan was to issue papers in Russian, French, and Italian; Langeron himself supported the project. When the higher authorities delayed approval, Langeron took the risk of authorizing the publication of the *Messager*, and personally donated twenty-four hundred rubles to the venture. Although the paper was, as its title suggests, mostly filled with news of ship arrivals, commodity prices, and so forth; it also published verse and theatrical reviews and argued the merits of visiting singers. Provincial papers were strictly forbidden to publish political accounts or editorials; they could only reprint articles from the St. Petersburg and Moscow press.[146] In 1822, the *Messager* rashly printed an article concerning the Greek Revolution (Odessa was the seat of the Greek secret society for liberation, the Hetairia). Another article reported on the meeting of the Holy Alliance in Laibach. These audacious essays proved to be the paper's ruin. It was closed in November 1823.

Another early periodical was the *Troubadour d'Odessa*, founded in 1822. It was devoted to theatrical and musical events. It included scores for Italian operatic arias and music for piano, harp, and guitar. As early as 1821 and 1822, the city press issued almanacs and calendars in French and Russian. A theater notice dated 1822, printed in Russian and Italian, is on display today in the city's historical museum. After 1827, Greek grammars and literary texts were issued for the Greek School.

Clubs with comfortable reading rooms served those interested in perusing foreign publications, including newspapers. For two hundred rubles a year a citizen could retain membership in the Resursy Club, or for only fifty rubles a year could enjoy the privileges of the Khadzhibeiskii Club. In 1827, these two clubs merged to become the Commercial Club, a name befitting the port city.

In 1824, the *Journal d'Odessa* first appeared. This French-language biweekly continued publication until 1881.[147] In 1827, the *Odesskii vestnik* commenced publication. For a year or so, the paper was published in both Russian and French, but thereafter in separate editions for the two languages. Appearing three times a week, the *Vestnik* survived until 1894. A. G. Troinitskii, a statistician, was its editor from 1834 to 1857. Both papers printed *ukaz*es, economic news (such as exchange rates, ship rents, port traffic, customs information, and so on), and foreign news reprinted from the censored newspapers of the capitals. They also ran features on archeology, history, literature, science, and geography.[148]

In the 1830s the *Odesskii al'manakh* also appeared; it published not only local poets, but also noted Russian authors from all over the empire. The issue for 1840, for example, contained Lermontov's poem, "Angel." An even more scholarly publication was the *Novorossiiskii kalendar*, first appearing in 1832. After 1839, the Richelieu Lycée was its publisher, and many professors were contributors.

By 1850, Odessa could boast three printers, one lithographer, six bookstores, and forty-one institutions of learning. Odessa seems to have been more literate than most cities in the Russian Empire. It attracted educated, ambitious immigrants. Those aspiring to enter the merchant world had to learn and speak foreign languages and also acquire the rudiments of mathematics. Immigrants also desired to keep in touch with their homelands—and the best way was through correspondence and newspapers.

By the 1860s, the Richelieu Lycée had become very nearly a university in terms of the quality of its faculty, students, and curriculum. Even its facilities were expanded to include laboratories for zoology, chemistry, and physics. On commencement day its graduates gave speeches in ancient and modern Greek, Latin, French,

Italian, Russian, and Turkish.[149] By 1848, the Lycée had a seven-year gymnasium preparatory school attached to it.

Besides the various ethnic schools (Greek, German, Jewish, and Armenian, among others), in 1845 the city district possessed 114 schools, 387 teachers, 3,764 male students and 1,080 female students.[150] In 1839, the Society of History and Antiquities was founded and given permission to make excavations throughout the south. Many of its findings (barbarian and Greek) are still on display today in the Archeological Museum.

Private citizens also enlivened the cultural life of the city. Zolotov and Totti opened the Library of Novorossiia, Odessa's first public reading room. Gargarin built a theater bearing his name, which put on Russian plays and ballets.[151]

Odessa, as it grew, gradually acquired nicknames: Little Paris, the Southern Palmyra, the Second Petersburg, the Golden City, the Southern Beauty, the Capital of South Russia, Little Venice, Little Vienna, Naples, Florence, and the Queen of the Black Sea. These honoring titles give testimony not only to the city's physical beauty but also to the vitality of its intellectual and cultural life. Odessa's beginnings were very auspicious. Could it maintain its high level of achievements during the tumultuous years of the late nineteenth century?

CHAPTER SEVEN

Municipal Government and Finance in the Nineteenth Century

The town was fostered in every way by the Imperial Government, enjoying many privileges and immunities . . .
—British consul at Odessa, 1874

As a new city set in largely deserted territory, Odessa was critically dependent for its prosperity on the support of the imperial government. It also faced a critical problem in forming an integrated community out of its own rapidly growing but culturally disparate population. Politics were central to Odessa's life, and yet at the same time strangely neglected by large numbers of its citizens.

The Legacy of Catherine

In 1785, Catherine II had granted to the cities of the empire a Charter of Rights and Privileges; it had been in force for nine years at the time Odessa was founded.[1] The new statute of municipal government for the first time recognized cities in the Russian Empire as legal corporations. For the first time too, city inhabitants were considered "townsmen," with civic rights and privileges. Prior to 1785, town inhabitants were registered according to the same occupational or estate categories applied in the countryside. According to its stipulations, citizens fell into six categories: [1] residents who possessed property in the city; [2] merchants of all three guilds; [3] artisans; [4] foreigners from outside Russia and persons from other parts of Russia who were engaged in urban industries; [5] honorary citizens, professionals, artists, and capitalists with more than fifty-thousand rubles in assets; and [6] *posad* people, literally those settled in the town who were engaged in industry, crafts, or manual labor.[2]

In keeping with her enlightened ideas, Catherine was determined that cities in the empire should become models of stability, order, and progress. To this end, townspeople were authorized to regulate their own affairs within one of the six "corporations"; they could also elect officials to do all that was "necessary, profitable and useful" for the commonweal.[3] Every three years a general city council would be chosen, and each of the six groups would vote for representatives from its own ranks. The general council would then elect a single representative from each of the six groups; all six so elected would form an executive board. To qualify as a citizen and elector, one had to be male, be at least twenty-five years of age, and possess an income of at least fifty rubles per year.[4]

This symmetrical system looked attractive in theory, but proved difficult to implement. The gentry, the class in society with the greatest political weight, were not required to participate. Many citizens were indifferent, and nearly all of them inexperienced. The centuries-old tradition of central bureaucratic control over local administrations was not easily overcome.[5] The records do not show that the six-man council ever met at Odessa before 1801. Indeed, even after 1801, for a couple of decades, the six-man council counted a membership of only four. In 1818, Governor General Langeron spoke of the "vanished" general council. It is doubtful that it had ever appeared.[6]

In 1820, elections were held to fill the seats of the general council. Those electors in turn chose the six-man executive council. It consisted of four merchants, one artisan, and one _meshchanin._ The council complained bitterly to St. Petersburg that not a single noble living in Odessa took part in the election; the provisions laid down in 1785, in their experience, were not working. A second and last general council was elected in 1824. This council in turn, as required, chose the six-man executive board, and then expired. Over the course of the subsequent thirty-five years, this particular body did not appear again. The six-man board survived and soon assumed the name of city council.[7]

In Odessa, enfranchised citizens showed little or no interest in the electoral process and even less enthusiasm in standing for public office. Real power continued to reside with the governors general, and they reported to the tsar through the minister of internal affairs. Even the city police carried out the orders of the governor, and not those of the mayor or other city officials. The urban populace continued to manifest inertia, apathy, and distrust. In the 1894 centenary volume, Odessa's city officials lamented the lack of civic consciousness despite Catherine's good intentions:

> Quite naturally, Odessa's inhabitants saw in their electoral responsibilities only a painful obligation; they looked upon them as on a heavy duty which they strove in every possible way to avoid.[8]

All kinds of excuses were concocted to avoid serving. Between 1830 and 1832 only fourteen persons applied to run for office.[9] Service in office might sour the citizen's relations with his neighbors. Elected officials were required to assess and collect taxes, not so much to fund municipal improvements as to pay the assessments imposed by the central government. For example, the cities had to support troops garrisoned in their midst, to build jails, and to pay the rents and salaries of the governor general and others.[10] Elected officials were viewed as conduits through which local resources were drained off to support outsiders.

Governmental functions were expanding in the nineteenth century, and the governor general of Novorossiia soon found his reponsibilities overwhelming. To ease his burdens and to serve as liaison with the elected local officials, a new office was created, that of *gradonachal'nik* or city chief. He was given specific charge of the city and its immediate environs, called the *gradonachal'stvo*, an area of about 270 square miles.[11] Since the elected bodies met so erratically, his supervision lent needed continuity to the city administration. Even he could not personally handle the entire volume of city business, however. He resorted to appointing *ad hoc* committees, as needs might dictate; a Building Committee and a Medical Board looked after the city's development and health. The central administration was quick to take up the slack left by civic indifference.

Military Interlude

Catherine's charter remained in effect until 1863, although it was suspended during the brief reign of her estranged son Paul I (1796–1801) and again during the Crimean War (1854–1856). In the latter period, the administration of Novorossiia was given to Adjutant General N. N. Annenkov. Another adjutant general, Osten-Saken, assumed command of the troops in part of the Kherson *guberniia* (including Odessa) and in Bessarabia, and General Kruzenshtern became military ruler of the city.

During the war, Odessa withstood the attack of an Anglo-French squadron of twenty-eight ships. Appearing in the waters off the city on April 9, 1854, the fleet shelled Odessa all day long on April 10. The shelling caused some deaths and injuries and damaged, among other buildings, Vorontsov's palace. But Odessa's defenses withstood the onslaught. A battery commanded by an ensign named Shchegolev, implaced at the end of the Praticheskii Mole, although taking heavy enemy fire, sank three ships. The bravery of Shchegolev and his men is still remembered. Today, on the Primorskii Boulevard, alongside the monument to Pushkin, there is placed a cannon taken from the English frigate *Tiger*, disabled during the battle. Unable to break Odessa's defenses, the allied fleet withdrew. And the Peace of Paris in 1856 led to the restoration of civil government.

Government and Growth

Finances

As a true boom town, Odessa's city government presided over a race between soaring revenues and soaring expenditures. Its revenues derived from both regular and special sources. Like other cities, it received money from the rent of city lands, tariffs on exports and imports, liquor franchises, fishing rights, the sale of confiscated properties, fines, notarial fees, and so forth.[12] A special concession to Odessa was its right to retain all taxes on the sale of spirits, which it enjoyed from 1798 to 1808. As a free port, the city was allowed to charge and collect one-tenth of the normal customs receipts; after 1802, the amount was raised to one-fifth. The city's busy port provided other sources of revenue: a last (loading) tax, based on ship capacity; and an anchor charge. As mentioned, in 1803 the city was authorized to collect a fee of 2.5 kopecks per *pud* of exported wheat, raised ten years later to 5 kopecks.

Of all revenues, initially the most lucrative was the levy of one-fifth of the normal customs on goods taken into its free port. In 1834, for example, this income yielded one million rubles, or 82.4 percent of the city's total revenue for that year. Unfortunately, this splendid revenue lapsed when Odessa lost its status as a free port in 1857 (it retained residual privileges until 1859). To make up for the lost income, the city turned to taxing real estate. In 1894, there were approximately twelve thousand pieces of real estate in Odessa. They yielded 600,000 rubles to the state and nearly 3.5 million rubles to the city.[13] From 1864 to 1900 (when the records available to us terminate), this tax was the single most important source of revenue. As Table 7.1 shows, the property tax consistently provided a little less than one-third of the city's total revenue. By 1900, however, the money generated seems to have fallen to a little over 18 percent of the total.

Table 7.1

Income and Expenditures of Odessa's
City Government, 1864–1900
(In rubles)

Period	Total Income (Avg.)	Income from Real Estate (Avg.)	Exp. (Avg.)	Population (Avg.)	Per Capita Income	Per Capita Exp.
1864–68	659,328	185,683	854,798	123,713	5.33	6.91
1869–73	1,036,399	255,970	863,598	152,395	6.80	5.67
1874–78	1,322,047	372,180	1,623,329	195,760	7.75	8.29
1879–83	1,701,326	512,087	1,663,510	227,722	7.47	7.30
1884–88	2,452,254	713,302	2,576,707	266,254	9.21	9.68
1889–92	3,089,630	789,152	3,279,445	316,423	9.76	10.36
1900*	5,274,851	990,000	5,239,351	450,000	11.72	11.64

* Absolute values

Source: *Odessa*, 1895, pp. 794–95; *Smeta*, 1900, pp. 2, 56.

As might be expected, the city (and state) could not resist taxing the port's major source of wealth: exported goods. In June of 1861, the city dropped its old export tax in favor of a flat chage of one-half kopeck per *pud* on all exports. This revenue was set aside from the regular budget to be used only for paving and cleansing the streets, supplying clean water, maintaining street lights, and so forth.[14] From 1864 to 1892 (by 1900 it seems to have been lifted), the sum was almost always over 200,000 rubles with a high of over 600,000 in 1888.[15]

Until the 1860s and the reform of municipal government in Odessa, a good portion (perhaps as much as one-half) of the expenditures went for state services—maintenance of troops in the city, upkeep of jails, payment of governmental expenses, and so forth. In 1859, for example, sixteen items involving payments for state services amounted to 111,759 rubles.[16] On the other hand, expenditures

for public health, education and lighting took up only 7.4 percent of
the city budget in 1814, 12.47 percent in 1822, and not quite 14 percent in 1859.[17] In addition to these normal expenditures, from time
to time the city was asked to make extraordinary "gifts." Thus, the
people of Odessa gave aid to flooded St. Petersburg in 1824, and, at
the urging of Nicholas I, they built a hospital for the veterans of the
1827 Turkish War.[18] According to the city officials writing in 1894,
these unexpected expenditures were among the reasons that the
townsmen looked with skepticism on the advantages of "self-
government."

As Table 7.1 shows, the amount of collected and disbursed funds
on a per capita basis more than doubled between 1864 and 1900.
The largest single source of revenue, the real estate tax, more than
quadrupled. The fact that Odessa came to rely more and more on
property for income rather than on fluctuating trade is probably a
mark of the city's fading commercial fortunes. But it may also measure the success of the merchants in shifting the tax burden to others.

As in most cities in the nineteenth century, private citizens
assumed the chief responsibility for helping the poor and needy.
Given the ethnic diversity of Odessa, it is not surprising that most of
the charitable organizations and fraternal groups reflected ethnic,
religious, or occupational divisions. There were also, however, municipal charities. In fact, the first charitable organization in Odessa
was the City Orphanage, founded about 1808.[19] More typical, however, were the Evangelical Lutheran Almshouse, founded in 1826;
the Women's Charitable Society, organized in 1833; and the Jewish
Orphanage, established in 1868.

By 1894, there were twenty-two such charities. In addition, various groups supported sixteen Mutual Aid Societies. Jews and Christians, stonecutters, doctors, midwives, and musicians were among
those who pooled their savings to help their indigent, provide for
their widows, and bury their dead. There were even seven foundations to help poor students from primary school through the *gymnasium* and Novorossiia University. In all, private funds dispersed
for charity in 1893 amounted to 875,319 rubles. The city's contribution to charity was considerably less—only 528,988 rubles.[20]

Within the various ethnic communities were other supporting
institutions, not officially listed as charities, such as, the British
Seamen's Home and Institute, a project of the British consul general,
Stanley. Even the duke of Edinburgh contributed to its upkeep. In
1876, Stanley wrote to London that the home had been completed at

a cost of "13,000 rubles collected amongst the English residents and friends in England, and Russian well-wishers."[21] Americans, including a graduate of Harvard University by the name of Donald A. Lowrie, opened a YMCA in Odessa, but not until October 1917![22]

The Municipal Reform of 1863

In 1859, the city chief, Baron Pavel Mestmakher, in his annual report to the monarch, noted that during his sixteen-year residency in Odessa, citizens had participated but little in urban government. He took the matter to the then governor general, Count Stroganov, and with his agreement asked A. M. Bogdanovskii, a professor at the Richelieu Lycée, to draw up a report on the current state of the economy and government of Odessa.[23] Count Stroganov then took it upon himself to seek imperial approval for the extension of the St. Petersburg type of municipal government to Odessa. He noted that in western European cities and even in Constantinople, citizens took more initiative in local affairs than in Odessa.[24] The suggestion met with the approval of the minister of internal affairs; he commissioned Stroganov to invite Mestmakher to enlist a committee and to assume its chair. Seventeen citizens were entrusted with the task of designing an appropriate municipal charter for Odessa. Among the committee members were prominent Greek merchants such as Konstantin F. Papudov and Theodore P. Rodocannachi; the future mayor of the city, N. A. Novosel'skii; and at least one Jew, Osip A. Rabinovich. After thirty-five meetings, the committee made its recommendations on April 30, 1863. Their proposals went into effect exactly three years later. According to the city officials who recorded these events, the regulations were even more progressive than the St. Petersburg statute of 1846, which had served as their model. They also improved upon the Moscow city charter promulgated in 1862.[25]

To be eligible to vote, one had to be male, over twenty-one years of age, in possession of real estate or receiving a salary worth at least one hundred silver rubles, and a member of the merchant guilds or a member of the *meshchantsvo*. Out of a total population of 101,000 in 1863, only 2,657 persons, hardly more than 2.5 of the population, were eligible to vote. Those eligible voted within the three corporations named above. Each group elected members to the general council (*obshchaia duma*), which in turn elected three members from its ranks to sit on the administrative council; these nine members and the mayor constituted its membership. The mayor (*gorodskoi golova*) was elected by the members of the general council; he had to be at least twenty-five years and the owner of real estate worth a minimum of fifteen thousand rubles.[26] The general council supervised the day-to-day affairs of the city. It reported to the city chief, the governor general, and the minister of internal affairs. According to the city officials of 1894, this reform represented "a step forward." With great fanfare on December 19, 1863, the general council held its opening session in the great hall of the Stock Exchange. Even women were granted tickets to attend the gala affair.[27] The former governor general, Count Stroganov, who had been instrumental in obtaining the new charter, was elected mayor. He declined the honor; in his stead Prince S. M. Vorontsov, son of the former governor general, was invited by telegram and accepted.[28]

The new regulation remained in effect for nearly a decade. Reportedly, citizens (at least that minute portion of them who were enfranchised) showed interest, involvement, and productivity. The new government launched many of the period's successful projects—street pavement, piped water, gaslights, and others. The city government at Odessa seemed unusually successful; when the state contemplated a general reform throughout most of the empire in 1870, Odessa's charter served as part of the model.[29]

The new statute, put into effect in Odessa in 1873, governed most of the cities of European Russia and Siberia. Its novelty consisted in a provision that made wealth, rather than class or occupation, the sole basis for judging eligibility to vote. There were still three groups of electors, but the division was based on the amount of taxes paid by the individual; the vote was weighted according to the amount. The new council was called the *obshchaia gorodoskaia duma.* No more than one-third of the members could be non-Christian; the mayor, whom the council elected, had to be a Christian. More than one-half of the former council members were reelected to the new offices, including the former mayor, Nikolai A. Novosel'skii. Familiar names and faces cropped up among the office holders: Grigorii G. Marazli, the fabulously wealthy Greek property owner; Charles Sicard, descendant of the like-named nineteenth-century merchant from Marseilles; Avram Brodskii, the rich Jewish industrialist; and so on.

During this reform period, the mayor presided over both the larger council and the smaller executive board. Serving a four-year term, the mayor appeared to have more power than before. In theory at least, the city chief reviewed the legislation passed by the council and judged its legality. But if he rejected an ordinance, the council could now appeal the decision to a new intermediary body at the provincial level, presided over by the governor general.[30] Between 1863 and 1893, the new urban government introduced major city services and played a principal role in founding Novorossiia University, in building the new Opera House, and in enhancing the general comfort and beauty of the city.

There were great changes in the judicial system as well. In 1874, trial by jury was introduced. Beginning the same year, fifteen justices of the peace heard the ordinary criminal and civil cases. The officials were elected and the city paid each of them a salary of forty-five hundred rubles. The central government appointed and paid the judges sitting in the higher courts.[31] This regime survived twenty reasonably effective years until the counterreforms of Alexander III transformed it in 1892.[32]

The major change in the legislation of that year was to reduce the number of those eligible to vote and hold office. The reform raised the property qualifications and restricted the number of seats that Jews could hold to one-fifth or fewer, although they constituted one-third of the population. The spirit of self-government was seriously dampened; in 1894, the city officials commented:

> The mayor and his fellow members of the Municipal Council, as well as the city secretary were considered to be in state service. The city chief was charged with the duty to supervise, not only the legality (*zakonnost*), but also the correctness (*pravil'nost*) of the actions of the city administration.[33]

The first session of the municipal council, now much reduced in both numbers and power, took place in January 1893. From the terse description quoted above, written a year later, it is evident that the authors of the centenary book judged the change to be one for the worse. The thirty-year era of self-government had been, in the light of Russian history, but a brief interlude.

Self-Government—An Assessment

The correlation between municipal progress and the reform period of 1871–1892 is clear. The wealthy property owners worked hard to improve the quality of life at Odessa, from their introduction of paved streets to modern plumbing to horsedrawn trams. The "Southern Palmyra" appeared to travelers, officials from St. Petersburg, and the boastful Odessans themselves to be the most European of cities in the Russian Empire, the most beautiful, the healthiest, the most cosmopolitan and urbane.[34] Quite naturally, the city officials of 1894 congratulated themselves and their predecessors for a job well done. And indeed they might—up to a point.

Foreign visitors to Odessa were not so impressed with the efficiency of local government. A Belgian economist, Gustave Molinari, visited the city in 1860 and, in 1877, published letters relating his experiences. He particularly noted the absence of pavement, in a city of more than 100,000, with a revenue of over 800,000 rubles per year. He attributed the failures of local government to the heavy hand of the central administration:

> Whose fault is it? Should the responsibility for the evil be laid at the door of the of the governor general, the city chief, or the mayor? Not at all. The authorities are animated, in the highest degree, with the desire to do well, and the mayor in particular, M. J. [Iurko], has one of the liveliest and most fertile intelligences that I have met in Russia. From whence the evil? The evil has several causes, but the chief one is the excess of administration. Russia suffers above all from a plethora of administrative and regulatory rules. . . . In Russia . . . all is forbidden except what the law permits. . . ." [35]

His comments raise a question as to the type of urban government that could function most efficiently in the Russian Empire of the tsars. F. Frederick Starr discerns in Russian provincial government three possible strategies, which he identifies as "decentralization," "self-government," and "greater centralization." Decentralization meant "granting provincial bureaucrats more power and initiative." Self-government relied on locally elected bodies that would be empowered to manage local affairs. Under the policy of centralization, the imperial government tried to implement its policies with minimal local or provincial initiative. Starr himself seems to believe that under Russian conditions, decentralization, though it lacked a democratic basis, most effectively served local and regional interests.[36]

Molinari thought that centralization hampered the progressive governors of Odessa, but in fact, among major towns in the Russian Empire, Odessa had more successfully than others followed the model of decentralization. City government, to be sure, as Molinari noted, was still restricted by commands from the center, but it nonetheless enjoyed greater freedom than the regimens prevailing in the other principal cities. There were several reasons for this. The creation of the office of city chief relieved the governor general of

Novorossiia of a crippling load of routine administrative chores, which in other provinces resulted in what Starr calls "undergovernment."[37] Richelieu, Vorontsov, and (as we shall see) Stroganov had stature at court, were enormously wealthy, and won the confidence of the reigning monarch; they enjoyed wide powers and financial support.[38] They viewed the city and region as a whole from a disinterested vantage point. They understood the importance of good roads, railway lines, favorable tariffs, a modern port, and all the needed infrastructure of a healthy economy. And, for the most part, they could obtain favors, privileges, and money more swiftly than could a local group of municipal council members. For no matter what latitude these latter persons were given by the municipal charter, in the last analysis their actions had to meet with state approval.

A powerful governor general acted as a effective *amicus curiae.* The advantage of imperial favor was never more evident than during the rule of the last two governors general, that is, the last two of the old-style governors general, Stroganov and Kotsebu.

Stroganov

Born in 1795 of a prominent noble family, Aleksandr G. Stroganov was trained as an engineer. He fought in the War of 1812, but he preferred civilian posts to a military career. From 1815 to 1823, still a very young man, he served as city chief of Odessa. He returned to military service in 1834, and from 1836 to 1839 was governor general of Chernihiv, Poltava, and Kharkiv. He married a daughter of Tsar Nicholas I; his son was to continue this attachment to the royal family by marrying the sister of Tsar Alexander II.

In 1841–1842, he journeyed to Paris and took up the study of various scientific subjects, including anatomy. In France, and later in Belgium, he studied government administration, the organization of savings banks, and railroad management. He developed a keen interest in factory legislation and in the condition of the working class, which influenced his later policies.

Upon returning to Russia, he became a member of the State Council. At the outbreak of the Crimean War, he was military governor of St. Petersburg. And from 1855 to 1863, he served as governor general of Novorossia and Bessarabia.

In 1858, while holding that office, he petitioned the minister of internal affairs to guarantee to Jews "all the rights of native inhabitants" of the empire. He participated actively in the discussions preceding the emancipation of the serfs in 1861. In 1860, he invited the Belgian economist Gustave Molinari, whom we have just quoted, to give a series of lectures in which he presented the advantages of free over forced labor. Stroganov himself fought against the proposal that the serfs be liberated without land, and he publicly criticized the small allotments of land ultimately assigned them. He was singularly uncooperative with the imperial secret police in its efforts to track down alleged revolutionaries within his jurisdiction. He did not arrest those accused of writing for or distributing *Kolokol*, Herzen's illegal paper published abroad. His behavior was the more remarkable, as the journal was itself unrelenting in its criticisms of him.

Stroganov called for reforms that would increase municipal self-government.[39] Only the reform of 1863, however, gave substance to his urgings. His engineering interests are manifest in his sponsorship, in 1856, of the Russian Steam Navigation and Trading Company. As early as 1861, he was pressing for a railroad line to Odessa that would serve commercial as well as military purposes. He allocated 100,000 rubles to study the feasibility of building such a line. Alexander II appointed Stroganov to a committee to study plans for railroad building, but Odessa had to wait several years (until 1865) before the first railroad line was constructed. Even then, the line extended only as far as Balta.

He worked to improve the city materially. In 1860, he levied a new tax of one-half kopeck per *pud* on exports to help defray the expense of building bridges and new waterworks, paving streets, and installing gaslights. He helped develop salt industries along the nearby lymans (estuaries). He was dismayed when Odessa lost its status as a free port in 1859. The city, he protested, which had once enjoyed a high standard of living through the reasonable prices at its marts, suddenly was saddled with the highest living costs in the empire.

Well educated and cultured, Stroganov acquired a large personal library of fourteen thousand volumes, which he bequeathed to Novorossiia University; he was indeed one of its founders, as we will discuss later.[40] He retired from service in 1862; just before his retirement, the city conferred on him the honor of "First Citizen of Odessa for Life." He continued to reside in the city for more than thirty years, and died in 1891 at the age of ninety-five. Some of his descendants could be found among the city's population in the 1970s.

K. A. Skal'kovskii gives a shrewd assessment of Stroganov's personality:

Count Stroganov was an original character, a genuinely erudite, stubborn aristocrat. Possessing wide knowledge, especially in mathematics, he represented the combination of rare contradictions: on the one hand he was an enlightened administrator, on the other, rude.[41]

Kotsebu

"Adjutant General Pavel E. Kotsebu," as the 1894 history stated, "making use of the special confidence of the Emperor, benefited Odessa in no small measure."[42] Ruling over Novorossiia from 1862 to 1874, he continued and in some instances completed the constructive work of Stroganov. During his regime the paving of the streets in granite, the installation of gaslights, and the construction of the piped water system were completed. It was also under him that Odessa finally had a railway connection. He helped establish several new credit facilities and Novorossiia University.[43] He planned a bridge across the Quarantine Ravine to Police Street. Costing seventy thousand rubles, it was not completed until 1892, but it bore his name. It was a handsome arched iron bridge fourteen *sazhen*s, or ninety-eight feet, long.[44] In 1870, he attempted to have the state build a new hospital. In this he was unsuccessful. More gratifying, however, was the completion of an eye clinic in 1876; this too was named for him. The Pavlov Eye Hospital was the forerunner to the noted Filatov Eye Hospital of today.[45] Yet a third monument testified to his interest in the city—the Pavlov Asylum for the Care of Youths and Infants, founded in 1873. In 1878, he donated his own mansion on Staroportofrankaia Street to house the institution.[46]

The End of the Office

The office of governor general was abolished in 1874 as part of the sweeping imperial reforms of government. This loss, along with the abolition of the free port, removed the last privileges that had aided Odessa's great commercial expansion in the early and middle nineteenth century. S. Bernshtein, then a resident of the city, made the following observation:

> It is true that Odessa was favored by privileges. Over the course of 80 years she benefited from the special graces of the Sovereign. She grew under the cover and protection of great and talented administrators. The abolition of the porto-franco and of the governorship placed Odessa in the position of a youth finishing his education and left on his own.[47]

One might expect the English consul, familiar with Western democratic procedures, to applaud the abolition of this powerful office. Rather, he regrets its suppression:

> The post of governor general of New Russia of which Odessa is the chief town, has been abolished. This city has therefore lost the distinction of being the seat of a provincial government of the first class. Able men have always been selected for this post, and their names are dear to the memory of the community. The change which cuts off the succession of them is felt by many as a sort of social bereavement, for all confess that their presence in the place was a public benefit checking abuse and encouraging progress both moral and material.[48]

It was precisely that material progress that concerned the city's Committee on Trade and Manufacturing in 1875:

> The Committee think that the appointment not merely of a governor general, as formerly, but of one with the more exalted rank and powers of a Viceroy would be the best guarantee for the effectual carrying out of the measures they have suggested.[49]

In the same year, the British consul reiterated his doubts that the change was for the better:

> The town was fostered in every way by the Imperial Government, enjoying many privileges and immunities, and it remained a free port until 1854, when an annual subsidy was granted in lieu of this.[50]

With the abolition of the office of governor general, the former advantages of decentralization disappeared. In 1879, the new type of temporary governor general took office; he was now less a friend at court and more a force at home. These officials were primarily interested in maintaining law and order. The first to fill this post was Eduard Ivanovich Todtleben. He had constructed the fortifications at Sevastopol during the Crimean War, and his works helped the beleaguered city to hold out nearly a year.[51] After the war, he strengthened the Kronstadt fort in St. Petersburg, Kievan fortifications, and Black Sea forts, especially those of Mykolaiv; there, he developed a design for the defense of railroad lines. He had learned this new technique by studying German and French systems. One Belgian engineer, Brialmont, pronounced Todtleben the most brilliant Russian engineer of the nineteenth century. At any rate, his skills at military engineering were not required at Odessa, a commercial, not a military port. It is true that he committed

1,017,211 rubles for the improvement of the harbor, but by then, as we shall see, Odessa needed substantially greater help to maintain its place among the Black Sea ports.[52] The decade of the 1870s was very troubled at Odessa, with a financial crisis, a vicious pogrom, and the crushing of the first Russian industrial union. Todtleben had experience as a trouble-shooter; he had been sent to Kiev during the Polish uprising of 1863 and, after a year of service in Odessa, he served as military commander at Vilnius, another politically unsettled area. The suspicion hangs heavy that his repressions of social unrest were the chief qualifications earning him appointment as governor general of Odessa.

The succeeding temporary governor general, Alexander R. Drentel'n, was a general in the infantry.[53] Before being assigned to Odessa in 1880, he had been the commander of the Military District of Kiev. Since 1878, he had been the chief of the gendarmes in the Third Section of the Imperial Chancery. He remained in Odessa only one year, returning as Military Commander of Kiev; he died there in 1888. The official history of Odessa written in 1894 records nothing but his name and the dates he served.[54]

Alexander M. Dondukov-Korsakov, a general in the infantry, had once been an aide under Vorontsov and was a veteran in subduing the mountaineers of the Caucasus.[55] Also a veteran of the Crimean War, wounded in the storming of Kars, he had once been the governor general of Kiev, Podillia, and Volhynia. His most notable contribution to Odessa, recorded in the 1894 history, was his proposal that the Slavic Society be given a public reading room in the Stock Market. In April 1882, the reading room was opened. The Slavic Society flourished in Odessa. It held readings in its auditorium in the Slobodka-Romanovka district, a poor workers' neighborhood. It also held musical and literary events in the city auditorium, organized a nursery and various charities for Slavs.[56] After one year, Dondukov-Korsakov was also assigned to another military post.

In 1882, Iosif V. Gurko, a general, took up the position of temporary governor general of Odessa. A veteran of the Russo-Turkish war of 1877, he had been an outstanding officer in the cavalry. From Odessa, he went on to become the commander of the military district of Warsaw.[57]

General Kristofor K. Roop supervised the city for eight years—from 1882 to 1890. For the first three years, he bore the title of temporary governor general. For the last five, he claimed the old title of governor general; he was the last to bear it, as the office was abolished in 1890. The 1894 history credits him with confirming the charter of the city hospital and with improving its facilities. He also had a children's park built in the Alexander Park.[58]

These five temporary governors general within a decade (four of them serving only one year each) did little or nothing to improve the city's economy. They were not expected to do much more than to suppress revolutionary activity or any other unwelcome disturbances. Besides, it was precisely during these years, 1879–1890, that the Muncipal Duma was at the peak of its power. Richelieu, Langeron, Vorontsov, Stroganov, military figures as well, had as their prime objective and mandate the welfare of the region. Most of them remained for long periods in Odessa, putting down roots, and each of them was a man of learning and culture. The temporary governors general, on the other hand, were swiftly moved to other jobs; they could not become attached to the area.

An incident associated with the founding of Novorossiia University is instructive. Already by 1837, the Richelieu Lycée was well qualified to be recognized as a university. In 1859, the great educator, writer, and physician N. I. Pirogov, as head of the Odessa educational region, wrote a report and petition to the minister of public education, requesting that the Richelieu Lycée be made into a university. The minister seemed sympathetic to the idea, but replied that the entire operation would be too costly. In an effort to cut the costs of the lycée, the medical faculty was dismissed. The nobility of Kherson *guberniia* and of Bessarabia pledged to support such a university. They maintained that even then the lycée was not a burden to the state. It earned seventy-five thousand rubles yearly, and the state only spent sixteen thousand rubles in its support.[59] The petition was pressed when the tsar visited the lycée, but to no avail. Pirogov's successor, M. M. Mogilianskii, also attempted to win the favor in 1860, but without success.

Unexpectedly, St. Petersburg announced that Novorossiia University would be located in Mykolaiv. That rival city had powerful friends at court, including Grand Prince Konstantin Nikolaevich; the minister of public education, Golovin; and the minister of the interior, Valuev. They claimed that Mykolaiv was more centrally located within the region than Odessa. They proposed that the Richelieu Lycée could be converted into a higher technical or agricultural college. Finally, they advanced a third argument, which was no doubt crucial in the decision. Universities located in large cities were hotbeds of disorder. Not only were such cities difficult to monitor, but students frequently fell under the influence of "altogether undesirable elements of the population."[60] Clearly, the highest levels of the imperial government harbored much hostility and deep suspicions toward Odessa. The then governor general of Odessa, Count Stroganov, fought back, however. He wrote to St. Petersburg that "the opening of the university in Nikolaev [Mykolaiv] would be pernicious for Odessa, deplorable for the region and for the education of youth."[61] He argued that the nobility of Kherson as well as the merchant community of Odessa supported Odessa as the site. Furthermore, the nobles of Bessarabia regarded a university in distant Mykolaiv to be utterly useless to them. As for disturbances, when had there ever been any at the Richelieu Lycée? In the last analysis, it was probably the fact that Alexander II was Stroganov's son's brother-in-law that persuaded the tsar to grant on June 10, 1862, that the lycée would become Novorossiia University, a transformation which took three years to complete.

Odessa had need for such champions of its causes. To begin with, it had no long line of ancient noble families, well established and with myriad connections as in Moscow. Even St. Petersburg was some seventy years older and there was no dearth of gentry or high officials. Odessa was a parvenu among large cities; in fact, it was the largest of the new late-nineteenth-century cities. It had the further disability that, because of its large foreign and Jewish population, it was the target of active opponents almost from its founding. The criticism usually took the form of attacks on its rapid growth and predicted collapse. Sometimes, however, its foes were more open in their hostility. Odessa was allegedly the place whence riches were leaching out to foreign soils and where foreigners were taking the lifeblood out of hardworking Slavs, deriving enormous profits thereby. To these enemies of Odessa we shall return, but their vociferous and vituperative voices called for defense. We have seen some of the governors general who took up the challenge. What about the lesser ranks of appointed officials?

From 1820 to 1894, some twenty-two men served as city chiefs of Odessa. In the history of 1894, some are remembered only by names and dates, others receive more detailed attention. One of the best remembered was A. I. Levshin, who served from 1831 to 1837, a period spanned by the governorship of M. S. Vorontsov. Unlike Vorontsov, however, he was neither a member of the military nor of the nobility. He is described by the city officials of 1894 as "enlightened." In their words:

> From the beginning of his activities in Odessa, Levshin was occupied with many useful projects and later on, he directed his unsparing energies towards increasing the welfare of Odessa and its inhabitants.[62]

Indeed, his record looks good. He helped to found the *Odesskii vestnik* in the French and Russian versions. Like Richelieu, he was interested in afforestation; he planted large numbers of trees along the shores of the port and of Peresyp in a somewhat vain attempt to cut down on dust. The Peresyp groves are named for him. At his own expense, he took himself to Western Europe to study quarantines, factories, and other modern constructions, which he hoped to introduce into Odessa. He applied his observations to the renovation of the quarantine. He attempted to better the water supply by having artesian wells dug and by investigating how much it would cost to bring in water from the Boh or Dnieper. The young city's resources did not match the required sum. He was also unsuccessful in building a sugar refinery, but he did establish a foundry. When the status of free port was threatened, he helped to convince the authorities that it should be retained. Even before he became city chief, he undertook to supervise a census of the population in 1828; at the same time, he drew up a report on the state of the city's trade and industry. In every way possible, he used his position to promote the economic welfare of the city.

In addition to his support of the city's newspapers, he was also interested in educating the lower classes. He wrote to the emperor asking that free schools be established in the suburbs, particularly for the children of *mechshane* and of artisans. He also promoted in 1835 the Jewish schools for both boys and girls. In 1894, the city fathers concluded that the city "retains a very good memory of his activities."[63]

For most of the other city chiefs we have only scattered references.[64] Of course, most of what was recorded was complimentary. D. D. Akhlestyshev (1840–1848) supported the founding of the Philanthropic Society and a second public *gymnasium*. N. I. Kruzenshtern (1854–1856) founded an orphanage for children of the victims of the Crimean War. F. D. Alopeus and his wife promoted and supported the Alexander Orphanage. P. F. Mestmakher, as we have seen, helped the city to obtain a new city charter in 1863; he also contributed to the Alexander Orphanage. E. I. Velio (1863–1865) helped to establish a mental hospital in Odessa in 1892, many years after his term of office. Pavel P. Kossagovskii (1882–1885), who had asked the tsar to give the city funds for a mental hospital, is remembered for his aid in establishing a school for deaf children.

Fortunately, there remains in the Odessa archives a lengthy report written to the tsar in 1883 by Kossagovskii.[65] He began by describing the rapid growth of the city. He emphasized the fact that the government of the city was too caught up in attempting to pay off interest on its debts to improve the harbor. He urged the government to buy up as much waterfront property as possible to ensure control over the city's commercial development. He also expressed concern for the 170 mental patients currently residing in the city hospital; they needed, in his opinion, specialized care. He further noted the overcrowding of the prison, where inmates had recently gone on a hunger strike for better conditions. But the most pressing issue was that of the city police. When he took office, the Odessa police, although better paid than their counterparts in other provincial cities, had a long-standing tradition of disobeying orders. The lower ranks in particular were noted for succumbing to bribes from tavern owners in return for overlooking infractions of the law. But he had changed the staff of the police force. With no little pride, he told Alexander III that even the temporary Governor General Gurko before departing Odessa had praised Kossagovskii for his police reforms.

At the writing of the 1894 commemorative volume, the city chief was P. A. Zelenoi. He is cited for his creation of a life-saving station on the beach in 1885. Apparently Zelenoi was a genuine eccentric. He tweaked the ears of dignified citizens; he insisted that Jews doff their hats at him, and that they give up their seats in the trams if high officials needed them. He addressed them with the familiar "you" yet he was not unpopular within the Jewish community. He had declared publicly that he would never allow any harm to come to "his little Jews."[66] In the period following the fearful 1881 pogroms, this was no small promise. Leon Trotsky remembered him: "He combined absolute power with an uncurbed temper."[67]

The best city chiefs were actively involved in promoting economic development, organizing charitable services, and controlling the police; they also helped win benefits for Odessa from the state treasury. They could, of course, hamper the functioning of the municipal self-government and act as petty tyrants within the city. We have no record of these negative actions, however.

Between 1863 and 1893, the "golden age" as it were of self-government in Odessa, the office of mayor was filled by three incumbents. The first was Semen M. Vorontsov, son of the former governor general. His service to the city must have been satisfactory, for he was asked to run again, but declined. His four-year term seems less than brilliant, however, for the city fathers credit him with no significant accomplishments.

The following two mayors were quite dissimilar. The first was a Russian entrepreneur, a self-made man; the second was an enormously rich descendant of a Greek merchant family that came to Odessa early in the nineteenth century. Nikolai A. Novosel'skii began his business career in 1850, by founding a joint stock company, the *Caucasus and Mercury*, a sailboat line linking the Caspian Sea to the Lower Volga.[68] By 1853, he was managing director of the company. With the disruptions of the Crimean War, the business declined. After the war, he ventured into even more substantial enterprises. In 1856, he founded the Russian Steam Navigation and Trading Company (ROPiT). Initially, ships called at the ports of the Archipelago and the Mediterranean and even sailed as far away as England. Under various owners, the company endured until the revolution of 1917. He also developed telegraph links between Odessa, Rostov-on-Don, and other southern cities. Even earlier, the city had given him a monopoly on collecting salt from the city's lymans. His contract stipulated that he must produce at least one and one-half million *pud*s of salt per year and sell it at no more than fourteen kopecks per *pud.* With the aid of French machines, he was able to produce more than twice the volume, but he could not make a profit at the established price. Consequently, in 1866, he turned the operation over to the minister of finance, who, in turn, split up the property into seven sections, which were leased to private operators. In 1871, a joint stock company took over the Odessa salt works. At one time Novosel'skii was also part owner of a mineral-water factory. This was a man who knew the possibilities of exploiting the resources of a frontier area. At times the local press was critical of this "Chichikov" of Odessa (Chichikov was the entrepreneur in Gogol's *Dead Souls*) because of his multiple enterprises.[69]

Precisely for his business acumen and managerial skills, he was elected mayor of Odessa in 1867. He came at a time of crisis and decline; the port was in disrepair, maritime traffic was congested. The countryside was adjusting to the liberation of the serfs. The city's lack of pavement and good water had caused a crisis.[70] As it was, his term of office partially coincided with that of Governor General Kotsebu. They made a good team. They obtained several million rubles to improve the city and finally paved most of the streets, and built the modern sewer and water supply system. The railroad links were enlarged; gaslights were installed, and so forth. According to Konstantin Skal'kovskii, who knew Novosel'skii well, the credit for all of these improvements was to go to Novosel'skii and not the city duma, which fought him over many of these issues.[71] He faced not only their opposition, but also mounting criticism in the press. Allegedly, his ambitions for the city were too costly, his projects too risky. One of his chief critics was Mikhail P. Ozmidov, an architect and a member of the city council. Editor of the reactionary newspaper *Novorossiiskii telegraf,* Ozmidov attacked Novosel'skii's waterworks project in print. Novosel'skii, not a rich man, was too controversial a figure for the conservative property owners of the city council to tolerate. After eleven years of service, he left the city for St. Petersburg. K. Skal'kovskii called him the "Baron Haussman" of Odessa. In the capital, he became an important aide to Sergei Witte, a former Odessan himself, and then minister of finance. But the lure of enterprise continued to draw Novosel'skii. He returned to the Caucasus to develop oil and coal interests. He died in 1902.

The new mayor elected in 1879 was Greek, not Russian, rich and conservative rather than risk-taking; a life-long resident of Odessa, he contrasted with the peripatetic Novosel'skii. Grigorii G. Marazli, a bachelor, had a long record of service to the community.[72] Before becoming mayor, he had been a member of the city council for five years, and he was to serve the city as mayor for nearly a quarter of a century. While his family's fortune initially derived from trade, he was typical of those Greeks who abandoned commerce after the Crimean War and invested money in property and industry. On the tax register of 1873, Marazli owned more than a dozen pieces of choice real estate.[73] In 1889, he and several others, including the engineer Edmund G. Harris, applied to set up a joint stock company in the construction business with offices in Odessa, Kherson, Bessarabia, Podillia, Katerynoslav, and Taurida.[74] He also subsidized the publication of many books on Odessa's history. Here was a man confident of the future of his city and region.

As mayor, he attempted to introduce electric lights into the city.[75] He built a chapel in the Christian cemetery. He gave the city a historic palace, built in 1803 by Count Potocki. It became a museum, which it is to this day—the Museum of Arts on Korolenko Street. Another showplace, a mansion built in the 1850s, on Pushkin Street by the architect Otton, was also his gift to the city. In 1883, he engaged the architect Gonsiorovskii to build a huge public library on Stock Market Square. He built another enormous public reading room with two public schools attached, designed by Dmytrenko, also a gift to the city. He paid the architect Iatsenko from his own means to make an addition to the almshouse. He was particularly interested in gardens, so he gave one of his dachas, located four *versts* from the city, to the Odessa Branch of the Imperial Horticultural Society, which was founded in 1884. In 1886 and 1889, he had the architects Klein and Tokhvinskii redesign this dacha to make a school for studying botany, gardening, farming, and so forth. One building housed the students, teachers and dining hall. Another served as a workshop, and the third was a two-story church. Not only did this extensive area (five *desiatina*s) house a boarding school, but also the three hundred or more members of the Horticultural Society met there regularly to present scientific papers.

He showed his interest in science by equipping from his own pocketbook the bacteriological laboratory in the city. This was the first of its kind in the empire; there, the renowned scientist I. I. Mechnikov made his valuable experiments. Today Odessa University is named for Mechnikov. Marazli also initiated the publication of the *Novorossiiskii kalendar* in 1891, first edited by Ia. A. Iakovlev and then by A. S. Borinevich. To continue the list of his donations: he enlarged the public library to make room for its eighty thousand volumes. He built a children's park in the Duc's Gardens for the poor children of Moldavanka and Sloboda-Romanovka. In 1885, at his own expense, he built an addition to the Sturdza Almshouse for children. In 1870, in memory of his mother, Zoe Theodorovna, he contributed five thousand rubles to support girls sent to the Maria Theodorovna Orphanage. In 1892, he financed a retirement home for veterans and gave as a donation to the city a large night lodgings establishment for vagrants. Among his many charities, he gave large subventions to the City Theater, especially to support the Italian opera.[76] Clearly, this man loved his city and appreciated the opportunities it had opened for himself and his family. It was, in a way, fitting that at the hundredth anniversary of that commercial city, the descendant of a Greek merchant should have been its mayor. There is no doubt that while he was mayor, Odessa became more elegant and more comfortable, and even the poor were aided somewhat by philanthropy. But the poor were increasing in number. Despite the best intentions of the civic-minded, the clever, the enterprising, the generous, and the concerned citizens of Odessa, the fundamental economy of the city and environs was declining.

The limited self-government allowed to Odessa in the late nineteenth century thus proved incapable of promoting—or maintaining—the city's prosperity. Conservative office-holders were reluctant to invest in much needed, but expensive, enterprises such as dock improvements. Left to its own resources, the city could not marshal sufficient revenues. Under the old system, wealthy men holding the chief administrative posts were able to exert influence at court, and thus attract the large investments in regional infrastructures that continued prosperity required.

While the city was being decorated, the port was deteriorating. While education, arts, and entertainment enriched the lives of the middle class and the well-to-do, the severe problems of housing, sanitation, jobs, decent pay, and anti-Semitism were left ignored or unsolved. As Odessa established itself as a pleasant seaside resort, the railroads were passing it by. Simultaneously, rival cities in the Russian Empire and abroad gained ground on Odessa in terms of port facilities, railroads, favorable tariffs—all of which were reflected in volumes of trade. As we shall see, Odessa's enemies were numerous and powerful and her protectors all but departed. Odessa, "The Southern Beauty," was a fading beauty—the more she deteriorated, the more she adorned and embellished herself.

CHAPTER EIGHT

Agriculture and Industry, 1861–1914

It is well to remember that until the grain is in the barn there is always risk of drought, insect pests, parching winds during growth, and rains during harvest. Even though the grain as it stands in the fields be excellent, peasant troubles may render it impossible to gather or thresh it, rolling stock may make it impossible to place it on the market.
—Britsh consul, 1907

With regard to manufacturing industry, Odessa is perhaps not so favourably situated by nature. There are no mineral treasures in its immediate neighbourhood or cheap motive power. There is an abundance of capital, an intelligent population, and advantageous geographical position for the transport of raw materials and the sale of the manufactured articles.
—Odessa Committee on Trade and Manufacturing, 1875

The volume of grain exported through the port of Odessa continued to rise at nearly spectacular rates in the three decades following 1861. But this apparent continuity with the past in fact masks steady deterioration in Odessa's relative place among the ports purveying grain to the world. Worsening commercial fortunes made it all the more imperative for the city to expand its industrial base, but old obstacles remained.

Agriculture

Peasant emancipation in 1861 affected the agrarian community in Novorossiia less than in the older regions, where serfs were much more numerous. Some 344,213 *pomeshchik* serfs were liberated in the Katerynoslav and Kherson *guberniia*s in 1861. In these two provinces, private serfs equalled 31 percent of the population, while in the Crimea they made up only 6 percent. In contrast, at emancipation private serfs constituted about 60 percent of the population of the Smolensk and Tula *guberniia*s, and a full 70 percent in those of Podillia and Kiev.[1] Nonetheless, the new status of the country worker profoundly altered the shape of Novorossiia's agrarian economy, in both the short term and the long.

Unrest

At emancipation, the former serfs of Novorossiia were given only a fraction of the land they had traditionally worked and were also saddled with high redemption payments. In the Kherson *guberniia*, landlords acquired one-third of the former peasants' plots. In the region of Odessa, the size of these "cut-offs" was about 4.7 *desiatinas* per "revision soul." The redemption payments for land were 29.22 rubles per *desiatina*. At such a price, 19.5 percent of the peasants near Odessa opted for the free "pauper plots."[2]

Many peasants had expected to become at once full as well as free owners of the land. Their "misunderstandings" of the reforms provoked riots in the countryside. In a letter to the tsar, Governor General Stroganov reported:

> I do not hide from you, Sire, that a large part of the peasants at first were not in a position to comprehend your first law; for that reason, on some of the estates of Novorossiia there occurred misunderstandings, giving rise even to disorders, for the suppression of which it was necessary to call in the local authorities and even the military. Such disorders took place for the most part primarily in the Odessa and Tiraspol *uezd*s of the Kherson *guberniia*. In order to stop them it was insufficient to use the military for the pacification of the peasants; it was also necessary to give a reasoned elucidation of the new law to them. . . . Thus it was that almost all the disorders which occurred in the Novorossiia region had its roots in ignorance.[3]

Disillusionment with the reforms also provoked rioting among the serfs whom Prince Vorontsov had transferred to Novorossiia from his central Russian estates. In 1863, the British vice-consul at Kherson reported to his colleague at Odessa that about two hundred refractory peasants, formerly Vorontsov's serfs, had been punished by whipping and hard labor because they had refused to pay ground rent for the land allotted to them at emancipation. Eight companies of troops had been dispatched to villages in the Kherson *guberniia* and in the Crimea. He concluded that "disaffection among the emancipated serfs is likely to become general."[4]

If the former serfs were disgruntled with the reforms, in time they nonetheless came to accept them, probably because their new status did indeed mark a substantial improvement over their former condition. As early as 1863, the British consul reported that the provisions of the law were being implemented smoothly and peacefully. Landlords were doing their duty without murmer, and the peasants received "equitable and liberal arrangements."[5]

In 1865, the British vice-consul at Kherson also gave a favorable account of the condition of the former serfs:

> Most of the emancipated serfs are flourishing in the extreme and if any complaint is to be heard, it is from their former owners, who insist that the serf is far better off than they are, and in a fair way of accumulating wealth, which the landed proprietor can never hope to attain. The peasants naturally produce their crops at less expense and live on about a hundredth part of what the owner of the land is obligated to spend; a crop, under even a middling average will leave them well off, while it brings ruin to the proprietors, all of whom, with few exceptions, are reduced to borrowing money at ruinous rates of interest, in many instances engaging to deliver their crops for several years to come.[6]

For the peasants of Novorossiia there was this further advantage: the communal system was rarely implemented, or existed only in a modified form. Thus the peasant was free to adopt innovative methods without being deterred by communal adherence to ancient custom.[7]

The Cost of Labor

Emancipation had the immediate effect of increasing the costs of hiring agricultural laborers. Workers remained in short supply in Novorossiia, and they required substantial remuneration in order to meet their redemption payments. The landlords of the region had anticipated this difficulty. In the proposals they made to the committees redacting the 1861 emancipation legislation, they recommended that the serfs in the southern Ukraine be liberated without land, but that they be required to redeem their houses and gardens. This obligation would have tied them to their homes, without fields to work; the landlords would have been assured of a large pool of desperate workers, willing to work for little.[8] But the proposal was rejected, and landlords had to hire the help they needed on a free and, for them, unfavorable market.

The United States consul at Odessa was alert to this situation; he reported in 1862, "The emancipation of the serfs has increased the price of labor in this country."[9]

Two years later the French embassy in St. Petersburg sent this report to Paris:

Daily wages of the agricultural workers have gone up fabulously. Thus in the Odessa region daily wages of agricultural workers, which four years ago were from 20 to 30 kopecks, all of a sudden, reached one ruble (4 francs).[10]

High salaries increased the costs not only of raising grain but also of bringing it to port. Peasants had been required under a kind of *barshchina* or labor obligation to cart the lord's grain, but this service vanished with serfdom. Landlords now had to hire the haulers. Even as their costs were rising, the construction of railroads in the Austrian Empire and in the United States were dramatically cutting costs of transporting cereals in those countries. The United States consul observed, "It is now said to be a fact that wheat can be sold at Trieste at a less price than at Odessa."[11] The British consul expressed amazement that landlords did not insist on railway construction to provide them with a cheaper means to transport their grain. No doubt they knew of the government's reluctance to introduce this form of transportation. Instead, the landlords "resolved to support and uphold that class of wealthy peasantry now engaged in the transport of goods by bullock carts and who demand the construction of bridges, the repair of roads, and other privileges."[12] He calculated that taking grain a few miles to port cost more per quarter of grain than the freight to carry the same cargo to England.

The Ownership of the Land

Concerning the distribution of the land, the most immediate effect of emancipation was to increase the number of small property owners. The owners of large estates found it difficult to adjust to the conditions of a free market in labor and to the changing international market in grain. According to the French consul, the gentry were woefully lacking in business acumen and were rich and ruined at the same time. They possessed no knowledge of how to calculate production costs, he claimed. They mortgaged their land, "borrowing from all sides and at all rates," selling their crops one or even two years in advance of harvest. These men "buy as they sell and administer, that is to say, with the same ignorance and the same disorder." And he concluded, "this state of affairs has only grown worse since Emancipation."[13]

Some years later, the British consul claimed that easy credit for landlords contributed to their ruin: "Their estates have not in general benefitted from the large advances made by the banks, the greater part of the funds so obtained having been thrown away in Paris or elsewhere. . . ."[14]

But the difficulties of the gentry worked to the advantage of other segments of Novorossiian society. Table 8.1 shows the direction of change in the patterns of landownership in Novorossiia.

Table 8.1

Changes in Private Landownership,
Odessa County, Kherson *Guberniia*, 1869-1889
(Figures are in *desiatinas*)

Class	Acquired	Sold	Gain	Loss
Dvoriane and chinovniks	358,766	550,606		191,840
Clergy	1,635	684	951	
Merchants	15,251	4,943	9,308	
Meshchane and peasants	50,489	15,177	35,312	
German colonists	103,936	47,062	56,874	
Bulgarians and Greeks	19,564	16,386	3,196	
Foreigners	67,757	40,591	27,166	
Jews	131,116	69,590	61,526	
Others	3,616	6,109		2,493

Source: Borisov, 1893a, p. 76.

The disintegration of big holdings was particularly rapid in years of poor harvest, such as 1879, and during the war against the Turks (1877–1878).[15] In an official brochure issued by Finance Minister Sergei Witte in 1901, Ia. Stavrovskii stated that, in Novorossiia, peasants increased their holdings at the expense of the gentry ten to twenty times between 1877 and 1887.[16] Table 8.2 shows the cumulative losses of land experienced by the gentry in the entire *guberniia* between 1861 and 1891.

Table 8.2

Cumulative Losses of Land by the Gentry
of Kherson *Guberniia*, 1861–1891
(Figures are in *desiatina*s)

County	Losses	Percent
Odessa	547,061	57
Anan'iv	390,293	48
Tyraspil	567,280	36
Kherson	876,942	51
Ielysavethrad	757,941	41
Oleksandriia	373,693	33
Total	3,513,210	45

Source: Borisov, 1893a, p. 88.

Who purchased the land that the big owners were putting up for sale? Table 8.1 reveals that the Jews, German colonists, *meshchane* and peasants acquired the larger shares of the landlord estates. According to the compiler of these statistics, Jews actually gained 145,926 *desiatina*s (and not the 61,526 *desiatina*s listed). If that was true, Jews would have purchased about 75 percent of all the *dvoriane* land put on the market.[17] The reason for the difficulty in assessing how much land Jews really purchased is that according to the May Laws of 1882, Jews were no longer allowed to purchase agricultural land. Therefore it was often bought or leased under cover of a gentile name.[18]

Within the Kherson *guberniia*, Odessa county showed a higher rate of gentry sales (see Table 8.2) and a higher rate of Jewish acquisitions than the other counties. Table 8.3 (following page) indicates how diverse from county to county were the groups who purchased the 2,012,455 *desiatina*s the gentry of Kherson *guberniia* sold.

The data were taken from surveys by rural boards (*zemstvos*); as Borisov, who made the study, observed, these transfers resulted in the "democratization" of the land.[19] But the active market in land also drove up its value. Good farm land around Odessa was selling for as much as 200 to 250 rubles per square *sazhen* in 1900.[20] Moreover, while many persons were acquiring property, comparatively few were able to accumulate holdings large enough to support efficient agriculture. In 1891 in Kherson *guberniia*, peasants owned 100 *desiatina*s for every 162 belonging to gentry. The distribution meant that the peasants had insufficient land and the gentry insufficient labor.

The pressure of the population against the land is reflected in the inflation of rents:

1866: 5 rubles 65 kopecks per *desiatina* per year;
1901: 9 rubles 5 kopecks per *desiatina* per year;
1904: 12 rubles 42 kopecks per *desiatina* per year.

Table 8.3

Land Acquisitions by Non-Gentry
Purchasers, by County, 1869–1891

County	Years	Peasants & Meshchane	Germans	Merchants & Foreigners	Jews
Odessa	1869–89	35,312	84,400	9,308	61,526
Tyraspil	1867–89	33,359	77,294	7,189	12,670
Anan'iv	1858–90	42,518	84,806	16,029	29,928
Kherson	1875–90	125,924	50,034	31,773	4,966
Ielysaveth.	1871–91	109,323	31,737	23,604	27,708
Oleksandr.	1866–91	33,015	21,563	50,113	2,809
Totals		379,451	349,834	138,016	139,607

Source: Borisov, 1893a, p. 88.

The disorders of 1905 and the uncertain future of the tsarist regime prompted the gentry to sell off land even more rapidly than before. By December 1905, some sixty thousand *desiatina*s were sold, including property owned by the Italian Anatra and the Jew Brodskii.[21] But the ongoing "democratization" of ownership did not satisfy peasant hunger for land. From the summer of 1905, disturbances in the countryside were frequent. The chief of the gendarmes asked the military to send in seven companies of troops to maintain order.[22]

In 1911, an American journalist evaluated the situation in the countryside:

Southern Russia is developing very rapidly in population, in wealth, in the area of land cultivated and in the volume of grain harvested and coal produced. The large estates, which have comprised as many as forty thousand and fifty thousand acres, owned by non-residents among the nobility are being split up into small farms and sold to the tenants who actually work the land, through the assistance of agricultural banks which have been established by the Russian government.[23]

The Monumental Staircase (now
called the Potemkin Steps), built in
1837–41, in 1894.

The Main *(Glavnaia)* Synagogue,
finished in 1860.

The Roman Catholic Church,
completed in 1835, now a sports
gymnasium.

The Russian Orthodox Cathedral
of the Transfiguration, completed
in 1848.

The Sretenskaia Church at the
New Bazaar.

The Passage, a department store
built in 1898–99, still standing.

A summer house (dacha) at Small
Fountain at the seaside, ca. 1900.

The Velocipede Cycledrome, built
in the 1880s.

A health resort on the Andriievs' kyi
Lyman in the early twentieth century.

The New Stock Exchange, built in
the 1880s, now the Philharmonic
Concert Hall.

Alupka, M. S. Vorontsov's palace
in the Crimea.

The Duc de Richelieu, 1766–1822.

Stephen Ralli, Greek merchant,
ca. 1820–1901.

The *Vsia Rossiia*, the "All Russian" Business Directory for 1913, allows us to discern, if not the proliferation of small farms, then at least the diminished importance of big estates near Odessa. Table 8.4 shows the distribution of landownership for the two counties of Odessa and Kherson.

Table 8.4

Distribution of Landownership according
to Size, Odessa and Kherson Counties, 1913

Holdings in *desiatina*s	Odessa		Kherson	
	Number	Percent	Number	Percent
Over 5,000	4	0.9	18	4.48
3,000–5,000	3	0.67	17	14.23
1,500–3,000	22	4.94	45	11.19
500–1,500	68	15.28	132	32.84
Under 500	348	78.20	190	47.26

Source: Calculated from the lists of landowners given in
Vsia Rossiia for 1913.

For the American, this fragmentation of estates, very pronounced in the environs of Odessa, was not necessarily a sign of progress:

Many wise people think this is a bad policy, because the small farmer cannot handle labour-saving machinery, and thus multiply the capacity of his hands, but the socialistic policy of the duma is to feed the land-hungry, and every peasant demands a farm.[24]

In 1913, the American consul lamented this fragmentation of the land:

The tendency for land to be broken up into small holdings is becoming steadily more marked. Farms range from 20 to 60 acres and many of the small plots are from one to ten acres each. The smallest holdings do not permit the keeping of a horse or cow, except under some form of cooperation with neighboring farmers. ... The advocates of larger holdings, who are becoming more and more numerous, point out that the yield of grain per acre on the small holdings is less than on the larger ones, because of the lack of proper fertilizers and the impossibility of using modern machinery and implements, except through cooperation.[25]

This increased pressure of population on the land and the pauperization of the peasantry of the South Ukraine enlisted ever increasing support for radical schemes of land redistribution and gave strength to Odessa's own socialist movements. The British consul gave a succinct description of land distribution and agricultural production in one *guberniia* of Novorossiia—Kherson:

> ... in the province of Kherson 2,663,495 *desiatina*s, or about 7,990,000 acres belong to landed proprietors, and 30 per cent of these lands are sown with grain. About 26 per cent are devoted to the natural growth of grass for hay, and 44 per cent are waste lands attached to villages and hamlets. The proprietors, however, cultivate only one-tenth of the land themselves; the rest is let out to the farmers and peasantry. The latter class numbers about 125,000 souls, in possession of 415,000 *desiatina*s of land, and farming about one-eighth of the land of the above-mentioned proprietors; thus they have on average something over 6 *desiatina*s, or 18 acres, to cultivate per head. Each *desiatina* costs about 15 rubles (21 pounds) in cultivation on the average, including labourers, seed, harvest, threshing, transport, etc.[26]

Thus, even many big proprietors were cultivating their estates through small leaseholds, taking no advantage of possible economies of scale. As time went by, peasant and lord alike turned more and more to the production of cereals at the expense of stock or sheep raising or diversified crops. By 1881, grain cultivation in the southern steppe region of the country occupied 92.8 percent of all sown land.[27] Wheat represented 48.6 percent of all this grain, rye 19.2 percent, and barley 14.8 percent. The southern farmer was putting all his eggs in one basket, or, more accurately, he was wagering on grain. Beginning in 1881, the Odessa Statistical Committee, evidently interested in this trend, distributed forms to cultivators in the *gradonachal'stvo* to find out exactly how much land was sown with wheat and what the yield was.[28]

To be sure, domestic demand, especially for rye (the staple for domestic bread), increased with the advent of the railroads and the growth of urbanization and industrialization.[29] Increased production of maize, especially in Bessarabia, was reflected in export figures from the Black Sea ports. An American agricultural expert from the University of Wisconsin was hired by the *zemstvo* in Kishinev in 1910 to help them raise Indian corn. A procedure had recently been developed in Iowa for testing seeds of corn for fertility before planting. The expert, Louis Michael, arrived with campaign-type buttons which depicted a ripe ear of corn with the slogan (in Russian) "More corn for Bessarabia" printed around it. The American enlisted local youth into hundreds of clubs to demonstrate the efficacy of his method for testing the seed.[30]

Demand for Ukrainian grain in the export market remained strong, but there was one significant change. The price at port no longer primarily reflected the abundance of the harvest in the empire. Before 1874, in periods of poor harvests the cultivator could count on elevated prices to compensate somewhat for the scarcity in quantity. After about 1875, however, the world market in wheat dominated price schedules. Other producing areas could make up for shortfalls in Novorossiia. Thereafter, it was possible for the southern regions of the empire to produce a small harvest that would fetch a low price, thanks to competition abroad. In 1882, for example, the French consul at Odessa noted that when the price of wheat dropped in America, it went down two rubles per *chetvert* in Odessa.[31]

Crops failed in the area in 1875; shortages and famine came at the end of the 1870s; in 1885, there was a drought; in 1889 and 1890, poor crops; in 1891, a devastating famine; and in 1892, a new failure. According to one local expert, the increasing incidence of crop failures was no fluke of nature. Everyone recognized that increased settlement resulted in the destruction of woods with its resulting desiccation. But by planting wheat extensively, meadow grass and the moisture it retained were also eliminated. Rainfalls became scantier still and crops less abundant.[32]

From the 1870s until the end of the century, grain prices continued to fall. This depression of prices pushed some owners into ruin and others into modernization. The rate of land exchanges continued to increase. Rich German colonists, "improving landlords," and the richer peasants bought up property. Thus, while grain prices fell, land prices rose. In Novorossiia in the six-year period from 1883 to 1889, the price of a *desiatina* of land rose from fifty-five to eighty-two rubles.[33]

One reason for the high price of land was the availability of government loans to peasants to buy it.[34] Other reasons were speculation and land hunger. As the British consul stated in 1913:

> The price of land in South Russia has about quadrupled within the last generation, and often it has increased even more. . . . For this no sound financial reason can be found, since the price of labour on the one hand, and the price of grain on the other, do not leave in any ordinary year a sufficient margin of profit to justify it. Indeed, it will only be possible to justify the prices already reached by putting the land to more remunerative use than has been done hitherto.[35]

Mechanization

Since labor was so expensive, one way of attempting to compete with American, Indian, and Romanian grain was to adopt labor-saving devices. In this matter, however, as in so many others, the official governmental policy was ambivalent. It recognized the need for improved methods of agriculture, but its long-standing habits of protectionism—not to speak of simple revenue-gathering—stood in the way of duty-free imports. As late as 1898, high duties were placed on all kinds of imported agricultural machinery that competed with Russian manufactures. The tax policy wavered from year to year. The British consul was hopeful in 1899:

> . . . Agriculture remains in its initial state. The deplorable condition of the peasantry and the primitive methods of agriculture, to which the inadequate yield of the extensive grain areas of this country is commonly attributed, are evils against which the Government are endeavouring to provide remedies. Foremost among these may be mentioned the recent [1899] abrogation of customs duty on agricultural machines and implements, fertilisers, and other agricultural requisites; the establishment of stores for their sale on a system of easy installments in the more important rural districts. . . .[36]

American firms were the major suppliers of binders, reapers, mowers, and horse rakes. American reapers, made of malleable steel, cost between fifteen and seventeen pounds, a few pounds higher than Russian-made reapers, but the English consul felt, "the superior quality more than making up for the difference in price."[37] While Germans were more liberal in extending long-term credit and demanded only a small down payment, the Americans had more aggressive marketing techniques. They established, for example, a showroom in Odessa for American-made products. Even in plows the Americans came to be very competitive; they made them especially light to suit the rather small and weak Russian horse.[38] The disorders of 1905 and a regional economic slump dealt a hard blow to this merchandizing of agricultural machinery. First an observation of the British consul:

> The trade in agricultural machinery suffered severely from the war and disorders of 1905. The sale season, which begins in May, was cut short at the beginning of July on account of agrarian unrest. In some places disorders occurred, in others the extensive demands and threatening attitude of the peasants made landowners and farmers

uneasy for the safety of the machinery they already possessed and unwilling to risk further purchases. . . .[39]

Not only were there no new purchases, but defaults in payments for past purchases were common. One British firm "which deals solely with buyers of first-class standing, was only paid 42 percent of the October-November installments. It would be difficult to estimate the losses suffered by the more venturesome American and German firms."[40]

The American consul made his report for the same year:

> In connection with the machinery trade, especially that of agricultural machinery, it must be remarked, that there is an agitation going on amongst the laboring classes aiming at inducing them to view such machinery with particular disfavor, as unpardonable contrivances intended to enable the large landowners to become less dependent upon the often very grudging services of the agricultural laborers. Cases of deliberate damage of such machines are becoming more and more frequent, and may become a consideration which can seriously and detrimentally affect the important trade in machinery.[41]

Still, as late as 1907, the French consul insisted that what the Russians needed was not more wheat, but better wheat. To produce higher quality, they had need of machinery—and as long as high tariffs were charged on foreign tools there would be "a heavy obstacle to rational cultivation and [this] favors the attachment of the cultivator to his old tools."[42]

The next year, the British consul, in summarizing the trade in agricultural machinery over twenty years, remarked, "the times are changed: formerly you sat in your office and buyers came to you; now they sit at home, and you have to go and look for them."[43] Although the estates and farms of Novorossiia remained in need of workers in the early twentieth century, the sullen mood of the countryside threatened producers who adopted labor-saving devices. And peasants who were obtaining more and more land could not afford them.

Even the great hopes placed in the *zemstvos* ended in disillusionment. The government had subsidized many *zemstvos* to open stores with the latest models in agricultural machinery, fertilizers, and so forth. The peasants then could buy these aids to production at below-cost prices. As of 1906, however, throughout the South Ukraine the arrears of these stores to the manufacturers amounted to at least 4 million rubles.[44]

As the British consul commented:

For the sale of agricultural machinery the year 1907 was bad. The
year 1908 was worse. Some Odessa houses did not sell a single set.
. . . Two of the oldest established British firms are closing their Odessa
branch.[45]

By 1910 the resumption of imports was noted by the French consul:

American [agricultural] machinery is being imported more and more.
At present a steamer is unloading numerous crates which came from
Milwaukee.[46]

The good harvest of 1909 resulted in large orders of German,
American, and English farm machinery.

Farm machinery was one means for increasing yield. The use of
fertilizers was another. Here again, the small farmer was at a disadvantage. In 1910, the French vice-consul expressed disdain for the
Russian peasants, whose production was only one-fifth that of the
French. He also complimented the region's German colonists whose
production was striking compared to that of the Russians:

The Russian peasant, confident in the fertility of his black earth,
refuses to use the slightest bit of fertilizer and lets the soil deteriorate
little by little. Excessively addicted to routine, he never desires to use
imported improvements and indolent by nature, he works only the
minimum, happy to loaf during the numerous holidays which decorate
the Orthodox calendar.[47]

Writing in 1913, the British consul warned:

The population of Russia increases and eats more and more grain.
The export trade also grows. The wonderful fertility of the black
earth soil begins to show signs of deterioration. It is reckoned that for
food and fodder about 600,000 tons of phosphoric acid are taken
every year from the soil, but that not more than 165,000 tons are
returned to it. On a yearly average each acre of cultivated land gets in
manure one-sixth lb. of phosphoric acid. In Belgium the amount supplied is about 21 lbs. per acre. It is clear that if the Russian yield is to
be brought up to Western European standards, or indeed kept from
shrinking away, greater use must be made of phosphorites, phos-
phates, kali salts, Thomas slag, saltpetre and sulphate of ammonia.[48]

There was no lack of fertilizers in the vicinity. The city slaughter-house dried the blood of butchered animals and exported the powder abroad for fertilizer.[49] The problem lay in the conservative habits of the countryside.

In 1914, when our survey ends, the agriculture of Novorossiia showed both great promise and great confusion. Emancipation, followed by rapid population growth, brought about a proliferation of small, uneconomic holdings. Many Russian observers—and all the foreign consuls—recognized what had to be done: cultivators, aided by machines, should work larger fields by more intensive, modern means. But many estate owners were unwilling to take risks, and many peasants clung tenaciously to the old ways and were suspicious of change. The government was indecisive and vacillating. Time and stability might have brought a satisfactory resolution, but the year was 1914.

Industry

Odessa's growth for its first seventy years was based on commercial, not industrial, expansion. Once the serfs were emancipated in 1861, however, the new mobility of labor held out the hope that the city could expand its economic base through fostering industrial development. And a growing industrial base was needed to provide employment for the growing population of the countryside. But in its efforts to industrialize, Odessa had to face and overcome formidable obstacles.

Fuel, Water, and Raw Materials

A first great obstacle to Odessa's industrial development was the scarcity of waterpower and of fuel. The flat steppes offered few sites for water-turned mills. And the nearly total dearth of forests deprived the community of wood to heat homes in winter, fire industrial furnaces, or generate steam to drive engines. Many travelers comment on the odd materials the natives burned in their stoves: "dung, stalks of vegetables and herbs."[50] As early as 1840, a German claimed that only the rich could afford to burn wood; a pile six feet in height then cost one hundred rubles.[51] And in times of war, wood could not be purchased at any price. Supplies of wood were floated down the Dnieper River or came by sea from the coastal forests of the Crimea. Kohl noted the considerable variety of fuels offered for sale at the city's bazaars:

Wood from Poland and Bessarabia, coals from England, charcoal from
the country around Kisheneff, reeds from the Dnieper and Dniester,
straw from the villages on the steppe, and dried dung and withered
vine branches from the German colonies.[52]

Each of the various fuels had a special function: straw for ovens,
coals and wood for kitchens of the wealthy. The poor made do with
straw and dung. A mixture of straw and reeds heated the city's
bread ovens. The substances were combined with some care. Bricks
of dung and straw, mixed with a touch of Bessarabian oak and dried
in the sun, burned slowly and long. The natives knew how to cali-
brate the burning time of each of these mixtures, and changed the
blend for different uses. And like blends of tobacco, the odor was in
each case so distinctive that at night some peasants could identify
which villages they were approaching from the smell of burning fuel.

High fuel costs delayed the construction of steam-powered mills.
Most of Odessa's furnaces burned coal imported from England. In
1867, the cost of transport was a relatively high nineteen to twenty-
one kopecks per *pud.*[53] Anthracite cost from twenty-five to twenty-
seven kopecks per *pud* in Odessa, while in English ports the same
product cost only eleven to thirteen kopecks per *pud.*

Tariffs added to the cost of this imported fuel. The British consuls at Odessa complained repeatedly about the high rates charged on
coal and other commodities imported from England. In 1890, the
consul affirmed that the heavy duties placed on English coal obstructed the development of local industries:

> Although the Russian Government derives a considerable revenue
> from the duty on coal, and has the further object in view of encourag-
> ing an important native industry, its proximate result is so to raise the
> price of fuel as to inflict unnecessary hardship on the poor and to
> paralyze local industrial undertakings. Quite recently a flour mill near
> Odessa has stopped work owing to the dearness of coal, and it is
> expected that another will shortly follow suit, while a large glass-
> button factory has also found it necessary to close its workshops.[54]

The consul added that Odessa factories preferred English coal
despite its dearness, because of its excellent quality.[55]

Sometimes coal was so scarce and so expensive that many urban
houses could not be adequately heated during the winter. In 1889,
according to the British consul, the city chief of Odessa recommended to the municipal authorities that they keep a reserve of
500,000 *pud*s of coal in stock for winter emergencies. And this could

only be accomplished if a certain amount came duty free from England.[56]

In 1900, the British consul again called the heavy duty levied on British coal over the previous ten years one of the greatest "hindrances to the development of various industries."

The South Ukraine was slow to develop local supplies of coal. To be sure, it possessed rich deposits in the Donets basin. Peasants, utilizing primitive methods, had been extracting coal for some time. As early as 1829, Vorontsov brought coal from Bakhmut through Taganrog in the relatively small quantity of six thousand *pud*s. But the mines were not intensively exploited for industrial purposes until well into the second half of the nineteenth century. Anatole Demidov, an entrepreneurial aristocrat who had spent years abroad, undertook in about 1840 to investigate the nature and value of the coal deposits. The famous French engineer and economist, Frédéric Le Play, headed the expedition. But his report was so negative as to discourage systematic exploitation of this rich resource. An expert later commented: "The consequence of Le Play's mission was to delay the industrial development of South Russia for a quarter of a century."[57] By 1880, in the Donets region, 197 mines produced 86.6 million *pud*s of coal, but much was consumed as fuel by the new railroads.[58] Not only the poor quality of the coal, but also its high price, made it feasible to be used only for railroads, steamboats, and household consumption, not for ordinary factories. Even when Russian fuel was utilized, it could only be procured seasonally. In the fall, generally all available rolling stock was used to haul grain to Odessa.[59]

In 1909, the British consul provided a lengthy report on the mineral fuel of the Donets basin, which he declared to be plentiful. The principal kinds were hard anthracite and a soft coal. Some of the difficulties involved in the mining of coal were "the dearness of capital and the want of uniformity of the mineral." Another problem was that of spontaneous combustion. Most of the coal was taken by sea to Baltic ports for use by factories and steamers.[60] Not much of it, apparently, reached the southern region for industrial purposes. Protection against imported English coal was, he believed, no longer needed. The development of the Donets coal basin (producing some 8 million tons in 1900) was still not adequate for local needs: "all [the Donets coal] has found a ready sale, and in fact has been insufficient to meet the demand, persons requiring it having to wait for weeks or even months so that protection is no longer necessary."

In addition to fuel, most manufactures required a good supply of water. As one local historian observed in 1875, Odessa would have produced many more consumer items if there had been "ample water, cheap fuel and a comparatively cheap labor force."[61] Indeed, he continued, "Actually, only thanks to the [new] water supply in Odessa, there appeared such huge works as the brewery and winery of the Industrial and Trade Society, the starch and glue factory of Lekont and Co."[62] With the opening of the new pipelines from the Dniester, the price of forty buckets dropped from four to three kopecks. Nonetheless, the price was still too high for the profitable operation of many manufactures, such as paper making; the production of fifty *pud*s of paper required, for example, one thousand barrels of water.[63]

A. A. Skal'kovskii was alert to these shortages of fuel and fresh water as he was to most other aspects of the economic life of his native region. His words show the situation in the 1860s:

> We repeat that the chief obstacles to the development of factory and manufacturing industry were the insufficient fuels for steam engines which had to be procured at high price from abroad, for example, from England and the absence of running water for hydraulic power. Sea water quickly corroded all steam boilers and equipment, especially pipes. . . .[64]

In 1905, according to the report of an Italian journalist, the problems of shortages still remained:

> The town is not well situated for industrial development as coal, iron and naphta can only be obtained from a great distance, either by a roundabout railway route or by a combination of railway and steamship transport, which of course means heavy transshipment expenses.[65]

Labor

Labor had traditionally been in short supply in Novorossiia, and emancipation did not immediately direct to it a stream of workers looking for employment to the city. One reason for this was the legislation itself; it set lengthy periods for negotiating the redemption fees. Then too, only those peasants who were willing to accept "pauper plots" acquired full freedom of movement. Those who sought a larger share of the soil assumed heavy obligations to their rural communes in order to repay the compensation demanded of them. In effect, they could not depart without their neighbors' permission. Moreover, in Novorossiia, the great landowners, always short of workers, recruited peasants to work or lease their holdings. For most peasants there was work enough on the land. In fact, as Lenin himself noted, Odessa was a gathering place for workers, who offered their services for sale; landed proprietors went there to seek them.[66] The demand for agricultural laborers thus worked against the growth of an urban and industrial labor force.

To be sure, a heavy, seasonal movement of laborers continued. Men from the countryside found occasional employment as dockhands, cab drivers, or builders. In the 1870s, about three thousand masons, carpenters, and plasterers passed their summers in Odessa, working in the building trades. Some five thousand came to repair or load ships and still another twelve thousand came in search of odd jobs. As late as the 1890s, some five thousand casual laborers migrated to the city every year, and then moved out again.[67] At the same time, only about one-third of the city's workers were employed in factories. The others found jobs in services—maritime or land transport, small shops or businesses.[68] As a historian of the city's industries reported in 1875:

> Today, when the export of grain from our port reaches such a huge quantity, all the working hands concentrate on the docks and in the grain magazines. Pay is as high as five to six rubles per day. Consequently, industrial affairs suffer from insufficient workers.[69]

When crops failed, even larger numbers of rural people were drawn into the city. This drifting population, which floated in and out like the tides, did not readily assure a large supply of cheap and stable labor. As the British consul observed apropos of peasants employed in factories: ". . . at the first good harvest, they would nearly all run away from their employ."[70] Moscow was set within a densely settled region, which offered a large pool of labor. The region around St. Petersburg was thinly settled, but its poor soil did not compete for workers as did the black earth of the steppes. Odessa, in contrast, could not recruit from its countryside sufficient numbers of workers willing to settle permanently in the city. Rather paradoxically, these seasonal migrants depressed day wages, especially in periods when harvests failed in the countryside. They thus discouraged permanent settlement. In 1862, a year of dearth, the French consul recorded that unskilled labor received only fifty to eighty kopecks a day; in the year before, the workers had received 1.5 rubles a day for comparable services. As wages went down, thefts and assaults went up, and both movements detracted from the city's appeal.[71]

Since the Russian state had abandoned its former policy of inviting foreign colonists, Odessa faced an aggravated problem of recruiting labor. In a way, it competed with itself. The seaport, at the end of the nineteenth century, employed about three thousand men, who were not inclined to accept jobs in factories.[72] The small artisans were also earning enough remuneration to resist pressures forcing them into factories. The number of master artisans grew from 1,662 in 1863 to 2,415 in 1877. The number of apprentices remained more constant, rising only from 2,245 to 2,824 in the same period. In 1872, a bad year, some 4,272 apprentices enrolled in the city's crafts, but their numbers dropped when the economy failed to sustain demand.[73]

Odessa, to be sure, continued to attract immigrants, often from great distances, in mounting numbers, as the census of 1892 makes clear. Reports of high wages, low living costs, and amenable surroundings drew them to the city. Indeed, the majority of Odessa's factory workers came from central Russia and were not local people.[74] But many of these had no skills, nor even much familiarity with urban life. They swelled the ranks of the destitute or the marginally employed, and Odessa faced a problem not unfamiliar in modern economies—a shortage of skilled, and a surplus of untrained, workers.

A committee, investigating Odessa's industries in 1875, concluded:

> Special industrial education is a necessary condition for the development of manufacturing industry in Odessa and its environs. A technical school should therefore be established at Odessa, and the mass of the people should also be taught the elements of handicraft.

This was particularly required in "South Russia, where industrial undertakings are quite a novelty, and where the population is sparse and unsettled."[75] As late as 1899, the total industrial labor force numbered only 20,859, or about 5 percent of the total population (see below, Table 8.6).

Capital

Venture capital, like skilled workers, was slow to settle in Odessa. The prosperous landlords came to Odessa to sell their produce, hire workers, and buy their luxury goods. They left money behind, but not in industrial investments. They were themselves often in debt and uncomfortable with the ways of urban enterprise. Tradition and custom in Russia went against the entry of gentry into the world of industrial enterprise, unless, of course, on their own estates. Both before and after emancipation, manorial factories were not unknown in the South Ukraine. But in the environs of Odessa, there were few large estates and even fewer manorial industries.

If the wealthy wheat-growers neglected to invest in industry and the serfs lacked the means, what happened to the mercantile fortunes that the flourishing export trade generated? Hagemeister comments on this problem of capital:

> The South of Europe is much less rich in capital than the North; and the commerce of New Russia, which is entirely under the influence of the markets of the Archipelago and of the Mediterranean is deficient in this most important particular. The greater part of the merchants in our ports are Greeks and Italians; they have brought thither rather their industry and their connection, than any great amount of money. As long as the trade was confined to the exportation of corn, a small capital sufficed, because the purchases were made on the spot, or in the country, against advances of considerable amount.[76]

Those merchants who did not plow their profits back into commerce tended to choose land over industry:

> Many Odessa merchants have invested their capital in great estates, and like the Polish landowners, produce for themselves the [cereal] articles, which, as merchants, they afterwards export.[77]

Most of the foreign firms to which Haxthausen alludes were family enterprises, with officers and partners (usually brothers and sons) distributed widely across the international commercial world. Profits were also widely distributed among scattered family members. The profits everywhere tended to flow into other commercial enterprises and rarely into large industrial undertakings. A. A. Skal'kovskii complained that the inhabitants of Odessa were insufficiently alert to industrial opportunities. Few in the city, he affirmed, were willing to invest in enterprises that demanded patience and time, or, as he termed it, "affaires de longue haleine."[78] In the view of those who authored the centenary volume on Odessa, the merchants of the city had been attached to the grain trade for so long that they could not "transfer to the new ways of trade-industrial activities."[79] The French consul discerned lack of imagination on the part of the city's commercial community at the time of Ferdinand de Lesseps's visit. His talk on the commercial possibilities for the Black Sea region upon completion of the Suez Canal failed to stimulate wide interest:

> Odessa, despite its great reputation as a commercial and maritime city, has only its grain merchants who are *au courant* of the sigificant financial and industrial operations of the rest of Europe.[80]

Nor were the merchants much attracted to manufactures. There were, of course, some exceptions. The Rodocannachi invested in a jute factory, a steam mill, steamship lines, a metal plant, chinaware manufactures, and other industries.[81] The Ralli family tried a hand at banking. But, for the most part, Greek firms such as these favored diversification in their commercial ventures rather than long-term capital commitments in industry.[82] Even the biggest merchants tended to return their profits to commerce or to spend them in ostentatious living.

Speculation

Finally, the rapid growth of the city fueled speculation in real estate. In 1870, the American consul noted:

> Capitalists are everywhere investing in real estate, the universal belief being that Odessa and South Russia are destined before long to exercise a much greater influence upon European commerce and industry.[83]

The fever mounted in 1871:

> The exciting speculations in real estate, so well known in the Western cities of America, are now for the first time witnessed at Odessa. The same is true respecting the lands situated within a long radius from here. The richness of the soil and comparative mildness of the climate of South Russia, now that railway facilities for travel are afforded, are attracting a large emigration from the colder and less thrifty regions of the north. All real property has doubled in value within a very few years and the upward tendency is more rapid now than at any previous moment. Large fortunes are to be quickly made in this region of the world, by immediate investments in real estate.[84]

The coming of the railroad was a principal cause of this speculative fever:

The railway connections with Central Europe and with the interior of Russia have largely added to the floating population of Odessa and increased the permanent population and business of the place.[85]

The railroad made it possible to reach Vienna in forty-eight hours. Mail from London came in five days and from New York in fourteen whereas ten years earlier, it had taken a month to communicate with the eastern shores of the United States. (It currently takes three weeks.) In the twelve years of his consulate, Timothy Smith had never seen such a boom:

The great number of hotels and private residences needed to accommodate the increasing population has greatly stimulated activity in building and almost fabulously increased the prices of property and of rents. All is movement, commotion and *go ahead.*[86]

Writing in 1874, the British consul observed:

. . . housebuilding has throughout last year held a conspicuous place. The increasing wealth of the mercantile classes had led to a demand for houses of a superior description.[87]

Indeed, merchants not only embellished their houses, but some of them accumulated many. In 1873, the Greek merchant G. Marazli, known for his philanthropy, possessed at least eleven buildings worth nearly 300,000 rubles, or 0.7 percent of the value of all the private buildings in Odessa. Theodore Ralli owned fewer buildings, but the total value exceeded 900,000 rubles or 1.69 percent of the value of all private real estate in Odessa at the time.[88] The consul further noted that, as rents went up, banks loaned mortgage money easily, and "banks went on making advances on the security of new buildings and by the end of the year [1873], with the money thus obtained, 600 new blocks of first-class houses were erected."[89] In 1870, the number of private buildings was 7,778, representing a 30 percent increase over the 5,303 privately owned buildings registered in 1869.[90]

Inevitably, heated speculation prepared the way for financial crises. Odessa was the more vulnerable, as its commerce linked it closely to western Europe, and its own economy was sensitive to international business cycles. A financial panic, beginning at Vienna in May 1873, and soon spreading to encompass the capitalistic world, quickly reached Odessa. In October 1873, the French consul reported to his Foreign Ministry that "There is not a day in which there is not registered a new [bankruptcy] victim." These bankruptcies, in his opinion, were caused by the easy credit handed out by new banks in Odessa; the situation was further aggravated by the poor harvest in Novorossiia. The facility with which the courts declared bankruptcies also inflated the number. Thanks to the lack of thoroughness in conducting investigations and to unscrupulous lawyers, firms heavily in debt quickly distributed their assets to family and friends in order to be declared bankrupt and be absolved of their debts.[91]

Without credit or orders, commercial establishments either folded or faced near ruin. Without sufficient grain, peasants faced starvation. The crisis, extending into the spring and summer of 1874, helped provoke the movement of liberal youth known as the "going to the people." Hundreds of well-meaning young people journeyed to the south of Russia, in order to help the peasants improve their lot. They hoped to instruct the disadvantaged and raise their political consciousness. Many of the peasants did not await these unexpected benefactors but instead fled to the cities. Those who came to Odessa could not have arrived at a more inopportune moment—business was bad, industry was slowing down.

In October 1874, the American consul reported, "There have been during the past quarter some heavy failures of merchants."[92] Cultivators, people in transportation, brokers, nearly all within reach of the Black Sea and the Sea of Azov felt the hard times. The scarcity of money, interrupted trade, and languishing industry affected nearly all workers. Real estate banks, established during the recent boom years, folded, affecting business and consequently workers as well.[93]

In 1875, some thirty different enterprises in Odessa closed down.[94] Crop failures between 1873 and 1875 increased the number of unemployed still further. The underground newspaper *Vpered* devoted an article to the pitiful condition of Odessa's day laborers. Many of them felt that the recently installed elevated train, the *estakada*, was responsible for putting them out of work.

Foreign Investment

Given the diversion of local capital into land speculations and the uncertainties of the local financial markets, the chief investors in industry at Odessa proved to be foreigners—though not the foreign merchants. The French consul observed—certainly with exaggeration—that in 1864 all factories in Novorossiia were foreign. The largest wool-washing establishments, the mills, chemical factories, soap factories, candle manufactories, paper mills—all were, he claimed, in the hands of foreigners.[95] He continued:

> The sugar factories in the interior belong to the large proprietors, either Russian or Polish, it is true, but they are greatly supported by government decrees and funds; but it is well known even there it is the foreigner who is the principal support, for all the factories without exception, are run by French, English, German or Swiss managers and mechanics.[96]

With time, even the sugar refineries were largely of foreign ownership. The American consul reported that in 1910 there was one Belgian sugar factory in Podillia. By 1911, there were seven foreign refineries. Then, "four more works were taken over completely and controlling interests in seven others were secured by foreign capital during 1912. The Belgian company, Sucrier Général, at present owns shares in five Russian sugar factories, valued at $1,158,000."[97]

The French consul, with more prejudice than insight, asserted that Russians were incapable of becoming capitalists, claiming that the Russian was not a warrior, not a farmer, not a navigator, not a merchant, not an industrialist, nor even an organizer. His only genius, he averred, was for disorder, and Russian disorder was not like that of the Spanish, "but disorder raised to the state of a social institution."[98]

One of the chief sources of capital was foreign joint-stock enterprises. Foreign companies, British, German, and Belgian respectively, built the waterworks, the gaslights, and the tramway. As Table 8.5 (following page) shows, in 1899 there were eight Belgian stock companies in Odessa, one French, and one English. Most of them were new arrivals. The total capital investment was 12,181,000 rubles, nearly as great as the 15,282,928 invested by Russian stockholders. In addition to these joint-stock companies, there were about five hundred foreign industrial establishments.[99]

Foreign capital found its way to Odessa, but not in massive amounts. Government policy, through guaranteeing lucrative returns, worked to divert investments elsewhere. As the British consul noted in 1900, Belgian capital, amounting to many millions of pounds sterling, had been invested in South Russian mines. These undertakings produced large profits and afforded employment to many hundreds of Belgian experts.[100]

Table 8.5

Foreign Firms in Odessa in 1899

Firm	Nationality	Capital (in rubles)	Year Founded
Jacquot French Candle Co.	French	3,000,000	1881
Odessa Tramway Co.	Belgian	2,539,000	1883
Cotton and Jute Manufacturing Co.	English	1,000,000	1886
Bottle and Cork Co.	Belgian	750,000	1895
Metallurgical Co. of Odessa*	Belgian	468,000	1895
Tile Co. of Odessa	Belgian	375,000	1896
Oils and Chemical Products Co.	Belgian	1,500,000	1896
Iron Products, Foundry and Chain Mftrg. Co.	Belgian	1,612,000	1897
Omnibus Company of Odessa	Belgian	375,000	1899
Cement Company of Odessa	Belgian	562,000	1895

*No longer in operation.

Source: MAE, *RC*, 23, 1901, p. 31: "Mouvement maritime, industriel, commercial d'Odessa en 1899."

In 1875, in the midst of the depression, the Odessa Committee investigating the sad state of trade and manufactures concluded: "A complete reform in the industrial conditions of Odessa is the only means of averting its decline, and this cannot be effected without a thorough revival of credit which the existing local private banks cannot give and which Government alone can give."[101] Private credit banks, founded in 1870, had put their money into property, not industry. "Odessa was possessed with a mania for house property, which embellished the town with fine buildings, but a natural reaction followed. The money market became tight, bankruptcies followed one after the other, and this in its turn caused a reaction in the operations of commercial banks."[102] The committee, therefore, recommended that in the absence of private credit, the State should "create at Odessa an institution of the nature of the French 'Crédit Mobilier' and so develop a manufacturing industry." They concluded:

> To sum up in a few words, capital at Odessa must seek fresh forms of investment, and not adhere to its old track. Certain difficulties always

attend a transfer of capital, and they would be peculiarly felt here, where the majority of our capitalists are mistrustful and inexperienced, and whose knowledge of industry is limited.[103]

In commenting on this report, the British consul noted:

With regard to the institution of a "Crédit Mobilier" nature which the committee suggest should be introduced here, I apprehend such an institution is well suited to a country having abundance of skilled labour seeking employment, but at Odessa where the committee admit the population to be "sparse and unsettled," where the relations between employer and workman are ill defined, and all in favour of the latter . . . where the capitalists are "mistrustful and ignorant of any kind of industry"; where fuel is dear and water has to be bought, and where there are no markets in the vicinity for manufactures, I cannot believe with the committee that industrial undertakings will be developed to the extent they anticipate.[104]

The British consul went on to state that if industrial ventures were undertaken, "the capital made by the grain trade might be swallowed up." He proceeded to draw a dismal picture of industry at Odessa:

Iron foundries and engineers' establishments cannot compete with the agencies established here of English engineers such as Ransome and Sims, Clayton and Shuttleworth, Robery and Company. Soap and stearine candle manufactories, paper mills, linseed oil mills, saw mills have failed.

The proprietor of the only wool-washing establishment here was so dissatisfied with the result that he hanged himself, as did the principal importer of colonial goods.

Brewers, sweetmeat and Russian biscuit manufacturers, and distillers of spirits have done fairly well.

To expect Odessa to become a flourishing centre of manufacturing industry on an entirely artificial basis, may, I think, be considered a chimera.[105]

The consul admitted that "Odessa and South Russia generally would be benefited by the creation of a successful manufacturing industry . . . , but I cannot see the same grounds for anticipating success as the committee do." Not entirely unbiased, he believed that the economy would be better off if it would "free the import trade from the heavy tariff which now, except in years of exceptional prosperity, almost excludes it [prosperity], and to retain only sufficient [tariff] to give an incentive to good work, which is now absent, the consequence being inferior work at a high price."[106]

Patterns of Growth

Table 8.6 presents an overview of the number of factories, their employees, and their output across the last decades of the nineteenth century.

Initially, nearly all of Odessa's manufacturers were what we are calling "induced" industries; that is, they involved the processing of raw materials, which were for the most part locally produced. Thus, well into the 1890s, the chief factories produced tallow, flour, macaroni, starch, sugar, salt, alcohol, mineral water, margarine (popular, since it could be consumed on holy days), canned fish, soap, candles, bone meal, glue, leather, hats, jute sacks, paper, rope, plows, scales, white iron, furniture, bricks, butter, chemicals, vegetable oils, and dyes.

With cattle still fairly numerous as late as the 1860s, tallow remained one of the area's chief manufactures. A versatile lubricant, tallow had many uses. For example, the British packed the cartridges for their new Enfield rifles in tallow. They also supplied these rifles and cartridges to their Indian army of Sepoys with unexpectedly disastrous results. The Indian soldiers were expected to lick off the substance. The Hindus among them regarded the making of cow tallow as sacrilegious, and the Muslims looked on pig tallow with disgust. When officers tried to force them to lick the bullets spread with tallow, they provoked the great Indian mutiny of 1859.

An American woman commented on the manufacture of tallow within the confines of the city in the late 1860s:

> Next to the churches, the most prominent buildings were the great stone granaries and the slaughter-houses, where countless cattle—the gray herds of the steppe—are converted into tallow.[107]

Some of the poor beasts that brought grain to port to supply European tables with bread provided their candlelight as well!

The French consul recommended that the Russians might themselves manufacture candles, instead of shipping 70 million kilograms of tallow abroad each year. He further noted that the region could expand its exports in stearic acid, lard, bone charcoal, gelatin, glue, and other animal products, with slight effort. However, the South Ukraine continued to ship raw tallow in great quantities; for reasons previously considered, it was slow to claim from others these more specialized—and more remunerative—manufacturing processes.[108] Even in the 1890s, about 6 percent of all factory workers prepared animal products such as tallow.[109]

Table 8.6

Industries in Odessa, 1859–1914

Year	Number of Factories*	Number of Workers	Total City Population	Percentage to Total	Production in Rubles
1859	53	1,015	114,265	.09	3,374,750
1863	78				2,120,108
1867	79				5,655,262
1869	110		244,609		8,610,000
1873	159				12,660,391
1874	166	3,715			14,578,936
1875	167	3,807			16,269,412
1876	168				15,208,070
1877	151				10,905,797
1880	206		219,300		28,014,000
1884	218	6,820			27,356,711
1885	222	6,000	245,000	2.49	22,906,000
1890	334	9,000	313,687	2.86	28,154,000
1891	420	9,816	340,438	2.88	27,535,979
1893	424	11,500	340,526	3.38	32,918,000
1894	355	11,306	350,000	3.23	59,129,760
1896	410	15,715	400,000	3.93	40,515,000
1897	432	18,826	403,815	4.66	48,618,000
1898	478	22,178	410,000	5.41	61,373,000
1899	500	20,859	410,000	5.09	60,711,978
1900	484	20,220	450,000	4.45	58,961,000
1901	477	20,629	460,000	4.48	65,100,000
1903	430	21,630			72,229,689
1906	417		461,000		78,316,800
1907	371				50,282,684
1908	312	19,166	450,000	4.26	76,339,200
1910	359	18,734	520,000	3.60	86,000,000
1911	370		620,143		92,000,000
1913	405				95,000,000
1914	420		630,000		100,000,000

* Conventionally in Russian industrial censuses, a factory is an establishment employing more than fifteen workers.

Source: Compiled from *Odessa*, 1895, p. 224; *BPP*, 1904 C, 24; *BPP*, 1905 XCII, 21; *Otchet Odesskogo komiteta torgovli*, 1884, Appendix No. 11; GAOO, *f.* 3, *op.* 1, *d.* 73, *l.* 8; GAOO, *f.* 3, *op.* 1, *d.* 70, *l.* 75; GAOO, *f.* 274, *op.* 1, *d.* 12, *l.* 59; GAOO, *f.* 274, *op.* 2, *d.* 4, *ll.* 28, 39, 91, 175, 185–90; GAOO, *f.* 274, *op.* 1, *d.* 12, *l.* 73; Ekerle, 1916, pp. 67–71.

Predictably, the largest single sector of Odessa's early industry was food processing. At the end of the 1890s, this segment accounted for 66 percent of all industrial production, in terms of value. But it engaged only 29 percent of the workers, in 32 percent of the factories.[110] These statistics suggest that the food processing plants were highly mechanized. The new canning industry, which processed meats, fruits, fish, and vegetables, was growing:

> The Odessa industry [reported the British consul in 1904] in preserved foods has progressed in a manner surpassing even the expectations of the manufacturers, and is in strong contrast to the decay which has set in in other places, e. g. Reval, Riga and Libau. It has latterly received a large influx of capital.[111]

Flour was also one of the most important of the food products. It served the fast-growing urban population, and growing quantities were exported, notably to northern Russia (St. Petersburg), to Constantinople, Egypt, and Poland. The late arrival in Odessa of steam mills meant that the flour long remained expensive. At the end of the 1860s for example, Marseilles could import wheat from Odessa, mill it into flour, ship the flour to Alexandria, and sell it at lower prices than the flour shipped directly from Odessa to Alexandria.[112] Nonetheless, in 1869 flour milling was the largest industry in Odessa. There were twelve steam mills, which produced flour worth 3.6 million rubles.[113] By 1881, Odessa possessed twenty-one steam mills, and over 3 million rubles were earned from flour exports.[114] High freight rates added to the price. For example, in 1908, freight rates from Odessa to Alexandria were four times as high as from Marseilles to Alexandria.[115] In 1902, the flour industry in Odessa received a setback when one of the largest companies was almost entirely destroyed by fire.[116] The tobacco industry represented the second largest industry in 1869. Some fifteen factories produced 1.9 million rubles worth of goods.[117]

The first large sugar beet refinery was built in 1879. By 1894, some fifteen steam engines rumbled in its service. Its workers, who lived in factory housing, numbered 720. The factory even possessed an infirmary with fourteen beds. In 1891, Odessa exported 14 million rubles worth of sugar.[118] By 1905, there were two sugar refineries, employing a total of 1,274 persons. Most of the sugar was consumed in the southern regions. Persia, however, also purchased some as long as it was sent in the shape of "Marseilles loaves."[119] By 1910, the number of workers had increased to 1,522, and the value of sugar production had risen to 11,694,600 rubles, of which only about 2 million rubles were received from exports. The number of infirmary beds rose to twenty-two, and the factory now ran an elementary school for its workers.[120] But such large industrial establishments remained the exception. In 1869, by another count there were 6,618 workers and 121 factories producing 8.7 million rubles in goods.[121]

In spite of growth, Odessa lagged well behind the other great cities of the empire and abroad. A Russian scholar, who wrote an article on the economic situation at Odessa in 1874, noted too that Odessa contained three times fewer industrial workers than St. Petersburg and four times fewer than contemporary Berlin.[122] A quarter of a century later, the British consul assessed the industrial productivity of the city. Flour was no longer the leading product, but no industrial "take-off" had occurred either. His report showed that the seven most productive industries in Odessa were the sugar refineries, tea packing plants, paint and varnish factories, cork firms, tanneries, jute factories, and machinery and agricultural machinery works. The values of output of the sugar refineries (16,938,393 rubles) and of the tea packing houses (15,157,066 rubles) were both well more than double that of the third leading industry, the milling of flour (5,864,169).[123]

About 1900, Odessa was entering the second phase of its industrial expansion. By then, substitution industries were showing considerably more vigor than the manufactures processing vegetable and animal products, which had been the first to develop.

Foremost among these substitution industries was metallurgy. Metal products constituted 12 percent of the value of manufactured goods in the city in the late 1890s. Some 1,650 workers, or about 24 percent of the working force, were employed in metallurgical plants.[124]

To be sure, some of the larger enterprises were already quite venerable, with roots stretching back to the era before emancipation. Among them were the Ghen agricultural machinery factory and the Russian Steam Navigation and Trading Company dockyards. They were followed by the railroad repair yards (1864), the mechanical works of Bellino-Fenderikh (1875), Katz Scales (1881), the New Russian Machinery Construction Company (1884), the Shpolianskii Metallurgical Plant (1885), the Liul'ko Engineering Works, and the Shako Tin Factory.[125]

The history of these big and booming industries in the early twentieth century was singularly turbulent. Iron foundries, for example, fell upon hard times in 1902. The British consul attributed this decline to poor communications, and to a "syndicate of iron smelters" who controlled the supply of pig iron, fixed prices, and refused credit to private buyers.[126] The year 1905, one of war and revolution, severely depressed the economy. The British consul summarized the situation:

> The industrial and commercial life of Odessa is feeling the effects of the war. There has been a general curtailment of credit, and in a country such as this, where business is so largely dependent upon it, the result is easy to see. Firms accustomed to receive large credit now fail to obtain it, and have been forced to reduce the scale of their operations; factories are working short time and few branches of industry remained unaffected. . . . Those industries directly connected with the Far East were naturally the first to suffer. Before the war began there was a large Eastern trade in food-stuffs and other goods, but this has been greatly curtailed.[127]

Wartime disruption of communications and the draining of manpower harmed Odessa's industry, but industrial strikes and revolutionary activity (which we will examine further in Chapter 12) nearly brought it to a standstill, as the French consul recorded:

> Local industry also felt the effects of the general crisis. At the same time that factories saw their activity considerably reduced as a result of lack of orders, the demands of the workers became daily more numerous and the revenge of malcontents consisted of more or less prolonged strikes. All factories produced disappointing results; several even were forced to close because of their losses.[128]

The Russo-Japanese war depleted the thin ranks of workers. The British consul noted: "One direct result of the war . . . is the scarcity of labour caused by reservists being called to the colours to take the place of men who have gone on active service."[129] He further observed that even the absence of a relatively few skilled workers could adversely affect "industries where skill and experience are essential factors in production."

In time, at least by 1913, industries were drawing workers away from the mines, although certainly not in sufficient quantity. The mines themselves were often dependent upon peasants who worked in them only as a last resort.[130] The instability and expense of labor remained a hindrance, according to the American consular report of 1913:

Labor conditions in this district are somewhat peculiar. Workmen complain of the scarcity of employment, while employers unanimously assert that since 1905 it has been impossible to get any steady work out of their laborers. It is claimed that the actual work done by a laborer is three times as expensive as it was less than ten years ago.[131]

The years following 1905 saw only slow improvement—again largely because of strikes. Higher wages with no corresponding improvement of quality meant that local manufactures faced heightened competition and earned diminished profits. Local sugar refineries found their usual Persian markets flooded with north Ukrainian sugar. The preserved food industry slumped because the price of tin had risen.[132] The British reported that many firms went bankrupt.[133]

The French consul wrote of the year 1908 that high hopes had been entertained for a rebound from postwar doldrums. But these expectations had been disappointed. Significantly, construction had not resumed its activity. The paltry importation of chemicals also indicated a slowdown of industrial activity. He continued, "The lack of credit, the consequences of the political situation and the poor reputation of the place explain much."[134] All three of Odessa's match factories were closed down, and the tin factories worked only three or four days a week.[135]

There were 25 percent fewer factories in 1908 than in 1906, but the reduction in output was only 2.5 percent. Tea packing and sugar refining fell off sharply. Because smaller firms failed, the average annual output per factory increased.[136] Also, the average number of workers per factory increased; for example, in the textile industry the numbers rose from an average of forty-eight in 1906 to sixty-one in 1908, a phenomenon that Trotsky suggested made revolutionary agitation easier.[137] By 1913, however, smelting flourished in Odessa and in the region. Renewed railroad construction boosted their activity.[138]

In 1908, the British consul presented a lengthy report about the iron mines of Kryvyi Rih. He sketched the ancient history of the site as well as the relatively recent exploitation of the mines (some quarter of a century previously). He gave a list of valuable elements to be found there: iron ore, manganese, rock salt, kaoline, high-grade quartz sand for glass-making, coal, and so forth. "All that was wanted," he stated, "to tap these great sources was intellect, energy and capital." In his opinion too, "a good deal of which three requirements was eventually supplied from abroad."[139]

Despite the promise offered by the Kryvyi Rih region, the state of the metallurgical industry in Odessa seemed to him singularly gloomy:

> The general condition of the metallurgical trade was in 1909 most difficult. The purchasing power of the population has fallen off and orders were small; in the town there was little building, so that the demand could not keep pace with the producing capacity of the metallurgical factories. Exportation at a loss, reduced as against 1907— improved nothing.[140]

For all this tortured history, Odessa retained its reputation in metals, as the French consul remarked:

> Odessa is a fairly important center for mechanical objects. Besides, in the South in general, they make machines, machine tools, railway tracks, locomotives, agricultural machinery and material for the factories and railroads at Kiev, Odessa and Sevastopol.[141]

The thriving canning industry stimulated the production of tin plate, as the American consul informed his government in 1913: "For forty years, beginning with 1867, South Russia was the center of the tin-plate industry, and Odessa had more tin-plate factories than all the rest of the Empire. . . ."[142]

The exceptions to the general advance after 1906 were the cement industry, which had almost disappeared; glass manufacture which had been diminishing steadily since 1897; and brickmaking, which had fallen off after a drop in the construction business. But, by 1911, there was reason for cautious optimism concerning the city's economic prospects:

> The clearest sign that the disturbed years following 1905 are being forgotten and that confidence is being restored is the active resumption of house building. For several years building was practically stopped. Rents have risen and the population has increased. This together with the rapid construction of a network of electric tramways, has caused a great demand for new houses, of which many are built in parts recently reckoned as in the country.[143]

Not only house construction, but various other industries might be considered as barometers of the city's improving economic climate. The jute factory, one of the city's major industries, in 1908, produced 1,824,000 rubles of goods with 1,200 employees. Two years later, the same factory employees produced some 2,500,000 rubles of jute products with 1,240 employees.

Telephone communications were established from about 1911, and the trams in Odessa were at long last electrified. In 1912, a German, Arps, constructed a new plant, made up of eighteen buildings and employing two thousand workers. Importing raw materials from Spain, Australia, and elsewhere, the enterprise manufactured cork, linoleum, and capsules. An American company established still another large factory; it recycled rubber, principally from old galoshes. It exported $388,676 worth of reclaimed rubber, with a profit of $26,089. Some American soles and tires had once traversed Odessa's muddy streets![144] Plans were formulated to build a cold storage warehouse capable of holding 450 tons of poultry, game, milk, cheese, and eggs, and 540 tons of fish. Also envisioned was an ice plant, which would supply the city with 216 tons of ice every forty-eight hours.

In the 1910 Industrial and Agricultural Exhibition in Odessa, many saw a hopeful sign that the city's fortunes had turned the corner. Such a hope was expressed in the official catalogue:

To all it is known, that in the past few years Odessa, as a trade-industrial center, fell remarkably and even lost its former greatness. In order to take the city out of this grave and depressing condition, new forces, new energy are needed; decisive and powerful thrusts are needed which would force the city to repair itself and which would push it onto a new path.[145]

The French vice-consul was not as optimistic:

Commerce and industry of South Russia in general, and of Odessa, in particular, saw in it [the Exhibition] a means for animating somewhat the commercial activity of this city, already greatly diminished by the competition from Kherson and Nikolaev.[146]

An Italian journalist noted in 1906 that Odessa was a "città di traffico più che d'industrie."[147] Had he returned in 1914, he might have changed his mind. In 1907, Odessa produced 50 million rubles in value of goods. Seven years later that figure had doubled (see Table 8.6). While still only a small percentage of Odessa's population was engaged in industrial work, and most of the industrial products were consumed within the empire, there appeared to be promise of industrial expansion. Indeed, there was to be a great expansion—but only to serve the needs of war.

CHAPTER NINE

Foreign Export, Apogee and Decline, 1861–1914

> The song of Odessa has been sung. It will fall into decline and face a slow death.
> —P. S. Chekhovich, 1894, in reference to Odessa's port

Odessa had risen to prominence principally as a port of export for the characteristic products of the southern Ukraine. Inevitably, the export trade continued to play a major role in the city's development in the second half of the nineteenth century. It also functioned as a port of entry into the Russian Empire. In the late nineteenth century, however, two factors were slowly undermining its status as portal to the empire. The first was the aging of its port facilities; Odessa was falling behind rival harbors on the Black Sea littoral in its ability to handle bulky cargoes cheaply and efficiently. The second was the decline of the South Ukraine as a major supplier of wheat to the world.

The Far East

One of the more exotic of Odessa's commercial links tied it to the Far East and made it the tea entrepôt of the Russian Empire. In 1871, two years after the opening of the Suez Canal, Russian ships sailed through the canal to India and China and returned with tea, cotton, and gums.[1] The French consul marked the historic event: "Last March the steamer *Tshihatcheff* of the Russian Steam and Navigation sailed to China."[2] By August 17 of the same year, the ship had returned to Odessa with 56,000 *pud*s of tea. This was the first direct sailing between the Russian Empire (Odessa) and China (Shanghai). To celebrate the occasion, some 250 merchants, notables, and members of the Navigation Company assembled at a banquet. The most popular toast was to Ferdinand de Lesseps, to whom the exuberant merchants of Odessa sent a telegram of congratulations.[3]

A special maritime unit, founded during the Russo-Turkish War of 1877–1878 as a naval auxiliary, took up mercantile ventures at war's end with financial aid from the State. Since the ships were purchased through private donations, the unit was called the "Volunteer Fleet." Initially, it consisted of only seven steamers, but, according to the British consul, they were "fine fast boats of large carrying capacity."[4] They carried away "troops, convicts, emigrants and stores to Vladivostok, Saghalien [Sakhalin], and the Russian possessions in the Sea of Japan whence they bring back time-expired men, and frequently large consignments of tea from China."[5]

Kuprin, the writer, described a scene at the Odessa harbor:

In it were loaded on their way to the Far East, the yellow, thick-funneled steamers of the Volunteer Fleet that absorbed every day large trains of goods or of prisoners.[6]

In addition to the human freight, the ships carried sugar, cloth, agricultural implements, tools, and seeds for sowing. In 1898, the British consul claimed, "Odessa may be said to have become the centre of the tea trade in the country."[7] And Odessa had a near monopoly of Russian trade with Port Arthur and Vladivostok by the turn of the century. At that time there were about twenty-one outward sailings to the Far East each year. In 1900, for example, the Volunteer Fleet carried out about twenty-three thousand tons of general cargo, and thirty-four thousand of government stores. Private passengers were few—only 703. The rest were soldiers (over 17,000), emigrants (nearly 5,000), and convicts—438.[8] But even this trade encountered bad times in the early years of the twentieth century. As the United States consul explained in October 1903:

With the completion of the Siberian Railroad and owing to the enormous contraband traffic via Manchuria into Russian Siberia, these volunteer fleet steamers find but little cargo to transport from European Russia. For more than a year these steamers have been laid up at Odessa.[9]

Just before the war with Japan, the Volunteer Fleet planned to undertake runs between Naples, New York, and Rio de Janeiro, mainly for the purpose of carrying Italian emigrants to the Americas.[10] The war suspended expansion and indeed any commercial operations at all. After the war, the fleet resumed its tea trade but still relied heavily on government subsidies. In 1911, the British consul recounted its history:

> Ten years ago the trade to the Russian East was a matter of the first importance to Odessa; it developed as more and more emigrant peasants went Eastwards, and raised great hopes for the commercial and industrial classes in this town [Odessa]. Then came the war with Japan which brought this trade to a standstill. After the war the Russian Government made it a first care to restore prosperity to her possessions in the extreme East, and to that end introduced there free trade (*porto-franco*). Though this no doubt helped the Eastern possessions considerably, it ended the trade relations between Russia on the Pacific and Russia at home.[11]

With the subsequent abolition of these privileges, Odessa resumed her primary position in trading with Russian eastern ports; trade grew from about 1910. It seemed at first that Odessa's eastern commerce might compensate for losses in the West.[12] But, in the end, cereal export to the West determined the city's and the region's commercial fate.

The Western Trade

From 1860 to 1864, the total amount of wheat exported from Odessa was 77,846 million *pud*s. Over the five-year period 1885–1889, the total grew to 226,097 million *pud*s.[13] But even as it grew, the pattern of this trade was changing. Although it was little realized at the time, a significant break came with the Crimean War (1853–1855). During the war, the Russian government imposed an embargo on grain exports for two years. Nearly all the belligerents were prime grain purchasers from Russia. But in the end, use of the "wheat weapon" backfired. Europe had to search for a new breadbasket and found several. To make its *pasta* and *pane*, Tuscany, for example, turned to Spain, Egypt, and Turkey for wheat. The recourse was, to be sure, temporary. After the war, Tuscany, and ultimately most of the newly formed Kingdom of Italy, once more purchased wheat in large volumes from the Russian Empire. In the years immediately preceding World War I, between two-thirds and four-fifths of Italy's imported wheat came from the Russian Empire.[14]

On the other hand, during the embargo, England, France, and other northern European countries looked across the Atlantic for wheat. At American ports, the price of wheat in 1856 had soared to

2.4 times the level of 1852.[15] The steamboat and the railroad were diminishing distances and giving European purchasers access to the abundant produce of the New World.

As the French consul viewed the global trade situation in 1879:

> The development of steam navigation, the discovery by Maury of the periodicity of etesian winds which shortens considerably maritime crossings, the opening of the Suez Canal, the numerous migrations of peoples to new colonies, the introduction of machines to agriculture—all that in a short lapse of time—permit to the pioneers of the New World, to the farmers of the Indies, to the settlers of Algeria and to the squatters of New Holland to cultivate grain and to produce wool destined to invade the docks of London and the storehouses of Marseilles.[16]

As we have seen, the late construction of railroads in the empire placed wheat producers, with their carts and barges, at a distinct disadvantage. Not only was American wheat cheap, but it was clean and sorted by kind. Most important, Americans were willing and able to ship wheat flour, a commodity the Russians could not adequately prepare and market.[17] And in the mid-1860s, when Russia was attempting to adjust to the end of the war and the liberal reforms, the northern, wheat-producing American states, having lost their southern customers through civil war, offered more wheat than ever before to the world markets.

The French consul recognized the advantages that good transport gave the American farmers:

> In fact, although America does not possess land as endowed as that of the black soil of Russia, or as fertile as along the banks of the Nile, or the Ganges valley, it has learned, nonetheless, through the bold, enterprising and practical spirit of its citizens, to enhance the richness of its soil by using machines, by digging canals and building railroads to transport its products from the most remote parts of its interior as far as the wharves of its maritime cities.[18]

He dismissed as a foolish dream the hope that South Russia could compete with America. There was only one railway line linking Bessarabia and Podillia to Odessa. The inefficient carting cost fifteen kopecks per *chetvert* per day. He continued: " 'You pay,' wrote a merchant from London to one of his merchants here, 'to transport grain from your suburbs [of Odessa] to the ship four-fifths of the price from Chicago to New York.' "[19]

The entry of American wheat into European markets had the effect of shifting the grain market from London to Liverpool and from Marseilles to Le Havre and Nantes. There was no doubt—northern Europe was turning its back to the Mediterranean and was looking across the Atlantic.

With hindsight, the British consul pronounced in 1872: "England since the Crimean War has shaken off her dependence on Russia for several great articles of produce. . . ."[20] The dramatic shift by English purchasers from Russian to American wheat is reflected in the following figures. At the end of the 1860s and the start of the 1870s, Russia still supplied England with 35 percent of her imported grain. In the years before World War I, Great Britain imported from the Russian Empire only 14 to 16 percent of its cereal needs. By 1913, the figure had slumped to 9 percent. The United States, on the other hand, supplied England with only 6.2 percent of its needs in the early part of the century; in 1876–1880, American wheat accounted for 54 percent of England's imports.[21] Inevitably, the Black Sea ports keenly felt this constriction of their traditional markets.

Although the Russian share of the world market was declining, the absolute quantity of exported wheat increased five times from 1861 to 1913. The demand for cereals in an increasingly industrialized, urbanized Europe continued to grow. To help offset its declining share of the wheat market, Russia shipped greater volumes of rye, oats, barley, and corn. Germany, for example, in 1913 acquired 88 percent of its imported rye, 84 percent of its imported barley, 65 percent of its imported oats, and only 30 percent of its imported wheat from the Russian Empire.[22] This shift in foreign purchases from wheat to rye and other grains was a mixed blessing. World demand for these grains was not as strong as that for wheat, since these crops were more easily raised than wheat, and they commanded lower prices. Even the expansion of rye exports proved to be a temporary phenomenon. Over the years 1876–1880, rye accounted for 32 percent of Russia's cereal export, but by 1908 it had slumped to only 11 percent.[23] Shifting crops and changing customers left Russia ill-prepared to meet various crises it encountered in the closing decades of the nineteenth century. By 1917, "the grain shipped from Odessa was chiefly hard winter wheat and barley. Very little rye or oats and corn were exported through this port."[24]

The paradox is that reputation lasted longer than performance. The prospect that the Ukraine might serve as the principal breadbasket of industrialized Germany misled the Kaiser, as it later did the Führer. Why did the Russian Empire fail to maintain its supremacy as a wheat exporter? Three factors largely explain the decline: (1) poor quality control; (2) inadequate marketing procedures; and (3) inefficient transportation facilities.[25]

Quality Control

One of the most frequent complaints about Russian grain was its uneven quality. The complaints grew louder after emancipation. By all accounts the cereal arrived with a high admixture of impurities—sand, insects, and so forth. The practice of "stretching" the quantity of grain with admixtures of sand was so widespread that it even elicited a cartoon in Odessa's local humor magazine.[26] The varieties of Russian grain were so numerous that it was difficult to classify any single lot by type. In the United States there were five or six grades of wheat, and they were delivered to the buyer pre-sorted, by type and by grade. Russian wheat came in fifty to sixty types, making it difficult for the purchaser to specify his desired kind of wheat. A British consular report makes the problem clear:

> The American wheat, which is clean and of good quality, and not a mixture of several sorts as ours, is preferred to Russian corn even though the latter is cheaper.
>
> The ruinous practice we [at Odessa] have of mixing our wheat does us serious harm, discredits our corn, and prevents sales being made in advance except on conditions onerous to us. Almost invariably disputes arise between the receiver and the seller, and we have to pay heavy indemnities.[27]

Ten years later, the situation had grown worse:

> It is this diversity in the kinds of wheat which renders South Russia so favourable a field for the operations of the manipulator. When a merchant has contracted to deliver a cargo of wheat, he finds it impossible to furnish all of one quality, and he accordingly employs the middleman to buy different parcels which he mixes together until the product comes up to the required sample. It will readily be understood what opportunities are thus offered to unscrupulous agents to palm off inferior or damaged grain on their principals, who have to take extreme precautions against the fraud inevitable to the situation.[28]

Odessa's active Committee on Trade and Manufacturing was acutely aware of the problem of quality control and repeatedly drew attention to it in its reports throughout the 1880s.[29]

The middleman's reputation was not at stake through such acts of adulteration, for he represented many clients who, for the most part, did not realize that a good reputation would in the long run promote more business. For both producer and broker, the short-term gain was of paramount interest.

Apart from deliberate falsification, the quality of the grain suffered from moisture. Exposed to dampness when dragged in carts, heaped on railroad platforms, carried in open railway cars, and dumped on wharves, Russian grain often was soaked. Even after drying at additional expense, the grain was not of the same quality as before.

About 1890, the government hit upon a solution for both quality and moisture control: grain elevators. The first major experiment was to be in Odessa at the terminus of the South West Railroad Company, which was located about a mile outside the city.[30] Two large buildings were constructed at a cost of a half million rubles. About 12.5 million *chetvert*s of grain (100,000 quarters) could be sorted and stored there. The grain was weighed, cleansed, and sorted automatically and the whole installation was lighted by electricity. E. Leigh Harris, an English contractor, was in charge of constructing the elevators. Unfortunately, as soon as the buildings were completed, one burned to the ground and had to be replaced.

The goal was to induce producers to bring their grain in good condition in order to have it placed in the highest category possible. The bulk grain of uniform quality would then pass to the ports for further inspection and the buyer would be certain of homogeneous grain, since the opportunities for dishonest admixturing would be reduced.[31]

It was, unfortunately, only a beginning. Many elevators and sorting procedures were needed before clean grain could be obtained. In 1901, a V. G. Hertz, who seems to have been a large landowner in Bessarabia, made a report to the local *zemstvo* about purchase orders of grain:

> Mr. Hertz has just returned from a trip abroad to inquire into the reasons why longtime purchasers of Russian wheat have ceased to take them and now prefer grain coming from elsewhere. The response he received everywhere, he related, is that it is because of the uncertainty they experience in buying Russian products with regard to the exactness in filling orders. One can never count on [Russians], [or] on their good faith in making up any deficiencies in the order. . . . To renew mutual confidence, that is the first condition for regaining our former buyers.[32]

As late as 1917, an American grain expert noted that "most of the exporters operated warehouses of their own which have floors, usually of dirt, occasionally of wood, but only infrequently of cement."[33] The primitive and harmful procedures are described:

> These warehouses operated by all but the most important exporters were equipped with sacks, handpower fanning mills, wooden shovels, brooms, thermometers, samplers, and apparatus for determining weight per volume, and scales. The grain received in sacks was dumped on the floor in a pile. During warehousing, the grain was turned over continuously with shovels to keep it from heating. When grain continued to arrive beyond the storage capacity of the warehouse it was piled into heaps outside and covered usually with canvas but often was left uncovered. The storage of grain and this method of handling were typical throughout Russia.

The one elevator in Odessa serviced much of the grain that arrived by rail, however. Grain came in sacks (an added expense) "because the railway cars were not lined with matched boards to permit shipment in bulk as in the United States." Once the grain was dumped out of the sacks into the elevator, a more modern procedure was observed:

> Much of the grain arriving by rail was conditioned at the elevator and then loaded mechanically into self-dumping wagonettes. Trains of these wagonettes were run to the harbor over a spur of railroad several miles long to an elevated pier and the grain was discharged directly into the hold of an oceangoing steamer under the supervision of the elevator.

Thus, as late as 1917, the loading of ships in Odessa harbor involved a curious mixture of new and old techniques.

Short deliveries also damaged the reputation of Russian suppliers. The American consul at Odessa forwarded to Washington a translation of an article that appeared in a St. Petersburg newspaper; he added the following comment:

> . . . there comes a moment, such as frequently arises in the feverish grain trade, when the local market price is higher, and sometimes even much higher, than that at which the exporter has effected his sale abroad in advance. How does the exporter act? . . . Practice has found a simple way out of it. The exporter then ships to his foreign purchaser not all the cargo according to the contract, but with a more or less considerable "shortage," which in these cases always equals that same sum of money, which he lacks to fulfill his obligations. Yet

he advises his purchaser of having laden the stipulated quantity of grain.[34]

If the purchaser noted the shortage, the seller promised to make it good on the next shipment—a promise he maintained only if the price of grain had fallen sufficiently to allow him to do so without loss. These sharp dealings on the part of middlemen understandably made the buyer wary, and even weary.

Besides these voluntary acts of cheating on quality and quantity, chance happenings, *forces majeures*, also intervened. The villainous insects, never under control, and the vagaries of weather made for uncertain rhythms in the Black Sea grain trade. As the French consul wisely noted:

> There is a forgotten fact in the picture, but an essential one and that is the weather; everyone in Russia knows if there is no rain during the month of May, for example, or no snow in the winter and late frosts come in the spring, the harvests are instantly damaged.[35]

Of course the climate had not changed since emancipation, but more crops and more people were dependent upon it. And it failed frequently, as in 1889, 1891, 1893, 1898, and 1900. World wheat prices were so low in 1892 that it was not worthwhile for the merchants to export it. As a journalist wrote in 1905:

> The grain trade is naturally subject to great fluctuations, for it is dependent on the result of the harvest, which in Russia differs from year to year more than in any other country, and the trade is bound to be very uncertain in quantity.[36]

Marketing Procedures

The continued selling of estates by indebted nobles to richer peasants, colonists, Jews, and *meshchane* who could afford to buy machinery promoted the rationalization of agricultural production. Presumably, inefficient producers departed the steppe and the enterprising moved in. To a certain extent this was occurring; the French consul noted in 1894:

> The introduction, however, of agricultural machines on a vast scale and the transfer of property from the hands of indebted nobles to those of peasants who are taking advantage of low prices to enlarge their acreage, lead one to expect now a rather rapid development of a new class, that of middling peasant proprietors.[37]

One of the results of this multiplication of producers was an increased number of middlemen. In 1890, the British consul explained why the middlemen were so numerous:

The needy condition of the peasant proprietor, who is almost always in want of advances for meeting the demands of the tax-gatherer or for reaping his harvest, which can only be procured from the local moneylenders, his general improvidence and apathy, the enormous distances to be traversed, tracts as large as an average English county being frequently devoid of a railway, or even of a macadamised road, are so many obstacles in the way of the farmer shaking himself free from the middleman, on whose services he must continue to depend for many years to come.[38]

The new elevators were expected not only to improve the quality of the stored grain and to promote uniform sorting procedures, but in the design of the minister of finance, Sergei Witte, they were to reduce the role of middlemen. When the peasants or even the wealthy landowners brought their grain to the station elevators, strategically scattered throughout the countryside, they would receive for whatever quantity of grain they brought, credits for so much grain of a certain grade:

Such warrants being payable at all the Government banks will enable the procurers to obtain the actual market value of his produce without having recourse to the middleman, who, while taking advantage of the peasant's ignorance of the real value of his produce, forms only the first link in a chain of middlemen through which the grain is passed before it is shipped for its destination.[39]

The paternalistic attitude of the government was plain. They spoke of the elevators as a means

towards liberating the tiller of the soil from the meshes of a system of extortion and chicanery, which diverts the profits of husbandry from the industrious peasant into the pockets of the crafty middleman and the calculating speculator.[40]

Nearly a decade later, the British consul laid upon these middlemen chief responsibility for the lack of progress in South Russian agriculture:

So hopelessly in the hands of these intermediaries is the Russian peasant that it is scarcely possible to conclude a bargain with him except through their medium. Long accustomed to this standing source of evil, the agriculturist has ceased to realise the injury done to him by such financial transactions and has become utterly incapable of bettering his condition. It is therefore to be feared that for some time to come the Russian peasant will remain a stranger to prosperity, however mindful the Government may be of his welfare.[41]

Russian economists were aware of the problem. In 1890, A. Borinevich described the chain of middlemen: needy peasants sold their grain to small, local *skupshchiks* (petty buyers) who, through a *makler* (broker), sold it to a larger buyer, who, in turn, sold it in Odessa in the name of a "commissioner or exporter." He observed:

> Often the roles of the dealers of the grain trade are so entertwined, that it is difficult to distinguish where the *makler* ends and the commissioner begins, where the commissioner ends and the exporter begins.[42]

An American agricultural expert marveled at the marketing procedures of South Russia about 1905:

> In Russia, even near the great exporting city of Odessa, the method of buying and handling grain is of the crudest and most primitive kind. The grain is sold by the peasants to speculators or to merchants— country storekeepers, they would be called in America.[43]

While middlemen were proliferating in the countryside, a parallel phenomenon appeared in the city. In 1881, the city administration notified the ministry of internal affairs that the Stock Exchange alone supported sixty brokers, not to speak of all the independent brokers.[44] Some of these brokers evidently decided to enter the exporting business themselves directly as exporters. For just as the big proprietors were reduced in number, so too the large grain exporting firms were leaving Odessa.[45] These large firms were chiefly Greek companies with the Ralli and the Rodocannachi prominent among them.

As early as 1851, the Jewish firm of Fisherovich and Kogan attempted to break the Greek monopoly of the grain trade by lowering its profit to one ruble per *chetvert* of wheat and finally down to twenty-five kopecks. They also competed by achieving a rapid turnover, thus reducing storage costs.[46] In 1863, the British consul at Odessa reported to London that the Jews were "pushing the Greeks altogether aside, and they have become the first bankers and merchants of South Russia."[47] William Hamm, who visited Odessa in the early 1860s, likewise recorded that the Greeks had once held the major share of Odessa's commerce of wheat, wool, tallow, skins, and linseed. Now, however, he observed, "The Greeks are in great decline."[48] A citizen of Odessa wrote that Greeks (in both export and import) "held first place up to the 50's, but at the present time in this business they have gone back to a second level, leaving their place to the Jews."[49] This is almost a verbatim repetition of the words of an expert on the Odessa grain trade:

> The exporters, that is, the trade houses occupied with foreign trade in grain at present are for the most part Jews, at least, the very largest firms, belong to this nationality. This dominance of Jewish houses began not very long ago, but they were successful soon in moving aside to secondary importance the old Greek houses, which for the most part became bankrupt.[50]

There were several reasons for the departure of the Greeks. For one, as the grain export trade became more and more specialized, those firms that dealt only in grain won the lion's share of the business. The Greek firms dealt with many commodities and were important in importing goods to Odessa as well as in exporting. When Odessa ceased to be a free port in 1857, and when the empire adopted a more aggressively protectionist policy, imports became less significant in the total commercial activity. At the same time, British firms began to establish branches of their companies *in situ* at exporting ports to deal with exclusive agents, avoiding such firms as those owned by Greeks. Big family firms, such as that founded by the Alsatian Leopold Louis-Dreyfus, which were large-scale grain exporters, moved into Odessa. As Graham Rees explained it:

> This trend, towards increasing specialization by function in particular commodities rather than in particular areas, contributed to the decline of Greek control over trade in the Mediterranean. These merchants were ousted from Odessa by the Jews and the Germans while British corn merchants extended their influence very considerably and began to buy direct from native exporters in corn-surplus areas such as Russia.[51]

Even as their fortunes faded at Odessa, the Greek merchants, members of pan-Mediterranean family firms, moved on to more lucrative ventures. Textiles, in preference to grain, attracted them in the late nineteenth century. Ralli Brothers established branches in Calcutta (1851), Bombay (1861), and New York (1871). Its trade in India and America was primarily in cotton. In 1866, in a major reorganization, the firm gave up its business in the Russian Empire altogether; it fell to a company known as Scaramanga and Associates.

When the large Greek firms left Odessa, smaller Jewish traders took up the slack. They were superbly suited for this. They had much the same cohesiveness, family connections, and invaluable experience in intermediate business roles. And in this period, when grain exports resulted in slimmer margins of profit, they were willing to accept them.

The American consul thought it instructive to send a copy of an article he had translated from a St. Petersburg newspaper, describing the changes that had recently occurred in Odessa:

> In the matter of exportation from Odessa has taken place a remarkable evolution. Only a few years ago the grain trader in Odessa was a man with large capital, who conducted affairs exclusively at his own "risk and conscience." He purchased from his own money, and if on the exportation of the grain abroad he lost, then those were really his own personal losses. It is clear, that under these circumstances, where the capitalist himself bore all the consequences of the risk, he had to be a large capitalist, since the exportation operations of the grain export trade demanded large means. And we readily observe that in the near past there were here such exporters of grain as Baron Maas, Anatra, Ashkinasy, Ralli and others, and amongst the foreign firms, the Brothers Dreyfus, Brothers Walther. But a long series of unheard of failures of harvests brought such disorganization into the export trade, that in the stead of the former large profits, it began to give quite colossal deficits, and little by little the former large firms entirely stopped the grain operations.[52]

The article goes on to offer this analysis. As there were no longer large capitalist-exporters, only middlemen and brokers remained. But some banker, taking advantage of this situation, might propose to a broker, "You are an expert in the grain trade, but have no money. I have money, but cannot distinguish rye from barley. Let us form a company. I will furnish the money and you will purchase grain and sell it abroad. Of course the foreign exporter will only know you." The banker furnished the middleman with an office, typewriter, and telephone, and thus a business was born! The exporter loaded his merchandise, received his advance from the banker against the bill of lading, which the banker discounted with a foreign company. If the exporter paid for his own purchases, he received an advance from his banker to cover the cost of living and of expenses, on a moderate scale. But if the price of grain rose above the anticipated price for which the exporter received an advance from abroad, then he turned to the usual device of shipping cargoes with shortages. And in the end the foreign purchaser was the only one who lost, as the banker assumed no risk whatsoever, and the exporter "is a mere fiction behind which is screened the banker." The article concluded:

> As a result of all this, confidence in our grain export trade will doubtless be fully undermined and such difficulties will be engendered, which will place this, once splendid commerce, the only one in South Russia, in an impossible position.

An American agronomist who lived in the South Ukraine for several years made this comment in 1917:

> A makler, a peculiarity of Odessa grain trade, was an exporter who had nothing but an Odessa address and a collaborator or two in some West European market. He would obtain a sample of some lot of grain that might become available or he would fabricate a sample which he would send to one of his collaborators. The collaborator would then look for a buyer who was willing to sign a contract. The contract would be mailed to the makler who would then hunt for an exporter willing to pay him a commission for obtaining a contract for the purchase of a given quantity of grain. The exporter would then attempt to assemble a cargo that would more or less match the sample. Such cargoes usually went to arbitration. This gave Odessa a bad name as a grain exporting port.[53]

The common allegation was clearly that Jewish middlemen, exporters, and bankers were exploiting peasants and proprietors producing grain for export; they were ruining former large exporting firms in Odessa, and they were deceiving good customers abroad. In fact, of course, Jews were involved in this commercial sector, as they were in many others, but they were far from being the sole participants.

Transportation

One of America's great advantages in marketing its wheat was the early construction of railroads. In 1863, the French consul reported that a Greek, the head of one of the most important commercial firms of Odessa, lamented:

> It is useless to hold onto the illusion any longer that we can henceforth compete in the English market with American wheat. Whatever the harvest—good or bad—we must endure such long transports,

which are so expensive and during which we suffer so many losses, we must give up sending grain to London. It is to the advantage of our firms in England to buy wheat from the United States.[54]

The cost of carting (and drying soaked grain) and the losses en-route made the system more and more burdensome. Urchins cut holes in the sacks on carts with glass. Observers declared that one could follow the cart trails by the tracks of spilled grain.[55] The children picked up what they could pilfer to sell at the nearest grocer.

The railroad age began in Odessa in 1865 with the completion of the first stretch of road linking Odessa to Balta, a marketplace where goods were exchanged between the *guberniia* of Podillia and the *guberniia* of Kherson. In August of that year, the French consul reported that fifteen thousand men were laying the tracks.[56] Work was completed in September; the cost to the government was 7 million rubles—the rails alone cost over a million rubles.[57] The line would eventually link with Kharkiv and Kiev. The opening ceremony took place in December; two hundred dignitaries attended, among them the archbishop, Governor General Kotsebu, and foreign consuls. They had lunch during the trip to Balta and dinner while returning.[58] The one-way trip covering eighty-five *versts* lasted one hour and forty minutes. In addition to the Balta terminus, there was a small spur off to the village of Parkani, a Bulgarian colony on the Dniester near Bender.

By March 1866, the tsar approved the project to extend the line toward Kiev. Some thirty thousand military criminals began laying tracks. In 1869, the line from Balta reached Ielysavethrad and Krykiv (a port on the right bank of the Dnieper across from Kremenchuk). One of the first railroad bridges in Russia was constructed across the Boh at this time. In 1872, the railroad joined Odessa to Kremenchuk and to Kharkiv and thence to Moscow. This time, a railroad bridge was built across the Dnieper. Eventually, through Kharkiv, Odessa was linked to the two capitals and to Kiev.

No overall plan governed this construction, and it would be a mistake to assume that railroad building in the South Ukraine was designed primarily to carry goods to port cities. Many of the directions taken by the lines served strategic purposes.[59] One of the chief goals was to move troops as quickly as possible to the Turkish border.[60] This haphazard method of railroad building brought many disadvantages to Odessa. The crooked lines built in *ad hoc* spurts resulted in added distances from point to point. For example, the route was unnecessarily long between Odessa and Ielysavethrad. This was also true of the line to Katerynoslav; the distance measured

263 *versts* by post road, but 448 *versts* by rail. Even the railroad line to Kiev had a huge bulge that lengthened the distance from Odessa by 200 kilometers. As late as 1908, the government was planning to construct new lines that would shorten the distance between Odessa and Moscow from 943 to 733 miles and from Odessa to St. Petersburg from 1,212 to 1,095 miles, as well as cutting off 68 miles to Ielysavethrad.[61] It was to be completed by 1914. As the British consul noted in 1874, "Properly speaking, there is no network of railways in Russia. There are separate thread lines which run parallel to one another."[62] Unfortunately, as far as Odessa was concerned, by the time there was a real network, her greatest commercial days had past.

More disastrous for Odessa than excessive distances, however, was the fact that some lines did not connect to Odessa at all. Odessa was bypassed altogether in favor of other Black Sea ports. This was true of the Kharkiv-Mykolaiv branch, which carried grain from Poltava, Kiev, and Ielysavethrad to Mykolaiv. As the British consul said in 1881 of the proposed Kryvyi Rih-Taganrog-Kharkiv lines: "It will probably divert to Nicolaieff [Mykolaiv] much corn."[63] Other lines with favorable tariffs funneled grain from Kursk and Orlovsk *guberniias* to Baltic ports.[64]

In 1874, the British consul gave the high cost of railroad transport to Odessa as the chief reason for the diversion of wheat from Odessa to Königsberg. Grain could be carried more cheaply from the region around Kiev to Königsberg than to Odessa. And the water transport from Odessa to London cost three times as much as shipping out of Königsberg.[65] The French consul cited the paucity of local lines and the absence of networks and marveled particularly at the fact that, in a country so much larger than the others of Europe, the government would tolerate such high freight rates.[66]

It was costly to ship grain by train, but it was even costlier to have the shipments wait in idleness when the trains were halted by snow. The British consul reported in 1874 that twice that winter no train arrived at Odessa because snow blocked the tracks for a total of twenty days.[67] In 1879, he graphically contrasted the costs of transporting grain in Russia and America:

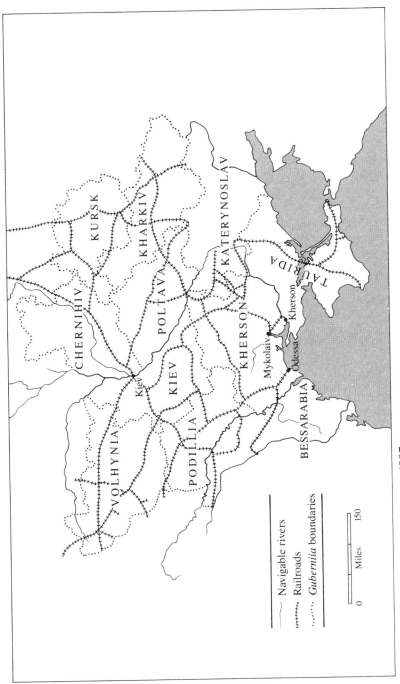

Railroads in the South Ukraine, ca. 1907

Table 9.1

Comparison of Shipping Charges
in America and the South Ukraine

America   The South Ukraine

1. Transport by river or canal of 10 *puds* (360 pounds) for 100 *versts*
   (in kopecks):

   7.35   22.5

2. Transport by railway of 10 *puds* for 100 *versts*:

   4.90   30.75

3. Shipment from warehouse of 10 *puds*, including sifting, weighing,
   etc.:

   3.00   40.00

Totals   15.25   93.25

Source: *BPP*, 1880, LXXIV, 863.

He sagely warned:

> Unless a better and cheaper system be found for conveyance from the
> interior to Odessa, and for shipment here, Russian corn must inevit-
> ably be driven out of the English market.[68]

Not only did the configuration of the South Ukraine's railways
hamper grain shipments, but its management also elicited complaints. An Italian observed in 1905:

> Another cause which arrests the growth of the trade is the imperfect
> organization of the Russian railways, which every year seem to be
> taken by surprise when the harvest season taxes their resources. End-
> less vans of grain are waiting on the sidings for weeks and months at
> a time, until the bewildered railway officials are able to cope with
> them; at every harvest season the newspapers are full of complaints
> about these delays, and wherever I went I heard bitter criticism on the
> management of the lines. Consequently, it is very difficult for foreign
> buyers to count on obtaining the promised consignments by a definite
> date.[69]

Despite the strain it placed on the railroad system, the quantity of
grain carried to Odessa by rail increased significantly. And the railroad itself enlarged the grain-growing region supplying Odessa.[70] By
1879, some 71 percent of all grain reached the port by train. As
Table 9.2 shows, in the 1880s the percentage fell to the 50 to 60 percent range.

Table 9.2

Means of Transporting Grain to Odessa, 1883–1888
Figures are in thousands of *pud*s.

Year	RR	Pct.	Water	Pct.	Cart	Pct.	Total
1883	33,413	54	21,300	35	6,932	11	61,645
1884	30,343	51	20,899	35	7,931	14	59,173
1885	61,876	65	21,230	22	12,034	13	95,140
1886	35,750	54	23,765	36	6,262	10	65,777
1887	67,254	66	31,037	30	4,128	4	102,419
1888	89,641	64	40,333	29	9,671	7	139,645
Average	53,046		26,427		7,826		87,300

Source: Borinevich, *Ocherk*, pp. 6–7.

In the decade of the 1890s, the railroads delivered to Odessa more than one-half of its total supply of grain only in three out of the ten years. Carts and barges carried the rest.[71]

The cereals carried by water came in river barges, which were in turn served by lighters. To facilitate the carrying of grain directly from rivers to port, a canal was built in 1900 from the mouth of the Dniester through a shallow estuary to the sea.[72] Until 1905, about one-half of the grain for export came to Odessa by water. But in 1907, according to the French consul, only one-fifth of Odessa's grain exports came by coastal craft. Kherson, which used to send the grain that came down the Dnieper to Odessa, began exporting grain itself.[73] Still, the American agronomist, Michael, writing in 1917, noted, "Much grain, however, arrived in bulk in small coastal steamers, sailing vessels, or barges. Such grain usually was loaded directly onto oceangoing steamers by floating elevators."[74]

The third chief means of conveyance remained the carts; of these the French consul wrote:

Carts, which one would have believed to have been dug up from primitive ages, are filled with 7 *chetvert*s, seldom more, and consigned to a man who knows nothing, who is responsible for nothing and who has no other care than to arrive first by dint of whippings and swearing.[75]

The Russo-Japanese War revealed how increasingly dependent Odessa had become on railway transport. The harvest of 1904 had been a good one. In 1905, however, virtually no rolling stock was available to carry cereals to port. It was needed in the East to carry troops and supplies to the war front. The tonnage carried by the South Western Railroad serving Odessa fell to one-half of what it had been in 1904. Both the American and French consuls listed the paucity of railroad cars as the chief obstacle to selling wheat. At the end of the year, most of the wheat was standing on railroad platforms.[76]

Given the lack of transportation, wheat prices soared at Odessa in 1904. For all southern ports, the price of wheat was 89.8 kopecks per *pud*; in 1908, it was 127.2, and it remained high for the rest of our period.[77] The entire year of 1905 was one of crisis following crisis—the October railway strikes resulting in vandalism of locomotives and wagons; the coal strikes; the mutiny on the *Potemkin*; the pogroms, and finally, in December, the post and telegraph strike. Since checks were little used and money transactions were usually effected by means of telegraph, it was a real blow to commerce to have sources of credit cut off.[78] All in all, as we shall see, the year 1905 was an exceptional one and a grim turning point for the city.

But once the industrial, military, and commercial crises had passed, problems remained. Foremost was the railroad situation: "The shortness of rolling stock," reported the British consul in 1907, "is still painfully felt."[79]

Even after rolling stock became available, the railroad system was not adequate for Odessa's needs. The French consul marked the weakness of the system in 1907:

> The port of my residence [Odessa] is besides, particularly at a disadvantage as a consequence of the defective construction of the single railroad line which ties it to the interior and which does not terminate in the centers of production except by way of multiple branches. . . . No one should be surprised if within a radius of 150 kilometers, the transport of grain to Odessa is generally carried out even at present by means of carts rather than [railroad] cars.[80]

Not only were the trains inefficient, but also alternate means provided no economic solution. We have seen the costliness and wastefulness of carting. The French consul declared water transport to be unsuitable. The cost of barges and lighters bringing grain to Odessa from the mouths of the Dnieper and the Dniester had risen from two and one-half kopecks per *pud*, reaching as much as four or five kopecks per *pud* in the autumn. And if grain arrived by barge, it had to be transferred to ships within eight to ten days, as there were no elevators to store it.[81]

The French consul concluded that the train would be the best means to transport grain if only the rates could be calculated to compensate Odessa for the circuitous routes involved. Even the proud author of a guidebook to Odessa in 1904 had to admit that rates based on *versts* favored Mykolaiv, which was served by direct lines.[82]

The paradox central to Odessa and the railroad that served it was this: the line did not penetrate directly into the grain-growing areas, and yet the insufficient rolling stock and the lack of grain elevators and storage units resulted in the system's inability to handle the quantity of grain already available to the port. As an observer noted in 1914:

> The railway communication has not until now kept pace with the requirements of the grain people, so the port has lost its former supremacy in this business.[83]

The Harbor

Odessa's natural harbor was one of the reasons Catherine ordered the construction of a city at that particular site. The port had initially been divided into two parts: the southern Quarantine harbor and the northern one, the Pratique, where coastal shipping docked. The entire harbor faced east. Gradually, these two harbors were divided and extended into new ones and the dock area spread out to cover about three miles of coastline. The southernmost harbor continued to serve as the quarantine port where foreign ships docked. Protected by an extended, curved mole, it was the largest, deepest, best-sheltered, and busiest part of the harbor. Through the construction of moles (1882), the port was further enlarged into the New Harbor and a coaling station. In 1884, the Petroleum Harbor was built next to the Pratique Harbor (see Map 11.1, p. 275). This new harbor began at the foot of the Peresyp coastline.[84]

In 1865, P. Beliiavskii made an inquiry into the condition of the harbors of Odessa. He concluded that the city had not maintained its port adequately. He chastised the government, saying that no other harbor in the entire world had reaped so much profit from its port and yet had plowed so little money back into it.[85] At the same time, A. A. Skal'kovskii noted that harbor improvements were the greatest need in order to increase exports.[86] The wharves were rotting and the loading and unloading devices were primitive. Had Odessa only continued the rate of progress it had attained within the first five years of its existence, Beliiavskii concluded, it would have been the leading port in the world. In 1861, N. A. Novosel'skii was charged with cleaning the harbor. He was given only 500,000 rubles for the five-year project. But by 1865 little had been accomplished, and plans were drawn for the port's improvement in that year. Governor General P. E. Kotsebu was to supervise a five-year project drawn up by a British engineer, Sir Charles Hartley.[87] Some 4,700,000 rubles were allocated for port improvements.[88]

The first task was to dredge the harbors. Ships coming in unloaded their ballast onto lighters, resulting in some spillage. Some captains even illegally dumped the ballast overboard. This spillage, as well as the natural seeping of mud, threatened to render the port waters dangerously shallow. Five million rubles were allocated for dredging and building moles to protect the harbors. By 1868, the British consul at Odessa reported that the dredging of the port was proceeding rapidly.[89]

By 1874, however, the work of enlarging the port was dragging:

> The harbour works still continue, but at a rate so slow that it would be hard to say when they will be finished. The plan designed by Sir. C. Hartley, if properly carried out, would, at a comparatively small outlay give to Odessa a safe, commodious harbour with 127 acres of sheltered water, in addition to the 95 it now possesses.[90]

Four years later, the British consul made a pessimistic report on the port, noting that it was not organized for extensive traffic, that the prices for freight had increased and were so fluctuating that the cost could double from day to day. The problem was not one of technology, all of which was available and which, if applied, could cut costs in half, but in the fact that "the port, unfortunately, is not under the sway of the municipal authorities."[91] Despite the municipal reforms of the period, the central government retained distant, uninformed control over this vital nerve of the city's economy.

In 1879, the Russian government sent Professor Orbinskii, a noted agronomist, to the United States to inspect the transportation system and the methods applied there for grading cereals.[92] The British consul who related this news feared that no matter what the report, the apathy of local merchants and farmers would prevent the installation of elevators on the docks of Odessa.

Orbinskii's report, written about 1881, rehearsed the harbor improvements made since 1869 in Odessa. Apparently the two new breakwaters proved to be a mixed blessing. They provided deeper harbors and safer berths in normal weather. But the calmer waters resulted in icier conditions, and this made it difficult for sailing ships and low powered steamboats to navigate. Icing of the port also delayed and detained ships, which had to pay for longer anchorage and longer storage. In 1888, a particularly icy winter, storage costs because of delays amounted to 155,000 rubles.[93] Ukrainian cities such as Kiev and Kharkiv, while closer to Odessa than to Riga or St. Petersburg, turned to the latter ports, whose navigable rivers allowed more docking space than the limited harbor of Odessa.[94]

The lack of storage space on the docks was another persistent problem. The carriage of grain from the magazines in the outskirts of the city to the docks was one needless cost that local authorities could eliminate by putting elevators on the docks. If an elevator could be built on one of the moles in the harbor connecting with the railway, grain coming by train, barge, or cart could be collected at ships' side. According to a French journalist, the cost for carrying grain from storehouses to the port in good weather was only ten kopecks per *chetvert*, but when it rained, it rose to seventy-five kopecks. He drew the obvious conclusion that, at times, it cost more to traverse Odessa's muddy streets than to cross the Black Sea.[95] As the British consul wrote in 1879, "The cost of manipulation between the railway station at Odessa and the port, which at present amounts to from 50 copecks to 80 copecks per *chetvert*, would, it is said, be reduced to from 20 copecks to 25 copecks."[96]

Orbinskii, in his 1881 report on Odessa's port, commented on the necessity to install grain elevators and to adopt the "American system." He noted that in 1879 an engineer had already proposed elevators as a substitute for the elevated railroad. Elevators could load twice as much grain in a day as the elevated railway, whose wooden piles presented a real fire hazard, especially in time of war.[97]

When at last the modern elevator was constructed, it was placed, as we have seen, not at the harbor, but some seven miles from the port. As the British consul explained:

> Of course the most rational course would have been to build elevators in the port where steamers could come alongside and take in grain direct, as in America, without further expense; but this arrangement would have done away with the necessity of the high level railway in which a large amount of capital is invested.[98]

The disadvantages of forwardness! Odessa had been so proud of its elevated trains along the docks. By means of six conveyers, eight meters above the port, grain was poured directly into the ships' holds. But still most of the grain had to be carried to the docks by carts. The elevated railway, or *estakada*, ran for about three and one-half kilometers. Elevators were needed so that regular trains could carry grain directly to them. The customs area was extensive, but there were no storehouses near the docks. The seven or eight floating elevators and the two floating cranes were not a satisfactory substitute. Nearly all goods except for some cereals had to be loaded by hand. This time-consuming procedure resulted in delays and additional costs.[99] Time and time again (in 1888, 1889, 1890, and 1894), elaborate engineering proposals were commissioned to indicate how the port and its storage space could be enlarged and how loading could be accelerated.[100]

The city fathers in 1894 appeared unaware of the true state of Odessa's harbor. In the centenary history they smugly commented that since 1870, the government had spent 7 million rubles on the harbor, "which at present is the best equipped in the Empire." In the next sentence, however, they admitted to "some deficiencies."[101] In the same year, the engineer Chekhovich spelled out what those deficiencies were: 1) the insufficient number of docks, so that waiting lines meant high anchorage and freight rates. 2) The extreme insufficiency of grain loading and unloading equipment. 3) The absence of specialized equipment to load wood, coal, gas, and cattle. 4) Lack of facilities for ship repairs. 5) Lack of ice-breaker equipment.[102]

In 1904, the British consul complained, "Warehouses are overflowing, and the merchandise lies in confused heaps on the quays."[103] And still four years later: "In good years the present harbour accommodation is quite insufficient."[104] He gives details:

> . . . early in August there were as many as 17 or 18 steamers waiting for berths, with an approximate detention of three weeks to a month for a berth, and it was not until well into September that the port became again practically normal. In certain cases steamers were in port more than 50 days (including the time waiting for berth and occupied in loading), and some even left partly loaded to complete at other ports. Many steamers lay at Odessa for 30 days (August) waiting berth and at last were sent elsewhere to load.[105]

In 1902 an English engineer, E. L. Harris, proposed improvements for Odessa's harbor, but the war with Japan put the project in abeyance. The effort was resumed in 1908. The project was to cost some 15.5 million rubles (to be covered by government bonds). A new grain harbor was to be constructed between the northernmost harbor—the Petroleum—and the repair yards next to the Pratique. It would contain fifteen new loading berths to accommodate twenty-one to twenty-six steamers at any given time. And there wagons carrying grain from the hinterland, from the railroad terminus, from the elevator, from the warehouses, from "Grain City," or from Peresyp would empty into transit silos where each cargo would be inspected. The silos would hold the contents of a single wagon so that the quality, weight, and destination of each could be ascertained. From the silos the grain would be placed in separate bins in elevators or loaded directly into the ships. In this way some 11,500 tons of grain could be loaded in ten hours. Electric lights on the docks would permit night and winter loading. Costs would thus be reduced from 4.89 kopecks to load a *pud* to from 3.45 to 1.75 kopecks per *pud*. Two major improvements would thus be achieved: ships would be loaded faster and more cheaply, thus avoiding delays; and the quality and weight of the grain would be controlled, thus restoring Odessa's good reputation on the world's grain market.[106] With reason, the British consul remarked that it was futile to plan improvements in the railroad system when the port could scarcely handle what grain already poured onto it. But then he recognized that if the harbor were improved, more grain would be welcome, but to achieve this, grain would have to be diverted from Mykolaiv.[107] In 1911, we learn that "work was confined to minor improvements to the wharves."[108] The project had been given to the State Duma for consideration. Some claimed that the militancy of Odessa's laborers, especially dock workers, impeded the installation of labor-saving devices. This was the opinion of an American agricultural expert:

> There is no other port in the world from which grain is shipped, except in Argentina, where traffic is interrupted by strikes as it is in Odessa. . . . Owing to the power of the laborers, very little progress has been made at Odessa in introducing modern methods of handling grain. There are no great elevators, as there should be from which the grain can be spouted into the holds of vessels. Nor is it likely there ever will be. Exporters say that it is possible to introduce modern methods at newer ports, but that prejudice makes it impossible at Odessa.[109]

Strikes not only interrupted trade, but in 1905 gained higher wages and shorter hours for Odessa's dock laborers, thus making the port less competitive with its rivals.[110]

Some observers attributed the lack of progress on Odessa's sea front to competition from other ports and the flight of private capital to less agitated harbors:

There has been a steady decrease [in population] during the last five years, which is due to the rivalry of other ports which are attracting trade because of better harbours, better railway connections and better facilities for doing business. The strong and violent socialist element in Odessa has also injured the city by frightening away capital and preventing the establishment of manufacturing industries because of the fear of labour strikes.[111]

To be sure, after the mutiny of the *Potemkin*, the docks were set on fire; about 9 million rubles of goods and wharf property were destroyed.[112]

Still others attributed the decline not to restless labor and emigrant capital, but to the State itself:

Odessa has not prospered so much in the last decade as formerly. The Imperial patronage has been transferred to Nicolaiev. Furthermore, Odessa is looked upon as one of the hotbeds of anarchy by the present government.[113]

Less threatening than revolution, but still more consistently bothersome for shippers were the thieves of Odessa, whose skills were legendary. The British consul warned in 1906:

It is necessary that masters of ships visiting Odessa should be very vigilant and constantly on the watch for thieves, who swarm in the port, and for whose attention nothing seems too big or too small.

From the brass fittings of a ship to a large tarpaulin, nothing is too heavy or too firmly fixed. Daylight is no hindrance to their operations, and in dealing with these thieves it is well to be to be very watchful, for life is cheap.[114]

In 1913, the American consul unwittingly wrote Odessa's epitaph over its docks: "The extensive harbor improvements, which for the past three years have been under contemplation, have not as yet been commenced."[115] Odessa declined as its rivals flourished.

Rivals

The shrinkage of Odessa's participation in the Black Sea grain trade is illustrated by the following figures. Its share in the total of the Russian Empire trade fell from 45 percent in 1897–1901 to 35.4 percent in 1902–1906, to 33 percent in 1907, and to 28.7 percent in 1908.[116] A glance at Table 9.3 below will show where the business was going.

Table 9.3

Black Sea Cereal Exports in U. S. Tons

City	1908	1909	1910	1911	1912
Odessa	730,845	898,571	1,268,117	1,650,162	744,746
Mykolaiv		1,521,990		1,577,762	1,029,838
Kherson	555,327	723,444		1,063,246	505,301

Source: Snodgrass, 1913, p. 182; MAE, *RC*, 1910, 26.

In addition to the above ports, there were many smaller ones on the Black Sea and the Sea of Azov, especially on the Crimean Peninsula. One new port, Khorly, bore the distinction of belonging entirely to a woman.[117] By 1911, this little port exported a substantial amount of grain (some 116,110 U. S. tons).[118]

The chief rivals to Odessa, however, were Mykolaiv and Kherson, although Rostov-on-Don was becoming a threat as well. Once a simple loading station, Mykolaiv became a permanent port in 1874. In 1889, an Englishman declared, "Next to Odessa, Nicolaef is the handsomest town in New Russia."[119] But by 1910, its population of nearly 200,000 was still only one-third that of Odessa. The port froze over more frequently and for longer periods than in Odessa and the port was more distant for European ships. The pilot charges were higher, and the port could not accommodate ships beyond a certain displacement. Nonetheless, Mykolaiv had the offsetting advantage of being better served by rail than Odessa. It boasted a harbor of 1,170 meters, which was to be enlarged by another 600 meters in 1910. Labor was cheaper; it was not given to frequent strikes.

Of Mykolaiv an American journalist wrote in 1906:

The convenience of the situation, the superiority of its harbour over that of Odessa and the favour of the imperial family and the clique of sycophants and speculators who hang around the grand dukes, gave it a preference among shippers, and since 1898, it has been growing faster than Minneapolis or Seattle. It has jumped from 18,000 to 200,000 population in a decade. During the same time it has acquired the largest shipping business in grain, manganese ore and coal in the Russian Empire and is booming along in an extraordinary manner. The population is increasing at the rate of ten thousand a year. The volume of business is gaining with even greater rapidity, the value of real estate has advanced 1,000 percent during the last eighteen years and the wealth of the community at a corresponding rate.[120]

According to the same journalist, the partiality of the grand dukes and the imperial court resulted in public works: a deeper harbor, grain elevators, favorable railway rates. This interest was rumored to be personal: "Grand dukes and their friends are heavily interested in real estate speculations at Nicolaef and have made enormous sums of money by advances in the prices of property." A second rumor had it that imperial circles wanted to ruin Odessa because of the large Jewish population: "Nearly all the business at Nicolaeiff is in the hands of the Russians; at Odessa the Jews control everything."[121] Jews were not even allowed to reside in Mykolaiv until 1859.

Apart from intrigue, the government had good reason for making improvements in Mykolaiv, especially in the dock area. After 1871, Russia could again equip military ports along the Black Sea and Mykolaiv became one of the largest naval stations there. Odessa was not a military port.[122]

The citizens of Odessa were outraged when Mykolaiv dared to call their city "a parasite of Mykolaiv." A series of debates, letters to newspapers, protests, and plans to improve Odessa's rail lines were published by the City Credit Society in an effort to stop the drift of trade to Mykolaiv.[123]

In 1917, Michael, the American agronomist from the University of Wisconsin, described how the mouth of the Boh River had been dredged so that ships drawing twenty-eight feet or less could dock at Mykolaiv. Most of the wharves were controlled by the Southern Railroad, which owned a wooden elevator. The elevator handled about 18 percent of the annual export. Grain was discharged into holds of ships by conveyor belt.[124] Closer to Kryvyi Rih, it also exported considerable amounts of iron ore.

The Cinderella success story was much the same for Kherson. Although it was not opened for commerce in modern times until 1902, its exports grew from 2 million francs in that year to 125 million in 1909.[125] Here too the government was not stinting in making improvements. Kherson, a few miles from the mouth of the Dnieper River, was limited in its growth only because of the depth of the river. Steamers went to Kherson to take on Donets coal and as much grain as the water's depth would allow.[126]

In 1910, the French vice-consul in Odessa noted with gloom that in the preceding year Mykolaiv had exported 100,755,765 *pud*s of cereals and dried vegetables; Kherson 45,012,686 *pud*s; and Odessa only 34,475 *pud*s. The city's exports, he complained, were "already greatly diminished by the competition from Kherson and Nikolaev."

These figures confirmed what he himself called "the commercial decline of Odessa."[127]

Table 9.4

Average Yearly Exports of Cereals in Thousands of Francs

Years	Odessa	Mykolaiv	Rostov	Novorossiisk
1891–1900	224,240	101,773	87,850	64,920
1901–1910	238,450	203,200	155,850	122,200
1909	181,100	291,700	252,000	232,256
1910	214,800	279,500	258,000	173,000

Source: MAE, *RC*, 1912, p. 4.

Decline, yes, but not a permanent one, according to the British consul in 1913:

> Though Odessa is the fourth largest town in Russia, with a population of over 500,000, it is approached by only one railway. This line runs north and west in the direction of Germany and Austria-Hungary and not towards the centre of Russia, so it is not in the best position for the conveyance of goods to Odessa for exportation. Nicolaiev and Kherson are in more direct communication with the centre of Russia, which is one of the principal reasons why, since the improvement of these two ports trade has been greatly diverted towards them. This will be in some measure redressed by the new railway from Odessa to Bakhmach, which runs north and east through new country and will much reduce the distance between Odessa and Moscow. This line should soon be opened. It will cross the River Bug at the town of Voznesensk. Between this town and Nicolaiev there is a large business in shallow draught barges.[128]

This sounded hopeful, but then he warned, "The exporters at Nicolaiev are already planning to tap the Odessa-Bakhmatch railroad at Voznesensk and to divert to the river what the line brings down from the interior. If they succeed, the new line will benefit Odessa but little." As if that were not enough, Kherson was trying to obtain a connection with the interior by a rail line to Kharkiv. Such a plan, which would cost 5 million pounds had already received official approval. The Odessa-Bakhmach railway was almost completed in early 1913. Its supposed benefit to Odessa was never tested, as it, like all railways, soon was in service of the war.[129]

The French consul also saw distinct signs of decline. He reported that in 1907 Odessa only accounted for 24.27 percent of all Black Sea exports instead of the 32.5 percent it had exported in the period 1897–1906. The exports of Kherson rose by some 9.7 percent in the same period, just about matching Odessa's loss.[130] The United States consul spoke in 1913 of Odessa's relationship with other Black Sea ports in the past and present:

In those days the three ports cooperated, and there was practically no competition. Odessa was then practically the only port that ocean vessels could safely enter, and the other two ports [Mykolaiv and Kherson] had to send their grain in barges to Ochakiv and Odessa to be loaded into vessels. Now the bars have been dredged away from the mouths of the other two harbors, and there is the keenest of competition between the ports. The total exports are fairly divided between them, but, as once before, Nikolaief gained the lead over the others in the quantity of grain shipped in 1912.[131]

The new railroad and new harbor might have given Odessa new life, but time ran out in 1914. There had been, however, one other trump that Odessa might have been able to play in its struggle for commmercial success. This was the attempt to issue bourse certificates guaranteeing the quantity and quality of grain exported from the city. A committee from the stock exchange would be delegated to act as controllers of export. Mykolaiv had adopted this measure and Kherson was following suit. But the army of middlemen in Odessa opposed this reform. Owners of grain storehouses opposed elevators, dock workers opposed modern loading devices, and the middlemen opposed elevators on the docks and the bourse certificates.[132] The imperial government could have overcome all these objections, but why should it favor an unruly city? The new darlings of the Black Sea possessed a more tractable labor force, modern equipment, and good railroads. The exporting firms were chiefly the large old Greek ones which, unlike Odessa's firms, survived the seventies. Fate, fortune, and imperial policies seemed to be frowning at the Southern Beauty. Ultimately, of course, it mattered little that Mykolaiv and Kherson, as well as some other Black Sea ports, were gaining on Odessa. All Black Sea ports suffered in 1912; bad weather resulted in poor harvests, and the British coal strike meant less shipping. Finally, because of the Balkan War, the Turks closed the Dardanelles. The Russian Empire was as powerless to open the Straits in 1912 as it had been in 1812.

The export of cereals through the Black Sea ports ended with the outbreak of the First World War, bringing to a close a cycle of stupendous growth and decline that had lasted more than a century. Odessa had been a leader in the expansion of this trade; appropriately, too, it gave early indication that this commerce was ebbing. New patterns in the international trade in cereals were emerging, in which Odessa—and ultimately the other ports of the Black Sea's northern littoral—were destined to play a diminished role. The worsening economy affected in turn the size of the city and the relationships of its constituent groups.

CHAPTER TEN

The People

[At Odessa] Russians feel a bit foreign; foreigners feel a bit Russian. Neither the one nor the other are exactly Russians or foreigners.
—Concetto Pettinato, 1913

Several characteristics distinguish the modern from the traditional city. The first and most salient is sheer size: in the nineteenth century, numerous cities were able to break through the demographic ceilings that had previously restrained their growth. The breakthrough was made possible primarily through effective measures of public health, which for the first time protected against endemic diseases. But unprecedented size in turn raised novel problems, both of social and cultural life. One problem that Odessa confronted even more than other communities was the preservation of peaceful and constructive relations among social classes and its large ethnic communities.

Numbers

Colorful and prosperous, by 1861 Odessa, with a population surpassing 100,000, was the third largest city in the Russian Empire (the fourth, if Warsaw is included). It was also on the threshold of still further growth. Rapid expansion came in the late 1860s and early 1870s. By 1873, Odessa's population had nearly doubled to 193,513. By 1878, with more than 200,000 people, the city overspread a radius of about seven miles.[1] In the twenty-five year period from 1873 to 1897, the population doubled again to nearly a half a million people.[2] Growth was then slowing, but not yet halted. The city's population at the outbreak of the First World War in 1914 was 630,000.

Table 10.1

Population of Odessa, 1861–1914

Year	Population	Year	Population	Year	Population
1861	115,567	1875	188,700	1891	310,438
1862	117,540	1876	194,500	1892	340,526
1863	118,412	1877	200,400	1897	403,815
1864	120,708	1878	206,500	1899	410,000
1865	116,917	1879	212,800	1900	450,000
1866	120,163	1880	219,300	1905	511,000
1867	127,775	1881	226,000	1906	461,000
1868	133,000	1882	233,000	1908	450,000
1869	139,462	1883	244,609	1910	520,000
1872	145,463	1887	271,000	1911	620,143
1873	193,513	1889	301,039	1914	630,000
1874	188,700	1890	313,687		

Source: GAOO, *f.* 274, *op.* 2, *d.* 4, *ll.* 72, 96; *f.* 274, *op.* 1, *d.* 12, *l.* 66. Borinevich, 1893, pp. 203–04; *BPP*, 1912–13, XCIX, p. 23; Smith, 1908, p. 51; Hume, 1914, p. 34.

Public Health, Public Works

As it grew, Odessa faced the whole panoply of diseases that everywhere threatened big and crowded cities. One menace corrected early was malaria. The city's own expansion helped reduce its presence. The draining of nearby marshes deprived the anopheles mosquito of breeding areas. Intermittent malarial fevers, common in the early city, go unmentioned in the medical chapter of the centenary volume on Odessa.[3]

As a port, Odessa was exposed to two major water-borne diseases: plague and cholera. Plague first appeared in 1812. Here the city's proximity to endemic centers of the disease in the east probably explains the repeated outbreaks. As late as 1902, bubonic plague affected forty-nine individuals, eighteen of whom died. The British consul described the measures taken:

Great attention was paid to the destruction of rats and to the cleaning and disinfecting of markets, lodging houses and all dirty dwellings, especially where cases had shown themselves.[4]

Cholera was even more difficult to control. The disease struck Odessa in the course of numerous "pandemics" between 1832 and 1894. In recalling his childhood, Konstantin Skal'kovskii reports: "When my old nurse Oksana died in 1843 from cholera, they laid her on a divan in the dining room, where we tranquilly took our meals. So much can be said for the hygiene of the time!"[5] In this, as in several other diseases, the chief protection was a clean water supply. Typhoid fever (spread through contaminated food and water) and typhus (carried by human lice) were also associated with crowding and with poor sanitation. It was feared in 1878 that the return of soldiers from the war against Turkey might lead to an outbreak of typhus. The troops were immediately whisked off to a remote quarantine, however.[6]

By the late nineteenth century, tuberculosis had become the city's principal endemic disease, and remained one of the most difficult to suppress. In 1895, it accounted for 10 percent of all deaths (still a moderate toll by the standards of many contemporary western cities). Its chief victims were adults between the ages of fifteen and sixty. Men were more susceptible to the disease than women.[7] The southern seaport of Odessa attracted many infected persons, who looked to the favorable climate in hopes of a cure. Poor, sick, male immigrants enlarged the ranks of the sick and dying.[8]

Within Odessa's population, the group or cohort that longest remained vulnerable to urban health conditions was babies and children. Diphtheria could strike children with mortal blows in the nineteenth century. After the 1877 war with Turkey, the British consul carried the sad news that in some villages such as Iburienka, near Kherson, not a child survived the diphtheria epidemic.[9]

Over the period from 1824 to 1827, the deaths of infants under one year of age accounted for 44 percent of all the city's deaths.[10] By 1851–1860, the rate had fallen to 28 percent, but thereafter infant mortality began to increase noticeably. In 1875, 13 percent of all of Odessa's deaths were babies under one month while 52 percent of all deaths were children under five years, a horrendous rate that obtained for 1874 as well.[11] Between 1867 and 1884, deaths in the first year of life had come to average 35 percent of all deaths.[12]

The tendency for infant mortality to remain high or even to worsen over the middle and late decades of the nineteenth century is observable in many American and European cities.[13] Perhaps the undercounting of infant deaths in the early nineteenth century and the improving registrations thereafter distorted the record. Still, it is odd that the same documentary fault should have been almost universally present.[14] Contemporaries, no doubt with reason, laid the principal blame for infant deaths upon inadequate maternal care. Migrants, including many women, were flocking into the cities in search of employment. Mothers who left the hearth for outside employment frequently had neither time nor energy to devote to the careful nurture of their babies. Nearly all commentators ascribed premature deaths of babies to improper feeding—the refusal or inability of mothers to nurse their babies, the indiscriminate use of solid food in infant feeding, the prevalence of the unhygienic *soska*, (a pacifier of prechewed rye bread tied in a dirty rag), and even, on occasion, recourse to drugs.[15] According to several doctors, wars or strikes that forced mothers to remain at home benefited babies even when food was in short supply.[16] At Odessa, too, experts in child care stressed the importance of mother's milk for babies. To send babies to wet nurses in the countryside—evidently a common practice at Odessa—condemned many of them to death.[17]

The heat of Odessa's summer gravely reduced the infants' chances of survival. In 1874, for example, the deaths of children under five years of age peaked in July with an average of 15.8 deaths per day (the figure for December was 5.9). Inhabitants five years of age and older died in greatest numbers in late winter and early spring (11.3 deaths per day in March) and survived the summer rather well.[18]

M. I. Finkel, writing about conditions in Odessa in 1865, maintained that the disease called *cholera infantilis* in the United States was the same as *gastro-enteritis epidemica infantum* in Odessa. Almost half the children dying before age three were its victims in Odessa and also, says Finkel, in New York, Philadelphia, and Washington.[19] C. E. Winslow, a modern expert on public health, stated that this summer diarrhea, "so prevalent in earlier days [within cities], was the product of two factors: the lower resistance of the infant due to summer heat and the toxic effect of decomposed or infected milk."[20]

The tardy reduction of infant mortality at Odessa prompts this observation. By 1895, the city had made great strides in improving the life expectancies of its inhabitants. But the better survival of infants depended as much upon social and cultural as upon physical changes. Poverty, illiteracy, superstition, ignorance of the proper care of babies, and perhaps indifference took a heavy toll of infants. The quality of the environment, supporting or threatening human life at Odessa, had cultural as well as physical dimensions.[21]

As late as 1870, death rates at Odessa hovered in the high thirties—occasionally, as in the cholera year of 1872, surpassing fifty deaths per thousand. Visiting in 1860, a French journalist summarized the city's chief defects:

> Odessa would be a charming city to live in, if it were paved and lit, if it had potable water, and if people didn't steal there as in a woods.[22]

After decades of struggle, the city finally succeeded in paving its principal thoroughfares. By 1862, the city authorities commissioned George Furness and Company of London to pave the streets with granite.

In 1868, the work was taken away from the English firm and entrusted to a Russian engineer. An English woman, visiting about 1870, found fault with his work:

> The pavement was of unequal merit—sometimes exceedingly good, at others, rough and uneven, and occasionally, it was altogether absent, and in the latter case, there intervened long stretches of mud and stones, difficult to traverse.[23]

In 1879, the French consul announced optimistically that all the streets of Odessa would be paved "in magnificent granite" within a year.[24] It took more time than that. By 1895, however, all the central area was paved and part of the outlying districts as well. The city fathers boasted, "The present pavement in Odessa is one of the best, not only in Russia, but also of Europe and has cost more than 10 million rubles."[25]

Odessa's efforts to obtain a plentiful supply of pure water had been equally long and even more critical for public health. The English traveler who had noted the uneven quality of Odessa's streets, commented on another noisome evil: "the want of fresh water, all that is really wholesome being conveyed to the town by an aqueduct, which is far from yielding a sufficient supply."[26]

Finally, after proposals made by many individuals and firms, a British company was given the task of providing the city with water.[27] By 1873, water from the Dniester was flowing through pipes into the city. The great event was marked by a ceremony during which the archbishop blessed the waters of the river.[28] Although in 1874, fewer than half of the houses were supplied by this water, by 1894, 71 percent of the houses in Odessa had running water. Only 45 percent, however, were connected to the city's sewer network.[29] When the system was new, it carried 2 million gallons of water a day. The British consul remarked on the benefits:

It is thus to be hoped that baths will be more frequently introduced into the houses here, and that the poorer classes will no longer be deterred by the cost of water from occasionally washing their clothes.[30]

He also gives an account of the accomplishment:

... the works were begun in March 1873 and notwithstanding physical obstacles of no ordinary magnitude, the rigours of a Russian winter, great difficulties at times in the way of labour, and unexpected restrictions on the free action of the concessionnaires, they were in ten months so far advanced that the inhabitants of Odessa for the first time saw water let loose at their doors by the turning of a cock, and running down the street in copious streams.[31]

Although the inhabitants of Odessa drew inestimable benefits from the new waterworks, Baedecker cautioned his readers visiting Russia not to drink the water at all, but to drink good wine or an occasional glass of vodka.[32]

By 1917, as the writer Paustovskii reported, the system was outmoded:

The water supply was very bad in Odessa in those days. It was pumped from the Dniester, some 60 kilometers away and the pumps were barely working. ... There was a little [water] in the pipes, not always, and only in the lowest lying sections of the city. These lucky districts were jammed from morning to night with lines of people from all over Odessa carrying pails, jugs, and tea kettles.[33]

But once the city had piped water and steam pumps powerful enough to move it freely, it could also adopt improved methods of sewage disposal. In 1876, the British consul noted: "A large open foul drain, which disgraces the town, has not yet been covered in."[34] Two years later, he concluded, "Odessa, which is exceptional in Russia in its general cleanliness and sanitary arrangements, though a Western medical inspector would find many faults in it, has not suffered so much [from diphtheria]."[35] In 1874, the major sewer system of Odessa had been completed. The very newness of the city facilitated rapid construction; no older and outmoded system obstructed the labors. In technical language, this was a "full floating system," which carried away both liquid and material wastes and storm waters.[36] It not only disposed of sewage, but drained the city streets. Odessa was the first large city in the empire to possess an efficient sewerage system. By 1899, the British Waterworks Company had doubled the length of sewer pipes within Odessa and established a second water pump at the Dniester; in 1904, the city purchased the waterworks.[37] In 1908, the sewerage pipes extended for 109 kilometers.[38]

In 1895, Odessa's administrators attributed the encouraging decline in the official death rate (from 37.9 per 1,000 in 1874 to 31.3 per 1,000 in 1880) directly to the new waterworks and sewer systems.[39] These officials also assembled statistics on various districts of the city, showing the percentage of houses with flush toilets and their mortality rates. These I have published elsewhere.[40] The coefficient of correlation between the percentages of houses with flush toilets and the district mortality rates is -0.893; in other words, as the percentage of homes with indoor flush toilets rises, the death rate shows a strong tendency to drop. Of course, many houses with flush toilets were also spacious, comfortable, and clean; the inhabitants probably ate better than the average residents of the city, kept servants, and enjoyed other advantages that promoted longevity.[41] While we cannot measure it exactly, the contribution of plumbing to the health of Odessa's people was nonetheless substantial.

With better medical knowledge came heightened awareness that disease was associated not only with sewerage, but also with dirt, lice, and poverty. In 1871, the City Committee for Public Health established six Sanitary Sections, distributed over the city. The purpose of these was to monitor the cleanliness of the air and water and to check the quality of food and beverages offered for sale. In 1877, for example, the Sections inspected 2,913 streets and public buildings.[42] In the last decades of the century, the authorities organized campaigns against the flophouses of the city; doctors were commissioned to visit them to inspect their sanitary conditions.[43] These and other measures seemed to have gained no small degree of success. The death rate from typhus was 16 per 10,000 in 1875; by 1895, it had been reduced to 1.5 per 10,000 out of an incidence of about 55 per 10,000. St. Petersburg, on the other hand, experienced 165 cases of typhus per 10,000 while Moscow had only 21 and Warsaw, even fewer—13.[44]

In spite of the continuing great loss of babies, the urban population of Odessa passed a milestone about 1880. After hovering around equilibrium, births registered a decisive advantage over deaths in the years 1874–1877, when nearly five thousand were added to the population by natural increase.[45] By the end of the century, Odessa's death rate was lower than that of the capitals. It was also lower than the contemporary death rates of Liverpool, Manchester, Le Havre, Danzig, Budapest, and Bucharest.[46] In 1904, the author of a guidebook to the city claimed that the death rate had fallen to seventeen per thousand, which, if true, would have made Odessa the healthiest major city in the empire.[47]

In 1908, however, a French author found that the city continued to face problems in public health:

> Odessa, as a large commercial and industrial city, always attracts masses of workers and people without resources who come here to earn their livelihood. This accumulation of men, of whom a great number remain without work and the misery of the lower classes of the population, inevitably create an environment where diseases of all sorts quickly spread.[48]

Crowding, with concomitant dangers to health, was a major preoccupation. Hospitals did not contain sufficient beds. Writing to Alexander III, city chief Kossagovskii stated:

> As far as healing is concerned, one cannot fail to see that the existing Odessa city hospital with 880 beds and the very helpful Jewish hospital with 120 beds do not fulfil the needs of the population which is proved by the constant appearance of new private hospitals in the city. The old architecture of the main hospital of Odessa in many respects does not suit the newest requirements of science. Nevertheless, some inconveniences have to be put up with because the erection of a new building would require too much money.[49]

By 1908, the number of hospital beds in the city had increased to two thousand, partly as a result of the building of a new hospital in 1902. By this time, the city could also boast of its eye clinic, a lying-in hospital (opened in 1908), and various private hospitals operated by religious or charitable groups such as the Jews, Evangelical Protestants, the Red Cross, and the Sisters of Charity. In addition, the First Aid Society, equipped with ambulances, and twenty doctors, supported by municipal funds, served the poor gratis.[50]

Demographic Characteristics

The New Arrivals

Immigration continued to be the principal reason for the city's rapid expansion from the late 1880s. This inflow came mainly from the Ukraine. Odessa had become an El Dorado for the poor of every sort—Ukrainians, Russians, Jews. One of Sholom Aleichem's imaginary, but wonderfully human characters, Menahem-Mendl, writes home to his wife in the 1880s:

> I want you to know it is simply not in my power to describe the city of Odessa—how big and how beautiful it is—the people here, so wonderful and good-hearted, and the terrific business one can do here.[51]

Another fictional character, Père Goriot in Balzac's novel of the same name, declares on his deathbed his intent to go to Odessa; he expected, this dying man, to make a fortune on the flour market.[52] Odessa attracted these entrepreneurial spirits. But it drew others as well, less prepared to find their fortunes, or even steady work, in the city. The weakening demand for wheat provoked what the Soviet historian Zolotov calls an "agrarian crisis in the last quarter of the nineteenth century," which drove many from the countryside.[53] But given worsening economic conditions, immigrants encountered increased difficulty in finding work. The lack and the insecurity of jobs aggravated ethnic relations and fueled agitation for radical social change.

Comparisons

About December 1, 1892, census takers, who seem for the most part to have been university students, surveyed Odessa's population.[54] They recorded some 338,690 souls, of whom 161,200 were females and 177,490 males. Of these numbers, some 58 percent claimed "Russian" as their mother tongue; the category apparently included Ukrainian and Belorussian, among whom the surveyors did not distinguish. Some 31 percent cited Yiddish as their mother tongue; 3.8 percent spoke Polish; 1.6, German; and 1.56, Greek. A sprinkling of other tongues was also heard, although in small proportions.[55] The "All-Russian" census of 1897 was done more thoroughly, on the basis of precise categories.[56] Thus, it distinguished among the speakers of Russian, Ukrainian, and Belorussian. In 1897, the speakers of these three principal Slavic languages made up 58 percent of the population—exactly the same as five years before. Yiddish, on the other hand, gained; it was recorded as the first language for over 32 percent of the population. There was a slight rise in the percentage of Polish- and German-speaking persons, but the percentage of Greek speakers was unchanged.[57]

According to the 1897 census, 166,345 individuals (41.2 percent of the population) spoke fifty languages other than the three principal East-Slavic tongues. (See Table 10.2.)

Table 10.2

The Ten Largest Groups by Native Language
in the City of Odessa, 1897

Language	Males	Females	Total	Pct. Total Population
1. Russian	104,173	89,081	193,254	50.78
2. Yiddish	61,156	62,530	123,686	32.50
3. Ukrainian	13,224	8,302	21,526	5.66
4. Polish	11,174	5,864	17,038	4.48
5. German	5,253	4,680	9,933	2.61
6. Greek	3,166	1,847	5,013	1.32
7. Tatar	970	459	1,429	0.38
8. Armenian	929	470	1,399	0.37
9. French	423	701	1,124	0.30
10. Belorussian	799	296	1,095	0.29

Source: *Perepis,* 1899–1905.

With only 56.7 percent of the population claiming Russian, Ukrainian, or Belorussian as their native tongue in 1897, Odessa was a much less "Russian" city than Moscow; there, 95 percent of the population spoke one of those languages. Even at St. Petersburg, for all its Western connections, 87 percent reported one of those languages as their maternal tongue.

The division of the population by religious belief also emphasizes the cosmopolitan character of Odessa's population. In 1897, only 56 percent of Odessa's people adhered to the Orthodox faith or some schismatic sect thereof; in St. Petersburg, 85 percent of the population were Orthodox, as were 93 percent of the inhabitants of Moscow. If we take either language or religion as an index, it could be affirmed that as late as 1897, Odessa was little more than half Slavic in its ethnic composition.

In 1892, only 45 percent of the population had been born in the city. In 1897, even fewer were native born Odessans, some 43.6 percent, a sign that the currents of immigration remained strong. But from 1897, Odessa's headlong expansion was slowing; between that year and 1905, the average annual growth rate was less than 3 percent. Its growth peaked and turned downward amid the social disasters of 1905—the subject of Chapter 12.[58]

In 1897, 57.78 percent of the population (all ages included) could read, a literacy rate somewhat lower than that for St. Petersburg

(62.6 percent) and slightly higher than the rate for Moscow (56.3 percent). In Odessa, however, literacy shows a distinctive association with age. In St. Petersburg, the literacy rate is highest among school-age children and diminishes at the older levels of the population. This certainly reflects the lack of educational opportunity in the past and probably also the continuing immigration of illiterate peasants into the city. In Odessa, the peaks of literacy are not found among the young school children. Rather, the highest rates are recorded in the groups between the ages of fifteen and nineteen, and between thirty and thirty nine. The delayed bulge in the literacy rate coincides, at least in part, with the age groups of the heaviest immigration into the city. The administrative, educational, mercantile, and cultural positions available in the city required literate persons to fill them. Perhaps even more than bureaucratic St. Petersburg, Odessa attracted those who could read.

In sum, in the late nineteenth century, the basic ethnic mixture of Odessa consisted of some few foreign nationals (in 1897, they numbered only 19,422), many Russians, some few Ukrainians and Belorussians, and nearly as many imperial subjects who spoke non-Slavic languages. It was indeed the modern Babel.

The division of the population by sex at Odessa shows several distinctive qualities. Like most cities fed by immigrants, men outnumbered women. Writing in 1860, Osip Rabinovich compared Odessa to San Francisco during the gold rush:

> . . . to Odessa as to San Francisco, a steady stream of men searching for luck and fortune flocked from all corners of the world. Here as there the community became at first a settlement of bachelors, drawn here for a chance at a handful of gold, living out in the open, without any constraints on their actions and limits on their desires.[59]

The sex ratio was not as sharply skewed in the Black Sea port as in the two northern capitals, however. The sex ratio for Odessa was 116 males for 100 females in 1897. At Moscow in the same year it was 133, and it was 120 at St. Petersburg. Apparently, the more intensive industrialization in the latter two cities strengthened the preponderance of males.

At Odessa, the sex ratio had recently registered a substantial increase; only five years earlier, in the census of 1892, it had stood at 110 men for every 100 women. The spurt in male numbers is especially evident among speakers of Russian and Ukrainian (the two groups, as mentioned, were not distinguished in the 1892 census). Between 1892 and 1897, males in this category grew in number by 13,425, but females only by 4,912. Unattached Russian and Ukrainian men were flocking into the city in the middle 1890s, some to fill jobs as industrial workers, but others to swell the ranks of drifters and the unemployed. Their presence no doubt added to the city's social volatility.

Age strongly affected distribution by sex. At Odessa, females nearly equal males during childhood, fall well behind them during young adulthood, and dominate the ranks of the elderly. For age sixty or older, the number of men per hundred women falls to only eighty-six. Odessa, like all large cities in the Russian Empire, attracted elderly women, many of them widows, some of them with means.

Economic advantages drew women into the city. Many young women sought employment in homes and shops, and more than a few became prostitutes in this seaport. In Odessa, as elsewhere, girls entered the labor force, especially domestic service, at a very young age. In 1897, out of every one hundred male workers in Odessa, only two were age fourteen and under. But nearly six girls of every one hundred female workers were fourteen and under. Starting to work earlier than males, they also worked longer, all the while for inferior pay. Thus, in 1875 the *Kievskii telegraf* commented that women factory workers usually received one-half or, in some rare cases, two-thirds the pay of men. In the jute factory, males received from eighty kopecks to one ruble, twenty kopecks per day, while women drew only from forty to fifty kopecks per day.[60]

Another reason for the relatively large numbers of women was cultural rather than economic. The Jewish population contained more women than men (their sex ratio in 1897 was 98). If the Jews are subtracted from the population of the city, then the sex ratio among gentiles in Odessa is 130, almost as high as Moscow's 133. Among the Russians at Odessa, men outnumbered women 120 to 100; among the Ukrainians, males held an even greater preponderance—159 to 100. The size of the Jewish contingent in Odessa, and the large number of women within it, thus lowered the sex ratio for the entire community. The predominance of males among Odessa's gentiles reflects the fact that many were students, soldiers, convicts and seasonal workers.

Why were there more women than men among the Jews? It may be that the Jews were concealing males in order to shield them from military conscription. The large plurality of male babies whom the Jews report at birth collapses during the years of military service, and this may well indicate a deliberate underreporting of young Jewish males. This persistent skewing of the reported sexes among the Jews bothered Odessa's chief statistician, A. A. Skal'kovskii, who tried to investigate the origins of the seeming error. One long-time Jewish resident, Marcus Hurovich, offered him, in a letter written in French, an explanation. Allegedly, Jewish parents were not as faithful in reporting the births of daughters to the rabbis as they were in declaring sons. For them, the birth of a son was cause for celebration, whereas parents were much less enthusiastic over the arrival of a daughter, and less concerned with public announcements of her birth. Hurovich recommended that Jewish parents be required to register all babies, in strict accordance with procedures laid out in the Napoleonic Code.[61]

On the other hand, one scholar has recently suggested that the preponderance of males among the Jewish infants was real and not a function of the reporting procedures. She argues that certain ritual practices associated with marital relations increased the chances that males would be conceived.[62] The theory is intriguing, although nearly impossible to test.

Be that as it may, there are also certain, less speculative reasons for the numerical predominance of Jewish women. The Jews, when they immigrated, seem to have done so in entire families.[63] Their households, as we shall see, contained large numbers of children and were not lacking females. It is, moreover, interesting to note that among the Russian women, 33.33 percent were independently employed, as opposed to only 19 percent of the Jewish women. This seems to reflect the peculiar strength of the Jewish household in Odessa.[64] Almost all adult Jews, male and female, married, and most married women remained at home. In 1892, only 4 percent of the male population were permanent bachelors, as opposed to 19 percent of the gentile males. Of females, seemingly all adult Jewesses married, while 8 percent of non-Jewish women remained single.[65]

Sex ratios can also tell us something about the cultural life of the city. Although the number of French in Odessa was small in 1897 (0.3 percent of the population), French women outnumbered males by nearly 164 to every 100 males. Those among them who were employed were nearly all governesses or teachers. The high literacy rates for Italian, American, English, and German women, compared with males of the same nationalities, indicate that Odessa attracted many trained and plucky foreign women who took up positions in the wealthy households and schools of the city. The relatively large numbers of women in Odessa and its attractiveness to the elderly testified to the elegance, amenities and cultural appeal of this southern seaport and summer resort and served to stimulate the demand for theater, music, fashionable clothes, and luxury commodities for which the city was justly famous.

The patterns of marriage observable in Odessa are also distinctive. Although women were present in somewhat larger numbers than in other towns, males showed no particular zeal to marry. Among the total population of males, only 45.36 percent were married in Odessa, below the 49.5 percent in St. Petersburg and substantially lower than the 57 percent found in Moscow—this despite the large Jewish population, who nearly all embraced matrimony. The most obvious explanation for this large proportion of bachelors in Odessa is the presence of a sizeable military garrison: 16 percent of the working male population were in the armed forces. Only 9 percent were so employed in St. Petersburg, and less than 5 percent in Moscow. Odessa was founded with a view to defending the imperial frontiers, and it remained an armed outpost in 1897, not only against exterior foes but also for the repression of domestic insurgency.

The census of 1897 allows us to investigate, although indirectly, the fertility and the natural increase of the various components of Odessa's population. We can calculate ratios between the numbers of young children in the population and women of child-bearing age. These child-women ratios indirectly reflect both the fertility of women and the survival of their offspring, and give us a rough but usable way of measuring the comparative success of the various ethnic groups in rearing children. The age categories utilized in the census require that we consider women between twenty and thirty-nine as representative of all women able to bear children. In Table 10.3 we have calculated ratios between women in that age category with babies less than one year of age, and then with children from one year to nine years inclusively.

Russian women were considerably more prolific than Ukrainian, Polish, or German females. For every 100 babies born to the Russian women and surviving up to age one, there were 87 Ukrainian, 73 Polish, and 65 German babies born and surviving.[66] One factor here was the large number of unmarried, employed women among these last groups. German women, for example, frequently served as teachers and governesses, and many no doubt returned home to marry. Then, too, with the exception of the Germans, these last groups were generally on a lower socio-economic level than the Russians, and this apparently affected the size of their families. On the other hand, Russian women were distinctly less fertile than Jewish wives; for every 100 babies born and surviving in Russian families, there were 127 Jewish babies. We shall presently examine some of the reasons for this remarkable contrast.

Table 10.3

Women and Children in the City of Odessa, 1897

	Russians	Ukrainians	Poles	Jews	Germans
Infants, to One Year	4,246	364	245	3,466	142
Children, Age 1–9	30,715	2,376	1,382	25,398	1,160
Women, Age 20–39	31,811	3,146	2,514	20,548	1,868
Ratios:					
Infants/ 100 Women	13.35	11.57	9.75	16.87	7.60
Index (Jews:100)	79	69	58	100	45
Children/ 100 Women	96.55	75.52	54.97	123.60	62.10
Index (Jews:100)	78	61	44	100	50

Source: *Perepis*, 1899–1905.

In spite of the considerable numbers of single males, the average size of households was comparatively large at Odessa. The census of 1897 does not give exact figures, so we must estimate average household size on the basis of aggregate information.[67] Although this limits the precision of the estimates, the figures still retain a comparative value. In Odessa, if we exclude those in convents, barracks, prisons, and other groups not based in the natural family, the average household size was 4.18 persons; the same figures, calculated by the same methods, are 4.01 for Moscow and only 3.78 for St. Petersburg.

Why were households larger in Odessa? We can only speculate about the answers. Single young men from distant areas were likely to lodge in the homes of relatives living there. The Jewish population in particular seems to have lived in large households, with members well balanced between the sexes and with relatively numerous children.[68] Perhaps, too, in this commercial city, young men remained long in their households of origin, as they acquired the training and awaited the success that allowed them to marry. Finally, the large average size of households may be an early sign of Odessa's slowing growth; its economy in 1897 may not have been buoyant enough to allow young people to marry at an early age and set up their own families. Large, complex households tend to be the mark of a stagnating, rather than a growing, economy.

The social divisions or *soslovies* (estates) of the population further differentiated Odessa from the two northern capitals; in the latter, peasants formed the largest single class.[69] Since there was no category for industrial laborers, these workers appear in the census as "peasants," since they were recent emigrants from rural areas. The fact that Odessa had comparatively fewer peasants among its inhabitants does not imply, as one might think, a greater degree of industrialization, but the contrary. The inflated numbers of those classified as *meshchane*—petty bourgeois—in Odessa, in comparison with the other two cities, indicate the vitality of trade and small crafts in the southern port and the large Jewish population.

The Ethnic Communities

The dominant social characteristic of Odessa is no doubt the presence in the city of large ethnic groups, differing one from the others in language and religion. Their presence affects all the aggregate statistics we have so far cited, and those statistics are therefore somewhat misleading, as Odessa was not a single, uniform society.

Slavs

The largest ethnic group comprised those speaking Slavic tongues. Among the Slavs, the Russians predominated; they formed almost exactly one-half of the population (50.78 percent in 1897). The figure may, however, be inflated by a tendency on the part of many non-Russians to report Russian as their native language and thus ascribe to themselves membership in the politically dominant group. In 1880, according to one observer, one-third of the family names in the city were Ukrainian, but in 1897, fewer than one of ten inhabitants reported Ukrainian as his/her mother tongue.[70] Although the exact size of the Russian component in Odessa's population is questionable, there can be no doubt that this was the largest single ethnic group in the urban population.

In terms of employment, more Russians living in Odessa are found in "private work and service" than in any other occupation. This category, while including some managers and employers, was largely made up of unskilled labor: servants, day laborers, and the like. The Russians so employed numbered 15,743 out of 75,983 males. The second largest occupational group of Russians (11,734) comprised those in the armed forces. In third place came the construction workers (5,824). Smaller, but still important groups of 2,000–3,000 Russians were engaged in the carrier trade (postmen, carters, and the like), the processing of food, carpentry and wood products, and the clothing industries. All these last occupations conferred relatively low status in the social hierarchy. But Russians were also well represented among those in government service (2,224), men who lived from stocks and savings (2,616), and those supported by land rents (1,954). These occupations conferred relatively high prestige. In sum, the Russians filled the lowest and the highest ranks of Odessa's society but were singularly absent on the middle levels of the social pyramid, where most shopkeepers and small manufacturers are found.

This distinctive distribution of Russians in Odessa's society partially reflects the pattern of Russian immigration into Novorossiia. The opening of this new territory had attracted land speculators, developers, and some nobles who were anxious to duplicate on the southern steppes the manner of life they had known in the central regions. In Gogol's *Dead Souls*, P. I. Chichikov purchased his "souls" ostensibly to settle them on land in Novorossiia; the government, he explained, granted free land to those who brought the labor to work it.[71]

The social position of Russians in Odessa was a microcosm of their status in the empire as a whole. They dominated the landholding aristocracy and government service and also helped to fill the lowest social orders, but they contributed relatively few members to Odessa's middle class.

Ukrainians formed another large group of Slavic speakers in Odessa. Although Odessa is located in the Ukraine, only 9.39 percent of its population were registered as Ukrainians in the city and suburbs. In the city alone, only 5.66 percent reported Ukrainian as their mother tongue. These percentages, as we have seen, may well be too low, but the Ukrainian component at Odessa is still surprisingly small. In founding Odessa, the Russian government deliberately encouraged Russians to move to the area, and it invited foreign settlers, but it did not actively recruit Ukrainians. Vladimir

Zhabotinskii, a Jewish intellectual, had this to say about Ukrainians in Odessa in the early twentieth century:

> Even if it was a city in Russia and in my time very Russified in language, Odessa was not really a Russian city. Nor was it a Jewish city, though Jews were probably the largest ethnic community, particularly when one takes into account that half of the so-called Russians were actually Ukrainians, a people just as different from the Russians as Americans from Britons, or Englishmen from Irishmen.[72]

The Ukrainians who immigrated to Odessa were predominantly poor, male, and ummarried. Very few were rentiers of any sort. Of the 11,172 Ukrainian men living in Odessa, only 224 were supported from interest on savings or stocks, and only 100 from land rents. In the first quarter of the nineteenth century, we know of at least two very wealthy Ukrainian capitalists—Iakhnenko and Symyrenko—but they were exceptions.[73]

More Ukrainians were in the military than in any other occupational category. About 14 percent of the males were to be found in the local quarries and mines (only 1.5 percent of Russian males were miners). Among Ukrainians, 12 percent were in manufacturing on a small scale and about 8 percent were in transport. The Ukrainian carter, the *chumak*, had long been a familiar sight on the roads to Odessa, driving grain-laden wagons from the hinterland to the port. By 1897, the railroad had largely supplanted the ox-drawn wagon, but Ukrainians continued to work on the still important river barges.

Few Ukrainian women came to Odessa as the high sex ratio (159) shows, and they appear with comparatively few babies in the census. Rates of child mortality must have been high among them.[74] These characteristics seem to be linked with their low socio-economic status.

Among the Slavic groups, there were some eleven hundred Belorussians in the city, exclusive of its suburbs, and a few Serbs, Slovenes, Bulgarians, and Czechs. The other sizeable Slavic group was the Poles, who numbered about seventeen thousand in the city itself. In their socio-economic position and their demographic characteristics, they resemble both the Russians and the Ukrainians. They included relatively more rentiers than the Ukrainians (259 Poles supported themselves from land rents and another 335 from interest and dividends), and some Poles appear in the skilled occupations of tailor, metal worker, and even medical doctor. But many Poles were also employed in low-level occupations. A large proportion (4,144) were soldiers. The second largest group (1,490) were day laborers and servants. The high sex ratio (191) and low child-woman ratios among the Poles would indicate a population predominantly composed of the poor.

The Jews

After the Slavs, the second major component of Odessa's population was the Jews. Table 10.4 shows the percentages of Odessa's total population made up of Jews since the foundation of the city.

Table 10.4

Percentage of Jews in Odessa's Total Population,
1794–1912

Year	Total Population	Jewish Population	Percent
1794	2,345	244	10.41
1827	32,995	4,226	12.81
1829	51,988	7,900	15.20
1841	73,888	10,775	14.58
1843	77,778	12,000	15.43
1854	90,319	17,080	18.91
1873	193,513	51,378	26.55
1880	219,300	55,300	25.22
1892	340,526	112,235	32.96
1897	403,815	138,935	34.41
1904	511,000	160,000	31.31
1912	620,143	200,000	32.25

Sources: GAOO, *f.* 274, *op.* 2, *d.* 4, *ll.* 26, 47, 68; A. A. Skal'kovskii, *TOSK*, 1865, I, 134–35; *Rezul'taty*, 1894; *Perepis*, 1899–1905; NACRO, 25 July 1905; and Fedor, 1975, p. 202.

Most of Odessa's Jews were Russian subjects, although there was a group of foreign Jews as well, chiefly from Austria. Subject to various civil disabilities, the Jews were frequently regarded as foreigners, but in fact they were, as we have seen, among the earliest settlers of the region.[75]

The sixties and seventies of the nineteenth century represented very nearly a golden age for Odessa's Jews. As one visitor remarked: "Judaism held up its head as it never dared to do in Moscow or St. Petersburg."[76] The same commentator further noted the

Figure 10.1: Percentage of Jews in Odessa's Population

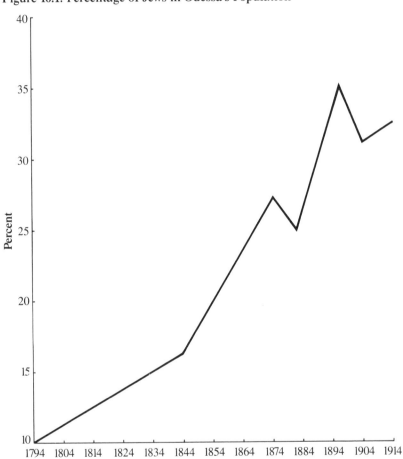

handsome synagogues, the participation of Jews in municipal management, and their contribution toward the social life and the culture of the city. Avram Brodskii, the merchant industrialist, for example, was one of the six men who formed the executive committee heading the city's government in 1873.[77] So satisfied were the Jews with their condition, affirmed the visitor, that few ever converted to Christianity. In 1863, the French consul reported that Jews were free to follow professions, and some became bourgeois notables. They could hold office and, in his words, were liberated from the "moral ghetto" in which they were confined elsewhere in the empire.[78]

From the 1870s, the status of the Jews deteriorated, even as their numbers continued to grow. Crucial in worsening the juridical, and in large measure the social, position of Jews at Odessa were the infamous May, "Temporary," or Ignat'ev Laws, promulgated in 1882.[79] They were the government's response to the issue of mounting racial tensions. They were designed to appease Russians who might otherwise turn to revolutionary activity against the regime. The laws were supposed to guarantee that Jews would no longer be in a position to exploit non-Jews. Consequently, Jews were severely circumscribed in their mobility; they could no longer reside in villages, even in the Pale. They were forbidden to purchase land outside the towns and hence could not live as landowners in the countryside. They could not work on Sundays or Christian holy days and thus gain a competitive advantage over Christians. While the laws were designed to place economic disabilities on the Jews, the political implications were far more damaging. The policy made it obvious that the government regarded Jews as second-class citizens; they were not accorded full legal protection against acts of extortion, harassment, and persecution perpetrated by gentiles.[80]

Oddly, the poverty as well as the prosperity of Odessa's Jews excited the resentment of others. The image of Odessa as an El Dorado for Jews and gentiles alike had flashed throughout the Pale, and the city was attracting numerous poor immigrants who found no opportunity for work at all. Crowded into Moldavanka, the Jews vied with all the other destitute laborers, artisans, and seasonal workers who were also seeking employment in Odessa. The bourgeoisie of Odessa could identify with their affluent Jewish counterparts, but not with the destitute, whose ranks seemed to be growing with frightening rapidity. The tragedy is that the majority of these poor Jews arrived during bad economic times. Agricultural production and transport had not yet adapted to the new demands of a capitalist economy. Commercial opportunities were shrinking even as the Jewish community was growing.

Numerous authors, Jewish and gentile, describe for us the turmoil that government policies induced in Odessa's Jewish community. An English minister observed in the 1880s that the status of the Jews had diminished in comparison to earlier decades. They were subjected to unprecedented "baiting." For example, a sign in a bathhouse proclaimed, "No dogs or Jews allowed to bathe here."[81]

Many Jews concluded that assimilation, or even accommodation, with the larger society was now impossible and chose to emigrate from Odessa and the empire. Others departed for St. Petersburg, where social and intellectual life was allegedly less oppressive.[82] Still others, such as Leon Pinsker, embraced Zionism and called for a Jewish homeland. A prominent physician and a member of the Odessa branch of the Society for the Promotion of Culture among Jews, a leading assimilationist group, Pinsker published (in German) his now famous *Auto-Emancipation*, a plea for establishing a national homeland for the Jews.

Many Jews belatedly embraced the nationalistic movement, as groups of Bulgarians, Greeks, Ukrainians, Poles, and so forth had done before them; all of them had made Odessa their headquarters. While the Bulgarians and the Greeks sought to free their homelands from Turkish rule, the last two groups saw the imperial Russian government as the enemy. Odessa's Jewish population, which counted in its ranks many wealthy, prominent, and powerful individuals, had strong incentives for supporting a regime that protected their persons and their properties. With the promulgation of the anti-Semitic laws, however, the tsarist government made it clear that it did not fully accept them as Russian citizens.

At the turn of the twentieth century, a Jewish intellectual named Vladimir Zhabotinskii pondered whether or not the Jews of Odessa could be regarded as assimilated. He concluded that they were and they were not: "In Odessa, everybody was an Odessan and everyone who was literate read the same newspapers and thought about the same Russian problems."[83] He then described his situation at the *gymnasium* when he was a boy in the 1890s. There were thirty in the class, representing eleven nationalities; ten students were Jews and not one was interested in the Zionist movement or even interested in Jewish civil disabilities, although they suffered from them. It had been difficult for them to attend the *gymnasium* and it would prove more difficult still to attend the university. Some of them studied Hebrew at home simply because their fathers insisted, much as some youngsters reluctantly take piano lessons. When it was possible to study Jewish religious history at school, only three of the ten signed up. The choice of these young Jews was assimilation:

> Yet at the same time, we all lived in rigidly separated national groups, especially we Jews. Without any propaganda, without any ideology, we ten Jews used to sit on one row of benches in class, next to one another. . . . In the '90s, even anti-Semitism drowsed—not, Heaven forbid, in the government, but in society. We were quite friendly with our Christian classmates, even intimate with them, but we lived apart and considered it a natural thing that could not be otherwise. . . . The five Poles, I recall, used to sit always in the "Polish corner," like the three Greeks, the three Armenians and the two Moldavians in theirs.[84]

Isaac Babel's experience at the Nicholas I Commercial School at Odessa was similar:

> The school was gay, rowdy, noisy and multilingual. There the sons of foreign merchants, the children of Jewish brokers, Poles from noble families, Old Believers, and many billiard players of advanced years were taught. Between classes we used to go off to the jetty at the port, to Greek coffee houses to play billiards, or to the Moldavanka to drink cheap Bessarabian wine in the taverns.[85]

Leon Trotsky also recalls his childhood in Odessa:

> In my school [run by the Lutheran church] there was no open baiting of nationalities. To some extent the variety of national elements, not only among the boys but among the masters as well, acted as an important check on such policies. One could sense, however, the existence of a suppressed chauvinism which now and again broke through to the surface.[86]

The censuses add to these literary descriptions a statistical picture of Jewish life at Odessa toward the close of the nineteenth century. According to the survey of 1897, the Jews remained chiefly traders and shopkeepers. Of the ten occupations in which most of their numbers were enrolled, four categories involved some kind of trade (in grain and other agricultural products, clothes, and general trade), and a fifth included middlemen or brokers. Jews were not, on the other hand, numerous in industry. Only in the manufacture of metal and wood products were their numbers significant. Over five thousand males (out of thirty-seven thousand) were engaged in the making of clothes. Presumably, these were tailors rather than industrial workers. Another three thousand men were employed as servants and day laborers, and slightly more than fifteen hundred served in the armed forces. Unlike the other ethnic groups we have so far considered, the Jews filled the middle classes of society. For example, in 1880 Jews formed about one-half the membership of the three classes of artisans: masters, journeymen, and apprentices.[87] They also owned many of the grocery stores and small retail shops of all kinds. Among professions, their numbers were also higher than their share in the general population. Many notaries, lawyers, pharmacists and doctors were Jews.

In many respects the Jews seem to have been the most stable component of Odessa's population. The sex ratio among them is nearly normal (ninety-eight men per one hundred women), and the Jewish household appears to have been large and cohesive. Unfortunately, this impression is in part illusory; the divorce rate was extraordinarily high among the Jews. A. A. Skal'kovskii, our indispensable statistician, wrote at length concerning the frequent divorces among Jews, and archival documents confirm his observations.[88] Jews easily divorced but quickly remarried. A few Jews married five times. He remarked on the ease with which divorce among Jews could be obtained. In 1876, for example, he cited 483 marriages among the Jews and 149 divorces; in 1877, 381 marriages and 147 divorces, so that approximately a third of the unions would end in divorce, a curiously modern statistic.[89]

Jews were also the fastest growing major group in the city. In 1873, members of the Jewish faith constituted 26.55 percent of Odessa's population. For 1877, Skal'kovskii noted that among the Christian population births exceeded deaths by 457 per year; the Jews, on the other hand, with a smaller population, registered a natural yearly increment of 473 persons.[90] By 1892, Jews constituted 32.96 percent of the population; and by 1897 their numbers formed 34.41 percent. Concurrently, the Orthodox population at Odessa declined from 64.79 percent in 1873 to 57.46 percent in 1892. It reached a new low of 55.93 percent in 1897. Despite all the efforts of Alexander III to promote Russification and Orthodoxy, Odessa was rapidly becoming a predominantly Jewish city. While this indicates that conditions were still favorable for some Jews in Odessa, it no doubt also contributed to the antagonism of many gentiles toward them.

The growth of Odessa's Jewish community was partially due to continuing immigration, but also to high fertility among Jewish women and comparatively low death rates among their children.

Table 10.3 shows that Jewish women of child-bearing age appear in the census with considerably more babies under age one than do the women of any other of the groups surveyed. If we compare the Jewish women with the number of older children, age one to nine, in the census, then the number of Jewish children increases in relation to two groups, the Ukrainians and the Poles, while remaining stable in relation to the Russians. This suggests that child mortality was particularly high among the Poles and Ukrainians, who included, as we have stated, many disadvantaged members of urban society. This high rate of infant survival among Jews was not entirely a function of affluence. Stable family life and the traditional care of Jewish mothers for their children no doubt also contributed. The Jewish family and child benefited from both cultural and material resources.[91]

Mortality rates for Jews had been lower than those for the general population well before 1897. In a survey conducted in the 1860s, the redactors noted that death rates among Jews were distinctly low.[92] The book commemorating the centennial of Odessa specified the advantage in 1895: between the ages of six and fifteen only five Jewish children per thousand died, whereas nine non-Jewish children perished. The authors calculated that the Jewish population in Odessa was growing at the rate of 36.4 per thousand, while the gentile population was increasing at the rate of only 21.4 per thousand.[93] Well before the census of 1897, contemporaries were aware of the remarkable growth of the Jewish community. A study of the census itself revealed that in the southern Ukraine, the population grew between 1881 and 1897 by 37.8 percent, but the Jews increased their numbers by 60.9 percent.[94] This expansion of the community was the combined result of immigration, nearly universal marriage, high fertility, and relatively low mortality.

For a time, economic success went hand in hand with increasing numbers. An American reporter who visited Odessa in the first decade of the twentieth century wrote that "all the wealthy classes are Jews." He gives us this remarkable description of their status:

There are more than 200,000 Jews in Odessa—exceeding one-third of the entire population—and, as everywhere else, they control the banking, the manufacturing, the export trade, the milling, the wholesale and retail mercantile and commercial enterprises. And naturally, they are hated by the Russians and envied for their success and prosperity. The prejudice against the Jewish population elsewhere as well as here is due to economic rather than religious reasons—simply because they are getting richer and more prosperous, while the Russians are losing ground in all the occupations and professions. They have wasted their capital in bad investments and dissipations and extravagance, and are forced to mortgage their property to the Jews to keep up appearances.

In the meantime the Jews have been securing control of all the profitable enterprises and lines of business in Odessa. Their sons show the same earnestness and zeal in the university that they show in the counting-room. Therefore, they make the best doctors and lawyers and engineers, and their services are in demand while the Russian members of the profession are idly waiting for business.[95]

Social turmoil, and then the great pogrom of 1905, poisoned the largely favorable atmosphere in which Odessa's Jews had lived. In the years immediately preceding the First World War, many Jews, fearful for their properties and even their lives, emigrated from Odessa and its hinterland. According to the Jewish Statistical Society, by 1904 the percentage of Jews in Odessa had dropped from 35 to 30.5 percent of the total urban population.[96] Shortly after the October pogrom of 1905, nearly fifty thousand Jews left Odessa.[97]

Jews fared well, but also suffered in Odessa. Shortly after World War I, Isaac Babel expressed these ambivalent feelings about Odessa, which both nurtured Jews and rejected them:

Odessa is an awful place. Everyone knows how they murder the Russian language there. All the same, I think there's a lot to be said for this great city, which has more charm than any other in the Russian Empire.[98]

Greeks

After the emancipation of the serfs, Greek merchants, as we have seen, slowly lost their predominance in the grain trade to their Jewish competitors, and most departed.[99] Some few, however, remained. Stephen Ralli, son of the American consul John Ralli, served in the city duma in the 1860s. He invested much of the family fortune in real estate, earning a reputation locally for hoarding large sums of gold and silver in his house. Stephen's twin sons, Peter and Paul, attended Novorossiia University, where they obtained law degrees.[100] Peter then moved to St. Petersburg and became a captain in the Imperial Guards. In 1910, Paul was president of both the Odessa Society for the Protection of Animals and the Odessa Discount Bank. He bought a large estate in Podillia, on which he experimented with new agricultural methods. He founded a sugar refinery on his lands and was one of the first employers to introduce the eight-hour work day. He also set up a clinic to look after the health needs of the workers. Paul was actively engaged in numerous charitable activities; once, he personally supported the musical training of a gifted female employee. As Paul had no sons, the name died out in the city with his death in 1911. As late as 1974, however, a niece and great-niece were living in Odessa.[101]

Theodore Rodocannachi, whose wife was from another prominent Greek family, the Mavrokordatos, appears among Odessa's most prosperous citizens. He and his son Pericles were sole or part owners of ten enterprises. These included steam-powered flour mills, a cotton thread and cloth factory, a brewery, a steamship line, a leather factory, several wineries, and a champagne bottling plant.[102] Their holdings represent a rare instance of commercial profits passing into industrial investments. Pericles became a member of the hereditary Russian nobility. Despite a reputation as a ladies' man, he remained a bachelor and died childless at Paris in 1899. No member of the family is mentioned in the city directory of 1910. Peter Ambrosevich Mavrokordato, presumably a relative by marriage, was president of the Society for the Study of History and Antiquities in 1910, however.[103]

The census of 1897 shows that only 1.3 percent of the population in Odessa gave Greek as their native tongue. The predominance of males (only 58.6 women for every one hundred men) shows that many Greeks were temporary residents. In the early nineteenth century, the enterprise of Greek merchants gave a powerful boost to the export of Ukrainian wheat. But most left the site when commercial opportunities beckoned elsewhere.

West Europeans

Italianate architecture, the Italian opera, a Roman Catholic church (now a sports gymnasium) are the lasting gifts of the Italian community of Odessa. It once formed an important segment of the population. Italians, as we have seen, even including Garibaldi in his youth, were quick to discern commercial opportunities in the Black Sea. Even sooner than the Greeks, however, Italian merchants withdrew from Odessa.

Still, in 1882, an Italian visitor to the city quickly felt at home at the Café Fankoni. There the Italians were speaking loudly in many dialects. The visitor was able to order his favorite Italian drink and read several Italian newspapers furnished by the café. He did note, however, that the Italian colony numbered only about one thousand, whereas in the 1840s and 1850s, there had been thirty thousand. Italians now go to America, he claimed, for in Odessa "the Jews have absorbed all commercial resources—all of them!"[104] By 1906, there were only two large Italian commercial companies, Marino and Anatra Brothers, although Italy remained a principal consumer of Ukrainian wheat.[105] In 1897, there were only 286 working Italian males in the city. Most were retail merchants of luxury goods, skilled artisans, or hotel and restaurant proprietors.

Frenchmen, also prominent in the days of the duc de Richelieu and Count Langeron, became fewer and fewer, although their language, tastes, and customs continued to influence high society. Most of the Frenchwomen living in Odessa in 1897 were governesses and teachers. French males worked principally in the metal-processing industry.[106] In all, there were only 319 employed French males.

In 1909 the French vice-consul explained:

The decline [in the number of French residents] has several causes. In spite of the influx of French capital into the industrial enterprises of South Russia, French influence diminishes from day to day. Odessa, founded by a Frenchman and entirely Gallicized, witnesses a diminution, every year, of the number of our nationals holding important industrial or commercial jobs. The French nationals known on the spot, and settled in the country for long years, disappear little by little, and our colony increases only by the influx, constantly increasing, of French men and women desirous of finding a position in teaching.[107]

The Anglo-American community was never large in Odessa. In 1865, the American consul announced:

There are several American families established here and in many shops, articles from the United States are offered for sale. It is a great recommendation if it is called "Americanskoe," e. g. petroleum, lamps, sewing machines, reaping machines, clocks, Indian rubber goods, oil cloth, codfish, rice, starch, etc. There would be a good speculation for some wide-awake Yankee to open an exclusively American store.[108]

The British consul reported in 1874:

As regards capital, Odessa may be said to have grown and to exist by means of English money; cut that off and the consequences would be stoppage and collapse. And yet, while English money is doing so much here and enriching so many, it is a singular fact that there is not a single English merchant or trader in the place. . . . The time has, in my opinion, arrived when an English merchant might well try his chance here. Our national character stands well in the country, and the recent alliance of our House with that of Russia acts on popular feeling here in the same way as it does in England.[109]

By 1897, however, there were only thirty-six persons who claimed English as their mother tongue. In 1906, some twenty-four Americans from all of the South Ukraine contributed $145 to the American Red Cross for the benefit of victims of the great fire and earthquake in San Francisco, California.[110] In 1913, the Anglo-American club, of about one hundred members, "more Anglo than American," provided a "comfortable retreat of superior insularity."[111] Just before World War I, it appeared that the Germans and Americans were the chief suppliers for Odessa's manufactured imports. An American noted in 1913, "The latest addition to the foreign colony are a few Americans with reapers and plows, steam or gas transaction-engines and the world-conquering automobile."[112] An American physician who went to Odessa during World War I was surprised to see two Black American jockeys at the racetrack.[113] By 1915, there were about four hundred British and thirty Americans residing in the city.

In 1874, the British consul stated:

In the mixed population of these parts, one of the most valuable elements consists of the German colonists who, numbering about 160,000, are descended from the settlers induced to come here in the time of Catherine II.[114]

The privileges that had enticed them to Russia had recently been cancelled, however, so that many of them emigrated with their families to America.[115]

According to the census of 1897, there were many German speakers in Odessa. Some 3,435 of them were Austrian subjects, 2,790 were nationals of the German Empire, and the rest Russian citizens. Many appear to be retired farmers from the nearby German colonies. Many were skilled workers in metal products, food-processing, carpentry, and the making of clothes. According to a city guidebook published in 1904, at least three German social organizations were flourishing: the Harmony German Social Club (principally for merchants), which put on amateur theatricals; the Club of Artisans and Manufacturers; and the Odessa Gymnastic Society.[116]

In 1908, the British consul noted:

> In South Russia, Russian is the language universally spoken. Other languages are widely known, especially in the large towns. For example, German can be spoken in every business house and in nearly all the principal shops in Odessa. French is known (more or less) by the upper quarter of the population. English is spoken by many of the upper classes and also (more or less) by seafarers, and by many business men; but undoubtedly Russian is incomparably the most used language and German stands in the second place.[117]

As late as 1914, a traveler gives an indication of the spread of German as a business language: "In the cosmopolitan cities of Odessa and Rostoff-on-Don, German speech is far more frequent than any other foreign tongue, for there are residents from every part of manufacturing Austria and Germany."[118]

All of these ethnic groups, and more, gave the city its distinctive cosmopolitan flavor and lent it their financial, physical, and intellectual resources. Moreover, the human diversity influenced the use of space in the city as well as its physical amenities.

CHAPTER ELEVEN

The Uses of Space

Odessa is making rapid progress in that material improvement which has already rendered it the best built, most cleanly, and best organized town in Russia.
—British consular report, 1876

Odessa in the late nineteenth century was not only one of the biggest, but also perhaps the most cosmopolitan of cities in the Russian Empire. It also could take pride in its physical beauty, partially assured by the sea but especially by its human design.

Architecture and Amenities

Streets and Buildings

In the second half of the nineteenth century the Nikolaev (now the Primorskii) Boulevard remained the most picturesque of Odessa's streets. At the south end stood the former Exchange, by then the city hall (Duma). The two-and-one-half story building cost the city sixty-five thousand rubles to build in 1829.[1]

On the north end stood the Vorontsov Palace; by 1906, it had become a engineering school. Next to this former palace stood Lloyd's Travel Agency where the city's elite could purchase tickets for their frequent trips abroad.[2]

Midway down the boulevard stood the classical semicircular buildings, embracing, like parentheses, Richelieu's statue overlooking the monumental staircase and the sea beyond. The wide, shaded boulevard, ("cool even at noon in the heat of midsummer") served as the gathering place for thousands of the city's inhabitants, who, like Italians on a *passeggiata* spent "the twilight walking to and fro, gossiping and even [indulging in] a liberal amount of flirting."[3]

Along the boulevard, on the south side, was the Hotel de Lon-
dres, then the best hotel in Odessa (as it is today). In 1904, it was
described as being equipped with all the newest European comforts:
salon, reading room, baths, telephones, electric lights, and good servants who spoke foreign languages.[4] The restaurant, where one could
obtain a five-course meal for two rubles, was reputed to be the best
in town (and still is), although one visitor there proclaimed it to be
the gloomiest dining room he had seen.[5]

By 1900, Bernadazzi had built the Bristol Hotel—today the still
handsome Krasnaia Hotel on Pushkin Street. In 1911, the Passage
Hotel advertised itself as the "largest and most comfortable in South
Russia." Located opposite Cathedral Square, it was in the business
and commercial district close to the Post Office and yet not distant
from the docks. In addition to a fine restaurant, there was a musical
salon, central heating, and an elevator.[6]

Odessa's outdoor life, especially in the summer, resembled that of
other southern European cities. Along the boulevard, on Catherine
Street (the main street leading into town at a 45 degree angle after a
jog behind Richelieu's statue), and on De Ribas Street (the first
major cross-street to Catherine Street) were numerous cafés:

> There are many cafés on the sidewalks, in the interior courts of the
> business section, and in the parks and squares. All night the air is
> filled with music and laughter, and pleasure-seekers turn night into
> day. One is inclined to wonder when the crowd of men he sees in the
> cafés and theatres attend to their business, but when the shops, offices
> and banks open in the morning at ten o'oclock, there seems to be no
> lack of customers and clerks and everybody is on the rush.[7]

On De Ribas and Catherine Streets also were the famous tea
shops, Robinat and Fankoni, where, according to an American,
"Everybody, in Odessa goes, at some time or other."[8] Favored by
ladies and considered the most fashionable was Robinat, although by
1910, Fankoni had a separate women's salon. Matrons and their
marriageable daughters strolled and shopped at the alluring stores
and then patronized Robinat or some other tea shop, the "rendez-
vous" for all the world on foot. In this area the stores were "bright
and attractive, and appeal to the shopper. Goods from all quarters of
the world can here be purchased, even if the price is high."[9] In
1898, a glass-covered arcade was built, sheltering twenty-four shops,
which gave Odessa's customers the latest word in shopping elegance
and convenience. This was the "Passage," the upper stories of

which contained the elegant hotel. The highly ornamented Passage still stands.

De Ribas Street was compared to Montmartre in Paris or the Nevskii Prospekt in St. Petersburg. There on any given weekday salesmen, office workers, merchants, dressmakers, and Greek and Tatar fruit peddlers could be seen hurrying to work. High school and university students, as well as their masters and teachers, were also hastening to class. No workingmen could be found there. Later in the day came the English nursemaids with children and the shoppers who looked in the windows or patronized the boutiques, pharmacies, libraries, banks, dentists, and specialty shops selling photographs or candy.[10]

Fankoni's, on the other hand, with its fine pastries and ices, attracted businessmen. As Kataev, a novelist from Odessa, unfolds the scene:

> At the corner of Langeron and Yekaterinskaya [Catherine] Streets . . . [was] the huge Fankoni Cafe where stockbrokers and grain merchants in Panama hats sat at marble-topped tables set outright on the pavement, Paris-style, under awnings and surrounded by potted laurel trees. . . .[11]

Another Jewish writer, Sholom Aleichem, has his hero, Menahem-Mendl, write his wife:

> Already I have access to all the business offices and am even privileged to sit in Cafe Fankoni, side by side with all the big speculators at the white marble tables, and order a portion of ice-cream, because in our Odessa, it is a custom that as soon as you sit down, up comes a man dressed in a coat with a tail and orders you to order ice cream.[12]

This fine blend of business and pleasure was characteristic of the city in 1912, as described by Kataev:

> The spirit of European capitalism reigned in the town center. There were black glass signs with impressive gold lettering in every European language at the entrance to the banks and company offices. There were highly priced luxury goods in the windows of the English and French shops. Linotypes clattered and rotary presses whirred in the semi-basements occupied by newspaper print shops.[13]

Kuprin, another discerning writer, conveys the same admiration for Odessa's center:

> ... the dressed-up, always holiday-like town, with its plateglass windows, its imposing monuments, its gleam of electric light, its asphalt pavements, its avenues of white acacias, its imposing policemen and all its surface of cleanliness and order.[14]

Wealthy Odessans lived predominantly in the central area, near the shops. Kataev presents a portrait of the rich as viewed by the fictional, middle-class Batchei family:

> Somewhere up above, beyond the Nikolayev Boulevard lay the bright, noisy, luring, unapproachable, intangible place which was referred to in the Batchei family circle with contemptuous respect as "the Centre." In the Centre lived "the rich," those special beings who travelled first class, who could go to the theatre every day, who for some strange reason had their dinner at seven o'clock in the evening, who kept a *chef* instead of a cook and a *bonne* instead of a nursemaid, and often even "kept their own horses," something indeed beyond human imagination.[15]

But even the rich could not afford to monopolize the central area. An American journalist describes the limestone buildings—one, two, or three stories (four at most):

> Most people live with their business. You will find a hardware shop, a dairy, a grocery on the ground floor of your dwelling, insurance offices and lawyers scattered through the upper floors, with the household of the tenants in the adjoining rooms.[16]

He might have added that in the cellars lodged seamstresses, carpenters' apprentices, and tailors, among others.

Among the great architectural monuments of the city was the Opera House, which stood a short distance behind the southern end of the boulevard. It was separated from the City Hall by the English Club. The old theater burned down in 1873, and a new one was built to take its place. Two Viennese architects (with the operatic-sounding names of F. Fellner and H. Helmer) began to construct the larger replacement in 1883 and completed it in 1887 at a cost of 1,300,000 rubles. Modeled after the opera house in Vienna, it was named the Odessa City Theater. An American in Odessa, viewing it, declared it to be "one of the finest in Europe."[17] The facade was (and is) Italian baroque; allegorical stone figures in groups decorated the exterior. In the niches were busts of Pushkin, Gogol, Griboedov, and Glinka. The large hall, in the style of Louis XVI, was richly decorated with gilded stucco designs and figures. Frescos on the ceiling depicted various Shakespearean scenes. In addition to the wide *parterre*, there were four tiers of loges, a dress circle, a balcony and a gallery.

The architects, remembering a tragic fire in the Ringstrasse theater in Vienna, provided the foyer with twenty-four exits, each one equipped with water supplies.[18] On the side of the theater was a lawn with fresh flowers and shrubs, patterning the city's emblem. (Today there are still floral designs at that site.)

Another major monument was the New Exchange, built in 1898 by A. O. Bernardazzi, who included in the design elements of flamboyant Gothic and even oriental style. Here is a description:

> ... a handsome building of oriental architecture [it] is a center of activity. The trading takes place in a splendid hall on lines similar to those of the board of trade at Chicago. The remainder of the building is devoted to sample rooms, committee rooms, reading rooms, and other purposes.[19]

The building of that large hall (60 meters by 120 meters) without supporting columns presented problems. That helps to explain why it was one of the costliest buildings in town. Its interior was paneled in cedar of Lebanon, its windows set in white Carrara marble. It now serves as the home of the city philharmonic orchestra.

Also in the center city was Novorossiia University (founded in 1865). Its main building was the former Richelieu Lycée, which was constructed in the Florentine style between 1852 and 1857.

In 1879, the French consul announced that Odessa would soon build one of the most beautiful railway stations in the world. It was to have a crystal roof and a separate pavillion for the imperial family.[20] Two years later, the British consul reported, "A handsome station is at last being built in place of the shed which has so long disgraced the town."[21] And indeed, as a triumphant symbol of the coming of the railroad age to Odessa, a huge neoclassical train station was completed in 1884 southwest of the center city. Nearly as large as the new city theater, it faced Pushkin Street on a large square. Here first- and second-class passengers found their entrances. The entrance for third-class passengers opened on Hay Square, while arriving passengers discharged onto Kulikovo Field Square. The chief facade was adorned with three arches and Doric columns. The exterior plaster work was especially intricate and the interior was no less elegant. The vestibule floors were laid with colored tiles and the pilasters and cornices were likewise brightly painted. The main hall boasted parquet floors and painted ceilings. The designers were Shreter and Bernardazzi and the builders were Shevtsov and Lonskii.[22] After its destruction by the Germans in 1944, a new, larger station, which maintained much of the old design, opened in May 1952.

By the early twentieth century, Odessa even displayed signs of modern architecture. The American consul described the new look of 1913:

> A noticeable feature of the new buildings is the use of sheet glass of larger dimensions than heretofore, although the general style of architecture is heavy. Most of the buildings are constructed of brick and cement, but there is a movement toward the use of iron and concrete, as in the United States.[23]

Despite the shortage of water in the city and the difficulty of growing trees, Odessa devoted ample space to parks, "the lungs of a city."[24] On the left of the Potemkin staircase was a children's park. No adults except mothers and nurses were allowed. There were special toys and amusements; we are told this park was open to all children—rich or poor—under supervision. On the right hand of the staircase were constructed tree-lined paths and artificial grottos made from the city's limestone. The pleasing winding paths and nooks on the bluff's incline afforded views of the sea as well as shade on a summer's day.

The City Park (the oldest municipal park) was directly in the center of the city between De Ribas and Preobrazhenskii Streets. There pavilions offered treats such as *kumys* (fermented mare's milk), milk, or ice cream to the thirsty. This was another favorite spot for children and their nurses. In the summer, part of the park became a *café chantant.* In the winter, an ice rink took its place. Today it is still a favorite resting spot for students, strollers, shoppers, and an informal club of elderly gentlemen who gather in the late afternoon, summer or winter. Friday night concerts from a bandstand (demolished in World War II but rebuilt by the Romanian government) in the center of the park attract audiences even in December! The Old Botanical Gardens were among the most pleasant places for a stroll. By the second half of the century, however, the City Nursery and City Asylum (which lay rather distantly beyond Kulikovo Field Square) had taken over most of the grounds, leaving only a small area open to the public.[25]

On the southwest side of the city, a relatively new park of large dimensions was opened by Alexander II himself on September 7, 1875. He planted the first tree (an oak), and the large space of more than twenty-four *desiatinas* was utilized for industrial fairs, bazaars, and so forth. After the assassination of Alexander II, the city spent thirty-five thousand rubles for a tall monument to the slain tsar, who had visited Odessa several times. He had favored the city with special tax privileges as well. The pedestal was designed by Bernardazzi; N. I. Baronov was the architect of the ensemble.[26]

There were five major sculptures in the city: Richelieu's statue; Pushkin's bust in front of the Town Hall; a large statue of Catherine II, crushing the Turkish emblem with her feet, in Catherine Square; a statue of Vorontsov in the Cathedral Square, and a monument to Alexander II in Alexander Park.[27] All but Catherine and Alexander II remain. In place of Catherine's statue today stands a huge monument dedicated to the Potemkin Mutiny of 1905. The base of the Alexander monument is today used to honor Taras Shevchenko, and Alexander Park has become Shevchenko Park.

Light and Transport

In 1866, gaslights were first installed in the city. Later, in 1880, the government tried a kind of electric light, called Iablochkov's candles. Not very effective, their use remained limited to the Primorskii Boulevard. By 1887, some electric streetlights were introduced. In 1894, the city officials boasted that nearly all the city was lit by gas. There were 2,142 gas lamps, but Moldavanka and Peresyp were still illuminated by kerosene.[28] In 1901, a German company was still providing gas illumination, despite talk of installing electric lights throughout the city. In most homes gas or kerosene lamps continued to burn; only the rich could afford paraffin. In the early years of the new century, a Belgian company brought electric lighting to the city.

In 1880, a Belgian stock company constructed the first horse-tramway line from Richelieu and Post Office Streets to the outskirts. Initially, the concession had been given to a French company, which in turn, sold it to the Belgian firm for twenty-five thousand rubles. By 1900, the company had built a system of eighty kilometers. Its capital was 6,770,786 francs; its annual profit more than a million francs. It was so successful (despite a bad year in 1899) that the city thought of purchasing the company and transforming the line completely into electric trams, an enterprise, which, it was estimated, would cost some 15 million francs. This project also interested German firms. Two companies from Berlin, Schuckert and Company and Union Company, made bids, as did Helios Company of Cologne. In the end, the same Belgian company that furnished the city with electricity provided a limited number of electric trams.[29]

A Belgian company likewise founded an omnibus service in 1899. German-made carriages offered passengers a more comfortable ride than the traditional droskies. These latter were backless, back-breaking vehicles, for hire at virtually every corner of the city for less than a half-ruble an hour, and were never completely displaced before the war. In 1914 they could still be heard rattling over Odessa's cobblestones.

By 1899, the city was actively engaged in providing its citizens with mass transportation. Thought was even briefly given to commissioning a Russian engineer to construct a cable-car line. Time was required before the citizens became accustomed to all these technological marvels:

> As they were crossing Greek Street, the drivers pulled up in terror to give way to a new and shiny electric tram-car, emitting cascades of sparks. This was the city's first tramway line, built by a Belgian company, connecting the center with the Industry and Trade Fair that had just opened in the wasteland near Alexandrov Park.[30]

Still, horse-drawn trams with their quaint awnings to shade riders from the southern sun endured alongside more modern means of transport. As late as 1917, an American physician remarked, "The horse cars at Odessa took one back twenty-five years to the primitive days of New York."[31]

Odessa, on the fringe of the empire, filled with free spirits and far from the stern gaze of Moscow and St. Petersburg, proved itself to be an experimental city. Precocious in its sewer system, quick to catch on to the wonders of electric transport, it is not surprising that it readily adopted other forms of locomotion as well. By the 1880s bicycles became popular. On the eastern side of the city beyond Old Free Port Street, practitioners of the new sport used the cycledrome for velocipedes.[32] A 1904 guidebook listed "The Odessa Society for the Lovers of Velocipedes."[33] In the same year, Paris received a report from the French consul at Odessa:

> The paving of the streets has not changed. The roads which lead to the very picturesque environs of the city continue to be covered with that dust and which, at the first rainfall, are transformed into deep

mud, but the bicycle has triumphed over difficulty. One sees it going about the city every day during the good season, mounted especially by young people, riders for pleasure, intrepid businessmen to whom the means of locomotion is of real help in a large city.[34]

By 1909, roller-skating came into vogue. A rink was opened in Kherson Street for the amusement of the "monde élégant." Citizens could skate outdoors on "les rares rues de la ville qui sont asphaltées."[35] At about the same time, automobiles from America, Germany, Italy, and France were finding an outlet in Odessa and environs despite the high duties placed upon them—for some models the tariff alone came to more than two hundred rubles. In 1904, there were about thirty autos, motorcycles, and delivery trucks circulating on Odessa's streets. Ten years later, 365 cars, 94 motorcycles, 33 trucks, and 1,828 bicycles were requisitioned from Odessa's citizens for the war. The French consul advised French manufacturers that the cars should be sturdy—to bear the rough paving—and lightweight—to avoid becoming mired in muddy roads.[36] He also warned that, as of 1908, the Russians themselves had installed their first automobile manufacturing plant. By 1910, British taxicabs were coming into use, as were motorbuses.[37] In the city directory of the following year, there were advertisements for Mercedes automobiles and motorboats.[38] In 1913, the United States consul reported that some eighteen to twenty different makes of cars were sold in Odessa. The Auto Club had recently sponsored an endurance, not speed, race to Sevastopol and return (some 795 miles). An American automobile took the cup.[39]

Aviation found its early admirers in Odessa as well. One of the city's colorful characters, a man by the name of Utochkin, nicknamed "Red," caught the fancy of two of the city's writers, Valentin Kataev and Iuri Olesha. The latter gives us a thumbnail sketch:

> Utochkin is supposed to be an eccentric and people somehow tend to laugh when they are around him. I don't quite understand why. He was one of the first to take up the bicycle, the motorcycle, and the automobile, and was one of the first to fly. . . . He was a champion, but in Odessa people looked upon him as the city's madman.[40]

Utochkin was not the only aviator. The French consul wrote to Paris in 1909, saying that a plane valued at thirty thousand francs had just arrived at Odessa on board a French ship; it had been purchased by the city's Aero Club. Not only were several people of Odessa interested in flying, but the Imperial Technical Society at

Odessa included a special section on aeronautics at its 1910 exhibition.[41] By 1913, two or three planes in Odessa were owned and operated by private persons.

Neighborhoods and Suburbs

Odessa did not have neighborhoods in the sense of ethnic and social self-segregated residential areas. As we have seen, the center city housed some of the wealthiest of the town and some of the poorest. As Bater noted in his book on St. Petersburg, social separation was more vertical than horizontal. The poor lived in cellars and attics; stores occupied the street floor; and the rich, the second and third stories.

Not only did the rich and poor live in propinquity, but they drank side by side as well. That is, the fashionable cafés, restaurants and tea shops of De Ribas Street found, welcome or not, one of the plebian pubs, Gambrinus, as their neighbor. Windowless, lit by gas jets and darkened with smoke, Gambrinus, as delightfully described by A. Kuprin, was a popular beerhall where dancing Ukrainians, Jews, sailors, and drunks passed an evening together. Like the living quarters of many of its inhabitants, it was subterranean. Its site, at the corner of Soviet Army and De Ribas Streets, is now occupied above ground by a jewelry store.

To be sure, most of the low taverns were down on the waterfront. Here, according to Kataev, were "the dives, doss-houses, second-hand shops, and dead-end lanes where tramps and down and outs, pale-faced and ragged, were playing cards or sleeping on the bare ground."[42] Oriental inns, gambling dens, and places where city thieves and sea smugglers could dispose of stolen goods, formed the nether side of Odessa. Kuprin parts the curtain on this seamy strip:

Here, too, were the many beershops, taverns, eating-houses and inns, with flamboyant sign-boards in every known language, and not a few disorderly houses, at once obvious and secret, from the steps of which hideously painted women would call to the sailors in hoarse voices. There were Greek coffee-shops, where one used to play dominoes and cards and Turkish coffee-shops where one could smoke narghiles and get a night's shelter for five kopecks.[43]

Moldavanka

Among the most distinctive of Odessa's neighborhoods was Moldavanka, located about four *versts* from the port. The district originated just beyond the circuit of the free port, according to the 1824 boundary. But the boundary soon included this area. (Odessa retained free port status until 1859.) Even after this privilege was abrogated, a large boulevard known as Old Free Port Street (*Staroportofrankaia*) continued to mark the former boundary. It also separated the rigorously geometric grid of streets, characteristic of the old center, from the looser pattern of the outlying districts. During the first half of the nineteenth century, Moldavanka was known principally as the site of the military barracks; it also contained the elegant country houses of many of the city's wealthy. Close to the free-port limits, it further served as a depot for contraband. The proximity of the old limestone quarries with their labyrinthian catacombs helped to give the district a reputation as a center for underground or underworld activities, in the literal and figurative meanings of the words. Today the catacombs are shown as the hiding place for World War II partisans.

From mid-century, the city's growing population pushed into this and other former suburbs in search of space. Many of the city's public institutions found convenient sites right on Old Free Port Street, between the old town and its former suburbs. These included the Technical Society; the Sretenskii Philanthropic Society, which founded a dining hall there; several public schools; the almshouse; the disinfectant chamber; the electric station; an artisan school; the Pavlov Eye Clinic; the city auditorium; and others. Indeed, this wide boulevard ringing the old center came to be called the "beauty's necklace" (the "beauty," of course, being Odessa), because it contained the community's civic jewels. Those jewels were its public schools, clinics, charitable societies, and public buildings.

In the early 1860s, however, a visitor remarked on the rustic character of Odessa's former suburbs:

> Two suburbs, that of Moldavanka and that of Peresyp [later to become an industrial sector] are remarkable for the magnificence of their country houses. In the former are found the institutions for noble young ladies and the *dacha* or farm of Richelieu.[44]

The poor in particular were becoming too numerous for the crowded center. According to the *Odesskii vestnik* for 1874, "many day laborers in Odessa spent the night right on the street in empty barrels, even in the rain."[45] The poor were pushing toward and then into the previously fashionable suburbs, such as Moldavanka. By 1900, property there cost eight to seventy rubles (averaging about forty) per square *sazhen*.[46] Not relishing such neighbors, the rich moved their dachas or villas still farther away from the city. Thus, Odessa acquired concentric rings of neighborhoods, the inhabitants of which showed vastly different levels of wealth. The dense center housed primarily the rich, with subterranean layers of poor. The houses became progressively more modest as one proceeded toward and through the newer suburbs. Around 1900, property could be acquired for only one to fifteen rubles per square *sazhen* in the less desirable areas such as Peresyp, Near Mills (Blizhnie Mel'nitsy) and Far Mills (Dal'nie Mel'nitsy), Slobodka-Romanova, and Grain City.[47] But at the farthest limit of the urban concentration, like frosting on a cake, was a thin but elegant ring of wealthy villas. Land, however, sold from twenty-five kopecks to fifty rubles per *sazhen*, depending on its proximity to the sea.

By the 1870s, competition for space in the city's center was already strongly mounting. The British consul reported, in 1873, for instance, that speculators were purchasing dwellings in the confident expectation that their value would soon double.[48]

Removal to Moldavanka proved to be especially attractive for the excess population. Moldavanka by then possessed gaslights, water-works, and a sewerage system. On the other hand, the absence of paved streets and the lack of fresh water severely handicapped growth along the seashore. Moreover, only wide Old Free Port Street separated Moldavanka from the city's core. Poor Jews in particular flocked there in great numbers. Many of the new arrivals, Jews and others, contributed to the district's old repute as a center of illegal doings. This is the reputation Moldavanka bears, for example, in Babel's amusing "Odessa Stories."

As late as 1917, Paustovskii described the district as ". . . a hang-out of thieves, receivers of stolen goods, small traders and many other characters with devious and dubious occupations."[49] In spite of its concentrations of Jews, Moldavanka was in no sense a ghetto—a district in which Jews were legally obligated or willingly chose to reside. An Italian visiting the city around 1913 makes this clear:

> Odessa has not even taken on the aspect of an international city. It doesn't possess a quarter diversely populated one from another. There is not even a Jewish quarter. . . . More than international, therefore [Odessa is] a-national, an esperanto city.[50]

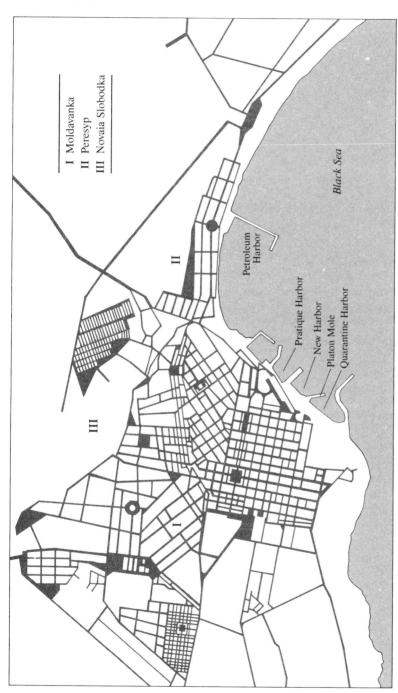

The City of Odessa, ca. 1895

I Moldavanka
II Peresyp
III Novaia Slobodka

Black Sea

Petroleum Harbor

Pratique Harbor
New Harbor
Platon Mole
Quarantine Harbor

To be sure, some quarters claimed larger numbers of Jewish residents than others. But marked ethnic neighborhoods, characteristic of many nineteenth-century cities, seem to have existed only in attenuated form at Odessa. Names—Italian, Greek, or Jewish Street—indicated not residential neighborhoods, but commercial centers, filled with shops and firms generally belonging to members of these ethnic groups.

The Periphery

As the city shaded off into suburbs, beyond the bands of poverty, the sparsely settled outlying areas retained a certain charm. Kataev described them in 1912:

> The typical provincial nature of this southern city had remained unchanged on the outskirts. There one could still find the small limestone houses with tiled roofs, the walnut and mulberry trees in the yards, the bright green booths of the soft-drink vendors, Greek coffee houses, tobacco shops, and wine cellars with a white lamp in the shape of a bunch of grapes over the entrance.[51]

Vodka shops were also there. Graters were nailed on nearby trees; customers could scrape off the wax stoppers on the bottles and try the beverage on the spot.

As industry came to Odessa, it settled primarily in two areas. Peresyp, to the northeast of the center, was a district about four to five feet above sea level, occupying about twenty-eight hundred *desiatina*s of land. Cattle yards and slaughter-houses were found there. This was also the site of Odessa's fair, held on the fourteenth of September. The district contained oil presses and steam mills, as well as factories preparing leather, candles, buttons, wine, industrial paints, and bottled water. Carts with heavy loads of grain lumbered to and from huge storehouses. In season, by way of the nearby railroad, the grain was taken to the waiting ships.

The second major industrial site was a district called Bugaevka. It lay beyond the Water Ravine (Vodnaia Balka), which cut across the western part of Moldavanka. Factories processing food, leather, and sugar, and the bottling plant for Odessa's "champagne," called "Excelsior," filled its spaces. Just to the south was a little village named Tyraspil Gate; it held so many large grain magazines that it earned the nickname, "Grain City."

Important settlements to the south of Tyraspil Gate were Far Mills, Near Mills, and Slobodka-Vorontsov. Earlier in the century, rows upon rows of windmills, set upon open fields, largely filled the space. But in the latter half of the century, factories, spewing forth clouds of smoke, dominated the landscape. As the city chief, Kossagovskii, reported to the tsar in 1883, the working class lived in the nearby villages of Dal'nyk, Usativ, Vorontsovka, and the neighborhoods known as Large and Small Fountain (Bol'shoi Fontan, Malyi Fontan).[52]

Abandoning their summer homes in the congested and industrializing suburbs, the rich moved to the farther fringes of the city and also to the seaside zones along the southern coast. The advent of the horse-drawn and then the electric tram gave both rich and poor a new mobility. As early as the 1860s, a tourist wrote that the estates of the rich were spreading over the surrounding rural villages, and that some used the houses all year round.[53] An American woman confirms his impression:

> At the latter season [summer] when there is neither shade nor coolness to be found in the city, all the wealthy people leave for their sea-side villas, or the watering places of the Crimea.[54]

A French horticulturalist was impressed with the seacoast villa belonging to a Greek merchant named Zarifi. It boasted "a house with walls painted light blue under the southern blue sky."[55] Another merchant, one of the wealthiest, an Englishman named Cortazzi, also had a lovely home, sheltered from winds by a small elevation and by many trees. Since it was nearly impossible to grow grass on the sandy soil, he planted low shrubs of a dark green color (*genièvre, sabine*). With its lanes lined with trees (chestnut and juniper), with terraces and gardens embellished by vases and statues, the dacha might well have been on the Italian or French Riviera. And the view his dacha offered of the Black Sea was no less enchanting.[56]

Murray's 1868 *Hand-Book for Travellers* advised tourists going to Odessa to drive to the race course outside the city and to visit the seacoast villas. One of the elegant homes had belonged to Count Langeron. Besides the lovely botanical gardens, the tourist could, on occasion, enjoy music or displays of fireworks.[57]

During the summer, the middle class frequently rented furnished rooms in the countryside, especially at the German colonies. In 1900, such rooms cost fifty rubles per month.[58] While the wealthy had their private strips of beach attached to or near their villas, and the middle class rented rooms, the public at large had their bathing establishments just south of the city. A chain of bathing beaches, warm water baths, and amusement parks there linked together; they bore romantic names—"Large Fountain," "Middle Fountain," "Small Fountain," "Arcadia," and "Delight." Restaurants on bamboo piles extended over the water; bandstands, shooting galleries, merry-go-rounds, and *kvass* (a thin sour beer of fermented rye) stands crowded the shoreline. These amusement areas were noisy and colorful. Even nature lent the area its own festive tints. In the spring, flowering yellow broom blanketed the cliffs. We recall that the Italians who first visited there in the Middle Ages called the area "Ginestra," that is, "broom." Also along the cliffs were wild roses, tamarisk, scratchweed, sweetbriar, lilac, and hawthorn. Crimean irises of every hue sprouted within the little valleys, and dahlias were in profusion.

While the southern shore was given over to bathing establishments and beaches, the northern shore offered bathing in the lymans or estuaries. The largest lymans were the Kulial'nyts'kyi and the Khadzhibeis'kyi. Because of polluted waters from industrial waste (emanating especially from slaughterhouses in the Peresyp), sea bathing was not as attractive as on the southern shores. However, rich in salt springs and mineral waters, abundantly supplied with the mud of estuaries, blessed for much of the year with a temperate climate, Odessa was predestined to become a health and vacation resort of wide appeal.

The Crimean Tatars had used mud baths as cures, but the inhabitants of Odessa apparently did not come to appreciate their medicinal qualities until the 1820s.[59] In 1833, during the regime of Vorontsov, the first sanitorium was built on the shore of the Kulial'nyts'kyi Lyman. The modest facilities could not meet the demands placed upon them by 1840. A new, larger, two-story building was constructed, but it was destined to see varied uses. During the Crimean War, the government requisitioned it as a barracks. The city government reacquired it in 1858 and made it into a hospital. But the establishment of a salt industry along the lymans led to its closing. The city reclaimed it in 1865; its facilities were expanded, with the addition of another building and fifteen cabins for mud and salt water baths. In 1892, a new, sprawling, grandiose health resort, located conveniently right across from a train station, was built to take its place.

Soon, new private bungalows, made of brightly colored limestone, sprouted up to take advantage of the spa industry. But the absence of piped fresh water limited expansion in the region of both major lymans.

The first sanitorium was built on the Khadzhibeis'kyi Lyman in 1866. It too was a branch of the Odessa City Hospital. Business boomed from 1887. The season for cures extended from May 15 to September 1. These resorts offered their clientele temperature-constant mud, steam, salt, sand, and mineral baths. Those willing to tolerate greater variations, and wanting to pay less money, could dip into the open lymans, and arrange their own cures. But they faced competition in their search for the waters. The sandbars of the lymans were exceptionally fertile, primarily because the city had taken to depositing part of its treated sewage there. It then leased plots to market gardeners.

In 1882, the Jewish Hospital opened its own spa where two hundred patients came annually for the baths. Children, from all ethnic groups and from all ranks of society (including orphans), had a special sanitorium of their own by 1888. Some 170 youngsters used their facilities each year. Doctors operated private clinics and recommended baths in the lymans. These many institutions, large and small, together generated a booming business, attracting about half their clientele from outside Odessa. Surrounded by sea and estuaries, Odessa made good use of its natural gifts, becoming a renowned resort and cure center on the Black Sea.

The Modern City

One hundred years after Odessa's founding, the city fathers proudly took account of the city's commercial structures. In all there were 9,786 buildings, including 661 stores, 3,600 shops, 413 restaurants, 127 bakeries, 55 tea shops, 371 spirit shops, 745 artisan workshops, and so on. [60]

During the second half of the nineteenth century, Odessa overcame the limits that traditionally repressed the growth of cities. Its attractiveness and its cultural and material advantages continued to draw outsiders to the city. The city fathers boasted of their achievements—the theater, the city auditorium, the Girls' Gymnasium, the girls' schools, the Artisans' School, about fifteen public schools, the psychiatric section of the city hospital, the lyman health resorts, and the city slaughterhouse. [61] Its growth was phenomenal in two directions. The population in its central districts reached new densities and the city also grew spatially. New modes of transport created here, as elsewhere, "streetcar suburbs." In its growth, it developed its own particular pattern of urban ecology: rich core, though still with a poor constituency; declining levels of affluence (but also less desperate poverty) as one moved outward; impoverished areas, but industrial areas as well, at the rim; and then, at the outer limits, and running down its coast, wealth again. The whole was attractive, and the life lived within it, for the most part, pleasant. *La belle époque* deserved its name at Odessa.

CHAPTER TWELVE

A Decade of Disturbance, 1904–1914

Odessa was perhaps the most police-ridden city in police-ridden Russia.

—Leon Trotsky

To observers of Odessa in the late nineteenth century, the city appeared to be the most cosmopolitan and progressive in the entire Russian Empire. In fact, beneath the calm surface tensions were mounting. In 1904 and 1905 strikes, riots, and pogroms shattered the social peace. Further strikes and an outflow of population marked its history in the years immediately preceding the outbreak of World War I. Its once successful social system was unravelling.

Ruffians and Revolutionaries

The flow of immigrants who filled the city included many poor and uneducated, but many intellectuals as well. Their one common characteristic was that they were male, young, adventurous, and disdainful of laws and rules. A. Kuprin, who at times lived in Odessa in "frightful lodging-houses," described some of the company he kept:

All these people—sailors of varied nationalities, fishermen, stokers, merry cabin-boys, port thieves, mechanics, workmen, boatmen, loaders, divers, smugglers—all young, healthy, and impregnated with the strong smell of the sea and fish, knew well what it was to endure, enjoyed the delight and the terror of everyday danger, valued, above anything else, courage, daring, the ring of strong slashing words, and when on shore, would give themselves up with savage delight to debauchery, drunkenness, and fighting.[1]

He also painted a vivid description of the stevedores who formed a sizeable segment of the population:

From the ships to the docks and warehouse and back along the quivering gangways the loaders ran to and fro, Russian tramps in rags, almost naked, with drunken, swollen faces, swarthy Turks, in dirty turbans, with large trousers, loose to the knees but tightened from there to the ankles, squat, muscular Persians, their hair and nails painted a red-carrot colour with quinquina. . . .

One visitor discerned in the population "adventurers and swindlers of the most ruthless kind, people who had learned their lessons in scoundrelism at Constantinople, Roumania and the Levant, and had grown grey in vices and crimes of every description."[2]

An ardent Russian nationalist visited Odessa immediately after the Russo-Turkish War of 1877; he describes the conditions that he says had prevailed there since the late 1860s:

[Odessa] was still a place of constant disorder and habitual lawlessness. Hopelessly involved in debt through the recklessness of its municipal administration, prevented from effecting any sort of consolidation by a constantly shifting population, held together by no ties of nationality or religion and visited, moreover, by periodical commercial crises, easily explained by the precarious nature of the grain trade, this town had degenerated into a focus of crime and dissolute excess, such as none of the governors-general, town prefects, or heads of police sent from St. Petersburg had even been able to master. Frauds and thefts of unprecedented extent, and murder and acts of violence committed in broad daylight, were daily occurrences. The attempts to curb the prevailing disorder remained nearly always abortive, the sea and the Roumanian frontier being near, and the number of professional thieves and receivers of stolen goods enormous. Neither the watchfulness and severity of Von Kotzebue, the former Governor-General, nor of Count Steenbock, the Chief of Police, had been able to check the evil, but after their departure it was worse than ever.[3]

The author no doubt exaggerates, but his strictures illuminate how high officials in the imperial government viewed Odessa. They accused the city of being "foreign," insubordinate, and deserving of punishment. They responded to its perceived faults by increasing still more the number of police serving within the city. And the imperial government punished Odessa in many ways: it denied the city favorable tariff rates, better railroad connections, and an improved harbor. This deprivation and the worsening economy further strained social relations among Odessa's classes and among its ethnic communities. Agitators of both the extreme left and the extreme right did not find it hard to incite these underemployed, often uprooted, usually impoverished and dissatisfied inhabitants to violent measures.

Odessa both produced and attracted radical intellectuals. Novorossiia University, located in Odessa, and several scientific and learned societies, such as the Agricultural Society of South Russia and the Society of History and Antiquities, provided focal points for political discussions and the exchange of ideas. Even the wealthy of the city, for the most part merchants, held more progressive views than the conservative landed gentry, who dominated society elsewhere in the empire.

Reformers and revolutionaries long found Odessa, with its easy communications abroad, a convenient headquarters for their political activity. Many of the Decembrist conspirators of 1825 had ties with the city. Repression quickly followed the aborted coup, but Decembrist literature could still be purchased at Odessa.[4] The Society of Independents, a liberal secret organization founded by members of the intelligentsia in the 1820s, may have included Pushkin.[5] As mentioned previously, as early as 1821 the Greek secret society, the Hetairia, was established in the city; it went on to plan the Greek national uprising against the Turks.[6] Bulgarian patriots (notably Vasil Aprilov) made Odessa a base for their efforts to raise Bulgarian national consciousness.[7]

Radical Movements

In the late 1850s, as the imperial government grudgingly recognized the inevitability of major reforms, it granted its citizens greater freedom of expression. This weak breeze of liberalism was enough to fan smoldering embers into revolutionary flames in Odessa. In 1861, a joint Polish and Ukrainian revolutionary committee set up its illegal headquarters in Odessa. From there it spun a conspiratorial network stretching to Kiev, Warsaw, London, Paris, and Genoa. The *Moskovskie vedomosti* called Odessa "the chief operational base of Polish activity and the international center for communications with all the revolutionary centers of Europe."[8] Participants in the Polish uprising of 1863 used Odessa as a point for reaching Poland and for departing abroad. Some Polish insurgents were exiled to Odessa.

Even some of the French communards, defeated in the great Parisian uprising of 1871, allegedly found their way to Odessa; the owners of a bottle factory offered employment to twenty-one of them, though they remained under close police surveillance.[9] Perhaps the presence of French communists made the police excessively nervous, for in that same year (1871) an English merchant by the name of Marx was arrested on the assumption that this was the notorious Karl. Advised by the English consulate, the indignant Marx brought suit against the police.[10] The police files yield other indications of official paranoia. In 1872, for example, they were carefully watching such seemingly benign organizations as the Italian Benevolent Society, the Women's Charitable Society, and the Lovers of Music.[11]

Odessa was the place of publication of a radical, though still legally printed paper, the *Odesskii vestnik*.[12] The liberal physician and educator, N. I. Pirogov, succeeded in shifting the sponsorship of the paper from the governor general to the Richelieu Lycée. The professors quickly used the paper as a forum for social criticism. One article, for example, lamented the waste of money on the merchants' luxurious balls, while the needy went hungry.[13] Even the "women's question" was aired; why, an author demanded, were women denied serious educational opportunities? Another unsigned article evaluated the wages of the working men of Odessa. Although 277 rubles were needed to support a family for one year, the average annual wage of laborers amounted to only 196 rubles, 30 kopecks.

These were dangerous words. The conservative commercial paper, the *Journal d' Odessa*, took up the gauntlet. It made it its business to publish conservative rejoinders to nearly all the liberal arguments of its rival. Several times the editors of the *Journal* hinted that the writers for the *Odesskii vestnik* were tainted with socialist sympathies. It is not surprising, therefore, that the city government eventually reclaimed sponsorship of the paper. Lest they be entirely muted, several of the contributors to the *Odesskii vestnik*, Professors A. Bogdanovskii and A. Georgiovskii, Pirogov himself, and other journalists such as I. Minitskii and O. Rabinovich, put out a collection of critical essays entitled the *Novorossiia Literary Collection*.[14]

During the Crimean War, many Russian officers and soldiers had spent time in the West, as prisoners of war. They became acquainted with the radical press, including some of Alexander Herzen's publications. With peace, they brought back to the Russian Empire a familiarity with this literature and created a demand for more. Odessa became a major point of entry through which Herzen's illegal paper *Kolokol*, published in London, was smuggled into the empire. According to a police report, it could be easily purchased for sixty kopecks.[15]

The true size of its readership is difficult to judge. Vorontsov's friend, E. S. Andreevskii, mentioned the publication several times in his diary, without concealing his admiration. In his estimation, had Herzen not turned to radical politics, he might have become a distinguished professor.[16] We do know of another faithful reader of the *Kolokol.* Carefully bound series of the paper today rest in the Odessa *oblast* archives; they are stamped with the *ex libris* Count Alexander Stroganov.[17] Marginal notes in the count's own hand betray his avid interest in the subversive sheet. No wonder, for his name appeared frequently on its pages. Herzen even published an open "Letter to Count Stroganov." Needless to say, he had little favorable to say, either to or about the count. As we have seen, however, Stroganov showed surprising tolerance toward those in Odessa who read or circulated the paper.

The rapid movement of men and goods through the port made censorship difficult—and the censors of Odessa had long enjoyed a reputation for corruption. Even the land frontier was difficult to patrol; contraband, whether in goods or ideas, slipped easily over the border. With reason, therefore, the writer F. F. Vigel referred to the "democratic republic of Odessa."[18]

Jewish liberals, reformers, and Zionists found Odessa hospitable to their movements. Numerous in the indigenous population, Jews were even more prominent among the students studying at the lycée and university. In 1859, student activists at the Richelieu Lycée founded a secret "Society of Good Goals" on the significant date of December 14, in memory of the Decembrist revolt. One of their good goals was to disseminate literature on social issues. Two years later at the same lycée, other students formed an even more radical circle. Students at Moscow University formed a similar group and even took the name, "The Odessa Circle."[19]

Despite its ostensibly small Ukrainian population, Odessa played a significant role in the Ukrainian national movement of the late nineteenth and early twentieth centuries.[20] In the late 1860s, a branch of Hromada ("Society") was founded at Odessa, on the model of the Hromada organized earlier in Kiev. Hromadas were loose associations that brought together intellectuals, students, and others interested in Ukrainian affairs. By the early 1870s they were developing programs of political reform, but the repressions of 1875 and 1876, and in particular the ban on the use of the Ukrainian language in publications, put an end to political agitation. Still, the Kiev Hromada, with the support of the Odessa group, did send Mykhailo Drahomanov to Geneva to serve as their official political representative in the West. They also tried to strengthen their organization and spread their ideas through organs such as the *Kievskii telegraf* (the Hromada's *de facto* newspaper) and the Southwest Russian Geographical Society (functioning from 1873 to 1875).

The Odessa Hromada was led by a very able group of individuals, including at first Leonid Smolens'kyi (a historian who taught for many years at the Odessa Military School) and Mykhailo Komar, a government official and an avid bibliographer.[21] In the 1890s many of the members cooperated under Komar's direction to compile a major Russian-Ukrainian dictionary, which was published in Lviv. In many respects the atmosphere in the city was conducive to Ukrainian cultural activities, as tsarist repression was less severe than in the older Ukrainian centers. From 1893 to 1897, the group helped to publish forty-four books in Ukrainian, and in the first years of the twentieth century the members put out a number of important Ukrainian almanacs.

After the 1905 Revolution, a second organization, called Prosvita ("Enlightenment") attempted to strengthen the movement's popular appeal through founding a library and bookstore. It published many books and two newspapers, *Narodna sprava* and *Visti.* Although the government suppressed Prosvita in 1910, a Ukrains'kyi kliub continued its work until 1914. The Hromada remained active until 1917.

These early liberal and radical organizations remained, however, largely confined to members of the educated classes. Only in the 1870s did the first labor organizations bring working people fully into the movement for reform or revolution.

Although Odessa was slow to acquire big industries, many artisans and apprentices lived within the city. Moreover, the urban economy was highly volatile and subject to frequent, violent downturns. Odessa was the first city in the Russian Empire to witness the formation of a politically active labor union. This was the South Union of Workers, founded in 1875.[22]

Students and intellectuals joined the effort to organize labor. In the 1870s, the "going to the people" movement, supported by liberal youth, met a cool reception. They then chose as the most promising targets workers belonging to artels. An artel was a workingmen's cooperative; the members travelled from town to town, especially during the summer, and were chiefly employed in construction. Most were in fact peasants who sought additional income through this seasonal labor. They seemed to the populists not yet "tainted by city life," as were factory workers. As peasants, they supposedly retained an affinity with the communal spirit of peasant society, and would be sympathetic to socialist ideas.[23] When they returned to their villages after the summer employment, they would carry with them socialist ideology.

Their very numbers were a distinct advantage. The building mania of the early 1870s drew many into town, and later the crop failures of the middle seventies pushed many more. According to Itenberg, the Soviet historian of the Union of Workers, some eighty thousand artel workers arrived in Odessa in 1873 and 1874 alone.[24] Typically, the revolutionaries who worked among the artel workers were also people who floated in and out of Odessa. N. Zhbunev, a revolutionary active within radical circles in Zürich, arrived in Odessa from abroad in 1873. He began his propaganda activities among the artel workers and was arrested in October 1874. Viktor Obnorskii worked briefly in a tin factory in Odessa and launched his educational work there, but escaped abroad in 1874. He later returned and was one of the union's founders.

University students also clandestinely organized study groups composed of factory workers; the meetings were held in rented rooms in ordinary houses. They taught the rudiments of mathematics, geometry, and Russian grammar as well as other elementary subjects. The transient workers were, however, difficult to educate. The students had greater success with workers employed in large metal-working factories. The big enterprises probably raised the workers' class consciousness, and the skilled nature of the work meant that most would have some education or at least high native intelligence.

A former seminarian set up a small lending library for the workers, replete with such radical publications as the journal *Sovremennik* (the *Contemporary*). Not only workers, but also the liberal bourgeoisie of Odessa read the *Contemporary*. In 1859, there were some 94 subscribers in the city, and in the following year, 114. No other city, not even the capitals, boasted so large a readership. In the entire *guberniia* there were 237 subscribers.[25]

The populist E. O. Zaslavskii, son of a nobleman of Saratov, lectured on political economy and history at one of these underground circles. His earlier efforts had been devoted to radicalizing the peasants. While he never completely abandoned the hope that the peasants would become agents of a revolution, he recognized the possibilities for revolutionary activity among factory workers. He lectured to them on N. Chernyshevsky's socialist (and feminist) novel, *What's To Be Done?*

It is not entirely clear why Zaslavskii moved from propaganda to labor organizing. Perhaps the collapse of industries around him prompted him to organize the metal workers of the Bellino-Fenderikh and Gullier-Blanchard plants. In its regulations the union set as its goal "to propagate the idea of the liberation of the workers from the oppression of capital and the privileged classes."[26] Two strikes were organized, one in January 1875 at Bellino-Fenderikh and then at Gullier-Blanchard in August. Possibly as a result of an informant's tip, the gendarmes intervened. The union did not survive the end of 1875. Various temporary offshoots were formed secretly in other south Ukrainian locations, but the movement was essentially suppressed.

During its brief existence, the union managed to set up a cooperative bath and a cooperative savings and loan institution; the money deposited also served as a strike fund. Many organizers were Ukrainian, and at least one was of Polish origin and another the son of an Italian immigrant to Odessa.[27] Itenberg argues that these minorities were better experienced in revolutionary tradition than were the Russians. They had a particular set of grievances against contemporary Russian society. Moreover, at Odessa the difficulties that industrialists faced in making their operations profitable tempted them to squeeze their workers as much as possible. Many of the workers, on the other hand, were drifters and trouble-makers. The Odessa Committee on Trade and Manufacturing in the year of the formation of the union hints at these factors:

> The relations then between employer and workman, their mutual rights and obligations should be clearly defined by law, which we consider to be of greater importance for the South than for any other part of Russia.[28]

As for the factories that joined the union, they would be heard from again in 1905.

Writing immediately after the Russo-Turkish War of 1877, Julius Eckardt describes the revolutionary atmosphere prevailing in the city:

> ... the revolutionary propaganda of the Nihilists found a more congenial soil on the coast of the Black Sea than at the neighbouring Kieff, and ... the dominant bad spirit infected the students when a union was founded at Odessa in 1865. Of their revolutionary sentiments the Odessa students had given evidence before the recent war, but after the outbreak of hostilities which all but destroyed the commercial industry of the seaport, it seemed as if town and university alike were possessed by an evil demon. A portion of the army being provisioned from Odessa, Jewish, Greek and Roumanian contractors and traders of the most suspicious kind thronged thither, and made the town a

scene of orgies, frauds, and crimes such as surpassed the utmost measure of former iniquities. The emissaries of Nihilism understood quite as well as the professional scoundrels of the place how to profit by this state of insecurity. Some of the police were bribed, the rest were intimidated and prevented from acting with energy. Placards appeared on the walls in public places openly inciting the populace to deeds of violence and disobedience against the government; clandestine printing presses prepared and circulated Socialistic pamphlets; small conspiracies were hatched in secret, whose members attacked with daggers and pistols the police who were sent after them. All this was done in the summer and autumn of 1877, and done with an insolence such as people were only accustomed to meet with among the infamous bands of robbers and thieves who infested subterranean Odessa, who prowled among the numerous caverns and passages beneath the plateau on which the city stands. So deeply had the spirit of insubordination corroded the population, that the Commercial Council was imprudent enough to take no official notice of the passage of the Guards through the town on their way to the seat of war, and to treat the household regiments of the Czar, accustomed to be welcomed everywhere with patriotic ovations, with a coldness scarcely to be distinguished from hostility. [29]

After the arrest of the members of the South Russian Union of Workers, several subsequent attempts were made to create unions, but all of them proved abortive. In 1879, for example, P. B. Axel'rod, then a young populist, later a well-known Menshevik, attempted to revive the South Russian Union of Workers. His chief goal, however, was the repartitioning of the land among the peasants. When this program failed to elicit much enthusiasm in Odessa, he departed. Leadership of the radical movement at Odessa passed largely into the hands of the populist movement known as The People's Will. [30]

With the failure of unions, only the artels remained to provide individual workers with some bargaining power. This was evident in the case of Odessa's stevedores. In his annual report to the tsar in 1883, the city chief, Pavel P. Kossagovskii recorded that some foreign shippers had attempted to take advantage of the dock workers, who were among the city's poorest inhabitants. They attempted to form a contractors' monopoly. But the workers themselves, many of them former seamen, requested permission to create their own artel with their own contractor. [31] They thus escaped even worse exploitation. Despite this small victory, the harbor area remained a scene of insubordination and violence.

The same report also casts light on the state of Odessa's police. The city chief had been required to reorganize thoroughly the police force, in fact to hire an entirely new one. Although the Odessa police were better paid than most provincial policemen, they traditionally were reluctant to follow orders. This demoralized and immoral staff was particularly susceptible to the liquid blandishments of the pub owners, who only asked that liquor law violations not be noticed. But in restaffing the police force, Kossagovskii reported, he had "taken appropriate measures to restore law and order."[32]

Of course, law and order were difficult to maintain in Odessa. Members of the People's Will were numerous there. An artisan school for poor Jews, called Trud, was run by the Jewish Philanthropic Society and served as a focal point for revolutionary propaganda. In 1893, the Social Democrats attempted to form a group, but in the following year, one of the leaders, Iosif Shif, was arrested. As P. Garvi, a Social Democrat, later a Menshevik, wrote in his memoirs: "This was the downfall of a large Social Democrat organization, one of the earliest and most powerful in Russia."[33] Perhaps Leon Trotsky had this failure in mind when he observed:

> Commercial, multi-national, loudly colored and noisy Odessa remained, to an extraordinary degree, far behind other centres in a political sense. In St. Petersburg, in Moscow, in Kiev, there were already in existence at this time [ca. 1890] numerous socialist circles in the educational institutions. Odessa had none.[34]

Several more attempts were made to form an underground unit of Social Democrats, in 1896 and again in 1898, but to no avail. Finally, in 1900 the Odessa Committee of the Social Democratic Workers' party was established. The new year of the new century had been a particularly disastrous one. The crops failed; trade came to a halt. Fortunes were lost and unemployment ran high. To make matters worse, it was a bitterly cold winter. When Garvi entered this fledgling group, it consisted mainly of Jewish workers and artisans. In fact, it was working with the Jewish poor in Moldavanka that caused him to reject the capitalist system. When he saw large families housed in cellar apartments without heat and without light, close by open latrines, he decided that only revolution could relieve such grinding poverty.[35] Some of his fellow organizers were former members of the South Russian Union of Workers and others had belonged to The People's Will. But still more had once belonged to the Jewish Labor Bund; it had a large number of members in Odessa but was not as important as the Bund in Vilnius, Minsk, Warsaw, and other cities with large Jewish populations.[36]

As early as April 1901, the Odessa Committee distributed a leaflet among the workers and soldiers of Odessa, inviting them to join in a mass demonstration on May 1. The committee demanded an eight-hour working day, the right to strike, a democratic government, freedom of speech and of the press, and equality before the law for all nationalities.[37] Perhaps because most members of the committee were Jewish, the response was most sympathetic among Jewish artisans and workers in small factories. On the other hand, most of the larger enterprises hired predominantly gentile workers, who remained cool to the summons. These included such government operations as the railway repair yards, the Russian Steam Navigation and Trading Company, and distilleries. Flour mills and the larger metal-working factories also contained few Jewish workers. Even Jewish manufacturers such as Brodskii hired mostly Russians and Ukrainians. This rigid separation of workers made it difficult to agitate across ethnic barriers except at pubs and through study groups.

Strikes

In the depression year of 1901, the unemployed dock workers resorted to violence. They expressed their fury by smashing store windows. At first they attacked only stores owned by Jews, but then the looting became indiscriminate. The government called out troops and Cossacks to disperse the crowds. Within two days more than a thousand persons were arrested, and order was, with difficulty, restored.

The bad economic times, misery, unemployment, strikes, and repression gave strength to the socialists, but heated ideological controversies also beset the movement. The émigré organization known as Iskra headed the radical wing and called for immediate revolution. Those who favored limited goals—shorter hours, higher pay, reduced fines, and better working conditions were known as "economists." Typical of these economists was M. S. Zborovskii, the leader of the Odessa Committee of the Social Democrats after August 1901.

Unhappy with the committee's conservative leadership, the radicals broke off to form their own groups. Most of these splinter groups proved to be ephemeral, and in time their members drifted back to the parent committee. There remained, however, an undercurrent of discontent over the economic orientation of the

Committee and its predominantly Jewish membership. Other revolutionary groups vied for the allegiance of the workers: the Social Revolutionaries after 1902; the Jewish Bund after 1903; and assorted groups of anarchists, Polish Socialists, and others.[38]

In February 1902, before a planned demonstration commemorating the fortieth anniversary of the emancipation of the serfs, the police arrested more than three hundred Social Revolutionaries and Social Democrats. The division within the socialist ranks and the government's harassment allowed a new form of workers' organization to take root in Odessa. This was the police-sponsored union of "Independents." The idea for such an unlikely organization came from Sergei V. Zubatov, then chief of the Moscow Okhrana the tsar's secret police. A loyal patriot and monarchist, Zubatov sought to better the lot of the Russian workers, while maintaining their allegiance to the tsar. He exploited the popular sentiment that the monarch was concerned for the welfare of the common man and eager to help the workers against their oppressors, the big industrialists. The Independent organization set out to promote workers' welfare and thus prevent their dissatisfaction from turning into political protest. The strategy, probably unique in the world, possessed a certain logic, although its implementation encountered formidable obstacles. Many tsarist officials did not believe that workers should be organized and trained in the arts of protest—for any cause. Zubatov's policy, known as *Zubatovshchina*, had been tried earlier in St. Petersburg and Moscow.[39] There too, the obvious aim was to win workers over to a legally recognized (and officially supervised) union and away from the subversive Social Democrats and other revolutionary parties.

In other parts of the Pale, notably in Minsk and Vilnius, a comparable organization, the Jewish Independent Party, worked to recruit Jewish workers and artisans, thus depleting the membership of the revolutionary Jewish Bund.[40] In Odessa, a charismatic leader and orator and an ardent Zionist, K. Shaevich, was amazingly successful in creating a branch of the organization in 1902. He drew adherents from all elements of the working class—Jews and gentiles, workers in artisanal shops and in large factories, railway workers, tram drivers, sailors, and stevedores.

The Odessa Committee of the Social Democrats had not effectively organized the large enterprises where most ethnic Russians were employed. But Shaevich and others managed to enroll more than two thousand workers in a few months. The pure economism of the organization's goals obviously had broad appeal;

and its semiofficial status offered it needed protection. To be sure, even the Independents had enemies in the government. The chief factory inspector of the Kherson *guberniia*, I. I. Popov, repeatedly attempted to block the movement. Both the local and the imperial police supported the Independents, but the local officials were divided in their attitudes, some sympathetic to the movement, others violently hostile. Fortunately for Shaevich and his enterprise, the city chief in 1902 was Count P. P. Shuvalov, who had long advocated improved conditions for the working class. He was warmly sympathetic to the Independents and aided them even in their strikes. But as the strikes grew more frequent, Lieutenant General D. G. Arsen'ev replaced him in office. Arsen'ev was not at all favorable to the Independents, and the then mayor, A. P. Zelenyi, was equally hostile. The policies of the government toward the labor movement remained vacillating and inconsistent, both locally and nationally. At St. Petersburg, Sergei Witte, only recently dismissed as minister of finance, had opposed the Independents, while V. K. Plehve, his archrival and the head of the state police, appeared to tolerate and even at times to favor them. [41]

The strike movement of 1903 gained greater momentum after the dismissal of Shuvalov. The Southwest Railway workers quit work on July 1, and the steamship personnel soon followed. [42] On July 17, some six hundred sailors from the Imperial Navy were brought from Sevastopol to load the mailboats. According to the American consul, Cossacks, troops, and regular police were keeping order in the city, but at first they did not directly interfere with the strikers. Next to join the protest were the tram drivers. [43] In quick succession, work stoppages closed the principal factories; by the end of July, they had taken on the dimensions of a general strike.

In this troubled summer, Odessa was not alone in experiencing crippling strikes. All the large cities of the Ukraine and the Caucasus suffered through similar stoppages. At Odessa, the strikers milled around the city in large groups. They gathered in the outlying parks, listened to speeches, and discussed the current crisis. In the parks, members of the Odessa Committee and other socialists and revolutionaries made inflammatory speeches, sang revolutionary songs, unfurled red flags, and urged the workers to put forward political as well as economic demands. The police stood by, but made no move to control the crowds; in consequence, there was surprisingly little violence. To be sure, strikers entered the smaller shops, inns, pubs, stores, and factories and forced sometimes reluctant workers to leave their jobs. But no pogrom or wanton destruction of homes and shops ensued.

Abroad, Lenin was elated over the general strike in Odessa. But even according to *Iskra*, the Social Democrats had failed to dominate the movement. On the whole the mood of the strikers was peaceful, even good-humored. Commissions set up by city officials carried on negotiations, which seemed to promise a favorable outcome. Nonetheless, as a precautionary measure, Lt. General Arsen'ev brought in additional troops and Cossacks to strengthen the forces of order. Not until July 19, after several weeks of work stoppages, did the authorities unleash the dreaded Cossacks and soldiers. That day the city chief published an official notification that no assemblies would be permitted. Between 6:00 and 7:00 in the morning a crowd variously estimated at fifteen thousand to fifty thousand persons had already gathered at the public gardens, however. Fights broke out between the Independents and the Social Democrats. When the latter began to hand out leaflets, the Cossacks and soldiers brutally dispersed the meeting, causing casualties.[44] A British observer maintained that the infantry and Cossacks "used their whips with such force that eight persons subsequently died of injuries received, and over thirty were permanently disabled. Some hundreds of strikers were also arrested and sentenced to imprisonment."[45] The same witness reported that Plehve gave "passive aid to the strike movement at Odessa in 1902 in order to lure the strikers to commit some outrage which might excuse a subsequent resort to armed force."[46] The account of the strike published in *Iskra* claimed that the soldiers had not molested the Independents. Allegedly, they and the police connived to lay the blame for the violence on the socialists.[47]

At all events, the great strike of 1903 was broken. The stevedores received wage increases from seventy kopecks to one ruble, sixty kopecks per day, and their work day was shortened by one and one-half hours, according to *Iskra*.[48] Other workers were not as fortunate. Some were discharged for being illegally absent from work for three days.[49] The loss of sixty thousand rubles in wages and 600,000 in production further depressed the city's economy, and tensions remained high. At this point, Plehve changed his mind and decided to suppress the Odessa Independents. Shaevich was exiled to Siberia, and Zubatov was dismissed in disgrace.[50] In disbanding the Independents, the government failed to respond to the legitimate demands of the workers; the imperial autocracy could no longer pretend to be the champion of the working people against rapacious manufacturers and capitalists. The chief beneficiaries of the demise of the Independents were the radicals, especially the Social Democrats.

The Revolution of 1905

The war against Japan, which began on February 8, 1904, provides the immediate setting for the violent events—strikes, mutinies, and pogroms—of 1904 and 1905.

After the July Days of 1903, Odessa's economy remained locked in depression. The harvest of 1904 was poor, and the export of wheat fell even below the levels of 1903. By the fall of 1904, the war against Japan was going badly and the economy was buckling under the strain. Fears ran rampant that France and Great Britain would intervene to aid their Japanese ally. The prospect that Russia itself would be forced to abandon the gold standard undermined confidence in the ruble. Capitalists sent their money abroad, and the normal sources of credit dried up. German banks, which played a prominent role in discounting paper for commercial and industrial enterprises, suspended this service, because of the monetary uncertainties. In Odessa, private banks provided most of the available credit, but they in turn depended on the Russian State Bank to rediscount the paper they received. With so many military reverses, it was not certain that the Imperial Bank could continue to provide this service. Observers noted that some 20 to 30 percent of commercial paper in Odessa could not be discounted.[51] The flight of capital and the shrinking of credit caused many commercial failures in Odessa. Without credit, local firms could not purchase goods abroad, and this led to further cut-backs in domestic production. More workers were laid off, and misery deepened. Individuals and firms could not meet the payments on their mortgages, and the bonds of the mortgage banks defaulted on their bonds. New mortgages were almost impossible to obtain, to the great damage of the construction industry. The American consul noted its depressed state in September 1904:

> The failure of building operations has thrown thousands of skilled workmen as well as ordinary laborers out of employment and this presents a situation which is not without danger to the country.[52]

The early and continued propaganda efforts of revolutionaries among the construction artels now yielded returns. In the events of 1905, construction workers were among the most vociferous protestors. Also prominent were the disaffected workers in the larger plants. By March, the huge Gen (Ghen) agricultural machinery factory, the Ulysses factory, and the Arps Cork Company had cut their work force down by one-half.[53] The jute factory and the stone quarries experienced significant layoffs. In April, about seventy men staged an illegal walkout at the stone quarries at Usatovo, near Odessa.[54] The price of stone had fallen, and workers who still had jobs faced a cut in salary. Brick factories closed down their operations. At the same time the price of bread was rising; the absence of many breadwinners at the front worsened the plight of many households. The forty-eight rubles a year received by the families of slain soldiers scarcely supported them.[55] Very few industries in Odessa benefited from war orders. Most depended for their prosperity on international trade, which the war had severely curtailed.

In the fall of 1904, several shots were fired at the city chief, Colonel Neidhart, as he walked on the Nikolaev Boulevard. By then thousands of working men were idle; crop failures continued; thefts and burglaries, always numerous in Odessa, reached new heights. The bad economic times were chiefly responsible, but governmental decisions also contributed. Seeking popularity, the tsar extended amnesty to all thieves not convicted of violent crimes. In Odessa, some 200 "notorious ruffians" walked out of the local jails. In addition, 180 recently released convicts in Kherson were given train tickets to Odessa! The American consul had cause to lament these decisions, as thieves twice broke into and robbed his own offices.

Bloody Sunday

In the closing months of 1904, the mood of the populace became more and more bitter. In early January 1905, news of "Bloody Sunday," when soldiers fired upon peaceful demonstrators in St. Petersburg, deeply shocked Odessa. The American consul reported:

> The brutality displayed by the authorities in St. Petersburg has brought to the front a movement which, with care, might have been held in abeyance for fifty years to come. I allude to a revolutionary movement among the peasantry and working class combined. The men who were murdered last Sunday were all workmen who came from the villages, peasants in fact.[56]

Neidhart immediately issued an appeal to Russian workers not to strike. Only Japan, he argued, would benefit, and a work stoppage would allow the enemy to take away markets in the Far East. Employers also would profit, for they were looking for excuses to shut down their plants; there was not sufficient demand to keep the factories open even three days a week. He also reminded the workers of the futile strike of 1903. "Let not your peaceful work be interrupted," he pleaded in ending his appeal.[57]

In a report to the United States ambassador in St. Petersburg, Robert S. McCormick, the American consul, describes the reaction of the people of Odessa to Bloody Sunday:

> I never knew the Russian public to be so united in their views in connection with the acts of the authorities in ordering the soldiers to shoot the workmen, their wives, children and inoffensive spectators last Sunday in St. Petersburg. All classes condemn the authorities and more particularly the Emperor. The present ruler has lost absolutely the affection of the Russian people, and whatever the future may have in store for the dynasty, the present Czar will never again be safe in the midst of his people.[58]

Within a few weeks, protests against the government multiplied. According to an account in *Vpered*, even a meeting of the Society for the Protection of Public Health, held in the city council hall, was transformed into an antigovernment rally, as it protested the pitiful condition of the working class. The mayor, A. P. Zelenyi, presided, and more than two thousand persons attempted to squeeze into the meeting. One of the orators claimed that most health measures had been mere palliatives. What the workman needed for his health was an eight-hour working day, free speech, freedom of association, and other liberties. The speeches grew ever more radical; in a kind of climax, the crowd rushed to the streets to demonstrate against the regime. They fanned out throughout the city, but the police, perhaps remembering the results of Bloody Sunday, took no action. On another occasion, a meeting of the Odessa Judicial Society served as a forum at which speakers expressed lack of confidence in the tsar, called for an end to the war against Japan, and demanded amnesty for political prisoners. Again, the crowd spilled out into the streets. Even at a meeting of nobles, the 5000 or so present (not counting the police) heard denunciations of the regime, to which the crowd responded with the cry: "Down with autocracy!" This time the Cossacks arrested about fifty persons, and some twenty-six were injured.[59]

These seemingly unpatriotic demonstrations spurred the reactionary and anti-Semitic gangs known as the Black Hundreds to increased activity. As early as February 1905, they were distributing pamphlets urging pogroms in Kiev, Odessa, Kherson, and Mykolaiv.[60] But as yet there was no mass response.

The Battleship Potemkin

The costly war dragged on through the late winter and spring of 1905 and blocked all commercial recovery. It entirely cut off maritime connections with the Far East. The lack of rolling stock obstructed the transport of grain (what little there was) from the hinterland to the port, and trade with western Europe remained sluggish. In the unyielding grip of misery, workers resorted to frequent strikes from April to June. By May, it appeared that a general strike would again paralyze the city. In a desperate effort to bring the workers back to their jobs, the government ordered that they be given Sundays off and that most be required to work no more than nine hours per day. From the middle of April until the end of June there were constant and general strikes of all wage-earners of all classes. At this critical juncture the mutinous battleship *Potemkin* sailed into the harbor. Eisenstein's classic film accurately shows the heroic sailors disembarking in the midst of chaos, and the mutineers certainly augmented the agitation in the city.[61] The populace went on a rampage; the focus of the agitation was the docks where lay the body of the dead sailor who had started the mutiny. For about a week fires burned in the port district; looting of the warehouses, ships, and shops appeared unstoppable. As some rioters burned docks, warehouses, ships, and the overhead railway, others were robbing trains. Estimates of losses run to over 9 million rubles—not a trivial sum for a city in severe economic crisis. The Customs House was closed for six days. An American journalist reported that about six hundred persons died in the tumult.

All this time the battleship lay at anchor. Finally, the mutinous sailors seized coal from private colliers, even as several battleships and torpedo boats steamed toward Odessa from Sevastopol. The *Potemkin* sailed out of Odessa, accompanied by a mutinous torpedo boat, to seek a haven somewhere in the Black Sea. One of the pursuing battleships mutinied, inducing rapture among the revolutionaries. Their joy was, however, short-lived, as the ship surrendered at Odessa. After consuming all of their coal, the sailors of the *Potemkin* put in at the Romanian port of Constanta. The authorities promised not to arrest the mutineers, and they were given five days to escape. The ships were returned to the Russian government.[62]

The October Manifesto

On August 25, 1905 (n. s.), peace agreements were signed at Portsmouth, New Hampshire, and this raised hopes that domestic order would be restored as well. But when Witte returned from the United States to St. Petersburg, he found, in his words, "complete chaos."[63] In the capital there was no transportation, water, lights, operating telephones, or railroads. Massive strikes continued in the provinces. By the second week of October, Odessa's economic life was once again paralyzed. In desperation, Witte and other ministers advised the tsar to grant a constitution, in order to stem the revolutionary tides. The resulting proclamation is known as the October Manifesto. In it, Tsar Nicholas guaranteed civil liberties and transformed the Duma from a consultative body into a legislature made up of elected representatives.

The concession did not produce all the hoped-for results. Most workers resumed their jobs; an improving economy also helped to restore social peace. But the Manifesto did not appease either the far left or the far right. Various rightist groups united to form the Union of the Russian People. They objected to the policy of liberal reform and were determined to punish those whom they considered responsible for the October Manifesto and for the economic upheaval of the past year. Or they used these reforms as an excuse to attack their predilected target—Jews. The very day after the issuance of the Manifesto, as if by a given signal, numerous violent pogroms erupted in the Pale: at Kishinev, Kiev, Kherson, Akkerman, Rostov-on-Don, and above all, Odessa.

Pogroms

In the first half of the nineteenth century, Odessa's many ethnic groups lived in mutual toleration and even in harmony. Within their own circles they shared social activities and religious worship and arranged for the education of their children; they promoted the welfare of their members through charitable and benevolent associations. Anti-Jewish riots had, to be sure, occurred—in 1821, 1849, 1859, 1871, and 1881. But the friction seems to have been initially limited to an animosity between Greeks and Jews, and the riots themselves did not take on monstrous proportions.

In the latter half of the century, Jews, as we have seen, came to constitute the second largest ethnic community in the city. Odessa's many Jews were for the most part assimilated, Russified, educated, and cultured; many (though far from all) were prosperous. In fact, one Jewish historian observed that the Jews "contributed more than any other nationality to Russifying Odessa, which, owing to its great foreign population was known as the most un-Russian city of Russia."[64] A Jewish expression for prosperity was "to live like God in Odessa."[65] A Lithuanian Jew who visited Odessa in 1861 was impressed not so much with the wealth of the Jewish community (which was considerable). Rather, he admired the fact that Jews walked calmly, with dignity and stateliness, through its streets. They conversed in the Café Richelieu, frequented the Italian opera house, obviously feeling comfortable and at home. In the words of one of them, Odessa was "the city in which Jews lived better and more pleasantly than in any other in Russia."[66] The Jews might well have walked proudly in their "Little Paris," for their talents, energy, and capital had contributed to its prosperity.

The growth in Jewish population was matched by their economic success in various sectors: in the ownership of land and factories, in the crafts and professions, and above all in trade. Once predominantly petty tradesmen engaged in local enterprises, the Jews by mid-century were becoming active participants in the international export-import business. This brought them into direct competition with the hitherto dominant Greeks.

This trend did not escape the sharp eye of A. A. Skal'kovskii, who wrote in 1865:

> Odessa's Jews are no longer content with small trade. Already 8 of their number are in the first guild and 16 in the second and 24 take part in banking operations on the Odessa Stock Exchange, where they have special freedom, although the means of some of them are still rather limited compared with the Greeks and the Genoese.[67]

In Skal'kovskii's opinion, the chief merchants were still Greek (some with Russian citizenship), Genoese and other Italians, Germans, Russians, and Jews. The ethnic Russians engaged for the most part in local commerce. They rarely traded on the Stock Exchange and even more rarely did they maintain direct contacts with Europe.

Between 1865 and 1870, Jewish merchants progressed even further. In 1871, the long-seething animosity between Greeks and Jews erupted into violence.

Pogroms, 1871 and 1881

The trouble began at the site of the Greek Orthodox church. The church stood on the corner of Troitskii and Catherine Streets, that is, in the heart of a heavily Jewish neighborhood. In 1910, a lawyer named M. G. Morgulis published in the Jewish press a detailed and vivid account of the pogrom, based on contemporary investigations and his own memories.[68] According to this source, Greek worshippers gathered in the courtyard of the church on Easter eve. This was, of course, an annual occurrence, as was the noise and revelry that accompanied the end of a forty-day fast and the renewed consumption of alcoholic beverages. But this particular year was marked by even more boisterous behavior. Random revolver shots, whistling, the breaking of bottles—all shattered the nocturnal peace of the Jewish neighborhood. Perhaps in retaliation, someone, presumably a Jew, threw a rock from beyond the walls of the courtyard; the rock struck one of the revelers, who fell down, perhaps from the injury or perhaps from intoxication. (Apparently, the crowd was largely composed of sailors.) His compatriots determined to take revenge. Some of them left the church precincts, accosted and struck the Jews they randomly encountered, and broke the windows of Jewish homes. Then they soon took to looting the shops and homes.

Whatever the provocation, the rampage continued for three days and three nights. The mob threw stones, broke windows, looted stores, and occasionally assaulted Jews themselves. Russian workers, artisans, artel members, and, according to the Jewish author, even some Jews joined the rioters. The lure of booty rather than religious fervor attracted the dregs of society. During the initial phases of this disturbance, the police kept out of sight. Indeed, the mob had deliberately attacked homes across from the main police station in order to "test the waters." When there was no reaction, the crowd fanned out through the city. A rumor was bruited about that soon the tsar would grant permission for all to seize Jewish property. With their greed aroused, even people from the surrounding countryside entered Odessa to join the looters. According to the same report, the forces of order—police, soldiers, and Cossacks—stood idly by as the pogrom progressed. Finally, the temporary governor general, who had stepped out on his balcony to address the populace, was himself struck by a stone. Only then did the authorities move to end the riots and restore order.

The American consul sent an extensive account of the events to Washington. Hostility toward the Jews, he explained, derived from the presence in the city of some forty to fifty thousand Jews and about half that number of Greeks. The Greeks were "doing generally the larger and better kinds of commerce."[69] In consequence,

> ... between the Jews and Greeks, therefore, there are constant jealousies and animosities, originating no doubt, mostly from differences of race and religion, but also, perhaps, excited and encouraged from the collision of business interests.[70]

He attributed the outbreak of violence to remarks made by Jews loitering outside the Greek church on Easter Sunday. Since violence broke out on the night before Easter, the writer's version has the ring of accuracy. The consul agreed, however, that the rioters were intent on destruction and not mayhem. The Jews did not attempt to defend themselves nor to take vengeance. Some fifteen hundred persons were ultimately arrested; some were publicly whipped in the marketplaces. The city government set aside funds to compensate Jews rendered destitute by the disorders.

The pogrom caused destruction of property worth millions of rubles. Six persons were killed, 21 wounded, and 863 houses and 552 businesses damaged or destroyed. As the Russian Orthodox bishop Dmitri wrote in a brochure denouncing the pogrom, "What they could not steal, they smashed. What they could not steal or smash, they burned."[71] What was the motive? Only a year earlier, a writer had noted, "Jews and gentiles live here in an atmosphere of fraternity and friendship." Morgulis, the author of the 1910 article (and one of the editors of the Jewish newspaper *Den*), attributed the pogrom to widespread resentment against the growing prosperity of the Jewish community. The new Jewish success in the grain trade, achieved at the expense of the Greeks, was especially grating. Since no physical harm had been intended, the destruction of property indicated that some Greeks felt the Jews had become too "puffed up." The Jews allegedly had taken on too many airs, and they "should be taken down a peg or two." The authorities had remained inactive because they initially viewed the battle as a fight between two foreign groups; as long as the interests of "nationals" were not involved, they saw no reason to intervene.

The central government, on the other hand, felt differently. It immediately became alarmed that the riots might have some revolutionary implications. It dispatched investigators of its own to make sure that the riots were not "a red speck on the horizon." As for the rioters themselves, Morgulis hints that they learned their lesson. The chaotic pogrom of 1871 would not be repeated. A decade later, the pogrom would be better orchestrated. The pogrom of 1881 would use destruction of property to impart a message to the government that the people resented Jewish "exploitation." It was to be a signal to the state that stiffer laws and restrictions on the Jews would be welcome. And indeed, it succeeded in that mission. Morgulis concluded with this observation:

> The pogrom of 1871 already hid in its womb its future phases. What for historians will be historical documents, for us contemporaries, all these pogroms were dreadful experiences, mixed with torrents of bitter tears and inconceivably horrible deaths. [72]

The American consul made this prediction:

> I think it not unlikely that new disturbances may take place and new persecutions may be directed against the Jews at some favorable moment hereafter, for the hatred of that race by both Greeks and Russians is deep rooted and in time, may possibly grow to intolerance. [73]

Unfortunately, the American consul's sentences proved insightful.

The pogroms of 1881, as Morgulis explained, had been so well timed and coordinated throughout southern Russia as to indicate that some sort of central organization was directing them. In his estimation the most likely ringleaders were members of the reactionary "Holy Brotherhood." The immediate causes are not difficult to locate. In March 1881, the tsar emancipator, Alexander II, was assassinated. Before his son, the new tsar, Alexander III, made public his views concerning the death of his father, reactionaries could vent their hatred against Jews and claim that their acts were retribution against the murderers of the tsar. Rumors circulated throughout the south that the tsar had ordered the destruction of Jewish property. [74] The riots broke out in Ielysavethrad in April, and at Odessa in May. Again, the riots continued for three days and three nights. Again, the local officials looked the other way. The minister of the interior, N. P. Ignat'ev, placed the following interpretation upon these events:

> The main cause of this movement lies in the economic situation. During the previous twenty years, the Jews have taken over trade and industry, purchased areas of land by sale or lease, and by means of their unity have succeeded in exploiting the main body of the poor,

hence arousing them to a protest, which has found distressing expression in acts of violence.[75]

The official response to this "exploitation" was of course the infamous May or Ignat'ev Laws issued in 1882, which we have examined elsewhere.[76]

The Jews reacted to the threatened violence by organizing a self-defense force, which was largely staffed by university students and by some few workers, and which included a fair number of Christians. But the existence of this private police force also lent credence to the charge that Jews were threatening the public order.

Pogrom, 1905

The racial atmosphere at Odessa remained surprisingly calm for more than twenty years after the pogrom of 1881, although there was a small disturbance in 1900. This period of relative peace proved to be only the lull before the most violent outburst of them all, the pogrom of October 18–21 (o.s.), 1905.

The October riots resembled the previous pogroms, but several new factors also intervened to worsen the violence. The old economic grievances were still there, but significantly, the highest tensions involved not so much wealthy Jews and their gentile competitors, as poor Jews and unemployed Christian workers. The war, the constriction of trade, and the cutbacks in industrial production had engendered high rates of unemployment within the city. Jewish merchants and industrialists were hated because they laid off workers in this year of depression. Ironically, they were also accused of filling the ranks of the radicals—the socialists, anarchists, and nihilists. Allegedly, Jews were unpatriotic; they did not support the war against Japan; they were also the ringleaders of the strike movement, which only increased the workers' misery. Suspicions of disloyalty, in sum, were added to the old economic rivalries and jealousies. The Ignat'ev laws, which made second-class citizens of the Jews, strengthened the popular sentiment that Jews were an unpatriotic and treasonous group. The failure of the local officials in Odessa to take quick action in repressing the disorders partially reflects this assumption that Jews were both disloyal and subversive radicals. It was no doubt also rooted in a conviction, shared by the local officials, that the imperial government would look with favor upon "punishment" meted out to Jews through the pogrom.

The mobs that joined the fray had their own economic, political, or religious agenda. Extremists on the right held the Jews responsible for the erosion of the tsar's autocratic powers. While the archreactionaries thought of Odessa's Jews as the leaders of the socialist movements, the leftists remembered them as organizers and enthusiastic supporters of Zubatov's police unions. The Jews had some influential friends at Odessa, notably among the liberal bourgeoisie and the university community, but they formed only a small part of the population.

The origins of the October pogrom go back to the disturbed summer of 1905. During the celebrated "Potemkin days," a state of martial law had been imposed upon Odessa.[77] The city chief, D. S. Neidhart, with the support of the commandant of the local garrison, Baron von Kaul'bars, wielded absolute authority over the city. Frightened by the disorders, the imperial government lifted the state of martial law in August, over the protests of Neidhart. The government next granted autonomy to the universities, removing them from the authority of the local administrations. At Odessa, the university at once became the center of political activism. Neidhart, stripped of his absolute power, appealed to the Ministry of the Interior, requesting that his powers be strengthened, but his petition was turned down. He was later to use this as an excuse for his failure to suppress the riots quickly. His toleration of the disorders was in part an act of retaliation for his own loss of power.

The first outbreak of violence occurred on October 14. The lecture halls had become the site of nearly continuous meetings, in which even nonacademicians were participating. Neidhart looked upon the meetings as subversive, but he was powerless to stop them. Several times he allegedly warned the rector of the university: "The lecture halls belong to you, but the streets are ours, and here things will be done without mercy—blood will flow." Unmistakably, he was thinking "pogrom." Whether he actively planned the pogrom remains an open question.

On the afternoon of the fourteenth, high school students, both boys and girls, tried to march to the university to join in the rallies. Police with drawn sabers waylaid them on the march and dispersed them, wounding several children. On October 16, as rumors reached Odessa about the events in St. Petersburg, other students tried to erect barricades, but the police again dispersed them, killing several and losing one of their own number. The wounded students were taken to the Jewish Hospital, and preparations were made for a public funeral for those who had fallen. But Neidhart abducted the bodies and had them secretly buried.

October 17, the day on which the Manifesto was promulgated, was ironically both "the Day of the Constitution" and the start of the pogrom. Crowds in the city celebrated the newly granted freedoms. Witnesses are not agreed as to whether or not these crowds unfurled red banners and other symbols of socialist revolution. Neidhart responded to the demonstrations by posting placards. On them he claimed to have received a letter signed by thirty thousand citizens, asking that the radical agitation at the university be suppressed. The rector called the placards a provocation and asked the military for troops to protect the university buildings. None were provided.

Neidhart responded negatively to a demand that a citizen militia be formed, but at the same time he ordered the police to remain off the streets—allegedly to protect them from shots fired from Jewish houses. Nor did he ask von Kaul'bars for help from the garrison of soldiers, as the law required him to do. He thus left Odessa's Jews completely without police protection.

In the early afternoon, crowds largely recruited from dock workers and city riff-raff gathered in the Dal'nitskaia region, the traditional capital of local hooliganism. The American consul telegraphed home the following description:

> Tuesday night October 31 [n. s.] the Russians attacked the Jews in every part of town and a massacre ensued. From Tuesday till Saturday was terrible and horrible. The Russians lost heavily also, but the number of killed and wounded is not known. The police without uniform were very prominent. Jews who bought exemption received protection. Kishenev, Kiev, Cherson, Akkermann, Rostoff and other places suffered terribly, Nicolaev also.[78]

The worst of the riots ran for the traditional three days, from October 19 to 21 (o. s.). The violence spread to the city center and to the suburbs, even into villages. The rioters showed masterful organization, as contingents in numbers corresponding to the size of the neighborhoods plundered. The looting occurred under the eyes and with the participation of policemen and soldiers in civilian garb. The Jewish self-defense forces did succeed in defending houses, and even entire streets and neighborhoods, but suffered heavy casualties and were eventually overwhelmed. The rioting worsened with each day, reaching a kind of climax on October 20. On October 21, the riots ended. Neidhart appeared on the streets and allegedly greeted the hooligans and told them: "Enough brothers, now go home."

Kaul'bars finally warned that his soldiers would shoot at all looters. Order was quickly restored.

After these events, Neidhart and Kaul'bars each tried to push the blame onto the other. Neidhart was forced to resign but was not otherwise punished.

Jewish casualties included 302 known dead (among them 55 from the self-defense forces and an additional 17 Christian members), many missing, and several thousand (perhaps as many as 5,000) wounded. Some reports claim the death toll reached 1,000. Property damage amounted to 3.75 million rubles. There were 1,400 ruined businesses, and some 3,000 artisan families were reduced to begging—in all, in Odessa and its surroundings, 42,975 persons suffered in one way or another from this historic pogrom.

According to an official report of the Odessa Jewish Central Committee to Aid the Victims of the Pogroms of 1905, the October pogrom was a large and unprecedented hurricane of hatred that swept through southern Russia and hit not only the poor, but also men of means to a great degree.[79] The committee helped 2,449 families, or 10,322 individuals, of whom roughly a third were under the age of ten years. Of the 2,549 families, 1,968 were attacked in their own homes. The committee collected 672,833 rubles; some 210,827 rubles were contributed by Odessa's Jews and 257,889 rubles came from abroad, including a sizeable donation from the Rothschilds.

An eyewitness, a young Polish Jew who had gone to Odessa as an apprentice to a brushmaker, gave this descriptive analysis:

> . . . the city was at that time the scene of frequent clashes between the unskilled laborers from the Russian villages, who earned small wages and were often out of work, and the Jewish shopkeepers or skilled workmen. The Tsar, I was told, wanted to exterminate us and had given orders that mobs should not be restrained too much from looting Jewish stores or injuring Jewish inhabitants. In Odessa several bands of young Jews had organized themselves into bands of defense, the most prominent being the butchers I had seen in action. When the alarm of a pogrom was sounded, they met by prearrangement, long knives in their hands and fought for their own lives and the lives of their co-religionists. Some of my new acquaintances said the priests were at the bottom of the trouble, others who had become Socialists told me that economic jealousy was the cause of the trouble.[80]

As a result of the riots, the American consul in December 1905 judged that some fifty thousand persons left Odessa:

As the greatest majority of these emigrants are Jews, i.e. members of the most mobile portion of the population, and at all times keenest on everything, that may be described as business, it need not be a matter of any surprise to find, that Odessa presents an appearance more dead than alive. And if the acute convulsions affecting the country continue, then this state of things may become still further accentuated.[81]

Indeed, after the pogrom of 1905, counter-revolutionary activity and anti-Jewish activity became so intertwined that it is difficult to separate the strands. Continuing economic troubles at Odessa sowed resentment against the Jews, who were held responsible for the unemployment. To the radicals, the persecuted Jews seemed likely allies against the common enemy—the tsarist regime. But the expectation proved ill-founded. In February 1906, when elections for the national Duma were being held, anti-Jewish riots broke out afresh. According to a proclamation issued by the "Hebrew Territorial Organization":

Amongst the wreckers were nearly all classes of Russian society: there were not only barefoot beggars, but also factory and railroad workers, peasants, chiefs of station, etc., amongst those who defended us Hebrews were only members of the learning youth, the victims who will be remembered. . . . But where were the organized workmen, where the Russian proletariat? They were not to be seen in the ranks of the "Self Defence." . . . We are showered with advice from good-natured assimilators of the Hebrews on one side and the leaders of the Hebrew laborers' organization on the other who tell us to be patient, but we have waited 2000 years. Antisemitism everywhere, everywhere Judophobism and now other comforters will come—the Palestine Zionists. They will also propose to you patiently to wait—to wait for "enlightenment" of the Turkish Sultan, for an expulsion of the Arabs from Palestine and until that time they will propose to our poor sufferers to remain in Russia and to the affluent to go to Palestine.[82]

For Jews, Odessa was not, as it had been, a comfortable home.

Aftermath, 1906–1914

Odessa's experiences in the last decade before the outbreak of the First World War closely paralleled those of the empire as a whole. Industrial peace was largely restored. There had been 13,995 strikes across the empire in 1905; in 1908, the number was only 892.[83] To be sure, Odessa, in reputation and probably in fact, saw greater labor unrest than other large cities. In May 1906, the sailors and firemen of the Russian Steam Navigation and Trading Company and of other shipping lines went on strike, demanding recognition of their union, a pay increase, and an eight-hour day. Peace was not fully restored to the docks until the following year. The French consul, as others had before him, observed: "These circumstances contributed not a little to increase the discredit which then weighed on Odessa and to deflect a part of the goods which feeds its traffic to the profit of its closest rival, Nikolaev."[84] Not until 1909 did restored labor peace combine with a good harvest to produce a measure of authentic prosperity.

In economic terms, Odessa's prospects by then seemed promising. Only one major strike, that of grain carriers, occurred in 1910. By 1911, the construction industry, which had suffered from the violence and the loss of population, had fully revived. The city acquired a system of tramways, which allowed the suburbs to expand. How Odessa's economy would have fared, had World War I not intervened, cannot be known. By 1910, it had already lost its preeminence in grain exports, and that type of commerce held little promise for the future. It had to seek other outlets for its entrepreneurial energies and other uses for its port. But international developments deprived these experiments of any chance of success. The war between Italy and Turkey (1911–1912) and then the Balkan Wars disrupted maritime commerce even before the outbreak of World War I in 1914. The entrance of Turkey into the war as a German ally in 1915 completely sealed the straits to Russian shipping.

Politically too, Odessa, like the entire empire, was moving in new directions after the revolution of 1905. The convocation of the imperial Duma in 1906 gave the empire a representative assembly for the first time, and helped to drain the violence out of political action, at least for a time. The Social Democrats had boycotted the elections for the first Duma but took part in elections for the second in the fall and winter of 1906. At Odessa, a coalition of Kadets (liberals), Mensheviks, and left Octobrists gained the seats. Most of the city's Social Democrats were in fact Mensheviks, and were primarily recruited from among the Jewish artisans, merchants, and shopkeepers. Only in the port district, in the industrial areas of Dal'nitskaia and Peresyp, and in the railroad repair yards and metallurgical factories had the Bolsheviks much of a following. The dominant political mood of the city could best be regarded as liberal. The ethnic tension that had produced the terrible pogrom of 1905 had surely not vanished, but government—especially the *gradonachal'nik* Tolmachev—now was strongly committed to the maintenance of public order. Where the new constitutional liberalism, at Odessa and in the empire, might have led, had war and revolution not intervened, is again impossible to know. After 1917, Odessa would have to seek resolutions to its problems within a vastly different economic and political order.

The experience of Odessa since the great reforms of 1861 is not a little paradoxical. Its commerce grew enormously over the last half of the nineteenth century, yet it lost relative position among the purveyors of grain to world markets. It also grew in numbers of people, but that growth slackened not long after 1900, amid the violence of strikes, revolutions, and pogroms. A historian such as Atlas argues that the city did not adapt quickly enough or well enough to the new conditions created by the great reforms. A principal reason for this failure was the strength of Odessa's "enemies"—highly placed persons in the imperial government who resented its non-Russian character, Western ways, political liberalism, and commercial prosperity. Be that as it may, in the early twentieth century, Odessa needed to lay out for itself new economic and political foundations.

Conclusion

Odessa was founded as a new city in a new land. It served as the principal maritime outlet to a rapidly developing region—New Russia—and the new Ukraine of which it was a part. It also quickly came to be integrated into a new world commerce in foodstuffs. The burgeoning industrial centers of Western Europe created an unprecedented market for wheat, and Odessa with the fertile black soils of its hinterland, was there to respond.

This dual role—outlet for the southern steppes, breadbasket to new industrial centers—made it a center of vital activity and of extraordinary growth through most of the nineteenth century. East and West, the age was one of booming cities, and Odessa for long held its place among, or surpassed much older rivals in its growth. Its success invited immigrants from both regions it served: the interior, whence came Ukrainians, Russians, Jews, and many other citizens of the vast tsarist empire; and from abroad, whence Greeks, French, Italians, and other westerners appeared in search of fortune. In its early history, Odessa was polyglot and cosmopolitan. Almost anyone who visited this great port would be sure to find someone ready to offer greetings in his or her native language.

Odessa did not succeed in maintaining this dazzling promise over the last decades of the nineteenth century and into the twentieth. Perhaps it was an exotic flower of early industrialism, doomed to fade as stabler plants took over the terrain. I do not think that this is so. Rather, I view Odessa as a door between economies and cultures. My research has recorded its opening. But the conditions, external and internal, that raised Odessa to eminence, shifted against it as the nineteenth century drew to a close. New suppliers of grain emerged, at great distance from Europe to be sure, but they were helped by new technologies of transport. Within the Russian Empire, problems of modernization affected and encumbered Odessa as well. Its trade needed efficient inland transport, mechanization of agriculture, greater productivity. Odessa failed to gain these advantages, as did the empire itself. Under conditions of a deteriorating economy, there was a final failure. Odessa could not meld its divided and angry citizenry into a cohesive unit, which might have given it more effective representation before the empire's rulers, and might have won for it the improvements it needed even to hold its traditional place in a competitive world.

My story ends somewhat sadly. But the ending is far from tragic. Odessa still holds a magnificent position on the littoral of the Black Sea, a place that since the age of ancient Greece has served as a door between peoples, societies, and cultures. In the long history of this region, only special circumstances have assured that this door would be used. May those times come again.

Notes

Chapter One

1. For the history of ancient Greek settlements on the Black Sea, see Gaidukevich, 1955; Shelov, 1956; Iessen, 1965; and Iailenko, 1975, pp. 188–98.

2. Cross and Sherbowitz-Wetzor (eds.), 1953, p. 53.

3. On Italian colonies and commerce in the Black Sea region during the Middle Ages, see Bratianu, 1919; Lopez, 1938; and the old but still useful survey, Heyd, 1885–1886.

4. Pegolotti, 1936, p. 42.

5. In 1413, for example, the Polish king Władysław II sent several shiploads of wheat down the Dniester River to the Black Sea, and thence to Constantinople, which was then withstanding a Turkish siege. See A. A. Skal'kovskii, 1850, pp. 83–84.

6. For the plans of a new fortress at Khadzhibei drawn by a Russian spy in 1766, see Borovoi, 1967a, pp. 130–36.

7. For an excellent analysis of Russian penetration into these areas, see Druzhinina, 1955, and idem, 1959.

8. On Russia's alleged "urge to the sea," now a largely forgotten issue in Russian history, see the discussion in Morrison, 1962, I, 49–50. The empire was in fact expanding in all directions.

9. Halm, 1943, I, 7 ff.; and Halm, 1961. For the impressions of a contemporary, see Weber, 1960, pp. 107 ff.

10. *Khersonu*, 1978, p. 5.

11. "Kherson," *BSE*, 46:121–22.

12. For the early history of Mariiupil, see Druzhinina, 1959, p. 79.

13. On Mykolaiv, see Halm, 1943, p. 10; Druzhinina, 1959, pp. 186–87; and for a near-contemporary view, Hagemeister, 1846, p. 2.

14. Weber, 1960, and Anthoine, 1805 and 1820.

15. See the comments of Sirotkin, 1970.

16. Harvey, 1938, p. 55.

17. Markevich, 1893, p. 24.

18. For the formation of the *guberniia*, see especially A. A. Skal'kovskii, 1850, pp. 34–41; also Druzhinina, 1959, pp. 53–57 and pp. 201–03; and Polons'ka-Vasylenko, 1955. For a more recent study, see the useful work by Shishmarev, 1975, pp. 24–75.

19. For a brief sketch of his career see *Proshloe Odessy*, 1899, pp. 9–10.
20. A. A. Skal'kovskii, 1837, p. 32.
21. The text of the *ukaz* is given in A. A. Skal'kovskii, 1837, pp. 33–35.
22. Smol'ianinov, 1853, pp. 43–44.
23. *Notizie*, 1817, p. 9.
24. *Istoricheskii ocherk*, 1889, p. xi.
25. *Proshloe Odessy*, 1894, p. 11.
26. Skal'kovskii claimed that the name "Odessos," meaning "great trade route," was given to the city by the Imperial Academy of Sciences. See idem, 1837, pp. 14 and 42. Some Greeks, such as Karabia, Raftopulo, Stomati-Lambro, and Gargoli were already living in Khadzhibei before 1794. See *Proshloe Odessy*, 1894, p. 7.
27. Barth, 1975. The book is primarily concerned with the boom towns of far-western America.
28. Nadler, 1893, p. 3; L. M. de Ribas, 1898, p. 233.
29. Luther, 1889, p. 7.
30. Scott, 1854, p. 335. For a description of the physical appearance of Odessa and its surroundings, see Fox, 1963, pp. 5–7; Shmidt, 1863; A. A. Skal'kovskii, 1850; Pavlovich, 1862; and *Odessa. Ocherk*, 1957, pp. 7–8.
31. NACRO, 15 Feb. 1862.
32. Armstrong, 1831, p. 24. It appeared to Vladimir Izmailov, who approached Odessa from the steppe in 1799, that all the buildings were floating on the sea. Izmailov, 1800–02, I, 359.
33. Moore, 1833, p. 19.
34. Koch, 1855, p. 259.
35. Mayakovsky, 1960, p. 62: "Eto bylo/ bylo v Odesse." He was referring to one of his love affairs.
36. One eulogist of the city claimed that its climate compared favorably with that of Paris, Vienna, Strasbourg, Cologne, Brussels, and Cambridge. See Moskvich, 1904, p. 68.
37. Author's experience. Green snow is evidence of how at times chilling continental weather surprised the city before autumn turned the colors of leaves; fallen green leaves colored the snow. See also *Odessa. Kniga*, 1911, p. 85.
38. Among the more famous complaints about Odessa's dust are Alexander Pushkin's lines beginning, "I lived then in dusty Odessa," from *Eugene Onegin*. In 1837, a Russian commentator observed: "From its steep eminence, Odessa commands a large bay, the dark blue waters of which contrast with the pale and arid appearance of the surrounding coast, invariably enveloped through the summer in whirling clouds of dust." Demidov, 1842, I, 290. The complaint is among the most common encountered in the travel literature. See Koch, 1855, pp. 259–60; Holderness, 1823, p. 77; and *Notizie*, 1817, p. 11.
39. On the other hand, in 1836, an English traveler noted that "the impalpable powder" raised by the slightest breeze was "considered so injurious to tender lungs, that the wealthy people having young families always

remove them to the country in the dry season. Before this practice was introduced, which was not till good physicians settled here, the town was considered very unhealthy." Bremner, 1839, II, 494.

40. Bremner, 1839, II, p. 483.

41. Ibid.

42. According to V. K. Kakhovskii, in a report to Catherine II in 1791. See *TOSK*, IV, 161.

43. *Notizie*, 1817, p. 36.

44. Ibid. pp. 10–11, ca. 1805.

45. Druzhinina, 1970, pp. 59–60. For a record of ice conditions in the port between 1848 and 1857, see Shmidt, 1863, I, 309.

46. Pinkerton, 1833, p. 121.

47. *Odessa*, 1895, p. 163.

48. Fox, 1963, p. 9.

49. *Stoletie*, 1894, p. 3.

50. *Odessa*, 1895, p. xiv; A. A. Skal'kovskii, 1837, p. 50, says the city received 311,822 rubles. For the same year the city received 405,000 rubles for the construction of docks. See Zolotov, 1963, p. 26.

51. *Proshloe Odessy*, 1894, p. 12.

52. Maria Guthrie, 1810, pp. 2–3.

53. Dearborn, 1819, p. 234.

54. Fox, 1963, p. 10.

55. Twain, 1911, p. 116.

56. Kohl, 1842, p. 419.

57. "In contrast to American cities which arose spontaneously (and at first only along the shore), the cities of Novorossiia were created for the most part at the initiative of the government [and] were situated throughout the entire territorial region. From the very beginning, they fulfilled entirely different functions—administrative, military, economic and cultural." Druzhinina, 1976, p. 74.

58. Skinner, 1973, p. 78. For the consequences of the lack of self-government, see Hamm, 1976a.

59. For a list of the names of the *gradonachal'niks* from 1797 to 1894, see *Odessa*, 1895, pp. 789–90. For the same period, on p. 791 there is a list of the *gorodskie golovy*, or the mayors of the city.

60. Druzhinina, 1970, p. 173.

61. There were some exceptions: about twenty to thirty small settlements in the Odessa area had been transferred from other *guberniias*. See Zagoruiko, 1957, I, 51.

62. *Odessa. Ocherk*, 1957, p. 15.

63. Beletskii, 1893, p. 126.

64. For the text of a Ukrainian folk song celebrating freedom found in Odessa, see Rudchenko, 1874, p. 117. For further discussion on the theme of freedom, see Druzhinina, 1970, Chapter II, especially p. 84, and my own comments in the article reviewing her book, Patricia Herlihy, 1974a.

65. Moore, 1883, p. 142. Some emigrants became criminals en route to their destinations. For example, the emigrants who mutinied on board ship, thus arriving in Kherson in irons, see Bartlett, 1974, p. 15.

66. *Odessa. Ocherk*, 1957, p. 24.

67. Haxthausen-Abbenburg, 1856, I, 429.

68. Druzhinina, 1976, p. 72. One historian argues that the existence of serfdom halted emigration of Russians to the South Ukraine, so that all the economic opportunities there went to foreigners. See Markevich, 1893, p. 31.

69. Smol'ianinov, 1853, p. 82.

70. *Odessa*, 1895, p. xvii. See also Kabuzan, 1976; Shishmarev, 1975; Bartlett, 1979; and Madariaga, 1981, pp. 362–63.

71. GAOO, *f.* 147, *op.* 1, *d* 77, *l.* 1.

72. Sirotkin, 1970, p. 74.

73. Levi, 1970, p. 302.

74. Orlov, 1885, pp. 104–22. Smol'ianinov, 1853, p. 40, lists names and provenance of early foreign merchants in the city. The copy of this volume in the Odessa State University Library is from the Count Stroganov collection. In the book are added several handwritten pages of historical material, probably in Stroganov's hand.

75. Shepelev, 1973, p. 18.

76. For commentary on the trade clauses in the treaty of Kuchuk-Kainarji, see Druzhinina, 1955, pp. 287–95. For Russia's commercial agreements with foreign powers from 1783 to 1787, ibid., pp. 183–84.

77. Sirotkin, 1970, p. 72.

78. Lobanov-Rostovsky, 1947, p. 85.

79. Sirotkin, 1970, p. 83. For Paul's interest in the Black Sea and the Mediterranean, see Saul, 1970, pp. 23–154.

80. Sirotkin, 1970, p. 85.

81. For comment, see *Account*, 1817.

82. See A. A. Skal'kovskii, 1837, p. 50; also Smol'ianinov, 1853, pp. 64 and 71.

83. See the discussion by Zolotov, 1963, p. 26. He quotes Minister Gagarin who is supposed to have said, "Without any doubt the port of Odessa is the leader on the Black Sea."

84. Ibid. p. 26.

85. Druzhinina, 1970, p. 340.

86. A. A. Skal'kovskii, 1837, p. 48, states that Odessa had a population of 9,009 by 1802. Orlov's estimate that Odessa's population was 20,000 by 1803 is surely exaggerated. See idem, 1885, p. 97.

87. In the late 1790s, Poggio, the father of the future Decembrist, was head of the city's merchants. Sperandeo, 1906, p. 324.

88. Smol'ianinov, 1853, pp. 77–79.

89. Druzhinina, 1959, p. 256.

90. Smol'ianinov, 1853, p. 78. The abundance of hard wheat gave a strong boost to the making of macaroni. Besides *pasta*, the factory produced *gallettes*, a type of hard biscuits often used for food aboard ship. See de Ribas, 1898, p. 240. Until 1939, Odessa was renowned for its macaroni production; see Fox, 1963, p. 15.

Chapter Two

1. On July 18, 1822, Byron wrote that in Cantos 7 and 8 of his *Don Juan* he had utilized in the adventures of his hero some true incidents from the life of the "late Duke de Richelieu, then a young volunteer in the Russian service. . . ." Lord Byron, 1928, p. 716. Perhaps it was Byron's association of Richelieu with Don Juan that led Pushkin to portray Richelieu as a "Don Juan" in "The Queen of Spades."

2. Pingaud, 1910, p. 346.

3. On this most prominent monument of Odessa, see the description in Hamilton, 1954, p. 234. While generally admired, the statue is not without its critics. In the 1860s, a German visitor claimed that a certain Mlle. Falcourt of St. Petersburg served as its model. "Viewed from one side," he stated, "the figure seems so miserable that wags claim that it seems to be saying: 'Give money here'." See Wilhelm Hamm, 1862, pp. 95–96. An English traveler thought that the statue possessed "an effeminate expression." See Bremner, 1839, II, 482. Another found fault with its size. Seen from below the vast staircase it "appeared crushed" and, in the opinion of the observer, either the statue should have been of colossal dimensions or else it should have been placed elsewhere. See Shirley Brooks, 1855, p. 18.

4. On Richelieu, see letters, notes and essays in *SIRIO* LIV, 1886. For further biography see Rochechouart, 1889 and its abridged English translation, Frances Jackson, 1920. One of the local historians, a professor at the Richelieu Lycée, wrote an appreciative essay, Mizhnevich, 1849; A. A. Skal'kovskii, 1837, pp. 115–19, cites as the source of his information, "Discours prononcé à la Chambre des Pairs de France par Cardinal Duc de Bausset, à l'occasion de la mort de M. le Duc de Richelieu, Paris, 8 juin, 1822." The best known biography is that by Crousaz-Crétet, 1897. For further bibliography, see Waliszewski, 1925, III, 253. The most recent biography is that by Cox, 1959.

5. She was imprisoned for royalist sympathies during a brief period of the French Revolution. In a memoir she wrote concerning her husband, there is no trace of rancor, see *SIRIO*, LIV (1886), 1–9. On the contrary, upon her husband's death, she asked for his heart, which she placed in the chapel wall of the chateau of Courtelles; it was eventually placed in her tomb. See Cox, 1959, p. 216.

6. The house must have been crowded, as the comte de Rochechouart, who lived with him, reported that fourteen persons resided in the duc's menage. They included three secretaries, foreign consuls, soldiers, merchants and the Abbé Labdan, Richelieu's former tutor who had also been

the tutor of the duc d'Engien. At the execution of the latter, the priest seems to have lost his mental equilibrium. He went to live with the kindly Richelieu, who treated him "with affectionate attentions." See Rochechouart, 1889, p. 87. The house was on the street later named for him (now Lenin Street).

7. Druzhinina, 1970, pp. 187–88.
8. Rochechouart, 1889, p. 87.
9. Cited in L. M. de Ribas, 1898, p. 311.
10. Sicard, 1886, p. 73, n. 5.
11. Ibid., pp. 33–34.
12. Rochechouart, 1889, p. 92.
13. Tarnopol, 1855, p. 59.
14. Haumant, 1910, p. 250.
15. Sicard, 1886, pp. 33–34, "Il aimait, favorisait, encourageait Odessa pour la Russie Méridionale et celle-ci pour Odessa." An English visitor in 1809 also noted that in administering both a city and a vast hinterland, he could closely coordinate agriculture and trade to their mutual benefit. Maria Guthrie, 1810, p. 27.
16. For the imperial edicts which established or reformed Novorossiia, see PSZ, 1830, XVI, 737 ff., no. 12149. See also ibid., no. 12211. Other edicts are calendared and summarized in Den, 1902, I, 272, 336, and 361.
17. Hommaire de Hell, 1847, p. 96. See AMAE, Mémoires et Documents, Russie, 8 March 1841, f. 129, for an account of how Count Vorontsov came to hire Hommaire de Hell, an engineer of the Ecole St. Etienne, to survey Novorossiia. For the changing names of the area ruled by the governors general of the region, see AOO, 1961, pp. 11–12, and my "Note on Geographic Terms," above, p. xvii. For a full description of the contemporary Soviet areas that once formed Novorossiia, see Istoriia gorodov, 1969, p. 17, n. 8.
18. In 1808, the comte de Rochechouart counted 203 "foreign" villages near Odessa: 106 German, 30 Tatar-Nogais, 13 Bulgar, 21 Russian dissenters, 25 Greek, and 6 Jewish. They contained a population of 300,000. See idem, 1889, p. 93.
19. Druzhinina, 1970, p. 154. For a detailed description of settlements in Novorossiia including statistics on the population from 1812 to 1835, see, most recently, Kabuzan, 1976.
20. In 1813, for example, in a move typical of his policies, he prevailed upon Alexander I to make immigration more attractive. See Druzhinina, 1970, p. 93.
21. Ibid., p. 95.
22. Zagoruiko, 1957–60, I, 53.
23. Druzhinina, 1970, p. 98.
24. Bartlett, 1974, p. 16.
25. Druzhinina, 1970, p. 95. Catherine had settled many Zaporozhian Cossacks on the southeastern shores of the Sea of Azov, especially at Ekaterinodar, to defend the former frontier against the Circassians. See

Rochechouart, 1889, pp. 95–96, for an account of how Richelieu was ambushed by some Circassians and barely escaped with his life.

26. Druzhinina, 1970, p. 96.

27. Ibid., p. 164.

28. See the entry, "Odessa," in *Jewish Encyclopedia*, 1905. For A. A. Skal'kovskii, see idem, 1837, p. 48.

29. The basic study of Jewish agricultural settlement in Novorossiia is by Borovoi, 1928. See also Druzhinina, 1970, pp. 149–54; Lerner, 1901, pp. 16–24.

30. Borovoi, 1928, pp. 45–47.

31. On colonization under Alexander I, see Bartlett, 1979, pp. 180–230.

32. See AMAE, Mémoires et Documents, Russie, Vol. XLIV, October 22, 1832, for a description of these communities by the French consul.

33. Druzhinina, 1970, p. 108.

34. AMAE, Mémoires et Documents, Russie, Vol. XLIV, October 22, 1832.

35. A. A. Skal'kovskii, 1848, p. 7.

36. For the history of the Serbs in the eighteenth century who had settled in the territory later to become part of Novorossiia, see Polons'ka-Vasylenko, 1955, pp. 41–102.

37. Druzhinina, 1970, pp. 119–20.

38. Ibid., pp. 120–26.

39. A large literature exists on German settlements on the steppe. Representative works are the following: Keller, n.d.; Stumpp, 1971; Bieneman, 1890; Lindemann, 1924; Pusarevskii, 1917; Friesen, 1911; Leibbrandt, 1928; Malinowsky, 1927; Druzhinina, 1966, pp. 573–78; and most recently, Bartlett, 1979, pp. 76–80, 189–212, 224–25, *et passim.*

40. Keller, n.d., p. 113.

41. Ibid., p. 21.

42. AMAE, Mémoires et Documents, Russie, Vol. XXVI, f. 20.

43. Keller, n.d., p. 28.

44. Ibid.

45. Ibid., p. 21.

46. Druzhinina, 1970, p. 141.

47. Ibid., p. 147. See too Shishmarev, 1975, pp. 136–44.

48. Holderness, 1823, p. 157.

49. Ibid., p. 160.

50. *JO*, 4/16 January, 1828.

51. Demidov, 1853, I, 350.

52. Druzhinina, 1970, p. 110.

53. Waliszewski, 1925, III, 249.

54. Kohl, 1844, p. 439.

55. Sicard, 1886, p. 83.

56. Rochechouart, 1889, p. 94.

57. Sicard, 1886, p. 30.

58. The duc's house on Richelieu Street fell apart from decrepitude on March 1, 1827. The house of the *gradonachal'nik* was built on the site. See Smol'ianinov, 1853, p. 147.

59. Maria Guthrie, 1810, p. 253.

60. Pingaud, 1910, p. 323. A. A. Skal'kovskii, 1837, p. 5 and pp. 120–22, discusses the population and number of factories, houses, etc. in Odessa in 1803.

61. Nadler, 1893, p. 5.

62. Mizhnevich, 1849, p. 24.

63. Zagoruiko, 1957–60, II, 46.

64. *Odesskii teatr*, 1977, p. 6. Among the foreigners who visited and reported on the theater, see Lagarde, 1812, p. 153 and Holderness, 1823, p. 77.

65. Rochechouart, 1889, p. 89.

66. Druzhinina, 1970, p. 196.

67. According to the anonymous Italian author of *Notizie*, 1817, p. 11.

68. Robert Stevens, 1819, p. 6.

69. Pingaud, 1910, p. 330.

70. Sicard, 1886, p. 73, n. 4.

71. Ibid., p. 34.

72. Krylov, 1865, p. 49. A. A. Skal'kovskii, 1837, pp. 240–44, discusses the proliferation of trees and plants in Odessa. To this day Odessa is marked by the great number of its trees. See also Druzhinina, 1970, p. 230. In the fall of 1812 he also helped lay out a large botanical garden along the shores of the Black Sea on the Crimean peninsula near the village of Mykyta. See ibid., p. 198 and p. 249.

73. Maria Guthrie, 1810, p. 271.

74. Lagarde, 1812, pp. 155–61.

75. Richelieu, 1886, pp. 369–70.

76. *Notizie*, 1817, p. 20.

77. According to the German doctor, Kohl, some sea captains ran the ships aground purposely, taking care to save themselves and their crews. Suitably bribed, the Turkish authorities would confirm their claims of shipwreck, and the captains would collect a handsome insurance settlement in Odessa. See Kohl, 1842, p. 423. Jesse claimed that five out of six insurance companies had failed. One gambler found a house with a view of the sea; he noted which ships appeared to be unseaworthy, and insured them heavily with hopes for shipwrecks and high profits. See Jesse, 1841, I, 227.

78. Morton, 1830, pp. 262–65.

79. Dearborn, 1819, p. 236.

80. Sicard, 1886, p. 72, n. 1.

81. Sperandeo, 1906, p. 327.

82. A. A. Skal'kovskii, 1837, p. 97. See also Harvey, 1838, p. 71, who cites and translates the *ukaz* of Alexander I; for a full discussion of Alexander's free trade policies, see Nadler, 1898. This short work, which praises the duc's liberal policies, especially his support of free trade and multinational colonization of Novorossiia, seems to be a thinly disguised attack on Tsar Alexander III and his policies of Russification.

83. Vol'skii, 1854, p. 77. Antoine Ignace Anthoine, 1805, 1820, p. 204. For total values of exports from the Russian Empire and the portions comprised by the Black Sea and Azov trade over the years 1802–1825, see Druzhinina, 1970, p. 338.

84. Hagemeister, 1846, p. 5.

85. Zagoruiko, 1957–60, I, 73.

86. Sicard, 1886, p. 37.

87. Zagoruiko, 1957–60, I, 743.

88. *Proshloe Odessy*, 1894, p. 23.

89. A. A. Skal'kovskii, 1865a, II, 39–124.

90. A. A. Skal'kovskii, 1865a, II, 111.

91. Batiushkov, 1886, III, 527–29.

92. L. M. de Ribas, 1894, p. 311.

93. Borovoi, 1967b, p. 146.

94. Atlas, 1911, pp. 6–7, and p. 31.

95. Ibid., p. 152.

96. It was entitled, "Al genio musicale della Signora Giustina Zamboni." Smol'ianinov, 1853, p. 165.

97. *OV*, 1845, Nos. 33 and 34.

98. *Odesskii teatr*, 1977, p. 6.

99. Batiushkov, 1886, III, 513.

100. Pingaud, 1910, p. 326.

101. For various accounts of the plague at Odessa in 1812, see Sicard, 1886, pp. 53–60; A. A. Skal'kovskii, 1837, pp. 352–53; Druzhinina, 1970, pp. 199–200; Lagarde, 1812, pp. 161–95; and Timiriazev, 1897, pp. 579–92.

102. Quoted by Druzhinina, 1970, p. 199.

103. Sicard, 1886, p. 58.

104. See Lagarde, 1812, p. 164 and p. 195.

105. Ibid., p. 164.

106. Zagoruiko, 1957–60, I, 74.

107. Comte de Falloux, 1860, p. 77.

108. *Murray's Hand-Book*, 1868, p. 251.

109. Waliszewski, 1925, III, 26.

110. Lobanov–Rostovsky, 1947, p. 364.

111. Ibid., p. 365.

112. AMAE, Mémoires et Documents, Russie, Vol. XIX, f. 410.

Chapter Three

1. On animal husbandry in the southern Ukraine, see A. A. Skal'kovskii, 1850, II, 337–92 for extensive statistics; see also the general remarks of Druzhinina, 1970, pp. 205–12 and 1981, pp. 64–65.

2. Crousaz-Crétet, 1897, p. 90. Also, A. A. Skal'kovskii, 1850, II, 354–57.

3. Shmidt, 1863, II, 199 ff. and A. A. Skal'kovskii, 1850, II, 257–58.

4. Jesse, 1841, I, 245. By 1842, Vorontsov's estates in the Crimea provided more than 7,000 *pud*s of fine-haired wool. See Indova, 1955, p. 36. By the mid-nineteenth century, Vorontsov had 30,000 sheep in the Taurida *guberniia*, 25,000 in the Katerynoslav *guberniia*, and 20,000 in the Kherson *guberniia*. See A. A. Skal'kovskii, 1850, II, 366–67.

5. Hommaire de Hell, 1847, pp. 37–38. Mary Holderness, 1823, p. 82, reported also that Rouvier was the first to introduce merino sheep to Novorossiia, and that Alexander I gave him a *desiatina* of land for every sheep. He thus had a flock of 50,000 on an estate of 50,000 *desiatina*s.

6. NACRO, 15 January 1843.

7. Druzhinina, 1970, p. 207.

8. Ibid.

9. Ibid. Shearing the sheep usually began in May and continued in the summer months. Prices for wool varied from 2 rubles 25 kopecks per *pud* per simple unwashed wool of a dark color to 32 rubles for washed *shlenskii* wool and up to 35 rubles for washed Spanish wool.

10. Druzhinina, 1970, pp. 208–29.

11. Zaionchkovskii, 1954, pp. 14–15.

12. Bagrov and Gradov, 1974, p. 14.

13. Gamba, 1826, I, 8–9.

14. Ibid., I, 24–25.

15. NACRO, 1 July 1844; 1 Oct. 1845; 1 Oct. 1846; 11 Oct. 1862; 2 March 1863. In 1862 the United States was the fifth best customer for wool from the South Ukraine. Ibid., 17 Oct. 1863: "... but of wool, a good portion has been sent either directly or indirectly to the United States." The United States purchased about one million rubles worth of wool that year.

16. Bremner, 1839, II, 488.

17. Hagemeister, 1846, p. 20.

18. See Herlihy, 1963, Appendixes I and II.

19. The figures are from Hagemeister, 1847, p. 220.

20. Hommaire de Hell, 1847, p. 38.

21. Bagrov and Grabov, 1974, p. 18.

22. Druzhinina, 1970, p. 206. For the various kinds of cattle, see A. A. Skal'kovskii, 1850, II, 342–45.

23. Druzhinina, 1970, p. 209.

24. Ibid.

25. A. A. Skal'kovskii, 1850, II, 347.

26. Kohl, 1842, p. 501.

27. Dana, 1969, pp. 49–50.

28. Kulisher, 1923, p. 284. *JO*, 1 Jan. 1835, noted that despite cheap production of palm oil in the English factories in Africa, England continued to import more tallow from Odessa each year.

29. ASF, Affari Esteri, Protocollo N. 266, Thom to Venturi, 7 Feb. 1834: "La mancanza del pascolo, costrinse i proprietari del loro bestiame, ha molto contribuito alla straordinaria abbondanza del sevo." Ibid., No. 2546, Rodocannachi to Serristori, 4 Feb. 1848, ". . . e siccome vi è penuria di fieno si teme che il bestiame ne soffrirà, lo che influirebbe tanto al minor prodotto della lana quanto all'incarimento del trasporto dei prodotti dell'interno."

30. Pinkerton, 1833, p. 138. In 1836, Robert Bremner found Odessa to be "one of the cheapest towns on the Continent; its markets are well supplied with beef and mutton of excellent quality . . . all kinds of poultry are cheap in Odessa." Idem, II, 510–11. Two years later, Kohl, 1842, p. 430, reported: "Odessa may be said with respect to food, to be in a constant state of repletion." As early as 1808, the Comte de Rochechouart wrote, "Food was very cheap at Odessa; butcher's meat of excellent quality was three sous the pound," 1889, p. 88. K. A. Skal'kovskii, 1906, p. 17, claimed that in the 1840s food was so cheap a family could be fed for one ruble a day and that dishes in restaurants cost only fifteen kopecks.

31. Exports of tallow from Odessa, except for the remarkable year 1851, remained relatively stable after 1837 at a value of about one million silver rubles. See Herlihy, 1963, Appendixes I and III.

32. AMAE, Odessa, VII, 10 Oct. 1852, f. 384.

33. A. A. Skal'kovskii, 1846, 233–44.

34. Kohl, 1842, pp. 432–33. At the same time an English visitor noted, ". . . the refreshing water-melons would of themselves make Odessa an elysium. . . ." See Bremner, 1839, II, 502. For the various kinds of melons: "Russian," "American," "Dukhobor," etc., see Druzhinina, 1981, p. 72.

35. *JO*, 25 Jan. 1858. Over twenty-seven thousand *chetverts* of peas and beans were exported in 1857, while in 1835 only about four thousand *chetverts* had been exported. See Hagemeister, 1846, p. 197.

36. *JO*, 15 Jan. 1858.

37. Early accounts of Black Sea commerce do not list linseed as an export article. See Oddy, 1807, I, 165: "The produce which can be exported from the Russian ports on the Black Sea and the Sea of Azoph are principally grain, oak timber, masts, hemp, flax, tar, tallow, hempseed oil, iron and sail cloth." Nor does Gamba, 1826, I, 9, list it. In 1834, the U. S. consul Ralli still called linseed a "new article," NACRO, 15 Jan. 1834.

38. NACRO, 15 Jan. 1834.

39. Kulisher, 1923, p. 282.

40. As early as 1828, the United States purchased directly from Russia linseed to the value of $32,290.00. NACRO, 15 Jan. 1834.

41. AMAE, Odessa, VI, 12 Sept. 1844, ff. 408–09. He reported that for the last three years 175,000 to 300,000 hectoliters of linseed had been shipped from Odessa and Taganrog, each at 10 francs 50 centimes per hectoliter.

42. For a detailed report on the methods of planting, harvesting, and use of sunflower seeds and oil, see 1912–13, *BPP* XCIX, 22–23.

43. AMAE, Odessa, VII, 24 August 1844, f. 403.

44. NACRO, 1 July 1854.

45. A. A. Skal'kovskii, 1846, pp. 232–33.

46. Indova, 1955, p. 36. For details on the types and quantity of vines grown in Novorossiia to mid-nineteenth century, see A. A. Skal'kovskii, 1850, II, 274–96.

47. Kohl, 1842, p. 432.

48. Jesse, 1841, I, 173.

49. AMAE, Odessa, VI, 29 May 1843, f. 314.

50. Bremner, 1839, II, 489.

51. According to a French report in the *Journal des Débats*, reprinted in *Il Corriere Italiano*, 14 Oct. 1854.

52. Ibid.

53. *Le Moniteur*, Sept. 1854.

54. Hagemeister, 1846, p. 8.

55. Cited in Sichynsky, 1953, p. 51.

56. Shmidt, 1863, I, 7 ff. provides an extended discussion on the kinds and qualities of the soil in the area.

57. Hagemeister, 1846, p. 101.

58. See A. A. Skal'kovskii, 1839, p. 18, and idem, 1850, II, 94.

59. This and the following statistics on population densities in Novorossiia are taken from *Statistische Tabelle*, 1859.

60. Haxthausen, 1856, II, 68.

61. Bagrov and Grabov, 1974, p. 15.

62. NACRO, 15 Feb. 1862.

63. The kinds of wheat raised in the southern provinces of the Russian Empire are discussed at length by Nebolsin, 1850, p. 13 ff.; A. A. Skal'kovskii, 1850, II, 77–83; Shmidt, 1864, II, 27–34; and Köppen, 1852, p. 74. The following travel accounts also contain much information on Russian cereals: Anthoine, 1805, 1820; Eton, 1805; Gamba, 1826; Dearborn, 1819; Hagemeister, 1846. More recent discussions of varieties of wheat may be found in Gorrini, 1918; Timoshenko, 1932; Borasi, 1939; *Céréales russes*, 1900. Hard wheat seems to have been unknown in classical antiquity, and first appears in the early Middle Ages; it was particularly suited to the dry steppe regions, and its low water content meant that it could be stored for long periods. On its early history, see Watson, 1981.

64. Hagemeister, 1846, p. 105. The French consul praises the hard wheat of Taganrog for the quality of the pasta made from it and for the ease with which it could be kept for a long time in good condition in storage, AMAE, Odessa, VII, 17 Aug. 1856, f. 462.

65. Dearborn, 1819, pp. 246–47.

66. Keller, n.d., p. 93.

67. AMAE, Odessa, VII, 17 Aug. 1856, f. 462.

68. Techniques of steppe agriculture are discussed at length in Köppen, 1852, p. 47 ff. He visited the black soil provinces of the Don region in 1850; Shmidt, 1863, II, 77 ff.; Pavlovich, 1862, p. 234 ff. As late as the twentieth century, the three-field system was used in the southern provinces of the Russian Empire. See Smith, 1908, p. 44.

69. Keller, n.d., p. 95; A. A. Skal'kovskii, 1850, II, 63.

70. NACRO, 1 April 1848. For A. A. Skal'kovskii's discussion of wheat-farming methods, see 1850, II, 55–65.

71. Jesse, 1841, I, 217.

72. Shmidt, 1863, II, 20.

73. Köppen, 1852, p. 47.

74. Haxthausen, 1856, II, 139.

75. See Milone, 1929, p. 9.

76. Extensive meteorological tables for the province of Kherson in the first half of the nineteenth century may be found in Shmidt, 1863, I, 562–71. A. A. Skal'kovskii also discussed climatic conditions in New Russia, giving yearly figures for wheat production. See 1850, II, 30–48.

77. NACRO, 1 January 1835.

78. AMAE, Mémoires et Documents, Russie, XLIV, 22 Oct. 1832, f. 40.

79. Druzhinina, 1970, p. 213.

80. Moore, 1833, p. 110. The American consul in 1848 describes the disastrous effects of a heat wave in the neighborhood of Odessa, although this would prove to be a banner export year, NACRO, 1 July 1848.

81. Haxthausen, 1856, II, 68–69.

82. Hume, 1914, p. 97.

83. Webster, 1830, I, 23; Armstrong, 1831, p. 23.

84. Armstrong, 1831, p. 23; Webster, 1830, II, 340.

85. Rzewuska, 1939, II, 320. Bremner, 1839, II, 500–01, tells of the efforts of a family to make enough noise to ward off the locusts; watering pans, shovels, pots, kettles, toasting-forks and tea-boards were all enlisted.

86. AMAE, Odessa, IV, 1 Oct. 1830, f. 281.

87. *JO*, 20 August / 1 Sept. 1827.

88. *JO*, 23 June / 4 July 1828.

89. Hume, 1914, p. 104.

90. Troyat, 1946, pp. 346–47.

91. Ibid., p. 349: "Les sauterelles volaient, volaient, / Puis elles se posèrent / Rampèrent, devorèrent tout, / Et de nouveau s'envolèrent."

92. A. A. Skal'kovskii, 1870, pp. 60–61.

93. AMAE, Odessa, IV, 1 Oct. 1830, f. 281.

94. Rzewuska, 1939, pp. 319–20.

95. Guillaume la Vasseur de Beauplan, cited by Sichynsky, 1953, p. 74.

96. A. A. Skal'kovskii, 1850, I, 166.

97. Ibid., p. 93.

98. Nebolsin, 1850, p. 194.

99. AMAE, Mémoires et Documents, Russie, XLIV, 22 Oct. 1832, ff. 35–36, for a description of the carts.

100. Brooks, 1855, p. 35. Three quarters and two bushels are about twenty-six bushels. Even in 1870 the carts' capacity had remained the same. An American woman noted that the carts held about twenty-five bushels of wheat. Proctor, 1900, p. 278.

101. AMAE, Mémoires et Documents, Russie, XLIV, 22 Oct. 1832, f. 36.

102. Hommaire de Hell, 1847, p. 19; Proctor, 1900, p. 278; Brooks, 1855, p. 38.

103. *Notizie*, 1817, p. 24.

104. Above, n. 101; Hommaire de Hell, 1847, p. 19.

105. Hommaire de Hell, 1847, p. 19.

106. Descriptions in Dearborn, 1819, I, 246; Nebolsin, 1850, p. 51.

107. AMAE, Mémoires et Documents, Russie, XLIV, 22 Oct. 1832, f. 6.

108. *Notizie*, 1817, p. 24.

109. Besse, 1838, p. 22.

110. According to another observer, Jesse, 1841, I, 195, forty thousand oxen came to Odessa with one million *chetvert*s of wheat. In making this calculation he was more interested in the number of flies carried than in the number of oxen. He decided that if each pair of oxen brought with it two hundred flies, then four million flies rode to town, some of which were disturbing his sleep each morning! Unfortunately, even now in the absence of oxen, flies abound. See K. A. Skal'kovskii for childhood memories of *chumak*s and their carts arriving in Odessa, 1906, p. 17.

111. ANP, F12, 2683. In 1820, the price of oxen was reported to be one hundred rubles a pair and a cart cost from twenty to twenty-five rubles. See Holderness, 1823, p. 315.

112. NACRO, 15 Feb. 1862.

113. AMAE, Odessa, VI, 13 March 1845, f. 434.

114. A. A. Skal'kovskii, 1846, p. 232.

115. AMAE, Odessa, VI, 13 March, f. 425.

116. AMAE, Odessa, VI, 17 January. Lt. General Potier's remedy for this cattle disease was to administer one bottle of *kvass* (rye flour fermented several days in water), four egg yolks, alum as big as a carrot reduced to powder, mixed with vinegar and copperas. He claimed to have saved twenty sick cattle with this recipe. AMAE, Odessa, VI, 13 March, f. 434.

117. A. A. Skal'kovskii, 1845, p. 1, n. 2. *CL*, 27 July 1847, mentioned that draft animals were dying on the way to port.

118. NACRO, 1 Oct. 1851.

119. AMAE, Odessa, VI, 24 April 1843, f. 301.

120. NACRO, 1 July 1849.

121. Dearborn, 1819, I, 246.

122. AMAE, Mémoires et Documents, Russie, XLIV, 22 Oct. 1832, f. 52. Also Jesse, 1841, I, 176.

123. Hagemeister, 1846, p. 101, who gives the cost of from two to six paper rubles per *chetvert*.

124. Ibid.

125. AMAE, Correspondance Commerciale, St. Petersbourg, XXX, 20 April 1839, f. 221.

126. Hommaire de Hell, 1847, pp. 18–19.

127. Reprinted in *CIBAVA*, 10 March 1847.

128. Oliphant, 1854, p. 236.

129. Giusti, 1858.

130. Ibid.

131. NACRO, 15 Feb. 1862.

132. Rozhkova, 1959, p. 269.

133. Il'f and Petrov, 1962, p. 73. The work was first published in 1932.

134. A. A. Skal'kovskii, 1845, p. 2, n. 2.

135. See below p. 217–22.

Chapter Four

1. Kabuzan, 1971, pp. 103, 139, 163.

2. In Russian law, a "juridically free" peasant could move as he wished, marry whom he wished, and own property of his own. According to Druzhinina, even those legal serfs in the southern Ukraine enjoyed a more liberal regimen than those in the central provinces. See Druzhinina, 1970, p. 169.

3. Cf. the incident recounted by Zagoruiko, 1957–60, I, 51, where peasants, rioting at the change in their status, were shipped in punishment to Siberia.

4. Holderness, 1823, 199.

5. Discussed in Druzhinina, 1970, p. 93, and Zagoruiko, 1957–60, I, 53–54.

6. A point made by Druzhinina, 1970, p. 368. G. P. Danilevskii, 1956, is a historical novel written in 1858, which tells the adventures and hardships of escaped serfs in Novorossiia.

7. Druzhinina, 1981, p. 42.

8. Discussed by Druzhinina, 1970, p. 167.

9. Pushkin describes him as "Half-milord, half-merchant / Half-sage, half-ignoramus / Half-scoundrel, it is to be hoped / That he will be whole, at last." Veresaev, 1937, I, 310.

10. Vorontsov, 1880, p. 588.

11. Zagoruiko, 1957–60, I, 51.

12. AMAE, Mémoires et Documents, Russie, XLIV, 22 Oct. 1832, f. 40.

13. Cited in Druzhinina, 1970, p. 169.

14. A. A. Skal'kovskii, 1865e, p. 243.

15. See above, Chapter 2, pp. 27–32.

16. See the comments by Pavlovich, 1862, p. 175, and Köppen, 1852, p. 93.

17. Haxthausen, 1856, I, 424.

18. Elliott, 1839, I, 122–23. The Mennonites settled on the Molochna River were given only about twenty-seven *desiatina*s per household. Cf. Keller, n. d., p. 95.

19. Quoted in Nebolsin, 1850, I, 196.

20. Ibid.

21. Köppen, 1852, p. 93.

22. Ibid.

23. See the unfavorable comment on the agriculture they practiced in Pavlovich, 1862, p. 175.

24. PRO, FO 63, 355, 28 Feb. 1848.

25. Indova, 1955, p. 41 ff.

26. For other examples of increased exactions of *barshchina*, see Druzhinina, 1981, p. 24.

27. Zaionchkovskii, 1954, p. 85.

28. Cited in Nebolsin, 1950, I, 194.

29. Lenin, 1967, III, 158.

30. Liashchenko, 1908, I, 173–79, and idem, 1952. See also Zionchkovskii, 1954.

31. Blum, 1961, p. 613 ff.

32. Not until the 1830s, however, did most colonists produce marketable exports. See Height, n. d., p. 91.

33. Kohl, 1842, pp. 418–19.

34. Jesse, 1841, I, 68 and 200.

35. Kohl, 1842, p. 420.

36. For comment, see AMAE, Mémoires et Documents, Russie, XLIV, 22 Oct. 1832, ff. 45–46.

37. Zagoruiko, 1957–60, I, 77. In 1845 alone, there were constructed twenty grain magazines. A. A. Skal'kovskii, 1846, p. 222.

38. AMAE, Mémoires et Documents, Russie, XLIV, 22 Oct. 1832, f. 25

39. Barker, 1855, p. 151.

40. AMAE, Mémoires et Documents, Russie, XLIV, 22 Oct. 1832, f. 47 ff.

41. For a description of fairs and their relation to the grain trade, see Druzhinina, 1970, p. 323. Zolotov, 1963, p. 164, affirms that the south Russian fairs were only weakly connected with the export trade. See my forthcoming study, "The South Ukraine as an Economic Region in the

Nineteenth Century," to be published by the Harvard Ukrainian Research Institute.

42. AMAE, Mémoires et Documents, Russie, XLIV, 22 Oct. 1832, f. 47 ff.

43. Zolotov, 1963, p. 170.

44. Ibid., p. 172.

45. Druzhinina, 1970, pp. 360–61.

46. Ibid., p. 364.

47. Atlas, 1911, p. 79, n. 1.

48. AMAE, Mémoires et Documents, Russie, XLIV, 22 Oct. 1832, f. 24.

49. Hagemeister, 1846, p. 74. K. A. Skal'kovskii also wrote that the Russian merchants of Odessa sold ropes, harnesses, and iron; according to him the only enlightened Russian merchant was Novikov. K. A. Skal'kovskii, 1905, p. 31. Jesse, 1841, I, 227, reports: "The principal foreign merchants here are Greeks, Italians and Germans; the only two English houses in the town when I was there have since ceased to exist."

50. Cited in Kulisher, 1923, p. 271.

51. A. A. Skal'kovskii (1808–97), over a long life wrote 276 books and articles on Odessa and Novorossiia, most of them crammed with figures. For biographical details and an appraisal of his studies from a Marxist perspective, see Borovoi, 1960, pp. 175–85. Borovoi labels him a reactionary historian, but betrays evident admiration for his productivity. See also an official biography in *Slavianovedenie*, pp. 306–07. Two older tributes are by another productive local historian, Markevich, 1900 and 1901. Skal'kovskii's son's memoirs also discuss aspects of his father's life, 1906, *passim.*

52. See also *Statistische Tabelle*, p. 75. Also, NACRO, 12 April 1856. Ibid., 20 Jan. 1860. It was possible for persons not members of a guild to participate in trade through purchasing a special license (*svidetel'stvo*). See Dikhtar, 1960, p. 11.

53. A visitor to Odessa noted in 1852 that the fee for joining the first guild was so high that only four new members had entered over the past four years. Oliphant, 1854, p. 235.

54. In 1808 the total of guild members was 204. "Svedeniia ob Odesse," 1839.

55. A. A. Skal'kovskii, 1845, p. 2. Of course, foreigners quickly assumed Russian citizenship when it was convenient for them, and just as quickly abandoned it.

56. *OV*, 1845.

57. Druzhinina, 1970, p. 257.

58. K. A. Skal'kovskii, 1905, p. 31.

59. Arsh, 1959, p. 142.

60. *Gosudarstvennaia vneshniaia torgovlia*, 1827.

61. *Odessa*, 1895, p. 791.

62. Arsh, 1959, p. 260.

63. I use the Italian form of spelling for Ralli instead of Rallis as that is the form commonly used in Western literature. The same is true for Rodocannachi instead of Rodokanaki. There is an anecdote told about Gogol who, upon first hearing the name Rodocannachi while visiting Odessa, inquired, "What's that—a surname?" When he received an affirmative reply, he remarked, "Well, it's God knows what, but not a surname. It's something you could use as a swearword like, 'Oh, you are such a rrrodokanaki!'." See Lerner, n.d., p. 325. The *Journal de St. Petersbourg*, 24 April 1845, lists Ralli's firm as the leader among sixty-six exporting companies. The Greek Rodocannachi was the largest importer.

64. *JO*, 28 January 1847.

65. NACRO, 29 October 1854.

66. Stephens, 1838, I, 260.

67. Moulake, 1964, p. 10.

68. His reports are preserved in NACRO, 1832 and ff.

69. NACRO, 30 May 1831.

70. Wickoff, 1880, p. 234.

71. NACRO, 1 March 1854.

72. NACRO, 20 Feb. 1857.

73. Moulake, 1964, p. 9.

74. Chapman, 1977, p. 38.

75. See below, p. 212–14.

76. A. A. Skal'kovskii, 1845, p. 5.

77. Ibid., p. 4.

78. Shmidt, 1863, p. 583.

Chapter Five

1. Post, 1977.

2. A. A. Skal'kovskii, 1837, pp. 45, 141; Zolotov, 1963, p. 33.

3. ASF, Affari Esteri, No. 2396. Letter dated 9 Feb. 1817 from Lebzeltern to Fossombroni: "The immense quantity of wheat which [Russia] possesses and which she has not been able to export since 1812 today finds considerable outlet on all sides. Exportation of grain already has climbed beyond 60 million rubles and the demands from the south of France and from Spain have not been satisfied and are still continuing. These circumstances have scarcely raised the price of grain in the interior where the stores are overflowing and have acted on the foreign exchange in the most advantageous manner for Russia and in a ruinous manner for foreigners who must liquidate their capital."

4. Hagemeister, 1846, p. 13. The high figure of fifty-two rubles is given by the French consul at Odessa, AMAE, Mémoires et Documents, Russie, XLIV, 22 Oct. 1832, f. 31.

5. Quoted by Giura, 1967, p. 51.

6. Pinkerton, 1833, p. 137, states that prices for wheat in 1819 fell to nine rubles per *chetvert.*

7. GAOO, *f.* 40, *op.* 1, *d.* 107, *l.* 83.

8. Fomin, 1829.

9. ASF, Affari Esteri, Filza 2514, 24 Dec. 1826.

10. Pinkerton, 1833, p. 137.

11. ASL, Governatore, Filza 875, 15 May 1821. See also Kulisher, 1923, p. 278.

12. ASF, Affari Esteri, Filza 1170, Protocollo 191, 19 June 1828.

13. Ibid. See also, for the Kingdom of the Two Sicilies, Giura, 1967, pp. 62, 64.

14. For the text, see *Recueil des traités,* 1791–1831, VIII, 143–52.

15. See the comments in ASF, Affari Esteri, Protocollo 196, 24 Dec. 1830.

16. ASF, Affari Esteri, Filza 1170, Protocollo 111, No. 43, 13 Nov. 1823.

17. Ibid.

18. ASF, Affari Esteri, Protocollo No. 224, 11 April 1832, and Protocollo 196, 24 Dec. 1830.

19. ASF, Affari Esteri, Filza 2472, Quaglia to Fossombroni, 11 June 1832.

20. Ibid.

21. ASF, Affari Esteri, Protocollo, Bi 507.38, Jan. 1857.

22. Concerning the maintenance of maritime lights, see ASF, Affari Esteri, Filza 2475, 27 Nov. 1838, and Filza 2476, 17 Sept. 1840. For a description of and complaint about Turkish health regulations, ASF, Affari Esteri, Filza 2476, 21 March 1840.

23. ANP, F12, 2644, "Report from the Select Committee on Bonded Corn (Grinding Act) together with the Minutes of Evidence and an Appendix communicated by the Commons to the Lords," 14 July 1842, p. 5.

24. NACRO, Ralli to Forsyth, 1 Jan. 1837. See also Albion, 1939, p. 93.

25. "Since the time that the commerce of the Black Sea has opened a new way, that is, after the year 1835, the foreign trade of this place has gradually been extended and consolidated; so that each year it exceeds the activity of the year before." Reprinted in *CIBAVA,* 10 May 1847.

26. NACRO, 1 April 1838.

27. ASF, Affari Esteri, Filza 2544, 1 March 1847.

28. ASL, Governatore, Filza 299, No. 1236, 23 Feb. 1848.

29. ASL, Governatore, Filza 323, No. 1640, Nozzolini to Pigli, 24 Jan. 1849.

30. Article included in ASF, Ministero delle Finanze, Capi Rotti, 16 April 1853.

31. NACRO, 1 Jan. 1854.

32. On the legislation, see Gras, 1915; L. Levi, 1872; and Galpin, 1929.

33. Kulischer, 1955, p. 733.

34. For further comment, see Vol'skii, 1854, pp. 102, 106.

35. For a lengthier depiction of the deposit trade in cereals, see Herlihy, 1976: 45–68, with bibliography. English mercantile commentators of the early nineteenth century call this commerce "the transit trade in corn." The equivalent French term is *expéditions par entrepôt.*

36. Vol'skii, 1854, p. 119.

37. According to the testimony of a grain merchant in London, given to a Parliamentary committee in 1814: "I have known many individuals, but one particularly, who has held his corn for five, six and seven years, because the price has not come up to his ideas of what it should have been." *Reports,* p. 79.

38. Hagemeister, 1846, p. 107. For average freight rates to the principal receiving ports from Odessa, see ibid., p. 27.

39. Baruchello, 1932, p. 591.

40. For a yearly list compiled from several sources, see Herlihy, 1963, Appendix VI.

41. See the comments of the Tuscan consul at Smyrna in 1856, who wondered at Turkey's failure to take advantage of her central geographical position, in order to become a maritime power. ASF, Affari Esteri, Filza 2555, 2 July 1856.

42. *Records,* 1833, I, 252.

43. Pavlovich, 1862, p. 271.

44. *JO,* 6 Nov. 1856. Earlier, the Spanish consul in Odessa wrote: "To tell the truth, those nations which do not have a treaty of commerce with Turkey can obtain access to the Black Sea for their merchant ships, by raising in Constantinople the flag of one of the four privileged nations." See Baguer y Ribas, 1832, p. v.

45. Report of the sales is in ASF, Affari Esteri, Protocollo 475.24, July 1854.

46. L. Levi, 1872, p. 293 ff.

47. According to Vol'skii, 1854, p. 145, the South Ukraine provided 315,594 quarters out of a total of 11,553,957 in 1846–1847.

48. Shepelev, 1973, p. 29. See also AMAE, Odessa, VI, 21 Nov. 1842, f. 285. The French consul in Odessa observed that passenger traffic from Odessa to Constantinople was largely in Russian hands.

49. ASF, Affari Esteri, Filza 2477, 29 March 1843.

50. *JO,* 27 Jan. 1858; ASF, Affari Esteri, Filza 2556, 24 June 1857. For a detailed report of the company, see Ralli's description in NACRO, 9 Jan. 1860.

51. It was entitled *Bolletino Commerciale della Compagnia Russa di Navigazione a Vapore,* and copies were frequently included in consular reports. See for example, ASL, Governatore, Filza 588 and Filza 628.

52. ASL, Governatore, Filza 673, 31 Jan. 1859.

53. NACRO, 12 Oct. 1858, ". . . there being no branch line yet to the frontier from the main line in any part of South Russia."

54. ASF, Ministero della Finanza, Capi Rotti 101, 10 May 1853.

55. Ibid., 27 Aug. 1858.

56. Bourdé, 1974, pp. 75–88.

57. On these industrial origins, see *Odessa*, 1895, p. 165. Blackwell, 1968, p. 41, discusses the terms for factory (*fabrika*s, *zavod*s) and concludes that tsarist industrial surveys did not use them consistently. Lenin's definition was that a factory had to include at least sixteen workers.

58. According to a survey of 1803, Odessa possessed a hair powder factory, two macaroni factories, three producing grape juice or bottled water, two wineries, two tallow (candle) factories, three brick works, two limestone ovens and twenty-three mills. See Zagoruiko, 1957–60, I, 73.

59. On the traditional freedom of Odessa's working class, see *Odessa. Ocherk*, 1957, p. 23.

60. GAOO, *f.* 2, *op.* 1, *d.* 62, *ll.* 2, 37–39. For the history of early factories in Odessa, see GAOO, *f.* 274, *op.* 1, *d.* 12, *f.* 57.

61. Druzhinina, 1970, p. 297. On Santsenbakher's soap factory, the first in Odessa, see Mel'nikov, 1875, p. 30. In 1896, the firm was still in operation. In addition to soap, it produced soda, beer, and ice. See *Al'manakh*, 1896, p. 13 of advertisements.

62. A. A. Skal'kovskii, 1839, p. 44.

63. GAOO, *f.* 3, *op.* 1, *d.* 70, *ll.* 75, 77.

64. *Odessa*, 1895, pp. 187–88.

65. AMAE, Odessa, VII, 12 Aug. 1858, f. 135.

66. A. A. Skal'kovskii, 1865e, p. 254.

67. Bremner, 1839, II, 502–03.

68. A. A. Skal'kovskii, 1865b, II, 272. In six years revenue from excise taxes on tobacco more than doubled—from 169,936 rubles to 420,000 rubles.

69. NACRO, 12 July 1856.

70. Kohl, 1842, p. 429.

71. Hommaire de Hell, 1847, p. 31.

72. A. A. Skal'kovskii, 1865e, p. 251.

73. Quoted by Zolotov, 1963, p. 145.

74. K. A. Skal'kovskii, 1906, p. 17.

75. For an interesting study of another great commercial port that failed to industrialize, see Scobie, 1972, 1064: "Despite the bustle and prosperity of the Buenos Aires environment in 1910, nothing stimulated industrialization, encouraged import substitution, or prodded landowners or merchants to invest capital in factories." There seem to be instructive parallels also in the history of Naples in the eighteenth century: see Chorley, 1965. See also Gilchrist, 1967.

Chapter Six

1. K. A. Skal'kovskii, 1906, p. 24.
2. The title of Langeron's play was *Manziello ou la révolution de Naples*, published in 1816 or 1819. See A. de Ribas, 1925–26, II, 32–40.
3. AMAE, Mémoires et Documents, Russie, XXI, ff. 211–15. For a brief sketch of his personality see Veresaev, 1937, I, 317–18. For further details on Langeron's difficulties with St. Petersburg concerning Odessa's free port status, see Morton, 1830, pp. 195–96.
4. *Odessa*, 1895, p. 790.
5. See Veresaev, 1937, I, 317, for the anecdote telling how Langeron absent-mindedly locked up Alexander I in his room and then proceeded to go out for a walk!
6. Pingaud, 1910, p. 421.
7. Odessa, 1896, pp. 74–75.
8. Ibid.
9. Pingaud, 1910, p. 422.
10. A. A. Skal'kovskii's unpublished manuscript, n.d., p. 38.
11. Mikhailovitch, 1931, p. 226. The anonymous author of a brochure, *Ville*, 1908, on the other hand, credited Odessa's progress to Langeron's skillful administration. See pp. 14–15.
12. Quoted in Alekseev, 1925–26, III, 58.
13. *Odessa*, 1895, p. 789. See also K. A. Skal'kovskii, 1905, p. 37.
14. Druzhinina, 1970, pp. 113, 148.
15. Troyat, 1946, pp. 272–78. For Inzov's relations with Pushkin, see Chereiskii, 1975, pp. 162–63, and Veresaev, 1937, I, 247–49: "Pushkin all his life remembered Inzov with fondness and gratitude."
16. Troyat, 1946, p. 311.
17. Pingaud, 1910, p. 444.
18. Atlas, 1911, p. 34.
19. Indova, 1955, p. 22.
20. Vorontsov, 1880, p. 40.
21. Ibid., p. 508.
22. Ibid., p. 528. Mikhail Vorontsov eventually became the third largest landowner of the Kherson *guberniia* with forty-five thousand *desiatinas* of land. See Druzhinina, 1981, p. 66.
23. Vorontsov, 1880, p. 533.
24. Indova, 1955, pp. 41–42.
25. Markevich, n.d., pp. 6–9.
26. Pushkin, 1937, XIII, 103.
27. Nolte, 1854, p. 453.
28. AMAE, Odessa, VI, 14 April 1844, f. 367.
29. Stephens, 1838, I, 261.
30. Hommaire de Hell, 1847, p. 11.

31. Indova, 1955, p. 36. For further comment on Alupka, see Webster, 1830, I, 64; Kohl, 1842, p. 463; Shipov, 1933, p. 450.

32. *Desiatidnevnaia poezdka*, 1848, p. 22.

33. Churchill, 1953, pp. 346–47.

34. Vorontsov, 1880, p. 558.

35. Ibid., p. 554.

36. For a detailed description of his expeditions, see AMAE, Odessa, VI, 8 March 1841, ff. 130–35. Hommaire de Hell eventually compiled a book, the *Report* frequently cited, for the tsar, which earned him the order of St. Vladimir, but then he left Russia for Moldavian service.

37. AMAE, Odessa, VI, 8 June 1842, f. 232.

38. K. A. Skal'kovskii, 1905, p. 37. One of Vorontsov's aides, M. P. Shcherbinin, wrote a reverential biography published in 1858.

39. AMAE, Odessa, V, 24 Oct. 1834, f. 188.

40. TsGIA, *f.* 385, *op.* 1, *d.* 7, *ll.* 9–11.

41. A. Skal'kovskii, 1870, p. 62; see too Straikh, 1911, pp. 5–6. Vorontsov left 130,690 titles in French, English, German, Italian, Polish, and other languages ranging from the sixteenth century to the nineteenth century to his son, S. M. Vorontsov, who gave the collection to the university library. See Skripnikova, n.d., p. 87.

42. TsGIA, *f.* 442, *op.* 34, *d.* 557, *l.* 1.

43. AMAE Odessa, IV, Dec. 1835, f. 237.

44. Webster, 1830, II, 342.

45. Borovoi, 1944, p. 43.

46. K. A. Skal'kovskii, 1905, p. 28.

47. Atlas, 1911, p. 35.

48. Ryndziunskii, 1958, p. 343.

49. Atlas, 1911, p. 25.

50. *Odesskii al'manakh*, 1839, pp. 9–10. Ferrier, 1841, p. 193 and Bremner, 1839, II, 486.

51. Jesse, 1841, I, 210–11.

52. Wegelin, 1845, I, 177.

53. K. A. Skal'kovskii, 1905, pp. 34–35.

54. Zipperstein, 1980, p. 42.

55. Hagemeister, 1846, p. 74.

56. Lyall, 1825, I, 162.

57. Tarnopol, 1855, p. 65.

58. AMAE, Odessa, VI, 24 Dec. 1843, f. 344.

59. Tarnopol, 1855, pp. 81–84.

60. Molinari, 1877, p. 236. Vorontsov succeeded in having the Empress Alexandra visit another synagogue in 1828. He wanted to establish good relations between Jews and Russians in Odessa.

61. Zipperstein, 1980, p. 56.

62. Orlov, 1886, pp. 104–22. For further comment on Greek settlement at Odessa, see Herlihy, 1979–80.

63. Quoted by Arsh, 1959, p. 211.

64. Cited in Herlihy, 1978–79, p. 399.

65. Moore, 1833, p. 149.

66. Shmidt, 1863, p. 863.

67. Arsh, 1959, p. 303.

68. AMAE, Odessa, V, 6 May 1836, f. 266.

69. Bremner, 1839, II, 497–98.

70. Zagoruiko, 1958–60, II, 51.

71. W. Hamm, 1862, p. 96.

72. Jesse, 1841, I, 182.

73. Ibid., p. 193. Also Tereshchenko, 1853, pp. 55–75.

74. Hommaire de Hell, 1847, p. 6.

75. *Odesskii al'manakh*, pp. 174–77.

76. Rzewuska, 1939, II, 321.

77. Golovin, 1854, p. 26.

78. K. A. Skal'kovskii, 1905, p. 29.

79. Atlas, 1911, p. 56.

80. Kohl, 1844, p. 425.

81. For comment, see Pinkerton, 1833, p. 137; Lagarde, 1812, p. 155; Morton, 1830, pp. 207–08; Webster, 1830, II, 347; Brooks, 1855, p. 22.

82. Rzewuska, 1939, II, 319.

83. A. A. Skal'kovskii, 1870, p. 49.

84. *JO*, 26 March / 7 April 1827.

85. Morton, 1830, pp. 207–08.

86. Jesse, 1841, I, 78.

87. Hommaire de Hell, 1847, p. 8.

88. For a description of the method, see AMAE, Odessa, VI, 23 March 1843, ff. 292–96; 30 August 1843, f. 328; 20 October 1843, ff. 334–36. Generally, hexagon prisms of wood were cut with a circular saw. Since there was no circular saw in Odessa, he made do with an adz. The diameter of each block was two centimeters wider at the base than at the top. The wood was strong enough to take frost nails and was placed together with sand and rock filling the cracks. According to its inventor, this system provided a paving which resisted heat, humidity, and cold. The cost was about six francs a square meter, as only cheap wood, such as pine, spruce, and linden was used. Wood had the additional merit of being soft on the horses' hooves.

89. For descriptions, see Scott, 154, p. 338; Hume, 1914, pp. 37–38; and NACRO, 23 Nov. 1860.

90. AMAE, Odessa, VIII, 6 May 1861, f. 250; 6 July 1861, f. 246; 1 Oct. 1861, f. 299.

91. In his memoirs, K. A. Skal'kovskii recalled the salty well water and the marble cisterns placed on tin roofs to catch precious water, 1905, pp. 4, 26.

92. AMAE, Odessa, IV, 24 June 1831, f. 310.

93. Finkel, 1865, I, 171–72. See also Herlihy, 1978, p. 435.

94. Jesse, 1841, I, 196.

95. Condor, 1826, p. 233. It was no better in the 1830s. Demidov complained that there was a "pénurie de l'eau potable," 1842, II, 292. Beginning in 1834 two entrepreneurs, Pichon and Wittenburg, did bring water from the Large Fountain (eight miles south of Odessa) and from the German colony of Lustdorf by means of steam pumps (built in England) and pipes to a reservoir in Odessa, but it too became inadequate. See *Odessa*, 1895, pp. 281–82.

96. Pinkerton, 1833, p. 136. In 1832, the Spanish consul at Odessa, Baguer y Ribas, wrote, "El mayor inconveniente que hay en esta ciudad es la falta de agua," 1832, p. 5.

97. Morton, 1830, p. 217.

98. Ibid., p. 287 and Shepelev, 1973, p. 25.

99. Rzewuska, 1939, II, 319. In 1859, all the cisterns dried. See W. Hamm, 1862, p. 105.

100. Jesse, 1841, I, 196. The water system was bad, but the sewer system worse. A traveler described it for us in midcentury: "The drainage of Odessa [is] a bricked channel, about two feet deep, open at the top, and with which the houses communicate by similar but smaller channels, crossing the footway, but usually covered by a board. As these larger channels turn the corners of the streets, it is frequently necessary to cross them, to the continuous disgust of the organ usually affected by such places, while the eye is also constantly annoyed by very loathsome sights." Brooks, 1855, p. 21.

101. Stephens, 1838, I, 261. Not only the doors, but also the chimney-piece and shutters were from the Mikhailov Palace where Emperor Paul was murdered. Vorontsov chose to build his city palace on the spot where Richelieu's humble house had once stood, just as Voronstov placed Alupka on the site of Richelieu's Crimean villa. See Morton, 1830, pp. 202, 198. For a detailed description of the vases, busts, and paintings adorning the palace, see Brooks, 1855, pp. 144–45.

102. Rzewuska, 1939, II, 322.

103. Wickoff, 1880, p. 254. One of the palace curiosities was the Turkish room. It had a light green Gothic roof and all around the walls were draped Persian and Turkish shawls. Persian divans and carpets completed the decor. The entire palace was open to the public on holidays. See Morton, 1830, pp. 202–03. In 1936, the palace became the Palace of Pioneers. About a decade ago, it nearly burned down for lack of water to fight the fire in the building.

104. Borovoi, 1967b, pp. 148, 150–51; Skripnikova, n.d. pp. 87 ff.

105. De Ros, 1855, p. 62.

106. Koch, 1855, p. 260.

107. Pingaud, 1910, p. 421.
108. Stephens, 1838, I, 259. This building is now the City Soviet of Working People's Deputies.
109. Ibid.
110. Jesse, 1841, I, 191.
111. Hommaire de Hell, 1847, p. 3.
112. Wickoff, 1880, p. 231.
113. In 1850 Odessa had seven restaurants. Haxthausen noted that even poor people "get their dinners from cook-shops in the bazaar." idem, 1856, II, 142–43.
114. Knight, 1839, p. 206.
115. Craven, 1873, I, 295–97. An American stated, "The Russians boast that this lazaretto is the finest in the world." He described the garden, the trellis, and the grating, called "Il Parlatorio," which separated the inmates and visitors when he was there in 1854. He also described the criminals in their fumigation procedure. See Guernsey, 1854, p. 10.
116. Stephens, 1838, I, 245–48.
117. Hommaire de Hell, 1847, pp. 3–5. Some twenty years later, the French consul in Odessa claimed that the quarantine was maintained for political, and not sanitary, reasons. With so many political exiles residing in Constantinople, Russian authorities were attempting to insure that none entered Odessa. With the telegraph to warn of disease, it should no longer be necessary, he felt, to detain persons so long for it only served to vex merchants, captains, and passengers and make the quarantine officials rich through bribes. See AMAE, Odessa, VII, 15 Aug. 1856, f. 457.
118. Jesse, 1841, I, pp. 54–62.
119. Knight, 1839, p. 206.
120. K. A. Skal'kovskii, 1905, p. 16. Another Englishman described the Opera House contract with the Quarantine as a matter mixing "meat and music." Brooks, 1855, p. 33.
121. Pinkerton, 1833, pp. 122–23.
122. Brooks, 1855, p. 24. Shishkina, 1848, II, 18, agreed.
123. Moore, 1833, p. 123; Armstrong, 1831, pp. 25–26.
124. Moore, 1833, p. 125.
125. Jesse, 1841, I, 65; for other comments on Odessa's hotels, see Hommaire de Hell, 1847, p. 6; Stephens, 1838, I, 236; Oliphant, 1854, p. 22; Ferrier, 1841, p. 64; Shishkina, 1848, II, 3.
126. Stephens, 1838, I, 263.
127. Hommaire de Hell, 1847, p. 7.
128. W. Hamm, 1862, p. 9.
129. Hommaire de Hell, 1847, p. 12.
130. Avdeeva, 1842, pp. 87–89. See too Kohl, 1844, p. 417.
131. Barker, 1855, p. 155.
132. Sperandeo, 1906, p. 331, claims that two Italian architects, Rossi and Toricelli, designed the staircase.

133. Zagoruiko, 1957–60, II, 46.

134. Koch, 1855, p. 260.

135. Jesse, 1841, I, 183; Sears, 1855, p. 171, repeated this as if it were his original observation.

136. Hommaire de Hell, 1847, p. 10. Later, a French visitor called the staircase "Babylonian," and attributed its building to Vorontsov's ostentatious response to Tsar Nicholas I's simple query: "Where are the steps going to the sea?" At that time there were only rough wooden steps. Today the staircase is not much used. For a few kopecks pedestrians can mount a covered escalator alongside the staircase.

137. Atlas, 1911, p. 33.

138. Jesse, 1841, I, 197, and Moore, 1833, p. 161. A series of Italian impressarios took charge of opera production in Odessa: F. Fiorini (whose productions were admired, praised, and rewarded by Alexander I in 1818); Montovani, Zamboni, Buonavoglia, and Cesare Negri. After 1825, a theatrical commission supervised the productions.

139. For details on Gogol's stay in Odessa, see Markevich, 1902.

140. K. A. Skal'kovskii, 1905, p. 10.

141. *Odesskii al'manakh,* pp. 182–87; Stephens, 1838, I, 262.

142. Atlas, 1911, pp. 51–52.

143. Lerner, 1902. For further details on Italian opera in Odessa, see *Odesskii teatr,* 1977, and Sperandeo, 1906, pp. 332–33. Not only opera stars, but also actors were rewarded handsomely for performing in Odessa. The English consul reported that "Mr. Aldridge, the English tragedian made about 2,000 pounds during his ten-day visit to Odessa." See PRO, FO 65, DCXLVII, 4 Feb. 1863.

144. On June 1, 1821, a Russian version, *Vestnik iuzhnoi Rossii,* appeared. But with only seven subscribers among the Russian merchants, the paper soon went out of business. See N. Lerner, 1901, p. 7.

145. Zagoruiko, 1957–60, I, 86.

146. N. Lerner, 1901, pp. 3–19; see also Borovoi, 1967b, p. 153.

147. Borovoi, 1967b, pp. 153–58. An English visitor pronounced it and its critical articles as "the very washiest of French flippancies." Brooks, 1855, p. 19. The Odessa State University Library possesses a complete run of the paper for the years 1838–1881.

148. The French ambassador at Constantinople was a subscriber and regularly forwarded the paper to Paris. AMAE, Odessa, IV, 2 April 1841, f. 141.

149. *OV,* 1844, no. 71.

150. Atlas, 1911, p. 49.

151. Ibid.

Chapter Seven

1. For an examination of Catherine's municipal reforms, see Ditiatin, 1875, pp. 415–72. See also Ryndziundskii, 1958, pp. 40 ff., for eighteenth-century city government and society.

2. Hittle, 1979, p. 221. For regulations governing cities in the seventeenth and eighteenth centuries, see Ditiatin, 1875, pp. 138–413.

3. *Odessa*, 1895, p. 67.

4. Hittle, 1979, p. 224. For a detailed description of the membership and functions of city institutions in Odessa before 1863, see *Odessa*, 1895, pp. 65–87, and Skinner, 1973, pp. 68–108.

5. Hittle, 1979, pp. 229–34.

6. *Odessa*, 1895, p. 77.

7. Ibid., pp. 75–77.

8. Ibid., p. 75.

9. Ibid., p. 77.

10. Ryndziundskii, 1958, pp. 95–96.

11. *BPP* 1875, LXXVI, 1299.

12. *Odessa*, 1895, pp. 101–02. Bernshtein, 1881, pp. 70–71, gives a partial list of Odessa's yearly revenues and expenditures from 1802.

13. K. A. Skal'kovskii, 1905, p. 48.

14. *Odessa*, 1895, pp. 116, 196.

15. Ibid., p. 116.

16. Ibid., p. 114.

17. Ibid., p. 107.

18. Skinner, 1973, p. 89.

19. *Odessa*, 1895, p. 709. For a recent survey of public and private charities in Russia, see Lindenmeyr, 1980. For Odessa's charitable societies, see *Odessa*, 1895, pp. 705–80. See ibid., pp. 798–801, for a list showing dates of founding, capital value, income and expenditures of Odessa's charitable institutions for the year 1894.

20. Ibid., p. 802. According to Lindenmeyr, 1980, p. 152, Odessa's province ranked third in the empire in the number of its charitable institutions.

21. *BPP* 1876, LXXIV, 436.

22. Wightman, 1928, p. 160.

23. *Odessa*, 1895, pp. 85–86.

24. For Stroganov's petition to the minister of internal affairs, see Ditiatin, 1877, pp. 507–86.

25. *Odessa*, 1895, pp. 86–87. For a detailed description of the regulations for municipal government adopted by Odessa in 1863, see Ditiatin, 1877, pp. 510–40.

26. *Odessa*, 1895, pp. 87, 789–90, for a list of Odessa's mayors.

27. Ibid., pp. 89–90.

28. Ibid., p. 91.

29. Ibid., p. 96, and Ditiatin, 1877, p. 540.

30. *Odessa*, 1895, p. 97.

31. *BPP* 1875, LXXVI, 1310.

32. *Odessa*, 1895, p. 99.

33. Ibid., 1895, p. 101.

34. Pregel, 1974, III, 205. Born in 1897 of Jewish parents in Odessa, the poet Sofia Pregel wrote of her youth: "I myself only felt good in Odessa. In other cities I could not have the Aleksandrovskii store, the library for Jewish salesgirls, the City Theater with matinees for students."

35. Molinari, 1877, pp. 234–35.

36. Starr, 1972; see chapter 3, "The Politics of Decentralization," pp. 110–84.

37. Starr, 1972, p. 34.

38. *AOO*, 1961, p. 11.

39. *Odessa*, 1895, p. lxxv.

40. See below, pp. 160–61.

41. Cited by Borovoi, 1974, p. 204.

42. *Odessa*, 1895, p. lxxv.

43. Ibid.

44. *Odessa*, 1895, p. 258. The iron was imported from Paris and the asphalt from Marseilles. E. G. Harris, one of the city's leading engineers, directed the project.

45. Ibid., p. 501.

46. Ibid., pp. 746–47.

47. Bernshtein, 1881, p. 73.

48. *BPP* 1874, LXVII, 1454.

49. *BPP* 1876, LXXIV, 450.

50. *BPP* 1875, LXVVI, 1298. Odessa retained some tariff priveleges until 1859.

51. *Entsiklopedicheskii slovar*, 1901, XXXIII, 664–65.

52. *Odessa*, 1895, p. 372.

53. *Entsiklopedicheskii slovar*, 1893, XI, 155.

54. *Odessa*, 1895, p. 789.

55. *Entsiklopedicheskii slovar*, 1893, XI, 17.

56. *Odessa*, 1895, p. 766.

57. *Entsiklopedicheskii slovar*, 1893, IX, 913.

58. *Odessa*, 1895, pp. 488, 687.

59. Ibid., 1895, pp. 602–04 and Atlas, 1911, pp. 83–88.

60. Atlas, 1911, p. 85.

61. Ibid.

62. *Odessa*, 1895, p. lxvi.

63. Ibid., p. lxv. He later became an aide to S. S. Lanskoi, minister of the interior, and advocated liberal terms for the serfs when the government was planning emancipation. He also advocated decentralization in order to give provincial governors more power. See Starr, 1972, pp. 120–38.

64. For a listing up to 1894, see *Odessa*, 1895, pp. 789–90.

65. GAOO, *f.* 5, *op.* 1, *d.* 388, *ll.* 12–25.

66. Motzkin, 1910, p. 110.

67. Trotsky, 1973, p. 58.

68. For Novosel'skii's career, see K. A. Skal'kovskii, 1902, pp. 302–13; also *Odessa*, 1895, pp. 86, 96, 98, 196, 220–23, 265.

69. K. A. Skal'kovskii, 1902, pp. 307–08.

70. Starr, 1972, p. 6, n. 9.

71. K. A. Skal'kovskii, 1902, p. 311; the American consul referred to "our very popular Governor-General Kotzebue," who had been transferred to Warsaw, but who had represented to the inhabitants of Odessa, "on a limited scale, the Imperial Majesty and Court." See NACRO, 1 April 1874.

72. *Odessa*, 1895, p. 791.

73. GAOO, *f.* 274, *op.* 1, *d.* 2, *ll.* 64–85.

74. Information supplied to me by Professor Thomas Owen. In 1903, Marazli sent two Greek books to President Theodore Roosevelt. See NACRO, 2 October 1903. Unfortunately, the consul does not give the titles. The president wrote Marazli a grateful letter of acknowledgment, saying that he would donate the books to the Library of Congress.

75. *Odessa*, 1895, p. 327.

76. Private communication from the late Professor M. M. Postan.

Chapter Eight

1. There might have been slightly more or less as these figures are for 1858, taken at the time of the tenth revision. See Druzhinina, 1981, pp. 14, 24.

2. *Istoriia mist*, 1969, v. 8, 17.

3. Shtraikh, 1911, p. 10.

4. PRO FO 257, XI, 5 April 1863.

5. PRO FO 65, DCXLVII, 4 Feb. 1863.

6. PRO FO 257, XI, 23 June 1865.

7. *BPP* 1876, LXXIV, 430.

8. Emmons, 1968, p. 194.

9. NACRO, 15 Feb. 1862.

10. AMAE, Mémoires et Documents, Russie, XLVI, 1 August 1864, f. 87, n.

11. NACRO, 15 Feb. 1862.

12. PRO FO 257, XI, 23 June 1865.

13. AN, F12, 31 July 1863. See also Confino, 1963, p. 176.

14. *BPP* 1876, LXXIV, 430.

15. Borisov, 1893, v. 2, pt. 4, 77.

16. Witte, 1901, p. 164.

17. Borisov, 1893, v. 2, pt. 4, 77.

18. Ben-Sasson, 1976, p. 883. Leon Trotsky tells how his father, a prosperous landowner, wanted to buy more land, but after 1882 was constrained to lease under the name of another. See idem, 1973, p. 86.

19. Borisov, 1893, p. 88.

20. *Vedomost,* 1902, pp. 81–82.

21. Shternshtein, 1955, p. 71.

22. Ibid.

23. Curtin, 1911, pp. 340–41.

24. Ibid.

25. Snodgrass, 1913, p. 173.

26. *BPP* 1875, LXXVI, 1022.

27. Zolotov, 1966, pp. 14, 17.

28. GAOO, *f.* 174, *op.* 1, *d.* 23. In 1872, the Imperial Agricultural Society of South Russia sponsored an exhibition to encourage gardening and vegetable farming in the area. See GAOO, *f.* 22, *op.* 1, *d.* 270, *l.* 33.

29. Metzer, 1974, p. 544.

30. For a fascinating account of the attempts of an American agronomist to help increase agricultural production in southern provinces of the Russian Empire, see the memoirs of Michael, 1979.

31. AMAE, Odessa, XII, 17 July 1882, f. 139.

32. Lazarovich, 1893, pp. 102–04.

33. Zolotov, 1966, pp. 28–29.

34. AMAE, Odessa, XII, 30 Oct. 1884, f. 253.

35. *BPP* 1912–1913, XCIX, 25.

36. *BPP* 1899, CII, 6.

37. *BPP* 1898, XCVIII, 11.

38. For a lengthy discussion of foreign agricultural machinery in the Odessa region, see *BPP* 1908, CXV, 14–15.

39. *BPP* 1906, CXXVIII, 11.

40. Ibid.

41. NACRO, 29 Nov. 1905.

42. MAE, *RC,* 1907, p. 5.

43. *BPP* 1908, CXV, 14.

44. *BPP* 1906, CXXVIII, 15 and *BPP* 1907, XCII, 12.

45. *BPP* 1909, XCVIL, 17. American firms fared somewhat better, as they pooled their resources, chartered entire steamers, and sent their wares to Odessa directly in two or three ships.

46. MAE, *RC,* 1910, p. 46.

47. MAE, *RC,* 1910, p. 4.

48. *BPP* 1912–1913, CIX, 25.

49. US. *DCTR,* 21 Aug. 1914, p. 1004.

50. Pinkerton, 1833, p. 138.

51. Possart, 1841, II, 821.

52. Kohl, 1842, p. 427.

53. Mel'nikov, 1875, p. 10

54. *BPP* 1890, LXXVI, 7.

55. *BPP* 1889, LXXX, 3.

56. Ibid., 2.

57. Lauwick, 1907, p. 11.

58. Parasun'ko, 1963, pp. 52–53.

59. Zolotov, 1966, p. 52.

60. *BPP* 1909, XCVII, 30.

61. Mel'nikov, 1875, p. 6.

62. Ibid., p. 9.

63. Ibid., pp. 9–10.

64. 1865e, p. 251.

65. Villari, 1905, p. 125.

66. Quoted in *Odessa. Ocherk*, 1957, p. 58.

67. Itenberg, 1974, pp. 37–38.

68. *Odessa. Ocherk*, 1957, p. 56.

69. Mel'nikov, 1875, p. 12.

70. *BPP* 1876, LXXIV, 433.

71. AMAE, VIII, Odessa, 28 August 1862, f. 449.

72. *Odessa. Ocherk*, 1957, p. 56.

73. GAOO, *f.* 279, *op.* 1, *d.* 4, *ll.* 4–35.

74. Mel'nikov, 1875, p. 13. Factory workers received fifteen to sixteen rubles per month, whereas in Moscow pay was no more than ten rubles. In fact, high wages and high costs for fuel and water tended to make Odessa's factories noncompetitive.

75. *BPP* 1876, LXXIV, 449. Mel'nikov, 1875, p. 12, also suggested the need for technical schools. Only the Steam Navigation and Trading Company had established specialized training for its employees: a mechanical shop and courses for the training of foremen.

76. Hagemeister, 1846, p. 215.

77. Parasun'ko, 1963, pp. 52–53.

78. A. A. Skal'kovskii, 1865e, p. 254.

79. *Odessa*, 1895, pp. 223–24.

80. AMAE, Odessa, VIII, 14 Aug. 1858, ff. 101–03.

81. Information supplied by Professor Thomas Owen, to whom I express my gratitude.

82. For recent examples of the contributions of grain firms to industrial investments, see Morgan, 1979, pp. 161–79.

83. NACRO, 9 July 1870.

84. NACRO, 28 March 1871.

85. NACRO, 7 June 1873.

86. Ibid.

87. *BPP* 1875, LXVII, 1438.

88. GAOO, *f.* 274, *op.* 1, *d.* 2, *ll.* 65–85. This document is a printed list of all the private buildings in Odessa. It gives the names of the owners, the

street, value of the property, and the assessment of four different taxes on the property.

89. *BPP* 1874, LXVII, 1438.

90. GAOO, *f.* 274, *op.* 1, *d.* 2, *ll.* 61–62.

91. AMAE, Odessa, Vol. X, 28 October, 1873, f. 221; also ANP F12, 7173, 711.

92. NACRO, 10 Oct. 1874.

93. NACRO, 3 July 1875.

94. Itenberg, 1974, p. 38.

95. AMAE, Odessa, IX, 15 Jan. 1864, f. 105.

96. Ibid., f. 106.

97. Snodgrass, 1913, p. 177.

98. AMAE, Odessa, IX, 25 Jan. 1864, ff. 106–07.

99. MAE, *RC,* 1901, pp. 23, 28–29, lists and classifies all these firms. According to McKay, 1970, p. 86, in 1899 ten of Odessa's twenty-nine companies were foreign and of these eight were Belgian.

100. *BPP* 1900, XCV, 8.

101. *BPP* 1876, LXXIV, 446.

102. Ibid.

103. *BPP* 1876, LXXIV, 447.

104. Ibid., 432–33.

105. Ibid.

106. Ibid.

107. Proctor, 1900, p. 277.

108. AMAE, Odessa, VIII, 20 May 1862.

109. *Odessa. Ocherk,* 1957, p. 57.

110. *Odessa,* 1895, p. 226.

111. *BPP* 1904, C, 26.

112. Zolotov, 1966, pp. 105–06.

113. Parasun'ko, 1963, p. 47.

114. Bernshtein, 1881, pp. 75–76.

115. *BPP* 1910, CII, 35.

116. *BPP* 1904, C, 26.

117. Parasun'ko, 1963, p. 47.

118. MAE, *RC,* 1894, p. 11.

119. *BPP* 1904, C, 26.

120. *Ofitsial'nyi katalog,* 1910, p. 65.

121. Parasun'ko, 1963, p. 47. For exports, see *BPP* 1911, XCV, 11.

122. Fedorov, 1878, p. 55.

123. *BPP* 1904, C, 24.

124. *Odessa,* 1895, p. 227.

125. *Odessa. Ocherk,* 1957, pp. 56–57.

126. *BPP* 1904, C, 25.

127. *BPP* 1905, XCII, 25. The U. S. consul also emphasized the disastrous results of the war, especially the absence of credit. NACRO, 5 Sept. 1904.

128. MAE, *RC*, 1906, p. 4.
129. *BPP* 1905, XCII, 25.
130. Snodgrass, 1913, p. 175.
131. Ibid., p. 179.
132. MAE, *RC*, 1907, p. 27.
133. *BPP* 1907, XCII, 25.
134. MAE, *RC*, 1908–1909, p. 55.
135. Ibid., p. 29.
136. Ibid.
137. For this and further details on various industries in Odessa, see *BPP* 1910, CII, 34–35. Sugar refining fell off as there was a bad harvest of sugar beets. And of Odessa's fourteen flour mills, only two worked at maximum capacity. France was exporting its flour to Turkey and Egypt, thus cutting Odessa from its former markets.
138. Snodgrass, 1913, p. 174.
139. *BPP* 1908, CXV, 29–31. He gives the number of mines, the names of the owners, and the amount of ore mined.
140. *BPP* 1909, XCVIX, 30.
141. MAE, *RC*, 1910, p. 44.
142. Snodgrass, 1913, p. 175.
143. *BPP* 1912–1913, XCIX, 11.
144. Ibid., pp. 178–79.
145. *Ofitsial'nyi katalog*, 1910, p. 1.
146. MAE, *RC*, 1910, p. 4.
147. Pettinato, 1968, p. 37.

Chapter Nine

1. *BPP* 1873, LXV, 1014–15.
2. AMAE, Odessa, X, 21 Aug. 1871, f. 124.
3. Ibid. In 1858, Ferdinand de Lesseps visited Odessa for a week. He lectured on how the Suez Canal, which he was building, would give great commercial importance to Odessa. He was invited to three banquets, one each given by the Russian Steam Navigation and Trading Company, the merchants of the city, and the nobility during which he was toasted as the designer of future commercial benefits for the city. See AMAE, Odessa, VIII, 15 August 1858.
4. *BPP* 1880, LXXIV, 862.
5. *BPP* 1890, LXXVI, 9.
6. Kuprin, 1920, p. 11.
7. *BPP* 1898, XCVIII, 7.
8. *BPP* 1902, CLX, 12. The French consul gave a similar report, MAE, *RC*, 1902, p. 20.
9. NACRO, 2 October 1903.

10. In 1906, the Russian Steam Navigation and Trading Company inaugurated a direct passenger and freight line to New York from Odessa. The voyage took twenty days. See *DCTR*, 12 September 1906, pp. 6–7.

11. *BPP* 1911, XCV, 10–11.

12. Chekhovich, 1894, p. 18, footnote.

13. Zolotov, 1966, p. 50.

14. Liashchenko, 1917, p. 67.

15. See the table of prices in Jourdier, 1863, p. 392.

16. AMAE, Odessa, X, 24 May 1879, f. 133.

17. Vol'skii, 1854, pp. 100–01. France and not the United States was the principal supplier of flour to England. See Rees, 1972, p. 130.

18. AMAE, Odessa, X, 24 May 1879, ff. 134–36.

19. Ibid., f. 147.

20. PRO FO 65, DCCCLX, 18 Feb. 1873.

21. Liashchenko, 1917, pp. 33, 316. For Italy, see also Timoshenko, 1932, p. 482.

22. Liashchenko, 1917, p. 91.

23. Jurowsky, 1910, p. 23.

24. Michael, 1979, p. 136.

25. See Herlihy, 1980, and Siegelbaum, 1980, pp. 113–51.

26. *Odesskii iumoricheskii al'manakh*, 1892, p. 32.

27. *BPP* 1881, XCIX, 543.

28. *BPP* 1890, LXXVI, 2.

29. Zabarinskii, 1894, pp. 112–13.

30. In 1878, some attempt was made to build an elevator, but it apparently was not successful. See *Das Handels-Museum*, v. 1, 24 June 1886, 289.

31. For frequent commentary on the problem of quality control of south Ukrainian grain, see *BPP* 1890, LXXVI, 2–3; *BPP* 1890–1891, LXXXVII, 3–4; *BPP* 1899, CII, 4.

32. AMAE, Odessa, XV, 4 May 1901, f. 403.

33. Michael, 1979, p. 136 for this and the following quotation.

34. NACRO, 28 March 1906.

35. AMAE, Odessa, XV, 4 May 1901, f. 402.

36. Villari, 1905, p. 124.

37. AMAE, Odessa, XIII, 30 June 1894, ff. 353–54.

38. *BPP* 1890, LXXVI, 4.

39. *BPP* 1890–1891, LXXXVII, 4.

40. Ibid.

41. *BPP* 1899, CII, 6.

42. Borinevich, 1890, p. 41.

43. Smith, 1908, pp. 46–47.

44. GAOO, *f.* 3, *op.* 3, *d.* 654, *ll.* 9–10.

45. Bernshtein, 1881, p. 74.

46. Information supplied by Peter Shaw.

47. PRO FO 65, DCXLVII, 4 March 1863.

48. W. Hamm, 1862, p. 103.

49. Ribas, 1894, p. 376.

50. Ianson, 1870, p. 288. See the comments to the same effect of the British consul, *BPP* 1890, LXXVI, 3.

51. Rees, 1972, p. 130.

52. NACRO, 28 March 1906. The article appeared in the *Torgovo-promyshlennaia gazeta*, 20 Nov. / 3 Dec. 1905.

53. Michael, 1979, p. 137. In 1887, several London firms wrote to the acting governor general of Odessa, Roop, protesting the practice of sending samples, which were subsequently not matched in quality as cargoes. Part of their complaint read: "The fate of Odessa as a great centre for the export of grain had fallen considerably in the estimation of foreign commercial men, but that they did not see their way to removing the evil, which might be attributed to the fact that firms, of no standing whatsoever in this city, cared little for the maintenance of the reputation of Odessa as a grain exporting centre." See *Board of Trade Journal*, v. 2, Jan. 1887, 50.

54. AMAE, Odessa, IX, 9 Feb. 1863, f. 21.

55. AMAE, Odessa, X, 24 May 1879, f. 147.

56. AMAE, Odessa, IX, 5 Aug. 1865, f. 182. For the history of the building of the railway at Odessa, see A. A. Skal'kovskii, 1865d, and Markevich, n. d., pp. 6–28.

57. AMAE, Odessa, IX, 16 Sept. 1865, f. 197.

58. Ibid., 17 Dec. 1865, f. 221; PRO FO 65, DCLXXXIX, 16 Dec. 1865.

59. See Markevich, n. d., p. 11, where he explains that the line was to keep close to Moldavia and Austria.

60. PRO FO 65, DCCCLX, 18 Feb. 1873.

61. Shimanovskii, 1911, p. 10; also *BPP* 1908, CXV, 16.

62. *BPP* 1874, LXVII, 1454.

63. *BPP* 1881, XCIC, 546.

64. Zagoruiko, 1957–60, II, 27. See also Metzer, 1974, p. 542. Wheat going to the Baltic area received rebates until 1893. But in 1894 the tariff rates on the Odessa line were still unfavorable. See Chekhovich, 1894, p. 16.

65. *BPP* 1874, LXVII, 1454.

66. MAE, *RC*, 1894, p. 7.

67. *BPP* 1875, LXXVI, 1299.

68. *BPP* 1880, LXXIV, 862.

69. Villari, 1905, pp. 124–25.

70. For a detailed description of the expanding areas that were tapped by the railroad in 1870, 1883, and 1888, see Zabarinskii, 1894, pp. 34–36.

71. Zolotov, 1966, pp. 48–49. The decline in the use of railroads brought to pass something the British consul deplored: "But one would hope than in the presence of such universal progress nothing so retrograde

will be seen as a return from railway to animal draft carriage." *BPP* 1874, LXVII, 1439.

72. *BPP* 1900, XCV, 13.

73. MAE, *RC*, 1910, p. 6.

74. Michael, 1979, p. 136.

75. AMAE, Odessa, X, 24 May 1879, f. 147.

76. NACRO, 25 Nov. 1905 and 10 March 1906.

77. *Vsia Rossiia*, 1913, p. 73. MAE, *RC*, 1906, pp. 3–4.

78. *BPP* 1906, CXXVIII, 7.

79. *BPP* 1907, XCII, 26.

80. MAE, *RC*, 1907, pp. 3–4.

81. Ibid., 4.

82. Moskvich, 1904, p. 73.

83. Hubback, 1915, p. 31.

84. Fox, 1963, pp. 17–18; for a description of the port in 1914, see Merry, 1915, p. 106.

85. Beliiavskii, *TOSK*, I, 266–89.

86. A. A. Skal'kovskii, 1865d, p. 165.

87. PRO FO 65, DCLXXXIX, 24 March 1865.

88. *TOSK*, 1870, III, 13.

89. PRO FO 258, VI, 24 Sept. 1868. Thirty years later Odessa purchased two British-built dredgers. See *BPP* 1900, XCV, 12.

90. *BPP* 1874, LXVII, 1452.

91. *BPP* 1880, LXXIV, 863.

92. Ibid., 1863.

93. Luther, 1889, p. 8. Governor General Stroganov in his report to the ministry of internal affairs in 1882 feared that the unemployment caused by icing of the port would stir up political agitation among the dock workers. See GAOO, *f*. 5, *op*. 1, *d*. 388, *l*. 15.

94. Orbinskii, 1881, pp. 2–3.

95. Molinari, 1877, p. 207.

96. *BPP* 1878–1879, LXXI, 1476. Progress was slow. The only improvement noted by the consul was the replacement of a rotting wooden quay by a stone one in 1887. The docks were still unlit at night. *BPP* 1889, LXXX, 4.

97. Orbinskii, 1881, pp. 13–14.

98. *BPP* 1890–1891, LXXXVII, 3. For a description of the *estakada*, or raised railway, built in 1866, see Luther, 1889, p. 9 and Shternshtein, 1958, p. 16, note.

99. *BPP* 1898, XCVIII, 9. Part of the delay was caused by the fact that ships were allowed to load as little as three hundred tons a day, when it was possible to load fifteen hundred tons.

100. Chekhovich, 1894, p. 5. As early as 1884, Odessa's Committee on Trade and Manufacturing called the port's facilities "obsolete." See *Otchet*, 1884, p. 95.

101. *Odessa*, 1895, p. 220.
102. Chekhovich, 1894, p. 5.
103. *BPP* 1904, X, 27.
104. *BPP* 1908, CXV, 16.
105. *BPP* 1909, XCVII, 20. In 1917, Michael also noted that Mykolaiv had overtaken Odessa as the principal port of grain export. See idem, 1979, p. 136.
106. *BPP* 1908, CXV, 16 and *BPP* 1910, CL, 38; also MAE, *RC*, 1910, p. 18. Many similar proposals had been made back in 1889 by a German engineer, but were not acted upon, see Luther, 1889, pp. 7–125.
107. *BPP* 1911, XCV, 11.
108. *BPP* 1912–1913, XCIX, 23.
109. Smith, 1908, p. 49.
110. MAE, *RC*, 1906, p. 4.
111. Curtin, 1911, pp. 327–28.
112. MAE, *RC*, 1906, p. 3.
113. Winter, 1914, p. 137.
114. *BPP* 1907, XCII, 22. There was an adage, "thieves come from Pera to Odessa to perfect their trade."
115. Snodgrass, 1913, p. 183.
116. MAE, *RC*, 1910, p. 3.
117. *BPP* 1909, XCVIL, 22–23.
118. Snodgrass, 1913, p. 183.
119. Michell, 1899, p. 136.
120. Curtin, 1911, pp. 336–38.
121. Ibid.
122. Zolotov, 1966, p. 187.
123. Shimanovskii, 1911, p. 33 ff.
124. Michael, 1979, p. 139. By 1911, Kherson was exporting 1,063,216 tons of grain, compared to 1,650,162 tons exported from Odessa. Snodgrass, 1913, p. 183.
125. MAE, *RC*, 1910, p. 21.
126. Michael, 1979, p. 141.
127. MAE, *RC*, 1910, p. 8 and MAE, *RC*, 1912, 4.
128. *BPP* 1912–1913, XCIX, 23–24.
129. Snodgrass, 1913, p. 178.
130. MAE, *RC*, 1910, p. 6.
131. Snodgrass, 1913, p. 182.
132. As early as 1874, the New York Produce Exchange abandoned the system of buying grain in parcels. All grain of like grade and quality was commingled and certified. See Morgan, 1979, p. 62. By keeping the system of parcels, Odessa's merchants paid more to store it in separate bins and more to ship it. They had to pay "mat money" to put mats between the separate parcels on board ships. See *BPP* 1910, CL, 23, and Smith, 1908, p. 50.

Chapter Ten

1. PRO FO 63, 18 Feb. 1873.
2. Moskvich, 1904, p. 69.
3. *Odessa*, 1895, pp. 433–569.
4. *BPP* 1904, C, 22–23.
5. K. A. Skal'kovskii, 1905, p. 5.
6. *BPP* 1878–79, LXXI, 1476.
7. *Odessa*, 1895, p. 452.
8. On this point see Sharlin, 1978, p. 127, and Bater, 1976, pp. 186–87.
9. *BPP* 1878–79, LXXI, 1476.
10. *JO*, 6/18 October 1828.
11. GAOO, *f.* 274, *op.* 2, *d.* 4, *l.* 22.
12. *Odessa*, 1895, p. 447. In 1883, 2,141 infants under one month died at Odessa, representing 26.8 percent of all deaths. In 1882, among the Jews 238 infants died at under one month, 11.9 percent of total Jewish deaths. In 1887, the rate remained at 11.6 percent, but in 1891 the rate fell to 11.3 percent. See GAOO, *f.* 274, *op.* 1, *ll.* 17, 22–23; *f.* 274, *op.* 1, *d.* 19, *ll.* 18–19; *f.* 274, *op.* 2, *d.* 15, *l.* 151. See also *BPP*, 1879, XXXI.
13. At Rotterdam, for example, infant death rates rose from early in the century until the 1870s, Van Dijk, 1978. In England and Wales the rate does not drop until after 1900, Rosen, 1973, p. 649. At Boston infant mortality rates increased gradually after the 1820s, Rosenkranz, 1972, p. 18. In 1853, at New York it was reported that "there was an alarming increase in infant deaths over the previous ten years," *Ely's Report*, n. d. pp. 92–93.
14. Kollmann, 1974, p. 28. There is further indication that infant mortality rates can regress, even in recent times. See Davis and Feshback, 1980.
15. Willoughby, 1893; Jarvis, 1873, pp. 206–09; Frieden, 1973, pp. 236–59. For a different view regarding the correlation of maternal neglect and infant mortality, see Dyhouse, 1978, pp. 248–68.
16. *Ely's Report*, n. d., p. 96. In a report dated 1875, the British consul ascribed the great death toll of babies in summer to the fact that mothers left their infants to gather in the crops. While this might help explain deaths of rural babies, it does not appear to be a factor in Odessa's death rates. See *BPP* 1875, LXXVI, 1313.
17. *Odessa*, 1895, p. 448. For a detailed description of how wet-nurse fostering increased infant deaths in Russia, see Ransel, 1973, pp. 189–217 and A. A. Skal'kovskii, 1865d, p. 17.
18. For average numbers of deaths by age, see *BPP* 1876, LXXIV, 1313.
19. Finkel, 1865, pp. 176–77. For a breakdown of the effects of seasons on mortality at smaller age intervals, see the table in Herlihy, 1978, p. 435.
20. Winslow, 1952, p. 122.
21. That poverty was not the exclusive agent of these high infant mortalities seems indicated by the fact that Jewish babies, many of them found in impoverished households, still survived markedly better than their gentile

counterparts. For the better survival of Jewish infants, see Rafalovich, 1843, p. 373. For educational and cultural barriers that obstructed improved infant survival, see Frieden, 1973, pp. 236–59; Richmond, 1977, pp. 237–59.

22. Molinari, 1877, p. 207.

23. K. B. Guthrie, 1874, II, 283.

24. AMAE, Odessa, XI, 20 June 1879, f. 191.

25. *Proshloe Odessy*, 1894, p. 44. After the eruption of Mt. Etna in Sicily in 1900, some of the black lava was used to pave Odessa's streets. See Ermolov, 1917, p. 18.

26. K. B. Guthrie, 1874, II, 282.

27. For a detailed account of the building of the waterworks, see *Odessa*, 1895, pp. 283–301. The Odessa Waterworks Company was a limited liability company with a capital of 800,000 pounds in 40,000 shares of 20 pounds each. Nearly all the shares were sold in England. Odessa's government guaranteed 6 percent interest on the capital and gave the company the concession for thirty-eight years, *BPP* 1874, LXVII, 1453.

28. AMAE X, 4 Dec. 1873, f. 230. In planning the new water supply system, a study was made of the Parisian water pipes. See GAOO, *f.* 274, *op.* 1, *d.* 12, *l.* 75.

29. *BPP* 1875, LXXVI, 1314; *Odessa*, 1895, p. 444.

30. *BPP* 1875, LXXVI, 1314.

31. Ibid.

32. Baedecker, 1893, p. xiii.

33. Paustovsky, 1964, p. 649.

34. *BPP* 1876, LXXIV, 436.

35. *BPP* 1878–79, LXXI, 1476.

36. The Russian term is *obshchesplavnyi*. Fal'kovskii, 1947, p. 272.

37. Spath, 1978, p. 347.

38. *Ville*, 1908, p. 27.

39. *Odessa*, 1895, pp. 442–43. In 1883, there was a slight rise in the death rate to 32 per 1000, a fact that the British consul attributed to the discharging of sewer drains into the open harbor in front of the city and to the insufficient frequency with which they flushed the sewers. But in 1886, it had fallen to 25.51 per 1000. See *BPP* 1884, LXXVI, 1379 and *BPP* 1887, LXXXV, 4.

40. See Herlihy, 1978, p. 432.

41. In 1874, there was a significant difference in the death rate per 1000 in the various city districts. The area of the wealthy—Bul'varnyi—witnessed 16.8 deaths, while the working class district of Slobodka-Romanovka was up to 52. See Itenberg, 1974, p. 40.

42. A. A. Skal'kovskii, 1878, p. 46.

43. *Odessa*, 1895, p. 435.

44. Bater, 1976, p. 351.

45. See *Statisticheskii vremennik*, 1872; GAOO *f.* 3, *op.* 1, *d.* 15, *l.* 10; A. A. Skal'kovskii, 1878a, p. 40. As late as 1877, one expert at a demographic congress included Odessa among the world's cities that were not maintaining their own numbers, Weber, 1899, p. 239, n. 2. This was not true according to local statistics. A. A. Skal'kovskii, 1878, p. 40, affirms that while the population of Moscow and St. Petersburg grew because of the constant influx of peasants, Odessa's growth was natural. Bater states that not until the turn of the twentieth century did births regularly exceed deaths in St. Petersburg, see 1980, p. 252.

46. *Odessa*, 1895, p. 445.

47. Moskvich, 1904, p. 1. On the city outskirts where the plumbing was more primitive, however, the death rate was 19 or 20 per 1000. Another author, writing in 1908, put the death rate as 20 per 1000, with an occasional drop to 14 or 15 per 1000. See *Ville*, 1908, p. 27. He concluded that Odessa occupied first place in the Russian Empire for its low mortality rate.

48. *Ville*, 1908, p. 22.

49. GAOO, *f.* 5, *op.* 1, *d.* 388, *l.* 21.

50. Ibid.

51. Aleichem, 1979, p. 10.

52. Balzac, 1866, p. 304.

53. Zolotov, 1966, p. 180.

54. *Rezul'taty*, 1894, p. 2, Tables I–XV.

55. Ibid., Table I.

56. *Perepis*, 1899–1905, Vol. 47. For further analysis of the demographic profile of Odessa in 1897, see Herlihy, 1977.

57. Ibid.

58. See below, pp. 301–310.

59. Zipperstein, 1980, p. 65.

60. Itenberg, 1974, p. 39.

61. GAOO, *f.* 274, *op.* 1, *d.* 12, *ll.* 27–28.

62. Guttentag and Secord, 1983, pp. 95–111.

63. The 1897 census shows that among Jews the sex ratio of those age 20–29 was 99 men per 100 women. Clearly, Jewish men did not immigrate unaccompanied by women.

64. The cohesiveness is also shown in the illegitimate birth rate among Jews, which was very low. See *Jewish Encyclopedia*, 1905, s. v. "Odessa." Also GAOO, *f.* 274, *op.* 2, *d.* 4, *ll.* 14–51. For example, on *ll.* 47–51, it is shown that of the 1,872 Jewish babies born in 1874 (1,225 males and 647 females), no illegitimate births were reported. Of the babies born that year in Odessa, 6,098 in all, there were 750 illegitimate births. On the problem of underreporting female births among the Jews, see below, pp. 244–45.

65. *Rezul'taty*, 1894, pp. 14–15, Table V.

66. These figures are comparative indices of the child-woman ratios, which result when the figure for the Russian babies is set equal to 100. The data on which this calculation is based are given in Table 10.3.

67. Households (*khoziaistvo*s) are grouped in the census according to the following number of persons: 2, 3, 4, 5, 6–10, and more than 10. It should be noted that these household figures include only the head of household and his relatives, not lodgers or servants. Without the complete, ungrouped distribution, it is impossible to calculate precisely the average household size. We estimate the average by adding to the distribution the number of one-person units (not regarded as households by the census takers) and by assuming an average size of 8 for all households in the category 6–10, and an average size of 11 in the category, more than 10.

68. The census gives no direct information on family size for the various ethnic groups. It does, however, list according to ethnic groups those employed in some occupation, whom it calls "independent," and those "members of the family" who were economically dependent upon them. The ratio of dependents to employed workers would thus reflect family size (of course, a single family could well have more than one member employed). For the city of Odessa as a whole, there were 146,064 independent men and 51,546 independent women, or a total of 197,610 persons. Again for the city proper, the male "members of the family" number 58,713, and the female 124,218, for a total of 182,931. The ratio of dependents to employed is therefore 0.93. Among the Jews, considered separately, there are 37,054 independent men and 11,970 independent women; and 24,102 and 50,560 male and female family members, respectively. Among the Jews, the ratio of dependents to employed is 1.52—more than one-third greater that that found in the entire urban population. Although we cannot convert these ratios into exact estimates of family size, it is manifest that the Jews were supporting numerous dependents in their households.

69. In the census of 1897, the population was classified by *soslovie* according to twelve categories.

70. Zagoruiko, 1960, p. 42, cites a book published in 1885, in which the author noted that one-third of Odessa's population bore Ukrainian names; one-third, Russian, Polish, Armenian, and Greek names; and one-third, Jewish and other names. Zagoruiko believed that the Ukrainians made up a large portion of the population, but he did not venture to say that they formed the major part.

71. Gogol, 1931, pp. 132, 199.

72. Dawidowicz, 1967, p. 398.

73. Zagoruiko, 1960, p. 36.

74. See above, Table 10.3.

75. See s. v. "Odessa," in *Jewish Encyclopedia*, 1905.

76. Frederic, 1892, p. 256.

77. *Odessa*, 1895, p. 100.

78. AMAE, Odessa, vol. 9, 4 Jan. 1863.

79. Rubinow, 1908, p. 492.

80. Raisin, 1915, p. 271.
81. Michell, 1889, p. 139.
82. Zipperstein, 1980, p. 269.
83. Dawidowicz, 1967, p. 398.
84. Ibid., p. 399.
85. Babel, 1964, p. xii.
86. Trotsky, 1973, p. 87.
87. Raisin, 1913, p. 294.
88. A. A. Skal'kovskii, 1878a, pp. 43–44. Also GAOO, *f.* 274, *op.* 1, *d.* 15, *ll.* 50, 137.
89. A. A. Skal'kovskii, 1878a, p. 44.
90. Ibid., p. 40.
91. Schmelz, 1971, pp. 77–78. See also Guttentag and Secord, 1983, pp. 91–95.
92. Finkel, 1865, pp. 181–82.
93. *Odessa*, 1895, p. 450.
94. Rubinow, 1908, p. 496.
95. Curtin, 1911, p. 4.
96. *Evreiskoe naselenie*, 1917, p. 72. The small divergences from the figures given in Table 10.4 reflect different estimates of the Jewish population.
97. NACRO, 14 Dec. 1905.
98. N. Babel, 1969, p. 26.
99. See above, pp. 212–15.
100. Markevich, 1890, p. xxxvii.
101. The author interviewed his niece Marfa Viktorovna Tsomakion in Odessa in 1974.
102. Taken from the industrial census compiled by Professor Thomas Owen, to whom I express my gratitude.
103. *Adres-kalendar*, 1910, p. 274.
104. Modrich, 1892, p. 542.
105. See Herlihy, 1977, p. 74, n. 61.
106. *Perepis*, 1899–1905, vol. 47.
107. MAE, *RC*, 1909, p. 72.
108. NACRO, 11 Nov. 1865.
109. *BPP* 1874, LXVII, 1455.
110. NACRO, 24 July, 1906.
111. Winter, 1914, p. 133.
112. Ibid.
113. Wightman, 1928, p. 150.
114. *BPP* 1874, LXVIII, 1454.
115. Ibid.
116. Moskvich, 1904, pp. 61–63.

117. *BPP* 1908, CXV, 35.
118. Hubback, 1915, p. 250.

Chapter Eleven

1. See GAOO, *f.* 274, *op.* 1, *d.* 2, *ll.* 9–21 for a list of all of Odessa's public buildings built before 1863. The survey indicates the date of construction, the cost, and who paid for the construction. For illustrations of historical edifices in Odessa, giving past and present names, see Selinov, 1930.

2. Kataev, 1957, p. 82.

3. Winter, 1914, p. 135. This passage appears to have been lifted from Curtin, 1911, pp. 332–33.

4. Moskvich, 1904, p. 14.

5. Merry, 1915, p. 113. E. E. Cummings, 1931, pp. 288-89, also expressed his admiration for this hotel, now called simply the Odessa Hotel.

6. *Odessa. Kniga,* 1911, p. 9.

7. Curtin, 1911, p. 329.

8. Adamson, 1912, pp. 902–43.

9. Winter, 1914, p. 136.

10. "Deribasovskaia ulitsa," *Al'manakh,* 1895, n. p.

11. Kataev, 1957, p. 84. The former Fankoni is now the Ukraina restaurant.

12. Aleichem, 1979, p. 32. In 1910, Fankoni advertised itself as supplyers of sweets to the Greek Court, see *Ofitsial'nyi katalog,* p. 16.

13. Kataev, 1957, p. 84.

14. Kuprin, 1920, p. 9.

15. Kataev, 1954, p. 64.

16. Curtin, 1911, p. 331. For an alphabetical list of Odessa's streets, classified into city sections in which prices per square *sazhen* are given for each area, see *Vedomost,* 1902, pp. 5–95. It was published by the Odessa City Credit Society.

17. Winter, 1914, p. 137.

18. Zagoruiko, 1957–60, II, 50. Although there were few wooden buildings in Odessa, it had its share of fires. One of the chief fire towers was above the police station. The number of balls hoisted on display indicated in which quarter of the city the conflagration was taking place. See Brooks, 1855, p. 133.

19. Curtin, 1911, p. 329.

20. AMAE, Odessa, XI, 24 May 1879, f. 191.

21. *BPP* 1881, XCIX, 545.

22. *Odessa,* 1895, pp. 426–27.

23. Snodgrass, 1913, p. 177.

24. A phrase attributed to Kajetan Felder, a nineteenth-century mayor of Vienna, by Schorske, 1981, p. 26.

25. For the development of the Botanical Gardens and the career of A. D. Nordman, who was largely responsible for them, see Druzhinina, 1981, pp. 73–74.

26. Kokhanskii and Zhelikhovskii, 1891, pp. 6, 24.

27. For comments on Odessa's old and modern monuments, see Il'f and Petrov, 1961, pp. 87–88.

28. *Proshloe Odessy*, p. 41.

29. MAE, *RC*, 1901, p. 26. For more information on Belgian companies in Odessa, see McKay, 1970, p. 86.

30. Kataev, 1957, p. 84. In 1893 the fare was ten kopecks. See Baedecker, 1893, p. 386.

31. Wightman, 1928, p. 167. In 1908, a contract was signed with the Belgian company, Société Anonyme des Tramways d'Odessa, to supply the city "with electric tramways in place of the present, archaic service of horse-wagons." The new service was to be in operation by the summer of 1911. *BPP* 1908, CXV, 16. It still was not completed in early 1913, although some $6,695,000 had been expended on it. See Snodgrass, 1913, p. 178.

32. *Odessa*, 1895, p. 41.

33. Moskvich, 1904, p. 63.

34. ANP, F12, Commerce et Industrie, 7173, Jan. 1904.

35. MAE, *RC*, 1909, p. 53.

36. Ibid., pp. 51–52. The French consul suggested that if French bicycle manufacturers could import parts and assemble them in Odessa, prices could be kept low and the product would sell well. See ANP, F12, Commerce et Industrie, 7173, Jan. 1904.

37. *BPP* 1910, CL, 40.

38. *Odessa. Kniga*, 1911.

39. Snodgrass, 1913, pp. 179–80.

40. Olesha, 1967, p. 124.

41. MAE, *RC*, 1910, pp. 55–56. The British consul reported that the Aero Club, founded in 1908, was a semimilitary group whose purpose was "to encourage aerial navigation, to organize ascents, to improve and build airships, to help inventors of aerial machines in every way, and to teach members to sail and navigate balloons and airships." Baron Kaul'bars, the commander of the Odessa military district, was its president. *BPP* 1909, XCVII, 37–38. See Snodgrass, 1913, p. 180, in which the U. S. consul reported that at Symferopil, the government had a school of aviation, hangars for one hundred planes of which several were of American make.

42. Kataev, 1957, p. 84.

43. Kuprin, 1920, p. 13. Prostitution and white slavery flourished in Odessa. See Kuprin, 1932, and Artamof, 1862–65, II, 300, who estimates that some seven hundred girls a year were sold for shipment to Constantinople. *Jüdische Elend*, 1903, claims that in 1903, 5 percent of Jewish women in Odessa were prostitutes.

44. Artamof, 1862–65, II, 211.
45. Parasun'ko, 1963, p. 176.
46. *Vedomost*, pp. 25–31.
47. Ibid., pp. 89–95.
48. PRO, London, FO 65, vol. 860, 18 Feb. 1873.
49. Paustovsky, 1964, p. 335.
50. Pettinato, 1968, p. 36.
51. Kataev, 1957, pp. 83–84.
52. GAOO, *f.* 5, *op.* 1, *d.* 388, *l.* 13.
53. Artamof, 1862–65, II, 298.
54. Proctor, 1900, pp. 273–74.
55. André, 1870, pp. 211–14.
56. Ibid.
57. *Murray's Hand-Book*, 1868, p. 253.
58. *Putevoditel*, 1900, p. 75. Kataev, 1954, pp. 11–17, described the summer rooms which the schoolmaster Batchei and his two sons rented in a German colony during the summer.
59. This and much of the following information is derived from *Odessa*, 1895, pp. 512–64. Baedecker, 1893, p. 38, recommended these spas for scrofula, gout, rheumatism, nervous disorders, and skin diseases. In 1908, the British consul advised people not to take the baths without professional advice as their effects were so strong. In addition to the above diseases, he claimed that the baths were therapeutic for rickets, ankylosis, chronic afflictions of bones, muscles, and joints; in chronic cases of catarrh of the mucous membranes, and for syphilis in advanced stages. *BPP* 1908, XCVII, 38.
60. *Proshloe Odessy*, p. 48.
61. *Odessa*, 1895, p. 138.

Chapter Twelve

1. Kuprin, 1920, pp. 11–12.
2. Eckardt, 1880, p. 329. In 1873, Odessa ranked third after Moscow and Kharkiv in the empire for its high crime rate. There were 11,037 criminal cases, mostly involving prostitution, rape, and liquor violations. See *BPP* 1875, LXXVI, 1310.
3. Eckardt, 1880, pp. 329–30.
4. Borovoi, 1974, p. 195.
5. Ibid.
6. Arsh, 1959.
7. Kashirin and Alekseev-Popov, 1963.
8. Itenberg, 1974, p. 40.
9. Ibid., p. 42.
10. Ibid.

11. TsGIA, *f.* 3851, *d.* 7, *ll.* 9–10.
12. Borovoi, 1974, p. 197. See also Klier, 1981.
13. Ibid.
14. Borovoi, 1974, p. 199.
15. Ibid., p. 203.
16. Ibid.
17. Ibid. The count obtained his copies through a bookstore in Constantinople.
18. Vigel, 1864–65, II, 107.
19. Borovoi, 1974, p. 201.
20. See *Entsyklopediia ukrainoznavstva*, 1949–78, II, 443–44.
21. Chykalenko, 1925, II, 2–15. These memoirs provide one of the most interesting descriptions of Ukrainian life in Odessa. The son of a wealthy landowner (a descendant of Ukrainian Cossacks) in the Kherson *guberniia*, Chykalenko describes student life in the city in the early 1870s. He left but returned to the city in the early 1890s; he provided much of the financial support for Hromada activities in Odessa and Kiev and abroad.
22. Itenberg, 1974 and Parasun'ko, 1963, pp. 299–309.
23. Itenberg, 1974, p. 196.
24. Ibid., p. 53.
25. Borovoi, 1974, p. 197.
26. Itenberg, 1974, p. 66.
27. Ibid., pp. 78–84.
28. *BPP* 1876, LXXIV, 449.
29. Eckardt, 1880, pp. 330–31.
30. Itenberg, 1974, p. 196.
31. GAOO, *f.* 5, *op.* 1, *d.* 388, *ll.* 18–20.
32. Ibid.
33. Garvi, 1946, p. 20.
34. Trotsky, 1973, p. 95.
35. Garvi, 1946, p. 15.
36. Tobias, 1972, pp. 8, 85.
37. *Revoliutsiia*, 1955, pp. 6–7.
38. Schneiderman, 1976, pp. 293–97.
39. Ibid., pp. 69–192.
40. Ibid., pp. 227–85.
41. Ibid., p. 167.
42. NACRO, 3 Aug. 1903.
43. Ibid.
44. Schneiderman, 1976, p. 331.
45. Drage, 1904, p. 28.
46. Ibid., p. 70.
47. *Revoliutsiia*, 1955, p. 339.
48. Ibid.

49. Ibid.
50. Schneiderman, 1976, pp. 350–54.
51. NACRO, 5 Sept. 1904.
52. Ibid.
53. *Revoliutsiia*, 1955, p. 567.
54. Ibid., p. 453.
55. Ibid., p. 569.
56. NACRO, 28 Jan. 1905.
57. Ibid.
58. Ibid.
59. *Revoliutsiia*, 1955, p. 474.
60. Piaskovskii, 1966, pp. 66–67.
61. *BPP* 1906, CXXVIII, 3.
62. Hough, 1960, pp. 182–86.
63. Kochan, 1966, p. 91.
64. Raisin, 1913, p. 255.
65. Zipperstein, 1980, p. xii.
66. Ibid., p. 169.
67. A. A. Skal'kovskii, 1865d, p. 108.
68. Morgulis, 1910.
69. NACRO, 22 April 1871.
70. Ibid.
71. Morgulis, 1910, p. 60.
72. Ibid., p. 66.
73. NACRO, 22 April 1871.
74. Morgulis, 1910, p. 51.
75. Ben-Sasson, 1976, p. 882.
76. See above, p. 253.
77. For this and much of the following, see Motzkin, 1910.
78. NACRO, 15 November 1905.
79. *Otchet*, 1908, p. 6.
80. Burrough, 1930, pp. 255–56.
81. NACRO, 14 Dec. 1905.
82. NACRO, 9 Feb. 1906.
83. *BPP* 1910, CL, 36.
84. MAE, *RC*, 1907, p. 3.

References

Abbreviations

AKV
    Arkhiv kniazia Vorontsova, Moscow

AMAE
    Archives d'un Ministère des Affaires Étrangères, Paris

ANP
    Archives Nationales, Paris

AOO
    Gosudarstvennyi arkhiv Odesskoi oblasti. Putevoditel. Odessa

ASF
    Archivio di Stato di Firenz, Florence, Italy

ASL
    Archivio di Stato di Livorno, Livorno, Italy

BPP
    British Parliamentary Papers; Commercial Reports, London

BSE
    Bol'shaia sovetskaia entsiklopediia, Moscow

CIBAVA
    Il Commercio, Industria, Belle Arti, Varietà ed Avvisi, Florence

CL
    Il Corriere Livornese, Livorno, Italy

DCTR
    Daily Consular and Trade Reports, Washington, D.C.

GAOO
    Gosudarstvennyi arkhiv Odesskoi oblasti, Odessa

JO
    Journal d'Odessa

JSP
    Journal de St. Petersbourg

MAE, *RC*
    Ministère des Affaires Étrangères. *Rapports Commerciaux des Agents Diplomatique et Consulaires de France.* Russie

NACRO
    National Archives, Washington, D.C.

OV
            Odesskii vestnik
PRO
            Public Records Office, London
PSZ
            Polnoe sobranie zakonov Rossiiskoi imperii, St. Petersburg
SIRIO
            Sbornik Imperatorskogo russkogo istoricheskogo obshchestva,
            St. Petersburg
TOSK
            Trudy Odesskogo statisticheskogo komiteta
TsGIA
            Tsentral'nyi gosudarstvennyi istoricheskii arkhiv, Kiev
ZhMVD
            Zhurnal Ministerstva vnutrennykh del

I. Sources

(a) Manuscript

AMAE
            Archives du Ministère des Affaires Étrangères, Paris.
ANP
            Archives Nationales, Paris.
ASF
            Archivio di Stato di Firenze, Italia.
ASL
            Archivio di Stato di Livorno, Italia.
GAOO
            Gosudarstvennyi arkhiv Odesskoi oblasti, Odessa.
NACRO
            National Archives, Washington, D. C.
PRO
            Public Records Office, London.

Skal'kovskii, A. A.
     n.d.   Opyt statisticheskogo opisaniia Novorossiiskogo kraia
              (unpublished manuscript), GAOO, *f.* 137, *op.* 1, *d.* 11, *ll.*
              1–42.
TsGIA USSR
            Tsentral'nyi gosudarstvennyi istoricheskii arkhiv, Kiev.

(b) Printed

Account
     1817   *An Account of Odessa Translated by an American.* Liver-
              pool.

Adamson, Sydney
    1912   "Odessa—The Portal of an Empire," *Harper's Monthly Magazine*, 115: 902–43.

Adres-kalendar
    1910   *Adres-kalendar odesskogo gradonachal'stva na 1910 god.* Odessa.

AKV
    1870–95 *Arkhiv kniazia Vorontsova.* Moscow.

Alcock, Thomas
    1831   *Travels in Russia, Persia, Turkey, and Greece, 1828–9.* London.

Aleichem, Sholom
    1979   *The Adventures of Menachem-Mendl.* New York.

Al'manakh
    1896–1902 *Iuzhno-russkii al'manakh.* Odessa.

André, Edouard
    1870   *Un mois en Russie.* Paris.

Anthoine, Antoine Ignace
    1805, 1820 Antoine Ignace Anthoine, Baron de Saint Joseph, *Essai historique sur le commerce et la navigation de la Mer-Noire ou voyages entreprises pour établir des rapports commerciaux et maritimes entre les ports de la Mer-Noire et ceux de la Méditerranée.* 2 editions. Paris.

Armstrong, T. B.
    1831   *Journals of Travels in the Seat of War, during the Last Two Campaigns of Russia and Turkey; Intended as an Itinerary through the South of Russia, the Crimea, Georgia and through Persia, Kooristan, and Asia Minor, to Constantinople.* London.

Artamof, Piotre
    1862–65 Piotre Artamov, Comte V. De La Fite, *La Russie: Historique, monumentale et pittoresque.* 2 vols. Paris.

Avdeeva, K. A.
    1842   *Zapiski o starom i novom russkom byte.* St. Petersburg.

Babel, Isaak
    1948   *Benya Krik, the Gangster and Other Stories,* ed. Avram Yarmolinsky. New York.

Babel, Nathalie (ed.)
    1964   *Isaac Babel. The Lonely Years, 1925–1939.* New York.

Baedecker, Karl
    1893   *La Russie.* Leipzig.

Baguer y Ribas, Francisco
    1832   *Memoria sobre el comercio de los puertos del Mar Negro, y modo de entablar relaciones mercantiles con la Persia por Tiflis.* Madrid.

Balzac, H.
    1886   *Père Goriot.* Boston.
Barker, W. B.
    1855   *Odessa and Its Inhabitants by an English Prisoner in Russia.*
                London.
Beable, William H.
    1918   *Commercial Russia.* London.
Bellia, Vallentino
    1925   *Un viaggio in Russia: Ricordi del viaggio della delegazione
                torinese nel giugno 1913.* Turin.
Besse, Jean-Charles de
    1838   *Voyage en Crimée, au Caucase, en Arménie, en Asie-Mineur
                et à Constantinople en 1829 et 1830.* Paris.
Board of Trade Journal
    1866–1970 Commercial Department, Board of Trade. London.
Bolletino
                *Bolletino Commerciale della Compagnia Russa di Navigazione
                a Vapore.* Odessa.
Boucher de Crèvecour Pertes, Jacques
    1855   *Voyages à Constantinople.* 2 vols. Paris.
BPP
    1715–   *British Parliamentary Papers; Commercial Reports.* London.
Bremner, Robert
    1839   *Excursions in the Interior of Russia.* 2 vols. London.
Brooks, Shirley
    1855   *Russians of the South.* London.
Bunin, Ivan
    1951   *Memories and Portraits.* London.
Burrough, Harry E.
    1930   *Tale of a Vanished Land: Memories of a Childhood.* Boston
                and New York.
Byron, Lord George Gordon
    1928   *The Poetical Works of Lord Byron.* London.
Castelnau, G. de
    1820   *Essai sur l'histoire de la Nouvelle Russie.* 3 vols. Paris.
Chekhovich, P. S.
    1894   *Zapiski o nuzhdakh odesskogo porta i ego rasshirenii.* Odes-
                sa.
Churchill, Winston S.
    1953   *The Second World War: Triumph and Tragedy.* Cambridge.
Chykalenko, Evhen
    1925   *Spohady, 1861–1907.* 2 parts; Lviv.
CIBAVA
                Il Commercio, Industria, Belle Arti, Varietà ed Avvisi. Flo-
                rence.

CL

Il Corriere Livornese. Livorno.

Clarke, Edward Daniel
1816   *Travels in Russia, Tartary and Turkey.* 2 vols. London.

Conder, Josiah
1830   *Modern Traveller: A Popular Description of Russia: Geographical, Historical and Topographical.* London.

Corriere Italiano

Il Corriere Italiano. Vienna.

Coxe, William
1784, 1785, 1872   *Travels into Poland and Russia, Sweden and Denmark.* 3 vols. Dublin. 2 vols. London. 5 vols. London.

Craven, Mme Augustus
1873   Mme August (Pauline) Craven (née La Ferronnays). *Le récit d'une soeur.* 2 vols. Paris.

Cross, S. H., and Sherbovitz-Wetzor, O. P. (Trans. and Eds.)
1953   *The Russian Primary Cronicle, Laurentian Text.* Cambridge, Mass.

Cummings, E. E.
1931   *Eime.* New York.

Curtin, William E.
1911   *Around the Black Sea.* New York.

DCTR
1906–10   *Daily Consular and Trade Reports.* U.S. Department of Commerce and Labor. Bureau of Manufactures. Washington, D.C.

Dana, Richard Henry
1969   *Two Years before the Mast. Twenty-Four Years After.* Introduction by Richard Armstrong. London and New York.

Danilevskii, G. P.
1956   *Beglye v Novorossii.* Moscow.

De Ros, Lord
1855   Lord De Ros (William L. Lascelles), *Journal of a Tour in the Principalities, Crimea and Countries Adjacent to the Black Sea in the Years 1835–36.* London.

Dearborn, Henry S.
1819   *A Memoir on the Commerce and Navigation of the Black Sea and the Trade and Maritime Geography of Turkey and Egypt.* 2 vols. Boston.

Demidov, Anatole
1842   *Voyage dans la Russie méridionale et la Crimée.* 4 vols. Paris.
1853   *Travels in Southern Russia and the Crimea through Hungary, Wallachia and Moldavia during the Year 1837.* 2 vols. London.

Demidov, Prince Pavel Pavlovich
1844   *The Jewish Question in Russia.* London.
Desiatidnevnaia poezdka
1848   *Desiatidnevnaia poezdka na iuzhnyi bereg Kryma.* Odessa.
Dolgorukov, I. M.
1870   *Slavnye bubny za gorami ili moe puteshestvie koe-kuda v 1810
            g.* Moscow.
Drage, Geoffrey
1904   *Russian Affairs.* London.
Durland, Kellogg
1908   *The Red Reign. The True Story of an Adventurous Year in
            Russia.* New York.
Dvizhenie naseleniia
1867–84   *Dvizhenie naseleniia v evropeiskoi Rossii.* Statisticheskii
            vremennik Rossiiskoi Imperii. St. Petersburg.
Eckardt, Julius
1880   *Russia before and after the War.* London.
Ekerle, V. F.
1916   *Vol'naia gavan v Odesse, ee znachenie i ustroistvo.* Odessa.
Ekonomicheskoe sostoianie
1863   *Ekonomicheskoe sostoianie gorodskikh poselenii evropeiskoi
            Rossii v 1861–1862 g.* Pt. 1. St. Petersburg.
Elliott, Charles B.
1839   *Travels in the Three Great Empires of Austria, Russia and
            Turkey.* 2 vols. Philadelphia.
Ely's Report
n.d.   *Mr. Ely's Report on the Sanitary Condition of the City of New
            York.* New York State Senate, New York.
Emery, M. S.
1901   *Russia through the Stereoscope: A Journey across the Land of
            the Czar from Finland to the Black Sea.* New York.
Ermolov, Alexjei S.
1917   "Misure per lo sviluppo delle relazioni commerciali della
            Russia con l'Italia," *Monitore Italo-Russo.* II: No. 1 and 2.
            Rome.
Eton, W.
1805   *A Concise Account of the Commerce and Navigation of the
            Black Sea from Recent and Authentic Information.* London.
Evreiskoe naselenie
1917   *Evreiskoe naselenie Rossii po dannym perepisi 1897 g. i po
            noveishim istochnikam.* Petrograd.
Fedorov, I.
1870a   "O polozhenii rabochego klassa v Odesse," *Pamiatnaia
            knizhka*, pp. 89–105.
1870b   "Klimat Odessy i vliianie ego na obshchestvennoe
            zdorov'e," *Pamiatnaia knizhka*, pp. 107–25.

1878   "Nastoiashchaia chislennost odesskogo naseleniia v 1870–kh godakh," *Pamiatnaia knizhka*, pp. 47–63.

Ferrier, Alexandre
1841   *La Russie.* Brussels.

Feuille
1830   *Feuille de commerce de la Nouvelle-Russie.* Odessa.

Finkel, I. S.
1843   "O torgovle, promyshlennosti, prosveshchenii i obrazovanii odesskikh evreev," *OV*, Nos. 36, 37, 38, 39.

Frederic, Harold
1892   *The New Exodus: A study of Israel in Russia.* New York and London.

Gallenga, Antonio
1882   *A Summer Tour in Russia.* London.

Gamba, Piero
1826   *Voyage dans la Russie méridionale.* Paris.

Garvi, Petr A.
1946   *Vospominaniia sotsial-demokrata.* New York.

Geddie, John
1882   *The Russian Empire, Historical and Descriptive.* London.

Giusti, V.
1858   "Il Progresso in Russia e l'agricoltura in Italia," *Il Commercio*, issue of 10 November.

Gogol, Nikolai
1931   *Dead Souls.* London.

Golovin, Ivan
1854   *The Nations of Russia and Turkey and their Destiny.* London.

Gorky, Maxim
1929   *Chelkash and Other Stories.* New York.

Gosudarstvennaia torgovlia
1827   *Gosudarstvennaia vneshniaia torgovlia 1826 goda v raznykh ee vidakh.* St. Petersburg.

Guernsey, A. H.
1854   "The Steppes, Odessa, and the Crimea," *Harper's New Monthly Magazine*, 9: 1–20.

Guide
1913   *Guide de la compagnie russe de navigation à vapeur et de commerce.* Odessa.

Guthrie, Mrs. (K. B.)
1874   *Through Russia: from St. Petersburg to Astrakhan and the Crimea.* 2 vols. London.

Guthrie, Maria
1802   *A Tour Performed in the Years 1795–6 through the Tauride, or Crimea.* London.
1810   *Lettres sur la Crimée, Odessa et la Mer d'Azov.* Moscow.

Hagemeister, Julius de
  1846   *Report on the Commerce of the Ports of New Russia, Mol-davia, and Wallachia Made to the Russian Government in 1835.* London.
Hamm, Wilhelm
  1862   *Südöstliche Steppen und Städte.* Frankfurt am Main.
Handels-Museum
  1886–1936 *Das Handels-Museum.* Vienna.
Haxthausen-Abbenburg, Baron August von
  1856   *The Russian Empire: Its People, Institutions, and Resources.* 2 vols. London.
Henderson, Ebenezer
  1826   *Biblical Researches and Travels in Russia.* London.
Holderness, Mary
  1823   *New Russia: Journey from Riga to the Crimea by Way of Kiev . . .* London.
Hommaire de Hell, Xavier
  1847   *Travels in the Steppes of the Caspian Sea, the Crimea, the Caucasus, etc.* London.
Hubback, John
  1915   *Russian Realities.* London.
Hume, George
  1914   *Thirty-Five Years in Russia.* London.
Ianson, Iulii E.
  1870   *Statisticheskoe issledovanie o khlebnoi torgovle v odesskom raione.* St. Petersburg.
Ienisha, A.
  1844   "Mediko-topograficheskoe opisanie goroda Odessy," *ZhMVD*, 6: 83–114; 7: 169–207.
Il'f, I. A. and Petrov, E. P.
  1961   *Sobranie sochinenii.* 5 vols. Moscow.
  1962   *The Golden Calf,* trans. John H. C. Richardson. New York.
Istoricheskii ocherk
  1889   *Istoricheskii ocherk Odessy. K stoletnomu iubileiu so dnia zavoevaniia.* Odessa.
Izmailov, V. V.
  1800–02 *Puteshestvie v Poludennuiu Rossiiu.* 4 vols. Moscow.
Izvestiia
  1877–94 *Izvestiia Moskovskoi gorodskoi obshchei dumy.* Moscow.
Jackson, Frances
  1920   *Memoirs of the Count de Rochechouart, 1788–1822.* London.
Jarvis, Edward
  1873   "Infant Mortality," *Fourth Annual Report of the State Board of Health of Massachusetts.* Boston.

Jesse, William
    1841   *Notes of a Half-Pay in Search of Health: Russia, Circassia, and the Crimea, in 1839–40.* 2 vols. London.

JO
    1824–81 *Journal d'Odessa.*

Jourdier, Auguste
    1861   *Voyage agronomique en Russie: Lettres et notes sur une excursion faites en 1859–1860.* Paris.
    1863   *Voyage agronomique en Russie: Lettres et notes sur une deuxième excursion faite en 1860–1861.* Paris.

"Jüdische Elend"
    1903   "Das jüdische Elend in Odessa," von H. M. *Jüdische Statistik,* Berlin. pp. 287–92.

JSP
    1846–48 *Journal de St. Petersbourg.*

Kalendar
    1835–93 *Novorossiiskii kalendar.* 11 vols. Odessa.

Kataev, Valentine
    1954   *A White Sail Gleams.* Moscow.
    1957   *The Cottage in the Steppe.* Moscow.

Khersonu
    1978   *Khersonu 200 let, 1778–1978: Sbornik dokumentov i materialov.* Kiev.

Knight, William
    1839   *Oriental Outlines or a Rambler's Recollections of a Tour in Turkey, Greece and Tuscany in 1838.* London.

Koch, Charles
    1855   *The Crimea and Odessa: Journal of a Tour.* London.

Koch, Karl
    1865   *Die Krim und Odessa: Reise-Erinnerungen aus dem Tagebuche.* Leipzig.

Kohl, J. G.
    1844   *Russia, St. Petersburg, Moscow, Kharkoff, Riga, Odessa, the German Provinces on the Baltic, the Steppes, and the Interior of the Empire.* London.
    1847   *Reisen in Südrussland.* 3 vols. Dresden and Leipzig.

Köppen, P.
    1844   "Russlands Gesammt—Bevölkerung im Jahre 1838," *Mémoires de l'Académie,* 5: 49–232. St. Petersburg.
    1845   "Über den Kornbedarf Russlands," *Mémoires de l'Académie* 5: 490–580.
    1852   *Statistische Reise in's Land der donischen Kosaken durch die Gouvernements Tula, Orel und Woronesh im Jahre 1850.* St. Petersburg.

Kraszewski, Josef I.
1845–46 *Wspomnienia Odessy, Jedyssanu i Budzaku; dziennik przejazdki w roku 1843 od 22 czerca do 11 wrzenia.* Vilnius.

Krylov, N.
1865 "Topograficheskoe opisanie g. Odessy," *TOSK* I.

Kuprin, A.
1920 *Sasha,* trans. Douglas Ashby. London.
1932 *Yama (The Pit),* trans. Bernard Guilbert Guerney. New York.

Lagarde, Le Comte de
1812 *Voyage de Moscou à Vienne, par Kow, Odessa, Constantinople, Bucharest et Hermanstadt; ou lettres adressées à Jules Griffith.* Paris.

Lauwick, Marcel
1907 *L'industrie dans la Russie méridionale.* Brussels.

Lee, Robert
1854 *The Last Days of Alexander and the First Days of Nicholas.* London.

Lyall, Robert
1825 *Travels in Russia, the Krimea, the Caucasus, and Georgia.* 2 vols. London.

MAE, *RC*
1892–1912 Ministère des Affaires Étrangères. *Rapports Commerciaux des Agents Diplomatiques et Consulaires de France.* Russie.

Mayakovsky, Vladimir
1960 "The Cloud in Trousers," *The Bedbug and Selected Poetry,* trans. Max Hayward and George Reavey, ed. Patricia Blake. New York.

Mel'nikov, N. P.
1875 *Fabrichnaia statistika goroda Odessy.* Odessa.

Merry, W. Mansell
1915 *Two Months in Russia, July-September, 1914.* Oxford.

Michael, Louis Guy
1979 *Russian Experience 1910–1917.* Privately published by Pauline McD. Michael.

Michell, Thomas
1899 *Russian Pictures.* London.

Modrich, Giuseppe
1892 *La Russia: Note e ricordi di viaggio.* Turin and Rome.

Molinari, Gustave de
1877 *Lettres sur la Russie,* Paris.

Moore, John
1833 *A Journey from London to Odessa with Notices of New Russia, etc.* Paris.

Morgulis, M. G.
1910 "Bezporiadki 1871 goda v Odesse (po dokumentam i

lichnym vospominaniiam)," *Evreiskii mir*, Dec. 1910, pp. 42–66.

Morton, Edward
1830   *Travels in Russia and a Residence at St. Petersburg and Odessa in the Years 1827–1829.* London.

Moskvich, Grigorii
1904   *Illiustrirovannyi prakticheskii putevoditel po Odesse.* Odessa.

Murray's Hand-Book
1868   *Murray's Hand-Book for Travellers in Russia, Poland and Finland.* 2nd ed. London.

Nadler, V. K.
1893   *K izucheniiu istorii goroda Odessy.* Odessa.

Nebolsin, G.
1850   *Statisticheskoe obozrenie vneshnei torgovli Rossii.* St. Petersburg.

Nevinson, Henry W.
1906   *The Dawn in Russia or Scenes in the Russian Revolution.* London and New York.

Nolte, Vincent
1854   *Fifty Years in Both Hemispheres, or Reminiscences of the Life of a Former Merchant.* New York.

Notizie
1817   *Notizie di Odessa scritte dal Sig. L. C.* Florence.

Oddy, J. Jepson
1807   *European Commerce.* Philadelphia.

Odessa. Kniga.
1911   *Odessa. Adresnaia i spravochnaia kniga vsei Odessy.* Odessa.

Odesskie novosti
1884–1916   *Odesskie novosti. Illiustrirovannoe prilozhenie k gazete.* Odessa.

Odesskii al'manakh
1839a   *Odesskii al'manakh na 1839 god.* Odessa.
1839b   *Odesskii al'manakh na 1840 god.* Odessa.

Odesskii iumoristicheskii al'manakh
1892   *Odesskii iumoristicheskii al'manakh s karikaturami.* Odessa.

Ofitsial'nyi katalog
1910   *Ofitsial'nyi katalog fabrichno-zavodskoi khudozhestvenno-promyshlennoi i sel'sko-khoziaistvennoi vystavki v Odesse 1910 g.* Odessa.

Olesha, Yuri
1967   "The Chain," *Envy and Other Works*, trans. Andrew R. MacAndrew. New York.

Oliphant, Laurence
1854   *The Russian Shores of the Black Sea in the Autumn of 1852.* New York.

Orbinskii, R. V.
    1881   *Iz otcheta R. V. Orbinskogo o nastoiashchem polozhenii khlebnogo vyvoza iz Odessy.* Odessa.
Otchet
    1908   *Otchet Odesskogo evreiskogo tsentral'nogo komiteta po okazaniiu pomoshchi postradavshim ot pogromov 1905 goda.* Odessa.
Otchet komiteta torgovli
    1884   *Otchet Odesskogo komiteta torgovli i manufaktur za 1884 god.* Odessa.
    1891   *Otchet Odesskogo komiteta torgovli i manufaktur za 1890 god.* Odessa.
OV
    1828, 1831–94 *Odesskii vestnik.* Odessa.
Pallas, P. S.
    1802–1803   *Travels through the Southern Provinces of the Russian Empire in the Years 1793–1794.* 2 vols. London.
Pamiat
    1884   *Pamiat odesskoi vystavki 1884 g.* Odessa.
Pamiatnaia knizhka
    1870–78   *Pamiatnaia knizhka odesskogo gradonachal'stva.* Odessa.
Paustovsky, Konstantin
    1964   *The Story of a Life.* New York.
Pegolotti, F.
    1936   *La pratica della mercatura*, ed. Allan Evans. Cambridge.
Perepis
    1899–1905   *Pervaia vseobshchaia perepis naseleniia Rossiiskoi imperii, 1897 g.* 80 vols. St. Petersburg.
Pettinato, C.
    1968   *Nella Russia degli zar.* Rome.
Pinkerton, Robert
    1833   *Russia or Miscellaneous Observations on the Past and Present State of That Country and Its Inhabitants.* London.
Possart, P. U.
    1841   *Das Kaiserthum Russland.* II, *Topographie.* Stuttgart.
PSZ
                Polnoe sobranie zakonov Rossiiskoi imperii. St. Petersburg.
Pregel, Sofiia
    1973   *Moe detstvo.* 3 vols. Paris.
Primorskie porty
    1980 *Primorskie torgovye porty evropeiskoi Rossii.* Ministerstvo torgovli i promyshlennosti. Otdel torgovykh portov. Trudy torgovykh portov. vyp. XXIV. St. Petersburg.
Proctor, Edna
    1900   *A Russian Journey.* Boston and New York.

Proshloe Odessy
    1894   *Proshloe i nastoiashchee Odessy. Izdanie Odesskoi gorodskoi auditorii narodnykh chtenii ko dniu stoletnego iubileia g. Odessy, 1794–1894.* Odessa.
Pushkin, Alexander
    1937   *Polnoe sobranie sochinenii.* Moscow.
    1964   *Eugene Onegin.* trans. Vladimir Nabokov. 4 vols. New York.
Putevoditel
    1900   *Illiustrirovannyi putevoditel.* Odessa.
Rafalovich, A.
    1843   "Meditsinskaia statistika Odessy za 1842 god," *ZhMVD.* 4: 344–85.
Rashin, A. G.
    1958   *Naselenie Rossii za 100 let.* Moscow.
Records
    1833   *Records of Travels in Turkey, Greece, etc. and of a Cruise in the Black Sea with the Captain Pasha in the Years 1829, 1830 and 1831.* 2 vols. Philadelphia and Baltimore.
Recueil des traités
    1791–1831   *Recueil des principaux traités d'alliance, de paix, de trève, de neutralité, de commerce, de limites, d'échanges, etc. conclus par les puissances de l'Europe tant entre elles qu'avec les puissances et états dans d'autres parties du monde depuis 1761 jusqu'à present.* Ed. G. F. Martens. Göttingen.
Reports
    1814   *First and Second Reports from the Committees of the House of Lords, Appointed to Inquire into the State of the Growth, and Consumption of Grain.* London.
Reuilly, J.
    1806   *Voyage en Crimée l'année 1803.* Paris.
Revoliutsiia
    1955   *Revoliutsiia 1905–1907 gg. na Ukraine. Sbornik dokumentov i materialov.* 2 vols. Kiev.
Rezul'taty
    1894   *Rezul'taty odnodnevnoi perepisi g. Odessy 1 dekabria 1892 goda.* Odessa.
Ribas, Aleksandr de
    1913   *Staraia Odessa: Istoricheskie ocherki, vospominaniia.* Odessa.
Richelieu, Duc de
    1886   "Mémoire sur Odessa, 1813," *SIRIO.* 54: 369–70
Risaliti, Renato
    1972   *Studi sui rapporti italo-russi (coi Ricordi di Viaggi inediti di Luigi Serristori).* Pisa.
Rochechouart, Louis V. L.
    1889   *Souvenirs sur la révolution, l'empire et la restauration.* Paris.

Rubinow, I. M.
1906   *Russia's Wheat Surplus.* Washington, D.C.
1908   *Economic Condition of the Jews in Russia.* Washington, D.C.
Rudchenko, I. Ia.
1874   *Chumatskie nardonye pesni.* Kiev.
Rzewuska, Rosalie
1939   *Mémoires de la Comtesse Rosalie Rzewuska (1788–1865),* ed. Giovannella C. Grenier. 2 vols. Rome.
SIRIO
1867–1918 *Sbornik Imperatorskogo russkogo istoricheskogo obshchestva.* 148 vols. St. Petersburg.
Scott, Charles Henry
1854   *The Baltic, the Black Sea and the Crimea: Comprising Travels in Russia, a Voyage down the Volga to Astrakhan, and a Tour through Crim Tartary.* 2nd ed. London.
Sears, Robert
1855   *An Illustrated Description of the Russian Empire.* New York.
Shcherbinin, M. P.
1858   *Biografiia general-fel'dmarshala kniazia Mikhaila Semenovicha Vorontsova.* St. Petersburg.
Shimanovskii, M. V.
1911   *Odessa-Bakhmach.* Odessa.
Shipov, N.
1933   *Istoriia moei zhizni.* Moscow.
Shishkina, Olimpiada
1842   *Zametki i vospominaniia russkoi puteshestvennitsy po Rossii v 1845 godu.* 2 vols. St. Petersburg.
Shmidt, A.
1863   *Khersonskaia guberniia. Materialy geografii i statistiki Rossii sobrannye ofitserami general'nogo shtaba.* 2 vols. St. Petersburg.
Sicard, Charles
1810   *Lettres sur la Crimée, Odessa et la Mer d'Azof.* Moscow.
1812   *Lettres sur Odessa.* St. Petersburg.
1886   "Notice sur onze années de la vie du duc de Richelieu à Odessa pour servir à l'histoire de sa vie," *SIRIO* 54: 27–79.
Sichynsky, V. (ed.)
1953   *Ukraine in Foreign Comments and Descriptions from the VIth to XXth Century.* New York.
Skal'kovskii, K. A.
1902   *Satiricheskie ocherki i vospominaniia.* St. Petersburg.
1905   *Za god.* St. Petersburg.
1906   *Vospominanie molodosti, 1843–1868.* St. Petersburg.

Smeta
  1900   *Smeta dokhodov i raskhodov g. Odessy na 1900 god.* Odessa.
Smith, Rollin
  1908   *Wheat Fields and Markets of the World.* St. Louis.
Snodgrass, John N.
  1913   *Russia, A Handbook on Commercial and Industrial Conditions.* Washington, D.C.
Société anonyme
  1900   *Société anonyme des Tramways d'Odessa. Statuts.* Brussels.
Spencer, Captain E.
  1854   *Turkey, Russia, the Black Sea and Circassia.* London.
Spisok
  1905   *Spisok chlenov Odesskogo obshchestva vzaimnago kredita na 1–e ianvaria 1905 goda.* Odessa.
Statistische Tabelle
  1859   *Statistische Tabelle des russischen Reiches für das Jahr 1856 in ihren allgemeinen Resultaten zusammengestellt und herausgegeben auf Anordnung des Kaiserlich-statistischen Central-Comité,* ed. E. Olberg. Berlin.
Stephens, John
  1838   *Incidents of Travel in Greece, Turkey, Russia and Poland.* 2 vols. New York.
Stevens, Robert
  1819   *An Account of Odessa.* Newport.
Stevens, Thomas
  1891   *Through Russia on a Mustang.* New York.
Sumarokov, P.
  1803–1805 *Dosugi krymskogo sud'i ili vtoroe puteshestvie v Tavridu.* St. Petersburg.
"Svedeniia ob Odesse."
  1839   *ZhMVD.* 8: 290–313.
Symonds, W.
  1841   *Extract from a Journal in the Black Sea in 1841.* London.
Tarnopol, Joachim
  1855   *Notices historiques et caractéristiques sur les israélites d'Odessa.* Odessa.
Tilley, Henry Arthur
  1864   *Eastern Europe and Western Asia.* London.
Timonov, V.
  1886   *Ocherk razvitiia odesskogo porta.* St. Petersburg.
TOSK
          Trudy Odesskogo statisticheskogo komiteta.
Trotsky, Leon
  1973   *My Life.* New York.

Twain, Mark
    1911   *The Innocents Abroad, or the New Pilgrim's Progress, Being Some Account of the Steamship* Quaker City's *Pleasure Excursions to Europe and to the Holy Land.* New York.
Ustav
    1898   *Ustav sluzhby na sudakh dobrovol'nogo flota.* St. Petersburg.
Vedomost
    1902   *Vedomost normal'nykh tsen na zemliu i stroeniia.* Odessa.
Vigel, F. F.
    1864–65   *Vospominaniia.* Moscow.
Villari, Luigi
    1905   *Russia under the Great Shadow.* London and New York.
Ville
    1908   *La Ville d'Odessa.* Odessa.
Vneshniaia torgovlia
    1827   *Gosudarstvennaia vneshniaia torgovlia 1826 goda v raznykh ee vidakh.* St. Petersburg.
Vorontsov, S. R.
    1880   *Pis'ma Grafa S. R. Vorontsova k synu ego.* AKV. 17.
Vsevolozhskii, N. S.
    1839   *Puteshestvie cherez iuzhnuiu Rossiiu, Krym i Odessu v Konstantinopl, Maluiu Aziiu, Severnuiu Afriku v 1836 i 1837 godakh.* Moscow.
Vsia Rossiia
    1913   *Vsia Rossiia, 1913 god. Spravochnaia kniga.* Kiev.
Washburn, Stanley
    1912   *The Cable Game.* Boston.
Wassiltchikov, A.
    1894   *Le comte André Razoumowski.* Halle-on-the-Saale.
Weber, Johann P. B.
    1960   *Die Russen oder Versuch einer Reisebeschreibung nach Russland und durch das russische Reich in Europa,* ed. H. Halm. Innsbruck.
Webster, James
    1830   *Travels through the Crimea, Turkey and Egypt; Performed during the Years 1825–1828; Including Particulars of the Last Illness and Death of the Emperor Alexander and the Russian Conspiracy in 1825.* 2 vols. London.
Wegelin, Daniel
    1845   *Erinnerungen aus Russland und dem Orient.* Zürich.
Wickoff, Henry
    1880   *The Reminiscences of an Idler.* New York.
Wightman, Orrin Sage
    1928   *Diary of an American Physician in the Russian Revolution, 1917.* New York.

Winter, Nevin O.
  1914   *The Russian Empire of To-Day and Yesterday.* London.
Witte, Sergei.
  1901   *Russia. Its Industries and Trade.* Glasgow.
Wood, Ruth K.
  1912   *The Tourist's Russia.* New York.
Zapiski
  1908   *Zapiski po delu o zakliuchenii dogovora s Bel'giiskim aktsi-*
            onernym obshchestvom. Odessa.
ZhMVD
            Zhurnal Ministerstva vnutrennykh del.

II. Archival and Bibliographical Guides

AOO
  1961   *Gosudarstvennyi arkhiv Odesskoi oblasti. Putevoditel.*
            Odessa.
Florovskii, V. V.
  1913   *Odessika. Bibliograficheskie materialy po istorii goroda*
            Odessy. Odessa.
Izvestiia
  1913–14   *Izvestiia Odesskogo bibliograficheskogo obshchestva.* 2 vols.
            Odessa.
Katalog
  1888   *Katalog kart, planov, chertezhei, risunkov, khraniashchikhsia*
            v Muzee Imperatorskogo odesskogo obshchestva istorii i drev-
            nostei. Odessa.
Materialy
  1927–29   *Materialy k bibliografii revoliutsionnogo dvizheniia v Odesse.*
            Parts I and II. Odessa.
Ribas, L. M. de
  1914   *Bibliograficheskie materialy po istorii Novorossii.* Odessa.
Spravochniki
  1978   *Spravochniki po istorii dorevoliutsionnoi Rossii.* Moscow.
Visnyk
  1925   *Visnyk Odes'koi komisii kraieznavstva pry Ukrainskii aka-*
            demii nauk. Odessa.
Zaionchkovskii, P. A. (ed.)
  1976   *Istoriia dorevoliutsionnoi Rossii v dnevnikakh i vospominani-*
            iakh 1801–1856. Ed. P. A. Zaionchkovskii. Moscow.

III. Studies

Albion, Robert G.
  1939   *The Rise of New York Port.* New York.

Alekseev, M. P.
1915–26   *Pushkin. Stat'i i materialy.* 3 vols. Odessa.
Andreevskii, I. S.
1839   "Literaturnaia letopis Odessy." *Odesskii al'manakh na 1840 god,* pp. 1–39.
Arsh, G. L.
1959   *Eteristskoe dvizhenie v Rossii.* Moscow.
1965   *Tainoe obshchestvo Filiki Eteriia.* Moscow.
Atlas, D.
1911   *Staraia Odessa, ee druz'ia i nedrugi.* Odessa.
Avaliani, S. L.
1912–14   *Graf M. S. Vorontsov i krest'ianskii vopros.* 2 pts. Odessa.
Babaitseva, Z. A.
1960   "O rasskaze M. Gor'kogo, 'Chelkash'." In: *Gor'kii,* pp. 49–72.
Bagrov, N. V. and Gradov, G. L.
1974   *Problemy razvitiia i razmeshcheniia proizvoditel'nykh sel severnogo prichernomor'ia.* Moscow.
Barth, Gunther
1975   *Instant Cities.* New York.
Bartlett, Roger P.
1974   "Foreign Settlement in Russia under Catherine II," *The New Zealand Slavonic Review.* 1: 1–22.
1979   *Human Capital: The Settlement of Foreigners in Russia, 1762–1804.* Cambridge: University Press.
Baruchello, M.
1932   *Livorno e il suo porto: origini, caratteristiche e vicende dei traffici livornesi.* Livorno.
Bater, James H.
1976   *St. Petersburg: Industrialization and Change.* London.
1980   "Transience, Residential Persistence, and Mobility in Moscow and St. Petersburg, 1900–1914," *Slavic Review.* 39: 239–54.
Beletskii, A.
1893   "Iz istorii zaseleniia Odessy," *Kalendar.* 2, pt. 4: 118–36.
Bel'for, D. S.
1956   "Profsoiuzy Odessy v revoliutsii 1905–1907 godov." In: *Sbornik,* pp. 29–52.
Beliiavskii, P.
1865   "Odesskii port," *TOSK.* 1: 266–89.
Belin de Ballu, E.
1965   *L'histoire des colonies grecques du littoral nord de la Mer Noire: articles publiés en U.R.S.S. de 1940 à 1962.* Leiden.
Ben-Sasson, H. H. (ed).
1976   *A History of the Jewish People.* Cambridge, Mass.

Bibliography 379

Bernshtein, S.
1881   *Istoricheskii i torgovo-ekonomicheskii ocherk Odessy v sviazi s Novorossiiskim kraem.* Odessa.
Bieneman, F.
1890   *Geschichte der evangelisch-luterischen Gemeinde zu Odessa.* Odessa.
Blackwell, William
1968   *The Beginnings of Russian Industrialization, 1800–1860.* Princeton.
Blum, J.
1961   *Lord and Peasant in Russia from the Ninth to the Nineteenth Century.* Princeton.
Borasi, L.
1939   *Grano duro e paste alimentari.* Vercelli.
Borinevich, A. S.
1890   *Ocherk khlebnoi torgovli v Odesse.* Odessa.
1893a   "Perepis Odessy 1–ogo dekabria 1892 g.," *Kalendar.* 2, pt. 4: 200–08.
1893b   "Kharakteristika ekonomicheskoi zhizni Odessy v 1891 g.," *Kalendar.* 2, pt. 4: 193–99.
Borisov, N.
1893a   "Dvizhenie chastnoi zemel'noi sobstvennosti v Khersonskoi gubernii (po dannym zemskoi statistiki)," *Kalendar.* 2, pt. 4: 76–88.
1893b   "Pervyi domennyi zavod v Khersonskoi gubernii," *Kalendar.* 2, pt. 4: 149–54.
Borovoi, S. Ia.
1928   *Evreiskaia zemledel'cheskaia kolonizatsiia v staroi Rossii.* Moscow.
1944   "Odessa k 150-letiiu so dnia osnovaniia," *Istoricheskii zhurnal,* 5–6: 41–48.
1958   "Polozhenie rabochego klassa Odessy v XIX i nachale XX v." In: *Iz istorii rabochego klassa i revoliutsionnogo dvizheniia,* ed. M. V. Nechkina. Moscow. pp. 308–18.
1960   "A. A. Skal'kovskii i ego roboty po istorii iuzhnoi Ukrainy," *Zapiski Odesskogo arkheologischeskogo obshchestva.* 1: 175–85.
1966   "Armianskaia gazeta v Odesse," *Istoricheskii zhurnal,* 3 (34): 294–98.
1967a   "Khadzhibei v 60-kh godakh XVIII v." *Zapiski Odesskogo arkheologicheskogo obshchestva.* 35: 130–36.
1967b   "Kniga v Odesse v pervoi polovine XIX v," *Kniga* 14: 145–59.

1974 " 'Kolokol' i obshchestvenno-politicheskaia zhizn Odessy v gody pervoi revoliutsionnoi situatsii," *Revoliutsionnaia situatsiia v Rossii 1859–1861 gg.* Pp. 194–206. Moscow.

Bourdé, Guy.
1974 *Urbanisation et immigration en Amerique latine. Buenos-Aires, XIXe et XXe siècles.* Paris.

Bratianu, G. I.
1929 *Recherches sur le commerce génois dans la Mer-Noire au XIIIe siècle.* Paris.

Braudel, Fernand
1955 *La Méditerranée et le monde méditerranéen à l'époque de Philippe II.* 2nd ed., 2 vols. Paris.

Brun, F.
1870 "Odesskoe obshchestvo istorii i drevnostei, ego zapiski i arkheologicheskie sobraniia," *TOSK*, 4: 69–101.

BSE
1957 *Bol'shaia sovetskaia entsiklopediia.* Moscow.

Cadot, Michel and Jean-Louis Van Regemorter
1969 "Le commerce extérieur de la Russie en 1794 d'après le Journal de Voyage de Baert du Hollant," *Cahiers du monde russe et soviétique*, 10: 371–91.

Céréales russes
1900 *Céréales russes (grains et graines)*, Ministry of Finance. St. Petersburg.

Chapman, S. H.
1977 "The International Houses: The Continental Contribution to British Commerce, 1800–1860," *The Journal of European Economic History.* 6: 5–48.

Chereiskii, L. A.
1975 *Pushkin i ego okruzhenie.* Leningrad.

Chorley, Patrick
1965 *Oil, Silk and Enlightenment: Economic Problems in XVIIIth Century Naples.* Naples.

Confino, Michael
1963 *Domaines et seigneurs en Russie vers la fin du XVIIe siècle. Étude de structure agraires et de mentalités économiques.* Paris.

Cox, Cynthia
1959 *Talleyrand's Successor: Armand-Emmanuel du Plessis Duc de Richelieu 1766–1811.* London.

Crousaz-Crétet, L.
1897 *Le duc de Richelieu en Russie et en France, 1766–1822.* Paris.

Crozat, J. F.
1910 *Rostoff-sur-le-Don et le commerce des céréales.* Paris.

Cukierman, Walenty
   1976   The Odessa School of Writers, 1918–1923. (Unpublished doctoral dissertation). University of Michigan.
   1980   "The Odessan Myth and Idiom in Some Early Works of Odessa Writers," *Canadian-American Slavic Studies*, 14: 36–51.

Davis, Christopher and Feshbach, Murray
   1980   *Rising Infant Mortality in the USSR in the 1970's*. U. S. Department of Commerce, Bureau of the Census. Washington, D. C.

Dawidowicz, Lucy S.
   1967   *The Golden Tradition: Jewish Life and Thought in Eastern Europe*. Boston.

Den, V. E.
   1902   *Naselenie Rossii po piatoi revizii*. 2 vols. Moscow.

Dikhtar, G. A.
   1960   *Vnutrenniaia torgovlia v dorevoliutsionnoi Rossii*. Moscow.

Ditiatin, I. I.
   1875, 1877 *Ustroistvo i upravlenie gorodov Rossii*. 2 vols. St. Petersburg and Iaroslavl.

Druzhinina, E. I.
   1955   *Kiuchuk-Kainardzhiiskii mir 1774 goda*. Moscow.
   1959   *Severnoe prichernomor'e, 1775–1800 g*. Moscow.
   1966   "Zur Geschichte der deutschen Kolonien in Neurussland," *Ost und West in der Geschichte des Denkens und der kulturellen Beziehungen: Festschrift für Edward Winter zum 70. Geburtstag*. Berlin.
   1970   *Iuzhnaia Ukraina 1800–1825 gg*. Moscow.
   1976   "Vozniknovenie gorodov," *Novaia i noveishaia istoriia*. 2: 69–76.
   1981   *Iuzhnaia Ukraina v period krizisa feodalizma 1825–1860 gg*. Moscow.

Dyhouse, Carol
   1978   "Working-Class Mothers and Infant Mortality in England, 1895–1914," *Journal of Social History*. 12: 248–68.

Emmons, Terence
   1968   *The Russian Landed Gentry and the Peasant Emancipation*. Cambridge.

Entsiklopedicheskii slovar.
   1890–1907 Brokgauz and Efron, *Entsiklopedicheskii slovar*. 41 vols. St. Petersburg.

Entsyklopediia ukrainoznavstva
   1949–78 *Entsyklopediia ukrainoznavstva*, ed. Volodymyr Kubijovyč. 2 vols. Munich, Paris, and New York.

Fal'kovskii, N. I.
   1947   *Istoriia vodosnabzheniia v Rossii*. Moscow and Leningrad.

Falkus, M. E.
1966   "Russia and the International Wheat Trade, 1861–1914."
            Economica, n. s. 33.

Falloux, Comte de
1860   *Madame Swetchine, sa vie et ses oeuvres.* 3rd ed. Paris.

Family
1978   *The Family in Imperial Russia: New Lines of Historical
            Research.* ed. David L. Ransel. Urbana, Chicago, and
            London.

Fedor, Thomas S.
1975   *Patterns of Urban Growth in the Russian Empire during the
            Nineteenth Century.* University of Chicago, Department of
            Geography Research Paper No. 163.

Finkel, Mark Il'ich
1865   "Issledovanie o smertnosti v Odesse, v desiatiletnii period,
            s 1851 po 1860 god vkliuchitel'no," *TOSK*, 1: 153–99.

Fomin, A.
1829   *O ponizhenie tsen na zemledel'cheskoe proizvedenie v Rossii.*
            St. Petersburg.

Fox, David J.
1963   "Odessa," *Scottish Geographical Magazine.* 79: 5–21.

Freibel, Otto.
1921   *Der Handelshafen Odessa.* Leipzig and Berlin.

Frieden, Nancy M.
1973   "Child Care: Medical Reform in a Traditionalist Culture,"
            Family, pp. 236–59.

1977   "The Russian Cholera Epidemic, 1892–93, and Medical
            Professionalization," *Journal of Social History.* 10:
            538–59.

Friesen, P. M.
1911   *Die Alt-Evangelische mennonitische Bruderschaft in Russland
            1789–1910.* Halbstadt.

Gaidukevich, V. F.
1955   "Istoriia antichnykh gorodov severnogo prichernomor'ia,"
            *Antichnye goroda severnogo prichernomor'ia. Ocherki istorii i
            kultury.* Moscow and Leningrad.

Galpin, William Freeman
1925   *The Grain Supply of England during the Napoleonic Period.*
            Philadelphia.

Gilchrist, David T.
1967   *The Growth of Seaport Cities, 1790–1824.* Charlottesville,
            Virginia.

Giura, Vincenzo
1967   *Russia, Stati Uniti d'America e Regno di Napoli nell' età del
            Risorgimento.* Naples.

Gor'kii
1960   *Maksim Gor'kii. Sbornik statei.* Odessa.
Gorrini, Jean
1918   *La Russie moderne et les rapports Italo-Russes.* Turin.
Gras, N. S. B.
1915   *The Evolution of the English Corn Market.* Cambridge, Mass.
Guttentag, Marcia, and Secord, Paul F.
1983   *Too Many Women? The Sex Ratio Question.* Beverly Hills, London, and New Delhi.
Hagemeister, J. von
1847   "Der Wollhandel in Russland," *Archiv für wissenschaftliche Kunde von Russland,* ed. A. Erman, 5: 217–22.
Halm, Hans
1943   *Oesterreich und Neurussland,* I: *Donauschiffahrt und -handel nach dem Südosten, 1718–1780.* Breslau.
1961   *Gründung und erstes Jahrzehnt von Festung und Stadt Cherson, 1778–1788.* Munich.
Hamilton, George Heard
1954   *The Art of Russia.* Harmondsworth, Middlesex.
Hamm, M. F.
1976a   "The Breakdown of Urban Modernization, a Prelude to the Revolution of 1917," In: Hamm, ed. 1976b: 182–200.
1976b   *The City in Russian History.* ed. Lexington, Kentucky.
Hanchett, Walter
1964   Moscow in the Late Nineteenth Century: A Study in Municipal Self-Government. (Unpublished doctoral dissertation). University of Chicago.
Handlin, Oscar
1941   *Boston's Immigrants, 1790–1865.* Cambridge, Mass.
Harvey, Mose L.
1938   The Development of Russian Commerce on the Black Sea and Its Significance. (Unpublished doctoral dissertation). University of California, Berkeley.
Haumant, Émile
1910   *La culture française en Russie, 1700–1910.* Paris.
Height, Joseph H.
n.d.   *Paradise on the Steppe: A Cultural History of the Kutschuran, Beresan and Liebental Colonists, 1804–1944.* Bismarck, North Dakota.
Herlihy, Patricia
1963   Russian Grain and Mediterranean Markets, 1774–1861 (Unpublished doctoral dissertation). University of Pennsylvania.

1974a   "Elena Ioasafovna Druzhinina, *Iuzhnaia Ukraina v 1800–1825 gg.*" *Kritika* 10: 157–62.

1974b   "Odessa, Staple Trade and Urbanization in New Russia," *Jahrbücher für Geschichte Osteuropas* 21: 121–37.

1976   "Russian Wheat and the Port of Livorno," *The Journal of European Economic History.* 5: 45–68.

1977   "The Ethnic Composition of the City of Odessa in the Nineteenth Century," *Harvard Ukrainian Studies*, 1: 53–78.

1978   "Death in Odessa: A Study of Population Movements in a Nineteenth-Century City," *Journal of Urban History.* 4: 417–41.

1979–80   "Greek Merchants in Odessa in the Nineteenth Century," *Harvard Ukrainian Studies.* 3–4: 399–420.

1980   "Odessa's Trade with Western Europe in the late 18th and the 19th Century," unpublished paper presented at the 15th International Congress of Historians. Bucharest.

1981   "Ukrainian Cities in the 19th Century," *Rethinking Ukrainian History*, ed. Ivan L. Rudnytsky. Edmonton.

1983   "Visitors' Perceptions of Urbanization: Travel Literature in Tsarist Russia," *The Pursuit of Urban History*, ed. Derek Fraser and Anthony Sutcliffe. London.

Heyd, W.
1885–86   *Histoire du commerce du Levant au moyen-âge.* 2 vols. Leipzig.

Hittle, J. Michael
1979   *The Service City: State and Townsmen in Russia, 1600–1800.* Cambridge, Mass. and London.

Hooson, David J. M.
1970   "The Growth of Cities in Pre-Soviet Russia," *Urbanization and its Problems*, ed. R. P. Beckinsale and J. M. Houston. Oxford.

Hough, Richard
1975   *The Potemkin Mutiny.* Westport, Connecticut.

Iailenko, V. P.
1975   "Zarubezhnaia istoriografiia drevnegrecheskoi kolonizatsii," *Voprosy istorii* 4: 188–98.

Iessen, A. A.
1947   *Grecheskaia kolonizatsiia severnogo prichernomor'ia.* Leningrad.

Indova, E. I.
1955   *Krepostnoe khoziaistvo v nachale XIX veka po materialam votchinnogo arkhiva Vorontsovykh.* Moscow.

Istoriia mist
1967–74   *Istoriia mist i sil Ukrainskoi RSR, Odes'ka oblast.* Kiev.

Itenberg, B. S.
1974 *Iuzhno-rossiiskii soiuz rabochikh.* Moscow.
Iz istorii
1964 *Iz istorii odesskoi partiinoi organizatsii. Ocherki.* Odessa.
Jewish Encyclopedia
1905 *The Jewish Encyclopedia.* New York and London.
Jurowsky, Leo
1910 *Der russische Getreideexport.* Stuttgart and Berlin.
Kabuzan, V. M.
1971 *Izmeneniia v razmeshchenii naseleniia Rossii v XVIII—pervoi polovine XIX v. (Po materialam revizii).* Moscow.
1976 *Zaselenie Novorossii v XVIII–pervoi polovine XIX veka, 1719–1858 gg.* Moscow.
Kashirin, G. A. and Alekseev-Popov, V. S.
1963 "K voprosu o roli Odessy v istorii sviazei russkogo i bolgarskogo narodov," *Izvestiia na narodnata biblioteka i bibliotekata Sofiiskiia derzhaven universitet.* vol. 3 (9). Sofia.
Kasperoff, M. V.
1900 "Le commerce des céréales," *La Russie à la fin du 19e siècle.* ed. M. W. de Kovalevsky. Paris.
Keller, P. Conrad, S. J.
n.d. *The German Colonies in South Russia, 1808 to 1904*, trans. A. Becker. Saskatoon.
"Kherson"
1970–78 "Kherson," *Bol'shaia sovetskaia entsiklopedia.* 30 vols. Moscow. 28: 41.
Klier, John D.
1981 "*Odesskii vestnik*'s Annus Mirabilis of 1858," *Canadian Slavonic Papers*, 23: 41–55.
Kochan, Lionel
1966 *Russia in Revolution, 1890–1918.* New York.
Kokhanskii, V. and Zhelikhovskii, N.
1891 *Pamiatnik Imperatoru Aleksandru II v Odesse.* Odessa.
Kollmann, Wolfgang
1974 *Bevölkerung in der industriellen Revolution. Studien zur Bevölkerungsgeschichte Deutschlands.* Göttingen.
Kulischer (Kulisher), I. M.
1955 *Storia del medio evo e dell'epoca moderna.* 2 vols. Florence.
Kulisher, I. M.
1923 *Ocherk istorii russkoi torgovli.* St. Petersburg.
Lazarovich, S.
1893 "Neurozhai 1891–1892 gg. i prodovol'stvennye nuzhdy v Khersonskoi gubernii," *Kalendar.* 2, pt. 4:102–17.

Leibbrandt, G.
    1928   *Die Auswanderung aus Schwaben nach Russland,*
                1816–1823: Ein schwabisches Zeit- und Charackterbild.
                Stuttgart.

Lenin, V. I.
    1960   *The Development of Capitalism in Russia.* Collected Works,
                3. London.

Leont'ev, A.
    1893   "K istorii zemlevladeniia Novorossiiskogo kraia," *Kalen-*
                dar. 2, pt. 4: 137–48.

Lerner, N.
    1901   *Pervaia odesskaia gazeta.* Odessa.
    n.d.   "Neskol'ko novykh slov o prebyvanii Gogolia v Odesse v
                1850–51 gg." Odessa.

Lerner, O. M.
    1901   *Evrei v Novorossiiskom krae.* Odessa.
    1902   *Odesskaia starina. Istoricheskie ocherki po dannym iz*
                arkhiva byvshego novorossiiskogo general-gubernatora.
                Odessa.

Levasseur, E.
    1911–12   *Histoire du commerce de la France.* 2 vols. Paris.

Levi, Giovanni
                "Les projets du gouvernement sarde sur les relations
                économique avec la Russie à la fin du XVIIIe siècle," *La*
                Russie et l'Europe XVIe–XXe siècles. Paris and Moscow.

Levi, Leone
    1872   *History of British Commerce and of the British Nation,*
                1763–1870. London.

Liashchenko, P. I.
    1908   *Ocherki agrarnoi evoliutsii Rossii.* St. Petersburg.
    1917   *Russkoe zernovoe khoziaistvo v sisteme mirovogo khoziaistva.*
                Moscow.
    1949   *History of the National Economy of Russia to the 1917 Revo-*
                lution. New York.
    1952   *Istoriia narodnogo khoziaistva.* 2 vols. Moscow.

Lindemann, K.
    1924   "Von den deutschen Kolonisten in Russland," *Ergebnisse*
                einer Studienreise, 1919–1921. Stuttgart.

Lindenmeyr, Adele
    1980   Public Poor Relief and Private Charity in Late Imperial
                Russia. (Unpublished doctoral dissertation). Princeton
                University, Princeton, N. J.

Lobanov-Rostovsky, Andrei
    1947   *Russia and Europe, 1789–1825.* Durham, North Carolina.

Lopez, Roberto S.
1938   *Storia delle colonie genovesi nel Mediterraneo.* Bologna.
Luther, G.
1889   *La transformation du port d'Odessa.* Brunswick.
Madariaga, Isabell de
1981   *Russia in the Period of Catherine the Great.* New Haven.
Malinowsky, J. A.
1927   *Die deutschen katholischen Kolonien am Schwärzen Meere: Berichte der Gemeindeämter über Entstehung und Entwicklung dieser Kolonien in der ersten Hälfte des neunzehnten Jahrhunderts.* Stuttgart.
Markevich, A. I.
1890   *Dvadtsatipiatiletie Imperatorskogo Novorossiiskogo universiteta.* Odessa.
1893   *Iuzhnaia Rus' pri Ekaterine II.* Odessa.
1894   "Odessa v narodnoi poezii," *Odesskie novosti,* no. 3047. Odessa.
1900a   *A. A. Skal'kovskii.* Odessa.
1900b   *Dvadtsatipiatiletie deiatel'nosti Odesskogo obshchestva dlia ustroistva deshevykh nochlezhnykh priiutov.* Odessa.
1901   *K biografii A. A. Skal'kovskogo.* Odessa.
1902   *Gogol v Odesse.* Odessa.
n.d.   "Zheleznye dorogi soediniaiushchie Odessu s ostal'noi Rossiei," *Al'manakh.* Odessa.
McGrew, Roderick E.
1965   *Russia and the Cholera, 1812–1832.* Madison and Milwaukee, Wisconsin.
McKay, John P.
1970   *Pioneers for Profit: Entrepreneurship and Industrialization, 1885–1913.* Chicago and London.
McKelvey, Blake
1973   *American Urbanization: A Comparative History.* Glenview, Illinois.
Metzer, Jacob
1974   "Railroad Development and Market Integration: The Case of Tsarist Russia," *The Journal of Economic History.* 34: 529–49.
Mikhailovitch, Grand Duc Nicholas
1931   *Le Tsar Alexandre I.* Paris.
Milone, F.
1929   *Il grano.* Bari.
Mirsky, D. S.
1926   *Pushkin.* London.
Mizhnevich
1849   *Biografiia gertsoga de-Rishel'e.* Odessa.

Mladenchestvo
1844   "O mladenchestve Odessy," *OV*, 1844.
Morgan, Dan
1979   *Merchants of Grain.* New York.
Morrison, John A.
1962   "Russia and Warm Water," *Readings in Russian History*,
              ed. Sidney Harcave. 2 vols. New York.
Motzkin, Leo
1910   *Die Judenpogrome in Russland.* 2 vols. Cologne and
              Leipzig.
Moulake, Chr.
1964   *Oikos Adelphon Ralli.* Athens.
Nifontov, A. S.
1974   *Zernovoe proizvodstvo Rossii vo vtoroi polovine XIX veka.*
              Moscow.
Odessa
1895   *Odessa 1794–1894. Izdanie Gorodskogo obshchestvennogo
              upravleniia k stoletiiu goroda.* Odessa.
Odessa. Ocherk
1957   *Odessa. Ocherk istorii goroda-geroia.* Odessa.
Odesskii teatr
1977   *Odesskii teatr opery i baleta.* Odessa.
Orbach, Alexander
1980   *New Voices of Russian Jewry: A Study of the Russian-Jewish
              Press of Odessa in the Era of the Great Reforms, 1861–71.*
              Leiden.
Orlov, A.
1885   *Istoricheskii ocherk Odessy s 1794 po 1803 god. Sostavil po
              dokumentam khraniashchimsia v moskovskom arkhive Min-
              isterstva iustitsii.* Odessa.
Parasun'ko, O. A.
1963   *Polozhenie i bor'ba rabochego klassa Ukrainy (60–90e gody
              XIX v).* Kiev.
Pavlovich, V.
1862   *Ekaterinoslavskaia guberniia.* Materialy dlia geografii i sta-
              tistiki Rossii, 6. St. Petersburg.
Piaskovskii, A. V.
1966   *Revoliutsiia 1905–1907 gg. v Rossii.* Moscow.
Pingaud, L.
1910   *Les français en Russie et les russes en France, 1700–1900.*
              Paris.
Polons'ka-Vasylenko, N. D.
1955   *The Settlement of the Southern Ukraine (1750–1775).* The
              Annals of the Ukrainian Academy of Arts and Sciences in
              the U. S., vols. 4–5. New York.

Portal, Roger
 1966   *La Russie industrielle, 1881–1927.* Paris.
Post, John D.
 1977   *The Last Great Subsistence Crisis in the Western World.* Baltimore and London.
Pusarevskii, G. G.
 1917   *Pereselenie prusskikh mennonitov v Rossiiu pri Aleksandre I.* Rostov-on-Don.
Raisin, J. P.
 1915   *The Haskalah Movement in Russia.* Philadelphia.
Rakhmatullin, M. A.
 1970   "Khlebnyi rynok i tseny v Rossii v pervoi polovine XIX v.," *Problemy genezisa kapitalizma.* Moscow.
Ransel, David L.
 1978   "Abandonment and Fosterage of Unwanted Children: The Women of the Foundling System," *Family,* pp. 189–217.
Rashin, A. G.
 1956   *Naselenie Rossii za 100 let, 1811–1913 gg.* Moscow.
Rees, Graham L.
 1972   *Commodity Markets.* London.
Ribas, A. de
 1925–26   "Pushkin i Lanzheron," *Pushkin. Stat'i i materialy,* ed. M. P. Alekseev. II: 32–40. Odessa.
Ribas, L. M. de
 1894   *Iz proshlogo Odessy.* Odessa.
Richmond, Julius B.
 1977   "The Needs of Children," *Daedalus* (Winter): 237–59.
Robinson, Geroid T.
 1967   *Rural Russia under the Old Regime.* New York.
Rosen, George
 1973   "Disease, Debility and Death," *The Victorian City: Images and Realities,* H. J. Dyos and Michael Wolff, eds. 2 vols. 2: 625–67. London and Boston.
Rosenkranz, Barbara G.
 1972   *Public Health and the States: Changing Views in Massachusetts, 1842–1946,* Cambridge, Mass.
Rozhkova, M. K.
 1959   *Ocherki ekonomicheskoi istorii Rossii pervoi poloviny XIX veka.* Moscow.
Ryndziunskii, P. G.
 1958   *Gorodskoe grazhdanstvo doreformennoi Rossii.* Moscow.
Saul, Norman E.
 1970   *Russia and the Mediterranean.* Chicago and London.

Sbornik
1956   *Sbornik posviashchennyi 50–letiiu pervoi russkoi revoliutsii 1905–1907 gg.* Odessa.
Schmelz, U. O.
1971   *Infant and Early Childhood among Jews of the Diaspora.* Jerusalem.
Schneiderman, Jeremiah
1976   *Sergei Zubatov and Revolutionary Marxism: The Struggle for the Working Class in Tsarist Russia.* Ithaca and London.
Schorske, Carl
1981   *Fin-de-Siècle Vienna: Politics and Culture.* New York.
Scobie, James R.
1972   "Buenos Aires as a Commercial-Bureaucratic City," *The American Historical Review,* 77: 1035–73.
Selinov, V. I.
1930   *Arkhitekturni pamiatnyky staroi Odesy.* Odessa.
Sharlin, Allan
1978   "Natural Decrease in Early Modern Cities: A Reconsideration," *Past and Present.* 79: 126–38.
Shelov, D. B.
1956   *Antichnyi mir v severnom prichernomor'e.* Moscow.
Shepelev, L. E.
1973   *Aktsionernye kompanii v Rossii.* Leningrad.
Shishmarev, V. F.
1975   *Romanskie poseleniia na iuge Rossii.* Leningrad.
Shternshtein, Ia. M.
1954   *U istokov revoliutsionnykh traditsii.* Odessa.
1956   "Bor'ba bol'shevikov Odessy za soiuz rabochego klassa i krest'ianstva v period pervoi russkoi revoliutsii." In: *Sbornik,* pp. 53–78.
1958   *Morskie vorota Ukrainy.* Odessa.
Shtraikh, Ia.
1911   *Iz epokhi osvobozhdeniia krest'ian.* St. Petersburg.
Siegelbaum, Lewis
1980   "The Odessa Grain Trade: A Case Study in Urban Growth and Development in Tsarist Russia," *The Journal of European Economic History.* 9: 113–51.
Siniaver, A.
1935   *Arkhitektura staroi Odessy.* Leningrad.
Sirotkin, V. G.
1970   "Le renouvellement en 1802 du traité de commerce franco-russe de 1787," *La Russie et l'Empire, XVI–XXe siècles,* pp. 69–101. Bibliothèque Générale de l'École Pratique des Hautes Études, VIe Section. Paris and Moscow.

Skal'kovskii, A. A.

1837   *Pervoe tridtsatiletie istorii goroda Odessy, 1793–1823.* Odessa.

1839a   *Istoricheskii-statisticheskii opyt o torgovykh i promyshlennykh silakh Odessy.* Odessa.

1839b   "Chetyre stranitsy odesskoi letopisi." *Odesskii al'manakh.*

1845   "La population commerciale d'Odessa," *JO* Nos. 27 and 28, and separately published.

1846   "Odesskoe gradonachal'stvo v nachale 1846 goda," *ZhMVD* 14: 213–50 and 413–42.

1848   *Bolgarskie kolonii v Bessarabii i Novorossiiskom krae.* Odessa.

1850a   *Opyt statisticheskogo opisaniia Novorossiiskogo kraia. Chast* I: *Geografiia, etnografiia, i narodonaselenie Novorossiiskogo kraia.* Odessa.

1850b   "Torgovaia promyshlennost v Novorossiiskom krae," *ZhMVD.* pt. 1, 29: 177–217.

1851   "Torgovaia promyshlennost v Novorossiiskom krae," *ZhMVD.* pt. 2, 33: 5–55.

1863   "O napravlenii zheleznykh dorog v iuzhnoi Rossii," *Severnaia pochta.* no. 49.

1865a   "Materialy dlia istorii obshchestvennogo obrazovaniia," *TOSK.* 2: 39–124.

1865b   "Aktsiznye uchrezhdeniia v Odesse," *TOSK.* 2: 269–84.

1865c   "Biografiia odesskoi zheleznoi dorogi." *TOSK.* 1: 291–310.

1865d   *Zapiski o torgovykh i promyshlennykh silakh Odessy.* St. Petersburg.

1870a   "Odessa za 40 let nazad," *TOSK.* 4: 47–68.

1870b   "Nachalo razvitiia zavodskoi promyshlennosti v Odesse," *TOSK.* 4: 145–57.

1870c   "Pochty i telegrafy v Odesse, 1808–1869 gg," *TOSK.* 4: 185–92.

1870d   "Odesskaia torgovlia v 1868 godu," *TOSK.* 3:126–31.

1870e   "Torgovlia, zavodskaia, fabrichnaia i remeslennaia promyshlennost v Odesse," *TOSK.* 1: 240–65.

1878a   *Odessa 84 god tomu nazad i teper.* Odessa.

1878b   "Odessa v 1870kh godakh," *Pamiatnaia knizhka,* pp. 37–46.

1878c   "Dvizhenie odesskogo naseleniia v 70kh godakh," *Pamiatnaia knizhka,* pp. 64–72.

1889   "Admiral de Ribas i zavoevanie Khadzhibeia, 1764–1797." Odessa.

Skinner, F. W.
1973   City Planning in Russia: The Development of Odessa 1789–1892. (Unpublished doctoral dissertation). Princeton University, Princeton, New Jersey.
1976   "Trends in Planning Practices: The Building of Odessa 1794–1917," In: Hamm, 1976, 139–159.

Skripnikova, L. V.
1970   "Nekotorye istochniki po istorii kolonial'noi politiki Anglii v Vest-Indee v pervoi treti XIX v.," *Voprosy istoriografii i istochnikovedeniia vseobshchei istorii*, 87–109. Dnepropetrovsk.

Slavianovedenie
1979   *Slavianovedenie v dorevoliutsionnoi Rossii.* Moscow.

Smol'ianinov, K.
1853   *Istoriia Odessy.* Odessa.

Solov'eva, A. M.
1975   *Zheleznodorozhnyi transport Rossii vo vtoroi polovine XIX v.* Moscow.

Spath, Manfred
1978   "Wasserleitung und Kanalisation in Grosstädten: Ein Beispiel der Organisation technischen Wandels im vorrevolutionären Russland," *Forschungen zur osteuropäischen Geschichte*, 25:342–60.

Sperandeo, G.
1906   "Gli Italiani nel Mar Nero," *Rivista d'Italia.* August: 325–42.

Stanislawski, Michael
1983   *Tsar Nicholas I and the Jews: The Transformation of Jewish Society in Russia, 1825–1855.* Philadelphia.

Stara Odesa
1927   *Stara Odesa. Arkhitektura prychornomoria.* Odessa.

Starr, S. Frederick
1972   *Decentralization and Self-Government in Russia 1830–1870.* Princeton University Press, Princeton, N. J.

Stoletie
1894   *Stoletie Odessy 22 avgusta 1894 goda.* Odessa.

Straten, V.
1925   "Ukazatel trudov, osnovannykh na odesskikh arkhivnykh materialakh," *Vistnyk Odes'koi komisii kraieznavstva pry Ukrains'kii akademii nauk.* No. 2–3: 162–66. Odessa.

Stumpp, Karl
1971   The German-Russians: Two Centuries of Pioneering. Bonn, Brussels, and New York.

Tereshchenko, A.
1853   "Odessa," *Zhurnal Ministerstva narodnogo prosveshcheniia* 78, pt. 2: 55–75.

Thiede, Roger Lee
1976   Town and Function in Tsarist Russia. A Geographical Analysis of Trade and Industry in the Towns of New Russia, 1860–1910. (Unpublished doctoral dissertation). University of Washington, Seattle.

Timiriazev, V.
1897   "Gertsog Rishel'e, odesskaia chuma 1812 goda," *Istoricheskii vestnik* 68: 579–92.

Timoshenko, V. P.
1932   *Agricultural Russia and the Wheat Problem.* Stanford, California.

Tobias, Henry J.
1972   *The Jewish Bund in Russia. From Its Origins in 1905.* Stanford, California.

Troyat, Henri
1946   *Pouchkin.* Paris.

Tugan-Baranovsky, M. I.
1970   *The Russian Factory in the 19th Century.* Trans. A. and C. Levin. Georgetown, Ontario.

Van Dijk, H.
1978   Urbanisation and Social Change in the Netherlands During the Nineteenth Century. (Unpublished paper distributed at the Seventh Congress of the International Association of Economic History, Edinburgh, Scotland).

Venturi, Franco
1960   *Roots of Revolution.* New York.

Veresaev, V.
1937   *Sputniki Pushkina.* 2 vols. Moscow.

Vernadsky, George
1936   *Political and Diplomatic History of Russia.* Boston.

Vol'skii, Mikhail
1854   *Ocherk istorii khlebnoi torgovli Novorossiiskogo kraia s drevneishikh vremen do 1851 goda.* Odessa.

Waliszewski, K.
1925   *Le regne d'Alexandre I.* 3 vols. Paris.

Watson, Andrew
1981   "New Crops and Farming Techniques," *Pathways to Medieval Peasants*, pp. 65–82. ed. J. A. Raftis.

Weber, Adna F.
1899   *The Growth of Cities in the Nineteenth Century: A Study in Statistics.* New York and London.

Willoughby, Edward
1893   *Handbook of Public Health and Demography.* London.

Winslow, C. E.
1952   *Man and Epidemics.* Princeton.

Yarmolinsky, Avram
      1969   *The Russian Literary Imagination.* New York.
Zabarinskii, P.
      1894   *Khlebnaia torgovlia Odessy s 1878 po 1892 g.* Odessa.
Zagoruiko, V.
      1957–60   *Po stranitsam istorii Odessy i Odesshchiny.* 2 vols. Odessa.
Zaionchkovskii, P. A.
      1954   *Otmena krepostnogo prava v Rossii.* Moscow.
Zbanduto, P. I.
      1960   "Gor'kii i odesskaia pechat 90–900kh godov." In:
                    Gor'kii, pp. 3–21.
Zipperstein, Steve J.
      1980   The Jewish Community of Odessa from 1794–1871:
                    Social Characteristics and Cultural Development. (Unpub-
                    lished doctoral dissertation). University of California, Los
                    Angeles.
Zolotov, V. A.
      1963   *Vneshniaia torgovlia Iuzhnoi Rossii v pervoi polovine XIX*
                    veka. Rostov University.
      1966   *Khlebnyi eksport Rossii cherez porty Chernogo i Azovskogo*
                    morei v 60–90 gody XIX v. Rostov University.

Index